PSYCHOLOGY AND CRIMINAL JUSTICE

Katherine W. Ellison and Robert Buckhout
MONTCLAIR STATE COLLEGE   BROOKLYN COLLEGE, C.U.N.Y.

Psychology and Criminal justice

HARPER & ROW, PUBLISHERS, New York
Cambridge, Hagerstown, Philadelphia, San Francisco,
London, Mexico City, São Paulo, Sydney

Sponsoring Editor: George A. Middendorf
Project Editor: Eleanor Castellano
Production Manager: Willie Lane
Compositor: Maryland Linotype Composition Co., Inc.
Printer and Binder: The Maple Press Company
Art Studio: J & R Technical Services

PSYCHOLOGY AND CRIMINAL JUSTICE

Library of Congress Cataloging in Publication Data

Ellison, Katherine W
    Psychology and criminal justice.

    Bibliography: p.
    Includes indexes.
    1. Criminal justice, Administration of—United States
—Psychological aspects.   2. Psychology, Forensic.
3. Criminal psychology.   I. Buckhout, Robert, 1935–
joint author.   II. Title.
HV8138.E58   364′.973   80–27205
ISBN 0–06–041024–8

PREFACE

Our aim in this book is to bridge a gap between two fields, each of which has its own traditions and establishments. We are not the first authors to attempt this task, nor will we be the last. The past century has been witness to a number of efforts to merge the interests of psychology and law, most notably by Hugo Muensterberg, who became a major public figure in his lifetime, aided by his willingness to reach out by writing for the educated layperson as well as for the professional.

The common ground to which we refer is human behavior, a vast area of knowledge that the psychologist attempts to understand and which the legal professional must try to influence. In our careers as psychologists we have tried to share some of the understanding of our profession with some unusually sensitive lawyers, judges, police officers, legal workers, victims and, yes, criminals. Our tools, at first, were the skills learned from our mentors in our profession. Our own outlook has been widened by the insights of "clients," who see human behavior from a different—not erroneous—perspective. Interdisciplinary research and application truly move on a two-way street.

"The law" is a bigger and more pervasive institution than any social science. The reader will find a deliberate selectivity in topic areas that relies heavily on the authors' experience. We have avoided some areas of interdisciplinary effort that might have led merely to an uninformed recitation of published work with which we have no direct experience. The interested reader may well find that our contemporaries who also work at the interface of psychology and law have given better coverage to areas such as the interaction of clinical psychologists with the court, the study of behavior control in corrections, the study of the formation of legal attitudes in children, and the dynamics of decision making in the court system. In these and other areas the names of June Louin Tapp, Michael J. Saks, Reid J. Hastie, Bruce D. Sales, Gordon Bermant, Ralph K. Schwitzgeibel, and Robert Sommers stand out as contributors to a growing number of pertinent books of considerable interest to students of psychology and law.

We have concentrated on those areas in which we have experience. Both of us have done extensive work in research and in practical application of the knowledge gained from that research, but we have tended to be on different sides in the advocacy process. Thus we have both worked with attorneys on criminal trials, one mostly with the defense, the other primarily with the prosecution. We regularly consult with and lecture to relevant agencies, one with lawyers' groups, the other with police, prosecutors, and citizens' groups. Our research is of a very applied nature, seeking to modify and extend the research findings of psychology to make them more responsive to questions posed by "clients."

This book was written to interest and educate the student of social science, the law or law enforcement student, and the practitioner—both in criminal justice and in psychology. We have tried to translate the research and our experience into an understandable language that befits the common ground on which we are trying to walk. To us this is a challenging and exciting field, and we hope that the reader will share our enthusiasm.

K. W. E.
R. B.

ACKNOWLEDGMENTS

Many people made this book possible by giving to us of their knowledge, experience, time, and labor. Just as we have attempted throughout the book to present a variety of viewpoints, so these people represent the range of the political spectrum as well as that of the legal and psychological perspectives.

Special thanks go to John Cross, an extraordinary person and an astute, creative, dedicated police officer. And to attorneys Nancy Baran, Stefan Baumrin, Ramsey Clark, Clinton Cronin, Elizabeth Defeis, Karen Galloway, Susan Goldring, Marc Hynes, James B. Kakoullis, William Kuntzler, Jeffrey Licker, Walter Marvin, Wilbur Mathesius, Chester Mirsky, Howard J. Moore, Sheldon Otis, Betti Sachs, Leslie Crocker Snyder, Richardson White and Richard Williams, as well as the dedicated attorneys, too numerous to list, with whom we have worked in public defender services and prosecutors' offices around the country.

Deserving of our thanks are members of police agencies and prosecutors' staffs: of the New York City Police Department's Sex Crimes Analysis Unit and others of the Chief of Detective's staff; of the New Jersey State Police Academy, of the SARA Unit of the Newark Police Department and of the Atlantic County, New Jersey Prosecutor's Office, and individuals like James Ahrens, Andrew Andoloro, Carolen Bailey, Ruth Dargan, Susan Durett, Mary Giachetta, Kenneth Hill, Henry T. O'Reilly, Gladys Poliakoff and Joseph Renne.

We also wish to thank our colleagues and students at Brooklyn College and the Graduate Center of the City University of New York, and at Montclair State College, especially Andrea Polans, Morton Bard, Matthew Erdelyi, Michael Fanselow, Mark Greenwald, Noreen Norton Reilly, Vincent Reilly, Miriam Slomovits, Steven Weg, and Lynn Williams.

Social scientists Richard Christie, George A. Miller, Jay Schulman, Judith Waters, and Philip Zimbardo have contributed to our understanding of the impact of psychology on legal settings.

Judith Corrao, David Ellison, Mary Elsworth, Diane S. Fordney, Bernie Schwartzberg Kettenbeil, Ann Moulton Miner, Courtney Mullin, Josie Smith, Julie Smith, John Wagner, Lila Wanderman, and Florence Weisberg have also contributed greatly to our effort. Finally, we acknowledge the efforts of that model of patience, our editor, George A. Middendorf and the entire staff of Harper & Row.

K. W. E.
R. B.

1

INTRODUCTION AND OVERVIEW

GENERAL INTRODUCTION

Law and psychology share a common focus: Both are concerned with
the understanding, prediction, and regulation of human behavior.
Despite this commonality of interest, different emphasis on these elements and a different mandate have frequently hindered active communication and collaboration between the disciplines and have even
led to charges of exploitation from both sides. We believe such enmity
is unnecessary—that each discipline has much to offer and gain from
an interaction that acknowledges the uniqueness of the other perspective and their common ground. It is the common ground that is the
subject of this book.

Our purpose in writing this book is not to champion the righteous-
ness of one perspective over the other nor to subordinate one to the
other. Our argument is that law and psychology are already immersed
in the same waters—the ripples of human behavior in a social environment. We hope to give to each discipline a clearer understanding of
the mandate and method of the other and of the possible areas of
interaction.

1

One stumbling block to communication between disciplines is the absence of a clear common language. Both law and psychology suffer from a form of arteriosclerosis: a clogging of communication channels with jargon, whose purpose may be to make one's own turf sacred by verbal fiat. "If you don't understand, you don't belong." Yet all twentieth-century guilds have come under close scrutiny for attempting to mystify the areas they claim as their own in order to "make knowledge precious" and to secure a monopoly on those areas. The increasing complexity of our tasks is, we hope, breaking down these barriers. As lawyers turn to social scientists for advice and social scientists refer to legal problems to clarify and illustrate their theories, we are encouraged and wish to share these common efforts with a broader audience. The reader will meet pioneers from both professions who have broken barriers between disciplines to forge syntheses of efforts toward creative and meaningful ends.

We propose to use the language of common experience and to discuss human behavior as it occurs in the environments touched by the law. Theories of human behavior, however admirably presented as abstractions in other works, will be examined once again as they become important to problems faced by the law and legal institutions. These problems will begin to come to light from an examination of some of the questions that members of the legal profession have asked psychologists, or into which psychologists have leaped unbidden:

Can psychologists predict whether an individual will engage in violence? What causes violence?

Can psychological training aid a police officer in his or her job? (What, indeed, is that job?)

How accurate is the eyewitness to crime? How can we tell the good from the poor witness?

What can psychologists contribute that will aid the criminal justice system in dealing with victims of crime?

When is a person competent to stand trial?

Can a study of community attitudes help to select a fair jury? What other methods might we use?

How can society deal with those who have been convicted of violent acts; especially, can society run a prison and apply a knowledge of human behavior to benefit society and help or change the criminal? How?

Questions of this sort have been posed by attorneys, judges, police officers, and concerned citizens. Psychologists, for their part, have looked to law and the criminal justice system for data to support or disconfirm their theories about behavior; They have looked to this segment of the "real world" for answers to questions such as:

How do people behave under stress, such as that caused by crime
  victimization and contact with the criminal justice system?
What can studies of legal problems tell us about the beliefs people
  have about causation?
What can we learn about the importance of organizational structure, especially in highly controlled environments, such as the
  prison? How important are the constraints of role in explaining
  behavior?
Do attitudes predict behavior (such as the behavior of jurors)?

We shall show how some of these challenging questions have been
addressed, either adequately or badly, and some of the changes the
answers have brought to criminal justice practices and psychological
theories.

We are addressing a growing group of social scientists who are
finding and creating new roles for themselves in and around the law.
We hope also to give the attorney, judge, police officer, or legislator a
readable guide to how the knowledge and skills of the psychologist
can be, and have been, employed in dealing with some of the problems
that confront the criminal justice system. (Although we focus on the
contributions of psychologists, we draw from all areas of social science
research, a necessity given the overlap in areas of concern.)

The growth of the psychological profession in the United States
over the past one hundred years has been marked by the involvement
of psychologists in virtually all areas of human behavior. Correspond-
ingly, the courts and legal profession have become the recipient of
society's unsolved problems, forced to deal not only with crime but
with every other social problem as well. Seen through the jaundiced
eye of columnist Russell Baker (1977), the landmark occurred in 1954
with the U.S. Supreme Court decision on desegregation (*Brown* v.
Board of Education). He laments:

> the Supreme Court's desegregation decision of 1954 opened a new
> way out for the politicians. If the courts could be forced to make the
> more troublesome political decisions, the politicians could escape retri-
> bution at least in this world, and even profit from denouncing those
> court decisions which particularly annoyed the electorate. . . . This
> hardly makes for a healthy political system. . . . It encourages the
> failure of the imagination.

Although we do not share Baker's pessimism, we do acknowledge
1954 as a turning point. The U.S. Supreme Court for the first time
heard and acted on the recommendations of social scientists and social
science research in reaching its historic finding that "separate but
equal" institutions were inherently unequal in their impact on people.
This decision was made in the face of conflicts of interest, history, bias,

confusion, and profound differences of opinion. The legal system has not been able to avoid these problems; social scientists have discovered that they can make useful contributions to the solutions of these problems through research. Whether the law or psychology is up to the task is a question that generates considerable controversy.

THE CRIMINAL JUSTICE SYSTEM

The criminal justice system is that group of institutions that deals with crime: police, courts, lawyers, prisons. It is a network of bureaucracies of incredible complexity, divided not only by functions and roles but also by jurisdiction. Generalizations that will cover systems housed in each of 50 states and hundreds of thousands of communities are not easy. Although statistical data on criminal justice systems are abundant, understanding these data, and the system they dissect, is thwarted by the sheer size of the endeavor and the frequent absence of meaningful standards of evaluation and inferences based on these standards rather than on propaganda (see Chapter 13). Criminal justice, like any other institution, monitors the information it makes public to foster its own survival. Thus the outward "face" of the criminal justice system will be much different from its "true nature"— if, indeed, the truth is discoverable at all. Our brief guide to the system presented in Chapter 2 is designed to acquaint psychologist readers with a typical pathway through the system followed by victims, witnesses, actors from within the system, and the accused.

PSYCHOLOGY

Psychologists have an image, too, as well as a rather loose bureaucratic structure. The person from the criminal justice system may have a somewhat mythical set of expectations about what a psychologist— or other social scientists—can or cannot do. We have attempted in our discussions on experts (Chapter 9) and in a guide to the consumer of social science research (Chapter 13) to acquaint the law student or professional with the services, skills, and knowledge available from psychology. On one end of the spectrum, the practitioner—therapist, test giver, correctional psychologist—is generally well known to the criminal justice professional as a participant in the process. Less well understood are the people who create the basic core of scientific knowledge, theory, and empirical data that has begun to have an impact on the criminal justice system, both through the practitioner and directly, as evidence in its own right.

PSYCHOLOGICAL THEORIES APPLICABLE TO THE LAW: THE ISSUE OF VIOLENCE

Few topics have done so much to bring social science and the law together as the attempts to understand the nature of violence. Political pressure on the criminal justice system is directed largely toward the control of criminal violence. Social scientists have added much to the understanding of violence—if not to direct solutions for it. We turn now to a discussion of research and theory on violence as an example of one area of mutual concern for psychologists and criminal justice professionals.

In the broadest sense of the term, *theories* are inventions to supply information where facts do not (yet?) exist. Our purpose is not to bury theories but to raise them wherever appropriate. As we reviewed the two literatures of law and psychology, we were fascinated by the overlap in concern. Social scientists will often reach for concrete examples from the world of law to illustrate or defend the practical utility of their theories. Lawyers will, if it suits their argument, cite theories of eminent social scientists.

These theories cannot be dismissed lightly, because they play an important role in guiding the behavior of social scientists and legal professionals (even if they fail to meet rigorous standards of scientific proof). The very structure of the law has always been founded on a prevailing theory of human behavior supplied, in earlier times, by the church and philosophy and supplied frequently today by the social and behavioral sciences as well as legal tradition.

In the past as now, there is much disagreement over whether the law is sufficiently up to date in considering psychological or other social science concepts. Indeed, as the criminal justice system is slow to change its ways—a trait shared by psychologists, who often cling to unproven and unprovable theories—any discussion of violence is invariably touched by the anecdotes ("war stories") and personal experiences of the participants.

The citizen equates violent crime most pointedly with fear and a sense of vulnerability. As we note in Chapter 3, the citizen turned victim becomes convinced that the world is no longer a safe place to live. Violence can change attitudes, as caricatured in that favorite New York City definition of a conservative in the 1970s, as a liberal who was mugged. The attitudes of police officers are affected by exposure to violent people and what many officers feel is people's willingness to sweep the dirt of society under the rug and not get involved. The corrections part of the system that houses violent people comes to breed cynicism and occasional violence in the keepers (see Chapter 11). The question of how to deal with criminal violence has been a major issue in political campaigns for decades and no global solution appears to have worked very well.

Even those individuals charged with defending those accused of violent crimes have not escaped the sense of despair that permeates the criminal justice system. Attorney Seymour Wishman (1977) writes of his cynicism about defending clients whom he knows or believes to be guilty of monstrous violence:

> One cost of the administration of criminal justice is the damage it does to the emotional and spiritual life of the lawyers. . . . My world is filled with deceit, incompetence, aggression and violence. I've had to adjust. . . . To be effective in court I must act forcefully and often brutally. . . . The trial itself is ritualized aggression between combatants. . . . Yet the dilemma is in deciding what to do with a father who bludgeons his daughter to death. . . . "But don't you take any responsibility for what the ones you help might do next?" they say. "Very little," I answer. But sometimes late at night, when I'm done. . . .

PSYCHOLOGICAL THEORIES OF VIOLENCE

A glance at any major newspaper gives examples of a variety of violent and criminal behaviors: A father brutally murders his six children; a federal prosecutor is caught attempting to sell stolen merchandise; two 14-year-old boys are arrested for the rape of an 86-year-old woman; a clergyman is convicted of fraud in connection with nursing homes that he runs. "Why do people do such things?" we ask. Often the answers have been simplistic to the point of cliché: "The trouble is he's lazy; the trouble is he drinks . . ." Social scientists, too, have been fascinated by criminal behavior and have proposed a variety of theories to explain it. (Nor, alas, have social scientists been entirely free of the tendency to simplistic answers; indeed, those explanations given by laypersons often are spawned by professionals.) Many of these theories have focused not only on criminality but also on the general topics of deviance, aggression, and violence (See Box 1.1).

Three major sets of etiological factors have been advanced to explain criminal behavior (Miller, 1969): genetic and/or physiological factors, psychodynamic or *intra*personal factors, and environmental or *inter*personal factors. Theories of aggression and violence differ in the relative importance that they attach to each of these factors.

GENETIC AND PHYSIOLOGICAL BASES OF VIOLENCE

Explanations for violent and criminal behavior that give great weight to genetic factors have long been popular with both scientists and the

---

BOX 1.1

A PROFILE OF VIOLENT CRIME

Violent crime in the United States is primarily a phenomenon of large cities.

Violent crime in the city is overwhelmingly committed by males.

Violent crime in the city is concentrated especially among youths between the ages of 15 and 24.

Violent crime in the city is committed primarily by individuals at the lower end of the occupational scale.

Violent crime in the city stems disproportionately from the ghetto slum.

Victims of assaultive violence in cities have the same characteristics as offenders: Victimization rates generally are highest for males, youths, poor persons, blacks. Robbery victims, however, are very often older whites.

Unlike robbery, the other violent crimes of homicide, assault, and rape tend to be acts of passion among intimates and acquaintances.

By far the greatest proportion of all serious violence is committed by repeaters. The exception to this is homicide.

SOURCE: U.S. National Commission on Causes and Prevention of Violence, Report, Vol. 13, pp. 37–44.

---

lay public. In 1875 Dugdale published his famous description of the Jukes family, a clan shot through with "crime, bastardy, immorality and laziness," as an example of the inherited nature of criminality. He asserted that 50 out of 709 of the members of this clan had come to the attention of the authorities for some kind of malfeasance or mischief. A similar family study claiming to give evidence of the genetic basis of criminality involves the Kallikaks (Goddard, 1914). The *pater familiases*, Martin Kallikak, Revolutionary War soldier, produced two sets of progeny: one begotten illegitimately on a feeble-minded tavern wench, the other of a woman of normal intelligence. His descendants by the left hand, Goddard noted, were given to feeble-mindedness and criminality, while those by his wife were ordinary, "decent" citizens.

In their eagerness to prove a genetic basis for depravity, Goddard and Dugdale both failed to realize that correlation does not imply causation, that several other explanations are just as plausible. Consider, for example, the effects of environment in each of these cases. The illegitimate child of a tavern maid certainly does not grow up in the same circumstances as children in a "decent" settled family. And the little Jukeses grew up in proximity to their Feaginesque progenitors. Nor did Dugdale take into account the large percentage of genes from unknown sources due to the bastardy he condemned in his subjects. Sadly, although both of these studies have been shown to have little more than literary merit—if that—their popularity has been little reduced (Miller & Buckhout, 1973, p. 161).

Another type of study that claims to confirm a genetic hypothesis about criminality is that which studies outward appearance (phenotype) as an indicator of genotype. In 1891 the Italian physician, Lombroso, claimed to be able to distinguish criminals from noncriminals by physical appearance. The criminal was degenerate, a throwback, somewhat apelike in appearance, with high, pointed head, retreating forehead, prominent eyebrow ridge (the "simian shelf"), and large ears.

Building also on the idea that genetically determined physical characteristics illumine manifold aspects of personality, Sheldon (1942) conducted an eight-year study of the relationship between physical type and delinquency. He concluded that there are important differences in body build not only between delinquents and nondelinquents but among the various kinds of delinquents, too. Further, the body builds characteristic of delinquents may also be found in their parents, ample evidence, for Sheldon, of a genetic basis for criminality.

Sheldon's work has been criticized on several grounds (Hall & Lindzey, 1970). The biographical sketches on which the personality ratings are based "leave the task of generalizing largely on the shoulders of the reader" (p. 370), and no other researcher has been able to obtain correlations as strong as those that Sheldon finds. Also, it must be remembered that body types are not permanent, as the Charles Atlas body-building advertisements remind us. Again, correlation does not imply causation: An alternative to the genetic hypothesis might say that society's myths about the personality that goes with a certain body build may have the strength of a self-fulfilling prophecy, so that people react differently to a husky person and have different expectations for him or her from those they have for a fat or thin person. Finally, any study of incarcerated persons has the problem of *restriction of range.* The people who actually go to jail for any crime are but a small fraction of those arrested for crime, not to mention those criminals who are never caught. Prison conditions, including lack of activity and prison food, may also change the somatotype.

The XYY Solution

As genetics has become a more sophisticated science, scientists have sought to skip the inferential processes and to make direct links between genetic abnormalities and criminality. Most famous of these studies have been those attempting to show a relationship between the chromosome configuration XYY and criminality. Several studies reported that XYY men were more common than would be expected by chance in institutions for the criminally insane (Witkin et al., 1976). The XYY male tends to be tall, white (it is uncommon among other races), to suffer from acne, to have reached sexual maturity early, and to be somewhat retarded intellectually. He was reported to be lacking in impulse control and to be less likely than average to be able to delay gratification. One theory for this was that the XYY male might have greater supplies of the male hormone, testosterone.

In a careful *epidemiological* study, Witkin and his colleagues (1976) demonstrated that XYY males, even those with arrest records, do not tend to be particularly aggressive. Their crimes tended to be against property rather than violent ones against persons. Further, they are similar to men with the chromosomal abnormality XXY in having slightly higher arrest rates than "normal" XY men. They point out that "people of lower intelligence may be less adept at escaping detection and so be likely to have higher representation in a classificatory system based on registered crimes. The elevated crime rate found in our XYY group may therefore reflect a higher detection rate rather than simply a higher rate of commission of crimes."

Even if the syndrome XYY is highly related to a tendency to criminal behavior, these individuals constitute only a very small fraction of the general population (about 3 per 1000) and of the number of people in prison. It does not explain most criminal behavior.

Another kind of study has attempted to find physiological or neurological explanations for violence. Physiological work with animals seems to point to the existence of "rage centers" in the brain. As early as 1892, Goltz noted that dogs whose cerebral cortex was removed surgically were quick to display anger. This work was refined by Cannon (1925) and more recently by Delgado (1970) and others. Although this work seems promising at first glance, it is not without problems. The effects of stimulation or removal of brain tissues differ from species to species (Valenstein, 1973), and the species that has been studied *least* carefully, for obvious ethical reasons, has been *homo sapiens*. Nor is the association between removal of a part of the brain and the occurrence of rage simple. Kluever and Bucy (1938) found that removal of the *amygdala* (an organ in the brain) of the rhesus monkey changed it from an unpleasant, irrascible animal to one that was playful and friendly (and oversexed). Memory, also was affected, and Kling, Lancaster, and Benitone (1970) showed that such monkeys, although less aggressive in captivity, behaved inappropriately when returned to the wild.

Genetic differences of the sort just mentioned are seen as deviations from the normal within the human, and other, species. A different kind of genetic explanation for aggression has also achieved widespread attention in recent years. This is the phylogenetic or ethological approach, represented by Lorenz (1966) and Tinbergen (1951) and in the popular writings of Morris (1968) and Ardrey (1961, 1966). Ethologists study behavior, particularly the behavior of animals, under natural conditions. They have tended to extrapolate from these studies of ants and greylag geese to the behavior of humans. They postulate that aggression against other members of the species (as well as against other species) is innate and inevitable in humans. Indeed, according to this view, aggression in humans differs from that in animals because the human's unique technological evolution into a lethal animal has outstripped the development of genetic inhibitions to aggression, such as those inhibitions that Lorenz (1963) describes in wolves. A wolf about to be vanquished in a fight with another wolf will bare his throat to the victor, making the kill, it would seem, easy. However, this action inevitably pulls the victor up short rendering him incapable of killing his rival. As LeFrançois (1974, p. 267) puts it, "a cynical expression depicting the human condition and reflecting this aggression is 'dog eat dog.' Ironically the expression would have been more appropriate as 'man eat man.'"

The anthropologist, Ashley Montague (1968) calls the extrapolation from other animals to humans a fatal defect of these studies: "arguments based on fish, birds, and other animals are strictly for them. They have no relevance for man." After discussing numerous inconsistencies in the work of Lorenz and Ardrey, he concludes:

> there is, in fact, not the slightest evidence or ground for assuming that the alleged "phylogenetically adapted instinctive" behavior of other animals is in any way relevant to the discussion of the motive-forces of human behavior . . . those who speak of "innate aggression" in man appear to be lacking in any understanding of the uniqueness of man's evolutionary history. Unacquainted with the facts or else undeterred by them they insist on fitting whatever facts they are acquainted with into their theories. . . .

Even the most hidebound adherent of genetic explanations for aggression recognizes some contribution from the environment. For ethologists, for example, this comes in the form of "releasers": situations that elicit behavior. The behavior of others can act as a releaser.

Freud, too, believed that aggression has its roots in instinct (1933). Although he had begun with the idea that aggression was a response to the thwarting of the pleasure principle (1920), his exposure to World War I lead him to postulate (1933) a death instinct (*thanatos*) that was a constant source of aggressive impulses and that tried to reduce the organism to its inanimate state. These wishes may be expressed directly, or may be displaced, as in hunting, or sublimated into such channels as sadomasochism in mild forms, such as satire, or in more obvious, virulent forms. This concept of aggression had enormous impact, as will be seen later in this chapter.

Freud's ideas on the roots of criminality also have had profound impact on the thinking both of professionals in law enforcement and corrections and of the public. He believed (1930) that guilt arising from oedipal conflict was the bedrock of criminal activity. Parricide and incest were the two great unimaginable crimes. The individual, mired in guilt over oedipal fantasies, seeks punishment to relieve his sense of guilt. His crimes are sublimations of the oedipal fantasies and by arranging to be caught and punished, he is relieved of that guilt. The idea that the criminal "really" wants to be caught, indeed, arranges for his own capture, is common in criminological literature (Abrahamsen, 1973). (The huge numbers of unsolved crimes and the general reluctance of suspects to confess spontaneously is but one datum refuting this idea as a major motivation for the majority of criminals.)

Freud and Company on Violence

Drawing on Freud and attempting to combine psychoanalytic insights with concepts from learning theory, Dollard and his colleagues (1939) introduced a frustration-aggression theory. In its first formulation this hypothesis defined *frustration* as anything that interferes with an ongoing goal response, and stated that *aggression* is always a consequence of frustration. Thus the occurrence of aggressive behavior is always evidence of the existence of frustration, and conversely, frustration always leads to some form of aggression. Although there is considerable evidence that frustration *may* lead to aggression, it soon became apparent that the original formula was too rigid: that aggression is but one possible consequence of frustration. To their credit, the Dollard group realized early that their original idea was inadequate and modified their position to say that instigation to aggression, rather than aggression itself, is the response to frustration (Miller, 1941). Whether or not this instigation results in overt aggressive behavior— that directed toward the injury of others—depends on factors such as

internal inhibitions and external events. Further, the strength of instigation to aggression varies, they postulated, with the amount of
frustration. The amount of frustration is a function of the drive
strength of the frustrated goal, the degree of interference with the
frustrated response, and the number of frustrated response sequences.
Thus the aspects of frustration remain active over a period of time,
and frustration from different events will accumulate.

Despite its flaws, the Dollard work proved heuristic. A classic
study by Barker, Dembo, and Lewin (1941) illustrated some of the
possible consequences of frustration. A group of preschool children
was first tested for creativity of play with ordinary toys, then allowed
to play with very attractive toys briefly. Next, the attractive toys were
put behind a wire screen, and the children were allowed to play only
with the original toys. Although many of the children became much
less constructive in their play, and some attacked the barrier, a few
became even more constructive.

Others have demonstrated that frustration, as defined by Dollard's
group, is not the only precursor of aggression. Bandura (1973) has
demonstrated that attack also leads to aggression, and Toch (1969)
and others have shown the power of an insult in bringing on aggressive behavior.

Berkowitz (1969), in particular, extended the frustration-aggression idea to expand the instigators to aggression to include a variety of
aversive events, of which frustration is but one. He also emphasized
the importance of a variety of aggressive cues in a given situation:
cues to tell the individual whether or not aggression is an appropriate
response. Thus Berkowitz and LePage (1967) found that subjects who
had been made angry attacked their tormentors more strongly when a
rifle and revolver were present in the experimental situation than when
neutral items—such as badminton racquets—were left lying around.

Many psychologists have taken the position that although the
capacity for violence may, indeed, be innate in human beings, this is
very different from claiming an instinct to violence. Aggression, they
hold, is a complex interaction of external events and brain condition.
Violence does not occur unless there is a suitable victim or an appropriate situation.

Environmental Factors in Violence

Social learning theorists who have studied aggression have focused on
the situations that teach or provoke aggression. They hypothesize that
much violent behavior is learned in much the same way that other
sorts of behavior are learned: by rewards, punishments, and, often, by
watching and imitating others—or what they call "modeling." Bandura

et al. (1971) believe that social behaviors are first learned by watching others, then these newly learned behaviors are either strengthened through reward or weakened by a lack of reinforcement or by punishment.

The classic experiment on the effects of imitation on aggression was done by Bandura, Ross, and Ross (1963). Their findings that children who had witnessed aggressive behavior tended to imitate it have been corroborated by a number of subsequent studies (See Box 1.2). Liebert and Baron (1972) found that exposure to television violence under experimental conditions caused increased interpersonal aggression in children. Field studies generally came to the same conclusion. Eron (1963), in a *correlational* study of relation of aggression to television watching (as reported by parents) found that third grade boys who preferred violent television were more likely to show aggressive behavior (as rated by their peers) than were those boys whose favorite shows were less violent. Interestingly, similar results were not found with girls.

Research such as that of Bandura has important policy implications for television programming, especially that aimed at children. Although there is some conflicting research evidence showing that in certain circumstances watching violent shows may have a *cathartic* effect (providing a vicarious outlet for the viewer's aggressive feelings), a review of the literature by Wurtzel (1977) concludes that "the vast majority of the laboratory and field experiments in the television violence area have suggested a relationship between violent material and subsequent aggression" (p. 233). (See also the review by Tannenbaum & Zillman, 1973.) An interesting addition to the work on imitation is the finding that many parents who beat their children, and husbands who beat their wives, were themselves battered as children (See Box 1.3.)

The French sociologist Gabriel Tarde was one of the first social scientists to study the effects of imitation in the experience that when a spectacular crime is reported in the media, others, of like nature, are likely to follow. He noted that following the publicity given to the case of Jack the Ripper similar cases of mutilation killings of women occurred in other parts of England. In more recent times, airplane hijackings have shown a similar contagion effect (Berkowitz, 1975), as have urban riots (Lieberman & Silverman, 1965).

Sociological and anthropological contributions to the understanding of violence have emphasized the importance of cultural and subcultural sanctions (Bateson, 1941). One of the more prominent of these is Marvin Wolfgang's (1967) notion of a "subculture of violence." Noting the disproportionately high rates of violent, assaultive crime in individuals of low socioeconomic status, below average IQ, in

BOX 1.2

VIOLENCE BEGETS VIOLENCE—AN EXPERIMENT

Bandura, Ross and Ross tested the effects of modeling under a variety of conditions on the behavior of preschool children. They divided the children into five groups. The three experimental conditions involved having a child observe either (1) a "live" adult model, with the child seated in the same room, (2) a movie showing a live model (called the "film" condition), and (3) a "cartoon" condition, in which the adult model was dressed as a cartoon character. Control conditions involved (4) an adult engaged in nonaggressive activity, and (5) no model.

In the three experimental conditions the model spent the ten-minute observation period attacking an inflated plastic punching-bag toy (commonly known as a "Bobo doll"), while ignoring other toys in the room. In the nonaggressive modeling condition (4), the model assembled Tinkertoys.

After watching the model or the film, each child was given a frustrating experience in order to instigate aggression. (For group (5) this was the beginning of the experiment.) The child was then placed in a room with a Bobo doll, other "aggressive toys," such as a dart gun, and some nonaggressive toys, such as crayons and paper. The child was left in this room for 20 minutes, and his or her behavior observed.

In the aggressive model conditions, (1, 2, and 3), the children imitated very closely, even to the words used, the behavior of the adult models. The type of model, live, film or cartoon, was not a significant factor in amount or form of aggression! Children in the nonaggressive model (4) and no model (5) conditions did not display such behavior, even though, remember, they, too, had been frustrated. Children who had observed the nonaggressive model (4) were much more likely to behave as she had than were the children who had not seen a model (5).

The authors point out that these responses occurred even though the children had not been rewarded themselves for aggressive behavior, suggesting that, contrary to traditional learning theory, external rewards may not be necessary to produce behavior.

REFERENCE: Bandura, A., Ross, D., and Ross, S. A. Imitation of film-mediated aggressive models. *Journal of Abnormal and Social Psychology*, 1963, *66*, 3–11 (a).

BOX 1.3

DOES VIOLENCE BEGET VIOLENCE?—
THE "REAL WORLD"

Dateline, Miami. October 7, 1977. The headline read: "Court Clears TV, Finds Boy Guilty in Slaying of Elderly Neighbor."

The defense had argued that 15-year-old Ronny Zamora was not guilty by reason of insanity of the killing of an 82-year-old neighbor during a burglary of her home. While insanity is not uncommon as a plea in murder cases where the identity of the killer is not in question, Zamora's attorney was suggesting a unique cause for the psychological state of his client: "voluntary subliminal television intoxication." Ignored or beaten at home, Zamora had spent so much time watching television, the story went, that death of a human being had little meaning for him, "no more than swatting a fly," one witness said.

The defense leaned heavily on the expert testimony of social scientists. Psychiatrist Michael Gilbert, who was allowed to testify before the jury, called Zamora "conditioned" by watching violent programs. In *voir dire*, with the jury absent, psychologist Margaret Hanratty Thomas, whom the defense called a specialist on the effect of television violence on the viewer, argued that the average American child views 18,000 murders on television by the time he or she completes high school. Television violence, she contended, is positively correlated with aggressive behavior. But unlike Gilbert, she had not "examined" Zamora; her testimony was to deal with hypothetical questions.

Judge Paul Baker refused to allow Thomas to testify as an expert witness who could establish a direct causal link between Zamora's 50 to 60 hours a week of television viewing and his psychological state at the time of the crime. His question to Thomas, "Have you ever conclusively linked any particular television program or any amount of television directly with a homicide?" elicited a response of "No," and the witness was dismissed.

The prosecution termed the defense strategy "hogwash." In his summary, chief prosecutor Tom Headly told the jury, "Someone could just as easily say they got too much violence reading the Bible."

The jury agreed. After only two hours' deliberation, they found Zamora guilty of first degree murder and lesser included counts of burglary, armed robbery, and possession of a firearm in the commission of a felony.

Ironically, television played another important role in the Zamora trial. Florida law had recently been changed to permit television broadcasts of court proceedings on a one-year-trial basis, and this case was the first to be so covered.

REFERENCE: *Record*, Bergen County, N.J., October 6–9, 1977; *Daily News*, New York, October 7, 1977; *Newsweek*, October 10, 1977.

disrupted families living in poor neighborhoods, Wolfgang and Ferracuti (1967) conclude:

> Within a portion of the lower class, especially, there is a "life-style," a culturally transmitted and shared willingness to express disdain, disgruntlement and other hostile feelings in personal interaction by using physical force. The repertoire of response to unpleasant stimuli is delimited for them; it is not simply that more stimuli are displeasing. And in this limited repertoire of alternatives, the ultimate weapon in efforts to control others, violence, not only is available but also has been incorporated into the personality structure through childhood discipline, reinforced in juvenile peer groups, confirmed in the strategies of the street. The aggressive male is socially "castrated" only for short periods of time in school, at work, and in other encounters with external control. But the fighting routine in his personal milieu is continued, for his subcultural group is prepared to use the same violence as he, to respond in similar fashion to his attack, to be governed by the same norms containing the same values. Within this value set, the external expectations of aggression more readily activate the internal physiological responses of excitation, and the circle of violence circumscribes a situation containing the essential ingredients for assaultive crime (p. 267).

Miller (1969) elaborates on the themes in lower-class culture that support violence. He concludes that the focal areas of concern of lower-class culture are related to (in order of importance): (1) trouble: law abiding versus law violating; (2) toughness; (3) smartness, that is, the ability to outwit others, to "con" others, a shrewdness versus gullibility dimension; (4) excitement; (5) fate, including the feeling of being controlled by the caprices of fortune; and (6) autonomy. Miller notes that the achievement concerns of the middle class are much less important in this scheme.

Criticisms of cultural and subcultural theories of violence stress that although violence may be more prevalent in some groups than in others—and, critics say, even that is questionable given the unreliability of crime statistics—the majority of the members of very violence-prone groups do not commit homicide or other violent aggressive acts. Even if one believes this level of analysis is appropriate, it presents the greatest difficulties for bringing about change. Finally, the epithets of racism and "classism" are frequently levelled at Wolfgang and his colleagues, by those who see subculture of violence theories as sophisticated ploys for "blaming the victim."

SUMMARY

As the reader will note, the development of relevant psychological theories is not a complete process. The theme of violence will be repeated throughout this book. Psychologists can help but they cannot substitute themselves for the criminal justice practitioner. We have examined many of the theoretical explanations of violence as psychologists view them, finding no panaceas. Older theories, based on genetic (or the more modern sociobiological) theories have been found to be seriously lacking in empirical support. Social learning theories appear to hold some promise, but the opportunity for learning violence may well differ for different classes of people, a situation that demands further sociological analysis. Psychologists and criminal justice professionals alike would do well to admit to a large degree of uncertainty about the causes of violence before endorsing seemingly compelling easy answers for its control.

Despite the lack of sound theoretical grounding, those of us who work in and with the system do not have the luxury of time to wait for complete solutions. We must do what we can with our limited knowledge and hope that, working together we may reach more viable solutions and paradigms consistent with our shared beliefs in the basic value and dignity of our fellow humans; this, ultimately, is our common ground.

2

INTRODUCTION TO THE
CRIMINAL JUSTICE SYSTEM

The *criminal justice system* is that part of our legal system "charged with the regulation, control and sanctioning of behavior established by the criminal law" (Shah, 1972). The behavior that is proscribed is carefully delineated, as are the penalties for transgression.[1]

In contrast to civil law in which an individual (the plaintiff) may bring suit against another (the defendant) whom he or she feels has wronged or injured him or her, a crime is considered an offense against the state, and the plaintiff in a criminal action is the people of the state, or, in federal cases, the United States.

At least four different goals have been given for regulating behavior through the criminal justice system (Meehl, 1970; Shah, 1972): (1) punishment, retribution; (2) individual deterrence, incapacitation, "warehousing"—removal of an individual from society and physical isolation to prevent that particular person, seen as a high risk by virtue of his or her previous actions, from committing further

---

[1] The civil justice system, the educational system, the military, the mental health system are examples of other institutions that have as part of their goals the regulation of behavior.

offenses; (3) general deterrence—to dissuade *potential* malefactors by threat or example; (4) rehabilitation and reform.

Meehl (1970) reminds us that these goals may be mutually exclusive, that no single method of dealing with convicted criminals can serve all four purposes at the same time. Thus set sentences with no possibility of early release may be consistent with an emphasis on retribution but inconsistent with aims at rehabilitation and reform.[2]

Unfortunately, too often the different parts of the system have lacked specific, coherent focus about their purpose. Some rules and practices show the effects of a punishment ethic, others, of the rehabilitation model. Psychologists have been particularly prone to get caught in this confusion of models; they may try to promote goals of rehabilitation in a system geared for punishment. The disastrous results of such inconsistency of models become evident in the chapter on prisons.

The decision as to what end the criminal justice system should serve is not in the hands of psychologists; it is, rather, a matter of social policy. Psychologists can provide input at a number of places in the system, including aid in evaluating the effectiveness with which the stated goals are being fulfilled.

FORM OF THE CRIMINAL JUSTICE SYSTEM

In the United States, the criminal justice system is an often confused and confusing mélange of codes and jurisdictions. Both the federal government and the various states have their own criminal codes, their own law enforcement agencies, courts and prison systems; counties, cities and other jurisdictions also have ordinances that govern behavior. Federal crimes include bank robbery, kidnapping, mail fraud, violations of antitrust statutes and interstate commerce rules, transporting women across state lines "for immoral purposes" (the Mann Act), transporting stolen autos across state lines (the Dyer Act), and violations of the individual's civil rights. (It was a broad interpretation of the Civil Rights Act of 1964 that allowed the federal government to become involved in the prosecution of what would ordinarily be a crime falling under the jurisdiction of a state: the murder of civil rights workers in the South). The states set laws regarding murder, forcible rape, and other proscribed sexual conduct—from obscenity to exhibitionism—robbery, many of the "white-collar" crimes such as

[2] Rehabilitation has been the watchword of the American correctional system for the last several decades. Current theory from psychologists, criminologists, and others involved in the area is tending away from the rehabilitation model, using as the reason the increasing weight of evidence that says a rehabilitation ethic not only has failed to prevent recidivism but has often denied individuals their constitutional rights.

price fixing (federal statutes involving interstate commerce may lead to some of these cases becoming federal offenses), larceny, certain traffic regulations, and the like.

Crimes are also classified according to seriousness; the most common distinctions being treason (usually a federal offense), felony, and misdemeanor. Felonies commonly are more serious and include violent crimes against the person, such as murder, forcible rape, and robbery. There is, however, tremendous variation from state to state, not only in the penalties for a given offense but even in the acts considered criminal.[3]

A LOOK AT CRIMINAL JUSTICE

The process from original complaint through apprehension and conviction of a suspect to release from prison is a long and complicated one. The criminal justice system is commonly thought of as divided into three segments: (1) police and similar law enforcement agencies, (2) administration of justice agencies—prosecutor, defense, court— and (3) correctional agencies (Shah, 1972). The steps that a case typically follows are outlined in Figure 2.1.

The formidable appearance of this structure belies the enormous amount of discretion possible in the system. Points at which discretionary judgments on the part of criminal justice officials are possible and common are found throughout the process and will be discussed in the following description. As a beginning, a second look at the enormous dropout rate between complaint and incarceration will give some idea of the potential.[4] It is at some of these points of discretion that psychologists and other "outside" professionals typically seek to study and influence the process.

The Police

The first step in the criminal justice process is the lodging of a complaint, usually by the victim,[5] with one of the country's 40,000 police

[3] These discrepancies become particularly apparent in the codes governing sexual conduct. In some states oral or anal sex even between consenting adults in privacy is a crime, as is sex between unmarried persons. In others, such acts are not part of the criminal code. In the past, forcible rape has carried the possibility of the death penalty in some states, five years in others, with ranges as wide as one-year imprisonment to death (Kling, 1965).

[4] Due to severe problems in record keeping, exact figures are difficult to obtain. However, it has been estimated that 80 to 90 percent of suspects arrested are never tried and only about half of the persons convicted are incarcerated (*U.S. News & World Report*, May 10, 1976).

[5] If an officer observes a violation, he or she, too, may lodge a complaint. This is particularly common in narcotics and gambling complaints.

departments or other regulatory agencies. It is the responsibility of the police to take the complaint, investigate, and collect evidence, close the case and clear innocent suspects, if necessary, make arrests where warranted, and, often, involve themselves in the preliminary court procedures such as booking. The officers will then testify at the various court proceedings.

INVESTIGATION OF COMPLAINT

The investigation phase begins with the complaint from the victim or witnesses. In many cases the victim calls the police department and the call is taken by a dispatcher. This person may be a "sworn" police officer or a "civilian" employee. Here is the first discretionary point. The dispatcher assigns the complaint a priority; in large, busy departments this may mean that some complaints will not receive a response for hours. The dispatcher may also make a decision to assign the complaint to the uniformed force or directly to detectives.

In most cases response is quick, and the interviewing of victim and witnesses, taking the formal complaint and official statement, is handled by uniformed patrol officers.[6] Here is another point where discretion may be used.[7] Depending on department policy and the seriousness of the charge, the officer, possibly after consultation with a supervisor, may (1) decide the charge is legitimate and worthy of further consideration or (2) "unfound" it: close it because of what he or she feels is insufficient evidence or because of a judgment that the witnesses are unreliable or not cooperative enough or alas, (3) not worthy of police intervention. In some large cities, for example, because of the volume of cases, the police will take the report but will not investigate further—dust for fingerprints, interview neighbors, and the like—any burglary in which the loss is less than a specified amount, say $2000.

It is not at all unusual for an officer to decide that an offense has, indeed, been committed but to let the accused go with a warning, to make referrals, or informally to adjudicate or mediate the dispute on the spot. This is especially true of disputes among neighbors and family members. Although the policy of informal arbitration in "domestic disputes" has been supported by many psychologists who work with police (Bard, 1969), it has come under intense criticism from members of feminist groups concerned with the problem of wife beating (Fields, 1978). They allege that the police do not take such complaints seriously and refuse to arrest a man who has assaulted his wife, leaving her helpless (Roy, 1977).

---

[6] These officers also are responsible, at this point, for protecting the crime scene, if appropriate.

[7] For examples of the use of discretion by patrol officers, see Rubinstein (1973).

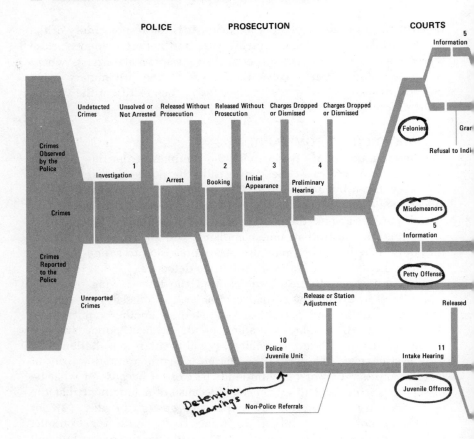

POLICE   PROSECUTION   COURTS

1 May continue until trial.

2 Administrative record of arrest. First step at which temporary release on bail may be available.

3 Before magistrate, commissioner, or justice of peace. Formal notice of charge, advice of rights. Bail set. Summary trials for petty offenses usually conducted here without further processing.

4 Preliminary testing of evidence against defendant. Charge may be reduced. No separate preliminary hearing for misdemeanors in some systems.

5 Charge filed by prosecutor on basis of information submitted by police or citizens. Alternative to grand jury indictment; often used in felonies, almost always in misdemeanors.

6 Reviews whether Government evidence sufficient to justify trial. Some States have no grand jury system; others seldom use it.

Figure 2.1   A general view of the criminal justice system. This chart seeks to present a simple yet comprehensive view of the movement of cases through the criminal justice system. Procedures in individual jurisdictions may vary from the pattern shown here. The differing weights of line indicate the relative volume of cases disposed of at various points in the system, but this is only suggestive since no nationwide data of this sort exist. (Source: *The Challenge of Crime in a Free Society: A Report by the President's Commission on Law Enforcement and Administration of Justice.* Washington, D.C.: U.S. Government Printing Office, February 1967.)

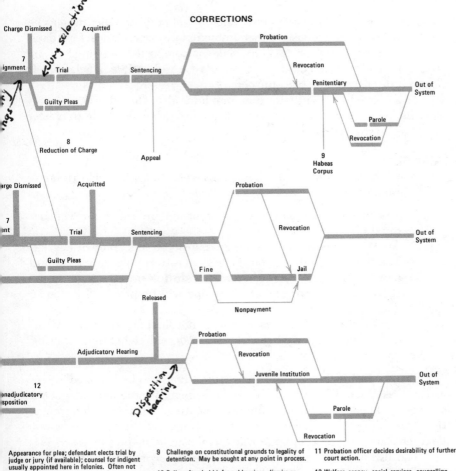

CORRECTIONS

Appearance for plea; defendant elects trial by judge or jury (if available); counsel for indigent usually appointed here in felonies. Often not at all in other cases.

Charge may be reduced at any time prior to trial in return for plea of guilty or for other reasons.

9 Challenge on constitutional grounds to legality of detention. May be sought at any point in process.

10 Police often hold informal hearings, dismiss or adjust many cases without further processing.

11 Probation officer decides desirability of further court action.

12 Welfare agency, social services, counselling, medical care, etc., for cases where adjudicatory handling not needed.

If the decision is made to continue with a case, and if an arrest is not made immediately, the case will be turned over to detectives and members of special investigative units, such as "evidence technicians," if the jurisdiction is large enough to support such specialists.[8]

If a person fitting the description of the offender is picked up within an hour of the crime, the witnesses may be asked to identify him or her in an informal, one person, on-the-street "show up." Other-

[8] Even if an arrest *is* made immediately, the bulk of the collection of evidence and further questioning of witnesses often falls to detectives. Another variation is that in some areas detectives and investigators attached to the county prosecutor's or district attorney's staff will assist in or assume the duties of further investigation.

wise, in crimes against the person, such as robbery, the victim may be taken to the station house, either immediately or within a few days, to view photographs or to help make a composite drawing.[9] If no arrest is made within a day or so, most cases, while officially left "open," are placed on a back burner.

If a suspect is found later than one hour after the offense, a lineup may be held.[10] Even after an arrest, the police often continue to collect evidence to strengthen the case.[11]

ARREST

Upon arrest, the suspect is advised of his or her constitutional rights—the "Miranda Warning":

1. You have the right to remain silent and refuse to answer any questions.
2. Anything you say may be used against you in a court of law.
3. You have the right to consult with an attorney at any time and have him or her present before and during questioning.
4. If you cannot afford an attorney one will be provided if you so desire prior to any questioning.
5. A decision to waive these rights is not final and you may withdraw your waiver whenever you wish, either before or during questioning.

The suspect is then taken to the station house to be "booked": The arrest is recorded officially and he or she is fingerprinted and mug shots are taken. The suspect may contact an attorney. An initial determination of charges to be filed is made at this time, but this decision is not final; charges may be dropped or added throughout the process.[12]

The listing of charges would seem a simple process; in fact, it is greatly influenced by the prevalence of "plea bargaining." The prosecution tends to include as many charges as possible, to give it some leverage in the bargaining process. (See Box 2.1.)

If they have not done so prior to the arrest, the police may

---

[9] If stolen property is recovered, the victim will be required to identify it as hers or his.

[10] It is not necessary for the suspect to be arrested: He or she may be allowed to appear in the lineup voluntarily and released or an arrest made only after the complainant has viewed the lineup. Lineups are frequently omitted if the police have independent evidence—identification from mug shots, fingerprints, the suspect was known to the victim—of the identity of the suspect.

[11] The report of the murder case involving the Manson family, by prosecutor Vincent Bugliosi (1974), gives some idea of the sort of work involved in the investigation and preparation of a complex case.

[12] Although the prosecutor has official responsibility for determining charges, the first listing is usually made by the arresting officer.

BOX 2.1

A POLICEMAN'S LOT

The following instructive example of the kinds of calls handled by a small-town police department was brought to the attention of the authors.

Unadilla, New York. Police report for the month of May 1978 . . . shows there were 121 telephone calls; 72 inquiries; 51 complaints; 6 dog complaints referred to dog warden; 1 assisted motorist; 15 calls from other police departments; 1 case concerning dog attacking livestock; 1 case concerning dog attacking another dog; 2 missing persons reported; 3 complaints of discharging firearms in the village; 1 call concerning lost wallet; 1 light found on at business place after closing hours, and 1 death notice given.

Also, 1 call concerning livestock on highway; 3 assisted other police departments with defendants; 2 complaints on abandoned vehicles; 1 injured dog report; 1 bonfire reported; 2 calls concerning trucks blocking street; 1 security check; 1 call on bad check; 1 illness notice given; 1 eviction complaint; 1 call on railway lights flashing; 1 case of stranded motorist; 1 license plate returned to owner; 1 deer complaint; 1 case concerning tree in highway; 1 exhibitionist reported; 5 larcenies investigated; 1 burglary; 4 harassments; 6 assaults; 1 trespass and 4 disorderly conducts.

Also, 2 family disputes; 2 criminal mischief cases; 1 arrested for harassment; 1 arrested for assault; 1 arrested for disorderly conduct; and 1 trip to Cooperstown jail.

13 violations and traffic summons were issued for the following: 2 unsafe tires; 7 speed; 1 studded tire; 1 exhaust violation; 1 no inspection and 1 inadequate exhaust.

question ("interrogate") the suspect at this point. He or she may, of course, refuse to answer questions and may have an attorney present at questioning.

Police and Human Service Delivery

Although the "law"-oriented portion of police work engages the imagination of both police and the public, the bulk of police work involves "order": up to 90 percent of police time is spent in order maintenance and service delivery—work not directly related to the investigation of crimes and the apprehension and conviction of malefactors. Many of the service delivery tasks involve complex skills in managing people. Included in service delivery are provision of emergency services—ambulance, first aid, delivering babies, rescuing cats from trees—missing persons, traffic control, family fights, death and illness notifications. Police are also called on to help with psychotics and attempted suicides, guard downed power lines, quiet noisy parties.

• The service delivery tasks, which are given, at best, only minimum structure by the law, involve the greatest exercise of discretion by police. They are also the areas in which training is most likely to be neglected and where psychologists have made some of their most important contributions to law enforcement—contributions that will be discussed further in Chapter 4 on interventions in policing.

The Administration of Justice: Adult Suspects

The administration of justice component of the criminal justice system includes municipal courts, which handle misdemeanors; state courts for trial and review on appeal of felonies; federal courts for federal offenses; the U.S. Court of Appeals for each of 11 districts, and the U.S. Supreme Court. Its personnel are the magistrates and judges, prosecutors and defense attorneys, and their staffs.

The American legal system is what is called an adversary system. In such a system, the court becomes a battleground, with the state on one side, the defendant on the other, and the judge serving as referee. The rules of the battle include certain constitutional guarantees, particularly guarantees to what is known as due process: the right to a public trial conducted in an orderly manner, the right to reasonable notice of charges, protection against self-incrimination, but the opportunity to speak in one's own defense, the right to confront and cross-examine hostile witnesses.

The burden of proof is on the prosecution: The state must prove the defendant's guilt "beyond a reasonable doubt."[13] The law places no burden on the defendant to prove he or she did *not* commit the act: He or she is presumed innocent until proven guilty.

In any discussion of the role of the prosecutor in the criminal justice process, it is important to remember that, at least in theory,

> there is a legitimate double standard in the criminal law. . . . The defense lawyer is supposed to do anything ethical to win for his client. The prosecutor, however, is held to a much higher standard. In recognition of the enormous power wielded by the prosecutor against any defendant, and because the prosecutor represents all of us in enforcing

---

[13] In a civil case the decision rule is "preponderance of the evidence," usually taken to mean a subjective criterion of 51 percent or more.

the community's moral code with its most drastic sanctions, the prosecutor's responsibility is not victory but justice (Schwartz & Jackson, 1976).

Under these standards, even if the defense attorney knows that his or her client is guilty, he or she may not decide to abandon the defendant. Even overwhelming evidence against the client does not relieve the attorney of his duty. He or she owes the client the best possible defense, short, of course, of perjury. He or she has no responsibility to make available to the prosecution evidence that might implicate the client. The prosecution, on the other hand, must provide the defense with any evidence it has that would exculpate the defendant and may drop the case at any point for insufficient evidence.[14]

Prosecution and law enforcement agencies typically work very closely together in the initial stages of investigation and of processing the suspect. Thus, although they are officially listed as functions of prosecution, the initial appearance and preliminary hearing may be handled largely by the police.

After arrest, booking, and questioning, the suspect is taken for an initial court appearance. Ideally, this occurs within six hours after arrest; it must be held without "unnecessary" delay. This hearing is usually in one of the lower courts, such as magistrates' court, justice of the peace courts, or municipal courts. These courts have jurisdiction over misdemeanors, as well as the preliminary stages of felony cases. At the initial appearance the accused is informed of charges, a plea of guilty or not guilty is entered, and bail is set. A review of Figure 2.1 reminds us that the prosecutor or the judge may decide at any of these stages that there is insufficient evidence or that some legal rule has been violated, and the accused may be released.

BAIL

The setting of bail is an important discretionary point. It also has been one where there has been wide latitude, great discrepancy from judge to judge, and much potential for abuse. The purpose of bail is to assure the suspect's appearance in court. Some judges, such as Judge Bruce Wright of New York, point out that the system places a particular hardship on the poor, others worry about turning potentially dangerous people back onto the streets. Depending on the circumstances, such as the seriousness of the charges, prior criminal record, employment history, family and community ties, recommendation of the prosecutor and the judge's subjective feeling about all these, bail may be set im-

[14] These rules, unfortunately, are not always followed, as Schwartz and Jackson and others demonstrate. For both sides, the quest for victory may get in the way of truth.

BOX 2.2

A ROBBERY IS A ROBBERY, AND . . .: LESSER INCLUDED CHARGES

A New Jersey man reports that a man came up behind him as he was opening the door to his apartment, stuck something—"I think it was a gun"—in his back, pushed him inside, and ordered him to give over his money. The victim handed over his wallet, which contained $25 in cash and five credit cards. The perpetrator took it and left. The victim turned around in time to catch a glimpse of him going down the stairs. He called the police.

A suspect was arrested when he tried to use the victim's credit card to buy gas. A gun was found in his jacket pocket.

Charges against this suspect might include (with penalties)

Charge	Maximum Fine	Maximum Sentence
Robbery	$5000	15 years
Assault with a deadly weapon	$2000	7 years
Unlawful use of dangerous weapon	$5000	10 years
Carrying concealed weapon	$1000	3 years
Unlawful entry	$2000	7 years
Possession of stolen property	$2000	7 years
Attempted fraud (misuse of credit card) (5 counts)	$1000	3 years (each count)

As the evidence against the suspect is strong, his attorney, with his consent, may work out a "bargain" with the prosecutor: the suspect will plead guilty to weapons possession and attempted fraud, and the other charges will be dropped. The prosecutor will suggest to the judge that the defendant be given a maximum sentence of ten years in prison. Usually the judge accepts the suggestion—even though he is not legally bound by it. A trial is averted.

SOURCE: New Jersey Police Manual, 1962.

possibly high or obviously in reach of the defendant, or the accused may even be released on his or her own promise to appear for trial, an option known as "release on one's own recognizance" (ROR).

If the suspect cannot make the bail, either on his or her own, or by arrangement with others such as bail bondsmen, he or she will be transferred to a local jail to await preliminary hearing.

Freedom during the stages of preparation for trial is a major

BOX 2.3

CRITERIA USED IN BAIL AND PRETRIAL RELEASE DECISIONS AS OF 1976

Decision Criteria	Total States Having Criterion
LEGAL FACTORS	
Nature of present charge	35
Probability of guilt/conviction (weight of evidence)	17
Possible penalty	4
Prior criminal record	31
Prior arrests	1
Prior record of court appearances	20
On probation or parole when presently charged	1
On pretrial release for previous charge	3
COMMUNITY TIE FACTORS	
General community ties	4
Age	1
Residence, length of residence	22
Family ties	23
Employment, employment history	22
Defendant's financial resources	29
Character	22
Reputation	5
Mental condition	17
Past conduct	1
Persons to assist accused in attending court	4
Addiction to drugs or alcohol	1
DANGEROUS FACTORS	
General consideration of pretrial dangerousness	2
Danger to self	5
Danger to others (other persons, witnesses)	7
Danger to community (public)	8
Likelihood of violation of law if released	5
GENERAL CONSIDERATION	
Risk of nonappearance	19
"Not oppressive", but "sufficient" bail	5

SOURCE: Goldkamp, John S. *Bail Decision-Making and the Role of Pretrial Detention in American Justice*, Utilization of Criminal Justice Statistics Project, Research Report Draft (Albany, N.Y.: Criminal Justice Research Center, 1977). Reprinted in *Sourcebook of Criminal Justice Statistics, 1978.* U.S. Department of Justice, Law Enforcement Assistance Administration, National Criminal Justice Information And Statistics Service (Washington, D.C.: U.S. Government Printing Office, June 1979).

advantage for defendants. Not only are they spared the psychological hazards of jail—and, remember, they are still considered innocent—they also find it easier to gather witnesses and prepare a defense, and so are less likely to be found guilty (Footlick, 1977). Detention may cost them their jobs and erode family and community ties.

PRELIMINARY HEARING OR GRAND JURY

At the preliminary hearing, usually held within a few days or weeks of the initial appearance, the prosecution must establish "probable cause," that is, present evidence that a crime has been committed and that the accused is the person who committed it. In this "pretrial discovery" the defendant and his or her counsel learn the nature of at least some of the evidence against him or her, information that allows them to start building their case.[15]

The Fifth Amendment to the Constitution guarantees that "No person shall be held to answer for a capital or otherwise infamous crime, unless on a presentment or indictment of a grand jury."[16] The grand jury varies in number from six to 23, depending on the state. Its job is to evaluate the evidence presented by the prosecutor to see if there is sufficient evidence to continue the case. If the grand jury determines there is sufficient evidence for an indictment, it returns a "true bill." If evidence is insufficient, a "no bill" is returned and the case will be dropped unless additional evidence is found, at which time the case may again be brought before the grand jury.

The grand jury is a fact-finding body, whose proceedings ordinarily are secret. The members of the grand jury may actively question witnesses themselves, and may have investigations conducted for them. (The victim often will testify.) The defendant may be called but usually is not. If called, he or she does not have to testify.

PLEA BARGAINING

One of the most important discretionary points in the processing of an accused person occurs at some time between indictment and trial. It is not part of the official process, nor is it shown in Figure 2.1. This is *plea bargaining*. The defense attorney and the prosecutor get together informally and work out a "deal" whereby the defendant will

---

[15] If a suspect is released at this time for insufficient evidence, it is still possible for additional evidence to be gathered and the case presented to the grand jury.

[16] Subsequent rulings, *Hurtado* v. *California* [110 U.S. 516 (1884)], allowed an "information" to take the place of a grand jury indictment. This is a document filed by the prosecutor in a trial court, and is common in misdemeanor cases.

plead guilty to some of the charges against him, and others will be dropped. The prosecutor will agree to recommend a certain sentence.[17] The defendant, of course, cannot be forced to accept any such "bargain". If he or she does, the prosecutor makes a recommendation to the judge. The judge usually accepts the bargain; in some cases he or she has even participated in the discussions over a possible plea bargain and may have guided it. However, the judge is under no legal obligation to accept any bargain.

During the time between the preliminary hearing and the trial, about 80 percent of the defendants charged with major offenses plead guilty (Saks and Hastie, 1978). The prosecution is particularly likely to be eager to bargain if its evidence is weak (Klein, 1976); the defense attorney will try to persuade the client to "plea" when the prosecution has a strong case, and, alas, sometimes when the defense attorney is a badly overworked public defender. Plea bargaining is also common when the process has been drawn out over a relatively long time, the defendant has been unable to make bail and so has been held in jail (even though, remember, the defendant is still considered innocent) for almost as long as he or she might have been held had he or she been convicted. In this case, credit may be promised for time already served as part of the bargain.

In addition to plea bargaining as an alternative to the formal legal process, there has been an important trend in recent years toward diverting certain offenders from the criminal justice system through a variety of programs. Social scientists have played important roles in the establishment, running, and evaluation of many of the projects.[18] Some of these will be discussed in later chapters.

ARRAIGNMENT AND PRE-TRIAL PROCESS

The next step in the process is called, in most jurisdictions, arraignment.[19] The *arraignment* marks the beginning of the formal trial process. The defendant, who now must be accompanied by an attorney in all but the most unusual cases,[20] is once again informed of his or her rights and of the charges against him or her. A plea is then entered:

[17] For a moving account of a prosecutor's thinking in a difficult plea-bargaining case, see Phillips (1977).
[18] For technical details about alternative programs, see Aaronson et al. (1977).
[19] In other jurisdictions the term "arraignment" is used for the appearance in which charges are listed, a hearing that occurs *before* grand jury.
[20] These include cases where a judge has ruled that the defendant may act *pro se*, that is, as his or her own attorney. Until this point the defendant can waive his or her right to be represented by an attorney.

guilty, not guilty, or *nolo contendere* ("no contest," which, although technically not an admission of guilt, has the same practical implications). If the defendant pleads guilty or *nolo contendere*, the judge will impose sentence, if he or she pleads not guilty, the trial process begins.

One of the first decisions the defendant makes is whether to be tried before a jury or by a judge or panel of judges (commonly called a "bench trial.") Most choose a jury trial. The defense counsel then may file any of a number of motions: to suppress evidence that may be in violation of the defendant's Fourth Amendment rights, to get a change of venue (move the trial to another location), to dismiss the indictment or complaint, or to "continue" the case until a later date, giving the defense more time to prepare for the trial. Psychologists have been particularly active in providing documentation for change of venue motions. (See Chapter 9.) The prosecution may counter these motions by evidence of its own, stating the reason that they should not be granted.

It is not unusual for several "continuances" to be requested and granted. This, it has been charged, is a defense technique to discourage prosecution witnesses, and sometimes it does have that effect. The trial is called for the sixth or seventh time, the victim fails to appear, and the defense calls for dismissal of the charges on the grounds of failure to prosecute. The various delays may mean that months elapse from the time of arrest until the trial begins. (Recently many states have tried to get major cases to trial much more speedily, in, say, a matter of two or three months.)

THE JURY TRIAL

Finally, the jury trial begins. The order of procedure is (1) jury selection; (2) opening statements, first by the prosecution, then by the defense; (3) presentation of the government's evidence against the defendant, with cross-examination by the defense of the prosecution witnesses; (4) presentation and argument of defense motions, particularly a motion for a "directed verdict of acquittal." This motion asks the judge to rule that the prosecution has not proved its case and that the defendant be acquitted. Such a motion is seldom granted.

The defendant is not required by law to bring forward any witnesses, or to say anything in his or her own defense. This is unusual; ordinarily the trial proceeds to (5) presentation of the defense case, in which witnesses are called and the prosecution now has the opportunity to cross-examine witnesses. The Fifth Amendment guarantee against self-incrimination means that even if the defense chooses to present a case, the defendant does not have to take the stand and testify. If he or she takes the stand, it may be possible to bring out evidence of any past criminal record. If he or she does not, such evidence may not be admitted.

After the defense rests its case (6) rebuttal witnesses may be called. First the prosecution and then the defense may call witnesses to counter evidence presented by the other side. Ordinarily, entirely new evidence may not be introduced at this stage.

After both sides have finished the presentation of their evidence, each gets to make a final statement, summing up the case from its point of view and, often, making an emotional plea to the jury. Most attorneys consider the final summation extremely important. The prosecution usually has the last word.

Now the judge "charges the jury": gives jurors instructions about the possible findings they may make (such as guilty, not guilty, not guilty by reason of insanity, guilty on some of the charges, not guilty on others, etc.), and the relevant law. The attorneys for both sides may make recommendations to the judge regarding the charge.

Finally, the case goes to the jury. Unlike grand jurors, petit jurors are passive during the presentation of evidence. They cannot ask questions or institute investigations, but must rely on the evidence presented to them. In all but six states, jurors must reach a unanimous verdict (U.S. Department of Justice, 1979). To help in their deliberations, they may ask to see evidence or for further instructions from the judge of legal points. Taking of notes by jurors during a case is usually left to the discretion of the judge. If the jury cannot reach a unanimous verdict within a reasonable time, they report to the judge that they are "hung." The judge may either send them back to deliberate further or declare a mistrial, whereupon a new jury is selected, and the process begins again. (Alternatively, the prosecution may decide to drop the case, at which point the defendant will be released for failure to prosecute.)

If, however, the jury reaches a verdict, they will so inform the judge, and the foreperson will deliver the verdict, either orally or in writing. If the verdict is "not guilty," the defendant goes free and can never be tried again for the same offense, even were he or she to stand up in court at that moment and openly confess guilt.[21] If the defendant is found guilty, the next step is sentencing. Although it is possible for the defendant to remain free on bail while awaiting sentencing, often he or she is taken ("remanded") into custody.

---

[21] Double jeopardy applies only within one court system, not across court systems, so that some acts violate both federal and state statutes, and an acquittal at the state level in no way influences the ability of the federal courts to try the suspect for the same act. In this way, defendants who were found not guilty of the murder of civil rights workers in state courts could still be tried in federal courts for violating the victims' civil rights.

SENTENCING

In some states the defendant will be sentenced by the judge, in others a jury, either the same one that decided guilt or an entirely separate one, will recommend a sentence to the judge. Before sentence is passed it is usual for the judge to order a presentence investigation by the probation department of the offender's history, psychological state, and criminal background. This report is presented, attorneys for both sides again have an opportunity to present arguments concerning appropriate severity of the sentence; occasionally the defense will call character witnesses.

Judges usually have very wide latitude in sentencing. The law will set a maximum, and sometimes a minimum for a given offense, but these can range as widely as from one year to life imprisonment. In many cases there is also the option of placing the offender on probation, or in one of the alternative facilities mentioned earlier.

THE APPEALS PROCESS

After sentencing, the defendant may begin to serve the sentence immediately, or may appeal. Appeal is possible whether the offender remains free on bail while the appeal is pending or is incarcerated. The case is then taken to an appeals court which does not hear witnesses, but studies the record of the trial, and decides if judge or attorneys committed any significant legal errors. If this court decides that an error was committed, it will reverse the lower court's decision and the defendant will be freed; if it finds no error, the decision will be affirmed. An intermediate step is also possible: A decision to reverse and remand means the defendant may be retried. If the first appeals court decides against the defendant, he or she can take the case to a higher appeals court and, ultimately, to the U.S. Supreme Court. The process may be stopped at the highest levels if the court refuses to hear the case.

The appeals process is exhausted, and the offender is given into the custody of the corrections system.

The Administration of Justice: Juveniles

Children, according to modern legal ideas, comprise a special category of human beings, with characteristics that merit special distinctions in the way others behave toward them. Because of their immaturity and malleability, they need and have the right to protection and supervision by parents or guardians and, if necessary, by the state (acting *in loco parentis*). This protection should allow a "second chance," that is, the right not to have to suffer for the rest of their lives for mistakes made during childhood.

Despite these protections for individual children, society has rights also. Society has demanded that children be made aware of the consequences of serious wrongdoing and that they be subjected to corrective measures. In especially serious cases, such as murder, rape, and armed robbery, it is becoming increasingly common to lower the age of responsibility and to try adolescents as adults, rather than to give them the special treatment usually accorded to children. This is one of the possible points of discretion in the administration of justice with juveniles: In serious cases a judge may decide, subject to state statutes, to put a teenager into the juvenile or the adult court systems.[22] In some states the child also may make this choice. All others under a given age, usually between 16 and 21, are dealt with in a special juvenile or "family" court. This court oversees not only cases that would be crimes were an adult involved but offenses peculiar to juveniles: "status" offenses such as curfew violation, truancy, running away from home, incorrigibility, and "being in need of supervision."

Unlike the adult system, the juvenile court is, at least officially, unambiguous in its mandate: Rehabilitation is seen as its goal. This is accomplished through protecting children from potentially harmful situations, such as neglect and child abuse, and from the ineradicable consequences of the criminal law. Children are not to be detained unnecessarily, or required to post bond. In most cases they are kept from contact with adult offenders; their records are kept separate and confidential and often are destroyed when the individual reaches majority. Unlike adults found guilty of criminal acts, they cannot be disqualified from holding office or holding various kinds of licenses later.

Because by law children are presumed incapable of self-determination or self-protection, their parents are notified immediately if they have come into contact with the law, and they or some other "friendly" adult must be present for questioning.

Because intent is a crucial part in the definition of a crime, and a juvenile is not considered capable of intent, a child under the jurisdiction of the juvenile court is never accused of a crime. He or she can only be guilty of "juvenile delinquency." Even the language is differ-

---

[22] Perusal of the FBI's Uniform Crime Report for 1976 gives an idea of the relative frequency of various dispositions in juvenile cases:

Total 1,569,626

Handled within police department and released	611,708	(39.0%)
Referred to juvenile court jurisdiction	838,503	(53.4%)
Referred to welfare agency	24,393	(1.6%)
Referred to other police agency	26,230	(1.7%)
Referred to criminal or adult court	68,793	(4.4%)

SOURCE: Kelley, Clarence M. *Crime in the United States*, 1976, p. 220.

ent: In New York, for example, the word "contact" substitutes for arrest, the formal accusation is called a "petition"; there is no trial but, rather, "fact-finding" in a closed court before a judge. A child who pleads guilty is said to have made an "admission," resulting in a "disposition," rather than a sentence. Reports by probation officers attached to juvenile courts and from the child's school usually play an important part in the judge's decision.

Until recently, judges in juvenile hearings had, because of the special status of juveniles, almost unlimited discretion in their handling and disposition of cases. Because the juvenile was not considered legally a criminal, the constitutional protections were not always applied. In the past 15 years, legal protections given to adults in *Miranda* [348 U.S. 436 (1966)] were also extended to children[23] so that they are not deprived of these rights in the desire to protect them. The courts have not expanded these rights to include the right to a jury trial [*In re Barbara Burrus*, 403 U.S. 328 (1971)].

In addition to juvenile courts, some states have "youth courts" to handle older adolescents. These are technically adult courts but use some of the safeguards of privacy of juvenile courts.

Corrections

The corrections component of the criminal justice system has the responsibility for persons convicted of an offense. It maintains jails, prisons, reformatories, and other correctional facilities, and oversees probation and parole.

Probation is a court-imposed sentence that involves reporting to a probation officer, often someone trained in social work or other human service delivery discipline, at stated intervals. Frequently, there are contingencies: The offender must have a steady job or attend school, a vocational training program, or be involved in some form of psychotherapy. Restrictions are placed on travel and, often, on acquaintances.[24] A person who violates the conditions of his or her probation may have it revoked and may be incarcerated.

Jails, run by city or county, typically hold offenders who are sentenced to terms of a year or less; convicted felons are incarcerated in penitentiaries run by the state or federal government. All corrections departments have several different institutions to which a felon may

---

[23] Decisions of particular importance in this area have been *In re Gault* 387 U.S. 1 (1967), *In re Winship* 997 U.S. 358 (1970), and *Kent* v. *United States* 383 U.S. 541 (1966).

[24] Unfortunately, in most jurisdictions probation officers have staggering case loads and are unable to monitor compliance with these restrictions.

be sent. A major difference in these is the degree of "security"; there are also units for the criminally insane. Unless the judge has specified the level of security, the felon typically is sent first to a reception center for testing and evaluation. He or she is then sent to the institution that is considered appropriate—or the institution closest in appropriateness that has space!—to serve the sentence.

At any time during incarceration, the prisoner or his or her attorney may file a writ of *habeas corpus*: a written court order directing that the prisoner be brought before the court to determine if there is adequate cause to continue to detain him or her. Typical reasons for such writs include the availability of new evidence that might exonerate the prisoner, evidence that he or she is being subjected to cruel and unusual punishment, or Supreme Court decisions that might affect him or her either as an individual or as part of a class (of, say, people under sentence of death).

Psychologists are, of course, involved in a variety of rehabilitation, education, and reform programs within the prison, as well as in research on the influence of the system, and searches for alternative structures. The promises and pitfalls of these programs are discussed at length in the chapter on prisons.

After serving the minimum sentence, a prisoner becomes eligible for parole. Parole board members are appointed from "the community." Although they are not official permanent members of the corrections department, they are usually drawn from individuals having experience with corrections: former law enforcement officials, clergy, mental health professionals who have had experience in the criminal justice system. They meet, examine the prisoner's records, including recommendations from parole officers who have investigated the case, and determine if the individuals may be released on parole or must continue in prison. There are few guidelines for making these crucial decisions, discretion is enormous, and decisions often seem arbitrary; much criticism has been focused on the parole process in recent years. Central to most of the criticism are the problems involved with prediction of dangerousness. These are discussed elsewhere in this book.

While few prisoners are released the first time they become eligible for parole, few serve out their full sentences; most are eventually released on parole. As with probation, parole usually involves a set of conditions. If the parolee violates the conditions—for example, if he or she associates with other known felons, moves without notifying the parole officers, or, particularly, is arrested for another crime—the parole officer may recommend to the parole board that parole be revoked and the individual returned to prison to serve out the remainder of the sentence. Like probation officers, the average parole officer oversees a large number of cases, and seldom has time for the full-scale investigations or counseling that are considered part of the duties.

SUMMARY

The criminal justice system, although formidable, is far from inflexible. Discretion is possible in decisions at many points. Aaronson and his colleagues (1977) have devised a matrix to show the potential alternatives open to a variety of actors in the criminal justice system at critical decision points. They define the decision points as:

1. Decision to define conduct as a crime.
2. Decision to focus attention on a subject.
3. Decision to arrest.
4. Decision to charge.
5. Decision to release defendant pending trial or disposition.
6. Decision on pretrial motions and applications.
7. Decision to try to accept plea.
8. Decision to sentence.

The actors they include are legislatures, police departments, prosecutor offices, trial courts, defense bar, public noncriminal justice and private agencies, citizen volunteers, probation and parole officers, and the appellate courts. Although psychologists are not mentioned specifically, they have had input at many of these levels and in other stages of the process, such as trial itself. In the following chapters we shall present a sampling of interventions by psychologists and other social scientists in the criminal justice system.

VICTIM AS EVIDENCE,
VICTIM AS CULPRIT,
VICTIM AS PERSON

People of the State of California v. *Edgar Smith* reads the legal case citation. As mentioned in Chapter 2 (Introduction to the Criminal Justice System), the plaintiff in a criminal action is not the victim or victims, but the state. Under such a system the victim of the crime comes to be known as the complaining witness and assumes the status of a piece of evidence (Brodyaga et al., 1975, p. 103). As such, he or she is fair game for either side in an adversary process. Until recently little thought was given to the possibility that the criminal justice process might be damaging to the victim as well as to the defendant.

In recent years, however, given impetus by the women's movement's concern for the plight of rape victims, organizations concerned with victim assistance have begun to operate. The victim of crime has become the subject of a variety of scientific studies, ranging from descriptive surveys to experiments aimed at concepts of causality. One common theme of the latter has been to search for behavior of the victim that may—or may not be seen by others to—precipitate the behavior of the offender. Thus the victim of crime assumes multiple roles and has become the subject of concern for both sides in the adversary system—for helping professionals and for social scientists. This chapter will describe the characteristics of victims and examine their multiple roles as evidence, culprit, and person.

WHO IS THE VICTIM?

The U.S. Department of Justice's Law Enforcement Assistance Administration through its National Criminal Justice Information and Statistics Service has, since 1971, been routinely conducting surveys of crime victimization. Although not without methodological flaws (McDonald, 1976; U.S. Department of Justice, 1977b), these surveys present perhaps the most complete descriptive data of crime victimization available. Some of the characteristics of victims surveyed in 1974 (U.S. Department of Justice, 1977d) are summarized below.

> Victimization rates for personal crimes of violence were relatively higher for males, younger persons, blacks, the poor, and for those separated or divorced. For personal crimes of theft, males, young persons, whites, and the more affluent were the more likely victims. With respect to personal crimes of violence or theft, men had far higher victimization rates than women.
>
> Young persons age 12–14 had the highest victimization rates for both personal crimes of violence and personal crimes of theft; beyond that age, the rates declined as age increased.
>
> Blacks had a higher robbery rate than whites, but the apparent differences for the other two personal crimes of violence (rape and assault) were not statistically significant.
>
> The rate for violent crimes was highest for black males, followed by that for white males, black females and white females.
>
> Divorced or separated persons had the highest rate for violent crimes, followed by those who had never been married, by married persons, and by those who were widowed.
>
> For personal crimes of theft, those who had never been married had the highest rate and widowed persons the lowest.
>
> The incidence of violent crime was highest among members of families with the lowest incomes; moreover, there was a tendency for the overall rate to decline with increased income.
>
> Family members in the most affluent group examined had the highest rate for personal crimes of theft.
>
> Unemployed persons were the victims of violent crime at a far higher rate than those who had jobs.
>
> The risk of victimization in personal crimes generally was the highest for central city residents and lowest for the nonmetropolitan population, with suburbanites ranking in between. The pattern was similar, although not so pronounced, for household crimes.
>
> Stranger-to-stranger violent crimes accounted for about two-thirds of the victimizations (p. 4).

Others have pointed out that not all people who report vicitimization are themselves blameless. As one writer (McDonald, 1976) put it, victim programs "frequently cannot even decide who is the victim. In many cases both parties are guilty of some criminal behavior. The 'victim' is merely the party who 'wins the race to the prosecutor's office'" (p. 64). Further, a study of victims of aggravated assault disclosed that 75 percent of all male victims had a police record themselves (Johnson et al., 1973). (This does not, of course, in itself lessen the legitimacy of their victimization).

It is also true that some alleged victims lie about crimes. How many are included in this category is not known, although analyses of rape cases indicate that lying at least for this crime is less common than many believe (Hursh, 1977).

THE VICTIM AS EVIDENCE

From the victim's standpoint, the first step in the criminal justice procedure is the definition of an act committed against him or her as a crime. A man standing on a crowded metropolitan street is hit sharply on the back. He looks around but is unable to identify anyone as a probable culprit. He might decide that the blow was an accident, an assault, or even an attempt to pick his pocket. A wallet that is suddenly noticed as missing might have fallen from pocket or purse, or have been stolen. A woman might consider a grab by a drunk who follows her from a bar as a "messy situation," an attempted assault, or an attempted rape.[1] Whereas the crucial point in the law is the intention of the offender, the victim's reading—or misreading—of that intention is the first step in the decision whether or not to report.

Reporting a Crime

Once she has decided the act was a crime, the victim's next decision is whether to report that crime to the police. At this point, the victim is "an important and influential criminal justice decision maker . . . the initiator of the criminal justice process" (Hindelang & Gottfredson, 1976). According to studies of criminal victimization (Ennis, 1976; U.S. Department of Justice, 1976a, 1976b, 1977), the majority of victims decide not to report (see Box 3.1).[2] The most

---

[1] Attempted crimes are perhaps the most likely to fail to be seen as a crime by the intended victim, according to the U.S. Department of Justice in its victimization studies (U.S. Department of Justice, 1977d, p. 1).

[2] Ironically, in some states, the person who fails to report a crime becomes a criminal him or herself. Laws requiring reporting are seldom invoked, however.

BOX 3.1

REPORTING OF VICTIMIZATION TO THE POLICE

A major community survey of victimization (United States Department of Justice, 1977d, p. 9). found that

The proportions of victimizations reported to the police ranged from 26 percent for personal larceny without contact to 90 percent for commercial robbery.

Roughly half of all rapes, aggravated assaults, or personal robberies were reported to the police.

There was no significant difference according to victim sex in the overall percentage of personal crimes reported; however, females were somewhat more apt than males to have reported violent crimes (rape, robbery, and assault combined).

Blacks reported personal crimes, as a group, slightly more often than whites.

For personal crimes as a group, those against teenagers were the least well reported.

Forty-seven percent of personal crimes of violence were reported, and there was a slight tendency to report offenses committed by strangers more readily than those by nonstrangers.

Homeowners reported household crimes (burglary, larceny, and motor vehicle theft combined) somewhat more often than renters.

Blacks were more likely to have reported household crimes, overall, than their white counterparts.

The burglary reporting rate was lower for poor people (less than $7500 annual family income) than for the more affluent, but this is not true for household larceny or motor vehicle theft.

The higher the value of losses, the more likely that household crimes were reported.

common reasons given for not reporting were the beliefs that nothing could have been done and that the crime was not important enough (U.S. Department of Justice, 1976c). Other reasons included the ideas that the police would not want to be bothered, it was too inconvenient or time consuming to report, the act was a private or personal matter, and the fear of reprisal.

Reasons given by victims who did report have been studied less frequently than those of nonreporters. Conklin (1975) concluded that "people do not call the police unless they are seriously wronged or have something to gain—for example, being able to collect on an insurance policy if a crime is reported to the police. The gain must outweigh the effort of calling police and the psychological cost of getting involved with the legal system . . ." (p. 157). Others disagree. In a study of victims who reported burglaries, Smith and Maness (1976) found that the most common reason for reporting was "obligation": a feeling of civic duty expressed in such phrases as, "It's the proper thing to do," "It's the only way we can have law and order," "There was no one else to call," and "I want to cooperate with the police."[3] Desire that the offender be caught was the second most frequently given reason, followed by personal protection and the wish to recover property. Insurance came fifth in percentage of respondents mentioning the reason at all (17 percent), and fourth as the most important one.

A community survey of victimization conducted in Portland, Oregon, by Schneider, Burcart, and Wilson (1976) found differences in reporting as a function of the crime. They concluded that

> minor property crimes . . . are more apt to be reported to the police if the victim (a) is more trusting of the police, rather than less trusting, (b) lives in an area where police enjoy good relations with the community, (c) is more integrated into the community in the sense that he or she is able to understand most of the local issues rather than only a few or none of them, (d) has participated in more activities sponsored by the Crime Prevention Bureau anti-burglary team.
>
> It is also interesting to notice that, for the minor crimes, beliefs about the ability of the police to catch the offender or recover the property are not important factors in a victim's decision to report incidents, and neither are attitudes toward the courts. In addition, whether the offender is a stranger or not seems to be irrelevant, as is also the question of whether the property was insured (p. 105).

In contrast, belief in the ability of the police to catch the offender and having insurance were important factors in the reporting of serious property crimes; these crimes were also more likely to be reported if the victim had lived in the city for a long time and believed the offender was a stranger. People who trusted the police and believed they had a chance of recovering lost property, who believed the courts would punish the offender if caught, and who understood local issues were more likely to report personal crimes.

The experience of the senior author with victims of sexual assault suggests another reason: the need to have society's stamp of legitimacy on the victimization, for someone in authority to know and acknowl-

---

[3] This was true both of persons who had insurance, of whom 39 percent reported "Obligation" as their first reason for reporting, and of those who had no insurance (50 percent).

edge one's outrage. "Obligation" also figures as a reason for reporting these crimes. Victims state that they reported because they hoped it would alert the police and other women to the danger.

Cooperating with Authorities

After a crime is reported, the victim who wishes to pursue the case has little formal say in the process that follows (DuBow & Becker, 1976). Now it is the police who decide whether a crime has been committed and whether enough evidence exists or the crime is serious enough to pursue an investigation. "Unfounding," the determination that no crime was committed, may occur as a result of a real misunderstanding by a "victim" about the law (as in a wife's attempting to charge her husband with rape in a state that specifically excludes husbands under the rape statute), because the police do not believe the victim, or consider him or her unworthy of their time, or in cases in which there is insufficient evidence (Coleman & Bottomley, 1976; Pepinsky, 1972; Hursch, 1977; Rubinstein, 1973). [Unfounding is also a convenient way for departments to reduce reported crime rates and increase reported clearance rates (Greenwood, Chaiken, & Petersilia, 1977).]

If the police decide to pursue the case, the collection of evidence is the next step. This may include physical evidence. If the crime occurred in the victim's home, the house may become a "crime scene" which the victim is not allowed to enter until the investigation is finished. Although the actual incidence of such drastic steps is rare, investigation texts advise police to cut up rugs or upholstered furniture showing stains of what might be blood or semen (O'Hara, 1973). More commonly, the victim's clothing will be taken for such tests. If an arrest is not made immediately, and if the victim did not know the offender, he or she commonly will be asked to report to the police station to view photos and lineups, or to help make a composite sketch. Interviews with detectives, and the taking of a formal statement may follow.

In many instances, the case ends here. While some crimes of violence, such as homicide (75 percent), aggravated assault (62 percent), and forcible rape (51 percent) are rather likely to be cleared by arrest, robbery (27 percent) and crimes against property seldom result in arrest (Webster, 1978, p. 161). Although victims report a desire to be informed of the progress or disposition of their cases,[4]

[4] Common dispositions include the decision to keep the case "open," but to suspend investigation, and the "closing" of the case by arrest of a suspect in another case.

such information is seldom provided consistently and often is difficult to obtain (Greenwood, Chaiken & Petersilia, 1977).

Prosecuting the Case

If, however, a suspect is identified and arrested, the case passes to the hands of the prosecutor. Because the prosecutor serves the state, not the victim, the interests of the victim are, at best, secondary to winning the case. An extreme example of the problems a victim may face because of his or her status in the adversary process is seen in the statement of an assistant prosecutor to the authors that he would be willing to sacrifice a victim's sanity to get a conviction. The uncooperative victim who fails to appear may, in extreme cases, find him or herself facing contempt of court charges, or detained as a material witness, and held under guard in a hotel room or even in jail.

One prosecutor (Ash, 1972) has said of the court system that it

> exhibits the natural human tendency to favor "insider interests" at the expense of "outside interests." Wherever minor inconvenience to "insiders" (judges, lawyers, court clerks, etc.) is to be balanced against major inconvenience to outsiders (witnesses, jurors, etc.) and the balancing is to be performed by insiders, insider interests will invariably prevail (p. 397).

The prosecutor may want to do his or her own interview of the victim, especially if he or she will testify at screening or preliminary hearings. The victim may be required to be present and testify at these hearings and before the grand jury (Brodyaga et al., 1975; Knudten et al., 1976). [How common this practice is is unknown; especially in less serious cases an officer often reads the victim's statement at these hearings. It is sufficiently common in rape cases, however, to warrant comment in a prescriptive manual for prosecutors (Brodyaga et al., 1975).]

Although plea bargaining may take place at many points in the criminal justice process, it most commonly occurs between arraignment and trial. The victim may be consulted about his or her wishes, but they need not be followed (Phillips, 1977). Sometimes victims are not even informed that a bargain has been made and that they will not have to be present or testify at court. Indeed, the victim often has difficulty ascertaining the status of the case.

Problems in Giving Evidence

Although speedy trial rulings have hastened the process over the past few years, in the past the average case that came to trial in large cities such as New York would involve a dozen delays (WCBS, 1976). One study of 1775 victims found that in 24 percent of the cases the case was rescheduled at least once; in 47 percent of these the victim was given no prior notification (Viano et al., 1977). Even with speedy trial provisions, attorneys for defendants, particularly those out on bail, may have their clients waive the right, knowing that delay causes witnesses to become frustrated and fail to appear, leading to the cases being dropped for nonprosecution. (This practice is known among attorneys as "aging the case.")

Even if the case has been "continued" several times, the victim is expected to be present each time a new trial date is set. In each of these instances the victim may be required to take time off from work, often a job that pays by the hour and does not provide compensation for court appearances. In one study, 53 percent of 1775 victims reported that they had lost time as a result of "system-related problems," with an average of two days lost (Viano et al., 1977). Thirty-one percent of this sample also reported income loss from system-related problems with an average loss of $127. Sixty-nine percent of the sample of 326 victims studied by Knudten and his colleagues (1976) said that unnecessary trips were a serious or very serious problem.

Knudten et al. (1976) also reported that 87 percent of their sample had to pay their own transportation or parking; for 12 percent transportation presented a difficulty. Although only 16 percent had a problem with child care, those who did rated it as a serious difficulty. Poor victims sometimes are forced to bring their children to court with them; the halls of many courts in urban areas are filled with restless children, adding to the already chaotic, tense atmosphere.

Nor is the potential cost to the victim limited to time lost from work and expenses connected with court attendance. If property was taken, or is needed for use as evidence, as may be the case if there were blood or semen stains and the like, it may be confiscated by the police. Often it will not be returned until the termination of the case. "One witness whose television had been stolen complained that the defendant had taken it for only two days but had kept it for five months." (Bloom, 1974). Eighteen percent of the Kundten group (1976) had property kept as evidence.

In most cases, the defendant's right to a public trial and to notification of the charges against him or her means that the name and address of the victim become a matter of public record. No statute requires that she or he be informed of her or his rights to protection from harassment that may result from this disclosure. Although exposure to "threatening or upsetting persons" was not a common problem (11 percent in Knudten's sample), victims who experienced it rated it as serious.

The defendant has the right to choose his or her own counsel.

Even those indigent defendants assigned a public defender may request of the judge that that counsel be dismissed and another appointed. Victims have no choice over the prosecutor with whom they must work and may have to deal with as many as a half dozen assistant prosecutors (Brodyaga et al., 1975). [In a few states, such as North Carolina, a victim may hire private counsel to assist the prosecutor. Such counsel serves at the discretion of the prosecutor (McDonald, 1976).]

At the trial itself, the defense attorney may attempt to lessen the onus on the defendant by vilifying the victim. Percy Foreman has claimed that "the best defense in a murder case is the fact that the deceased should have been killed regardless of how it happened," so that "the jury [is] ready to dig up the deceased and shoot him all over again" (Smith, 1966). Many victims have claimed that the attack itself was mild compared to the way they were treated in the criminal justice process (Burgess & Holstrom, 1974). Over 50 percent in one study reported mental or emotional suffering (Viano et al., 1977).

Despite the potential for problems, victims who go through the criminal justice process generally rate the performance of representatives of the criminal justice system as excellent or good, and over 80 percent say they would cooperate with them in the future if the need arose (Viano et al., 1977).

Although the victim has, as this analysis has shown, little formal say in the criminal justice process beyond the decision to report, he or she may have impact on an informal level. In all but the most serious cases, if the victim withdraws cooperation at any time during the process, the case will be dropped. Few prosecutors exercise their right to indict reluctant witnesses for failure to answer a subpoena.[5] Wealthy or politically influential victims may also put pressure on actors in the system to get their views heard.

In summary, the victim's place in the criminal justice system is first as "gatekeeper," regulating entry of many cases into the system. After that the victim serves as evidence that a crime has occurred and that the defendant was the offender. Although a crucial part of the process, the needs of the victim often have been secondary to those of the adversary system in its battle over the fate of the defendant.

The attitude of "benign neglect" toward the victim is beginning to change. In the past ten years, social scientists and criminal justice administrators have become increasingly concerned with the victim's problems and have begun to examine the victim–offender relationship in a new light.

---

[5] Many victims assure their ability not to proceed with a case by giving fictitious names and addresses (Cannavale, 1975; Ziegenhagen, 1976).

THE VICTIM AS CULPRIT

Research on victims has centered around three overlapping areas of interest. The first is the concern with examining characteristics of the victim, the victim–offender relationship, and the social climate to assess factors that might predispose certain individuals to victimization. This sort of inquiry has tended to be the purview of sociologists, criminologists, and psychoanalysts. Social psychologists have concentrated on attitudes about victims and clinical psychologists and other service deliverers have done the bulk of the work on the trauma of victimization and intervention techniques to minimize its impact.

Victimology developed in the late 1940s as a subdiscipline of criminology. Although originally conceived as a study reflecting "scientific concern for the plight of those victimized and exploited" (Weis & Borges, 1973), the emphasis has come to be an examination of the behavior of the victim as exculpatory evidence for the behavior of the offender: As Weis and Borges (1973) put it, the act becomes justifiable on the part of the offender, and the victimization "legitimate." These authors further contend that most criminological work could be called "victorology . . . reflecting more interest in the winners (lat. *victores*) than in the losers of criminal activities . . . and losing sight of victims" (p. 97).

The orientation of victim-as-culprit is seen in the work on victim precipitation by Von Hentig (1948), Wolfgang (1958), and Abrahamsen (1960) in homicide and Amir (1971) in forcible rape. Following psychoanalytic theory, most of these researchers feel that behavior is purposive and that victims are motivated by masochism—and even desires to commit suicide.

Wolfgang (1958) defines victim precipitation in homicide as situations in which the victim first used physical force against the person who subsequently kills them. A similar definition is used for victim-precipitated aggravated assault: the victim was the first in the encounter to use either physical force or insults. For rape, Amir (1971) uses the definition that the woman first agreed to sexual relations or clearly invited them by her behavior, but then reneged. A "bad reputation," drinking with the offender or using vulgar language and wearing suggestive clothing are also behaviors that have been considered precipitative in rape cases. Robbery victims "ask for it" by careless or ostentatious display of money or valuables, whereas burglary victims leave their homes "temptingly" open, and victims of auto theft "help a good boy go bad" (to quote a crime prevention advertisement) by leaving their cars unlocked or running.

Using these definitions, and working with data from a nationwide survey, Curtis (1974) calculated the incidence of victim-precipitated violent crimes. Victim precipitation was clearly evident in 20 percent of the homicides in his sample, 17 percent of the aggravated assaults, 5 percent of the forcible rapes, 6 percent of the armed robberies, and 9 percent of the unarmed robberies.

Alternatives to Victim Blaming

In contrast to the orientation that says that "in a way, the victim is always the cause of the crime" (Amir, 1971, p. 258) is the theoretical view that although there are indeed certain characteristics of individuals that increase the likelihood that they will be targeted as crime victims, the purpose of the law is to protect the weak, the incautious, even, as in the case of confidence games, the greedy against those who would exploit them: Characteristics of behavior of the victim do not excuse the offender. Thus old people are more susceptible than younger ones to robbery because of their physical infirmities and consequent decreased ability to offer resistance; certainly one cannot be blamed for growing old and infirm. Brownmiller (1975) argues fervently for this view of rape:

> I, . . . would consider the housewife (who lets a strange man into her house for a glass of water) and the hitch-hiker insufficiently wary, but in no way would I consider their actions provocative or even mildly precipitant. Similarly, most men seem to consider a woman who engages in sex play but stops short of intercourse guilty not only of precipitant behavior, but of cruel, provocative behavior with no excuse, yet I and my sister feminists would argue that her actions are perfectly allowable and quite within the bounds of human decency and rational decisions . . . (p. 354).

The tendency to blame the victim is not limited to victims of crime, but pervades a variety of explanations of causation. Jews have been held somehow responsible for their persecution by the Nazis (Hallie, 1971; Selznick & Selznick, 1969), the plight of the poor is sometimes seen by the middle class as the result of laziness or moral inferiority (Ryan, 1966), physical disability becomes evidence of moral defect (Goffman, 1963), and even natural disasters may be seen as punishment for sin (Rosenman, 1956).

Just World Theory

The interest of social psychologists in victims has been a by-product of attempts to understand the kind of attributions people make about causation.[6] Particularly relevant is that subset of attribution theory concerned with the idea of a "just world" (Lerner, 1965; Lerner & Simons, 1966). According to this theory, people have a strong tendency

---

[6] For a general discussion of attribution theory, see Shaver (1975).

to believe that one gets what one deserves, and deserves what happens to him or her. In a just world there will be a tendency to blame even objectively innocent victims for their fate as a way of maintaining cognitive constancy.[7] "Just world" research has tended to show a positive correlation between seriousness of the harm that befell a victim and the amount of blame attributed to him or her. For college students, at least, the more serious the calamity, the greater the amount of blame that will be attributed to the victim (Lerner, 1965; Walster, 1966; Rubin & Peplau, 1975; Jones & Aronson, 1973; Landy & Aronson, 1969). When people observe evidence of apparent suffering, some, at least, tend to conclude either that the suffering is exaggerated or is not really happening (remember the reaction of many Germans to the evidence of concentration camp murders) (Rubin & Peplau, 1975), that the victim is an undesirable person, or that the victim behaved badly and brought the suffering on him or herself (Lerner, 1970).[8]

Conversely, many people tend to believe in a primitive sort of social Darwinism in which those who are "winners" are morally superior and deserve what they get. This holds true even for physical attractiveness: Attractive people are seen as kinder, more sensitive, better natured and more intelligent than the less well endowed (Berscheid & Walster, 1974). As the Bible puts it, "For whosoever hath, to him shall be given, and he shall have more abundance; but whosoever hath not, from him shall be taken away even that he hath" (Matthew 13:12).

Although it is common, a belief in a just world is not universal. Rubin and Peplau (1975) have found that

> everyone may have a version of the just world belief in early childhood (Piaget's "imminent justice"), but some people outgrow the belief quickly and some apparently never do. Believers in a just world have been found to be more religious, more authoritarian, and more oriented toward the internal control of reinforcement than nonbelievers. They are also more likely to admire political leaders and existing social institutions, and to have negative attitudes toward underprivileged groups . . . (p. 65).

Effect of Other Victim Characteristics

The tendency to blame the victim may have interactive consequences for other attributions. The belief that characteristics of the victim influence not only how much the victim will be blamed for what hap-

[7] The reader who is unfamiliar with the theory of cognitive dissonance will find a clear synopsis in Bem (1970), Chapter 4.

[8] Of course, "just world" theory also may apply to an apprehended offender.

pened but also how much punishment will be assigned to an offender in a criminal case is a common one. Landy and Aronson (1969) found that simulated jurors gave the highest sentences when the defendant was "unattractive" in character and the victim "attractive," sentences were lowest when the defendant was "attractive" or "neutral" and the victim was "unattractive," and Jones and Aronson (1973) found that student "judges" would sentence a defendant to a longer imprisonment for the rape of a married woman than for the rape of a divorcee.

The mythology of attorneys also seems to hold that the decision of a jury will be affected by the character of the victim. This mythology may have some basis in fact. In their massive study of judges and juries, Kalven and Zeisel (1966) found that certain characteristics of the victim do seem to influence sentencing of an offender: drunkenness, and, in sex crimes, bad character in a victim seem to have the greatest effect in decreasing the sentence that will be given to a defendant. Williams (1976), in contrast, found that victim characteristics affected the prosecutor's decisions at screening and later in the case. However, the decision of whether the defendant was guilty or not guilty at trial did not appear to be influenced by the characteristics of the victim (p. 204). This finding may have been influenced by the possibility that the initial screening by the prosecutor weeded out the most "unsympathetic" victims.

All of the work just mentioned has used sentence as the dependent variable; none specifically asked both for sentence to an offender and how much the respondent felt the victim was at fault. In contrast, when Jones and Aronson (1973) asked both for a sentence for an offender and attribution of fault to the victim, they found a positive relation: higher sentence was found in the same situation that produced the greatest tendency to attribute fault to the victim. As with the others, this study used college students as subjects. In a somewhat similar study, Ellison (1976), using police officers, members of feminist organizations, and men and women from the general public as respondents, found little relation between fault attributed to the victim and sentence to the offender. Her results further contradicted not only the just world theory, but ideas of feminists about the differential blame attributed to rape victims: Robbery victims were not more likely to be blamed than were rape victims, victims who had received physical injuries were less likely to be blamed than those who were not injured. Women from the general public were far more likely than any of the other groups to attribute blame to victims under all conditions.

Thus, although there is abundant evidence that some people do tend to blame even innocent victims for what has happened to them, the tendency is by no means universal and may be affected by a number of contingencies and conditions as already detailed. In this, it does not differ from most other work in social psychology.

THE VICTIM AS PERSON: CRISIS THEORY

A third perspective has defined crime victimization as a traumatic event and has concentrated on the reactions of crime victims following the event with a view to discovering intervention techniques designed to minimize or overcome that trauma.

Crisis theory has provided the underpinning for most of this work. Modern crisis theory had its origins in the work in 1942 of Erich Lindemann (1944) with victims and families of victims of the Cocoanut Grove fire. This work has been expanded and elaborated greatly by Caplan (1964) and others to cover reactions to a variety of situations that involve important changes in a person's life.

The term "crisis" has been used very broadly; we speak of the energy crisis, a crisis in confidence, and so forth. In the psychological context, crisis is a subjective reaction to a stressful life event. It is the way a person feels when confronted with drastic, life-threatening changes or too much pressure. Even positive experiences, such as marriage, a new job, a new home, or the birth of a child can lead to crisis reactions. This is especially true if the individual experiences too many changes in a short time period.[9]

Definition and Kinds of Crisis

Crisis is a turning point in one's life, one from which the individual can emerge either psychologically damaged and less well able to cope, or strengthened, with skills that facilitate future coping. Thus some victims cope well even with severe crisis situations. Variables that determine the direction of crisis reaction include the extent to which it is life threatening, how long the stressor is present, the extent to which the community and significant others in the victim's life are available and able to give support, the reaction of authority figures to whom the victim turns, the victim's prior experiences with coping, personality style and strengths, and so forth and the number of other stressful events that have occurred in the recent past (Erikson, 1976; Caplan, 1964).

There are several different kinds of crisis, each with somewhat different dynamics and requiring somewhat different intervention strategies. *Developmental crises* (Erikson, 1950) are those that occur in the normal course of growth. These include such stages as adoles-

---

[9] For a fuller discussion of the impact of stressful life events, see Dohrenwend and Dohrenwend (1975).

cence and the recently popularized "midlife" crisis (Sheehy, 1976; Levinson, 1978).

A second kind of crisis is the sort that arises from constant exposure to stressful living situations: a disruptive family, a bad neighborhood, a stressful occupation. People may react to stressors of this sort with psychotic episodes, family fights, including battering, suicide attempts, and the like. They often require long-term counseling and even drastic life-style changes for resolution.

The third kind of crisis comes in reaction to accidental stressors: events that are sudden, arbitrary, so that the person asks, "Why me?" and unpredictable. Events of this sort include fires, floods, and other natural disasters, accidents, and sudden illness. Crime victimization by someone not an intimate is a crisis of this sort.

Crisis Reactions

All violent crimes against the person, and even some crimes that traditionally have been thought of as crimes against property, will precipitate a crisis reaction in the victim. The severity of that reaction and whether it is resolved with positive or negative consequences for the victim will depend on, among other things, whether the victim was put in fear of death or severe injury and the meaning of the particular crime to that individual. In this way, a woman who firmly believed that premarital sex of any kind would "spoil" or "ruin" her so that as "damaged goods" she would be an unattractive marriage prospect would react to a rape more violently than might a woman with a less rigid view of sexuality. A scientist, whose definition of herself was strongly related to her work, might view the destruction of crucial files as more traumatic than a rape. This is not to say that she would not be affected by the rape; any experience that so threatens life and control must be traumatic, but that the severity of the trauma is in part related to the victim's individual values.

For all victims, crime represents a loss of control. Burglary is an intrusion into an extension of self, the home. It breaches the individual's feeling of a place to go that is secure, a place one can order and furnish as an extension of her personality. Victims describe feelings of being dirtied, violated.[10] The home is no longer a secure place.

Crimes such as robbery, assault, and rape involve personal contact between offender and victim. The threat of injury or death becomes

---

[10] It is interesting to note that violation of the victim seems to be an important motivation of some burglars: More than half of all residential burglaries result in some damage to the property (Pope, 1977), and it is common to find that the burglar has defecated or urinated, masturbated into the linens or wantonly destroyed property (Bard & Ellison, 1974).

much more real. Feelings of contamination are particularly prominent in rape. The crisis caused by rape too often is exacerbated by the expectation—or reality—of public skepticism and stigmatization.[11]

Victims of crime respond in a variety of ways. Despite the contention of some defense attorneys that "that woman could not have been raped, she was too calm after the alleged attack," there is no single common behavior pattern for crime victims. Some, of course, cope magnificently and emerge unscathed or even strengthened. Others, unfortunately, do not. A list of some of the reactions seen in crime victims is presented in Box 3.2.

Despite this apparent variety, there seem to be common underlying psychological mechanisms at work in most victims.[12] Crisis reactions tend to occur in stages.[13] The first, the acute crisis phase, begins with the attack and lasts for a few hours or a day. It is characterized by

1. Denial: The first reaction immediately following the confrontation usually is denial—This couldn't be happening to me. This is followed by
2. Disruption: The individual's normal coping mechanisms no longer are adequate; he or she feels out of control.
3. Regression: Reverting emotionally to a state of helplessness and dependency characteristic of an earlier stage of development. An otherwise mature and effective person may behave in childlike ways.
4. Guilt: Sometimes straightforward, sometimes projected onto others such as family members, police, and expressed in statements such as, "If you had been out there doing your job this wouldn't have happened to me."
5. Distorted perceptions.[14]

---

[11] For discussions of the special problems of rape victims, see Brodyaga et al. (1975), Brownmiller (1975), Holstrom and Burgess (1978). It should be noted in this context that the only objective measure of the different treatment of rape victims that is often alleged is to be found in the inordinately low rate of convictions for rape (Kelley, 1977; Kalven & Zeisel, 1966).

[12] Material for the following discussion is drawn from the senior author's experience working with crime victims, and from Bard and Ellison (1974), Burgess and Holstrom (1974), Sutherland and Scherl (1970), and Symonds (1973).

[13] There is some disagreement about the exact number of stages in crisis: they may shade into one another, often imperceptibly. The following discussion of the crisis draws most heavily from Sutherland and Scherl (1970). The reactions of each stage are drawn from the experience of the senior author in working with victims, from Bard and Ellison (1974), Sutherland and Scherl (1970), and Burgess and Holstrom (1974).

[14] For a more complete discussion of perceptual distortions in crime victims and their importance in criminal justice procedures, see Chapter 5 on "Eyewitness Identification."

BOX 3.2

REACTIONS TO VICTIMIZATION

Reactions to victimization differ markedly from individual to individual.

The following are some of the behaviors that are common in people who are in crisis from severe accidental stressors, such as a violent crime. A victim may display several of the reactions at the same or different times.

Anger	Anxiety attacks
Extreme calm	Denial
Confusion	Self-hatred
Nightmares	Hypersensitivity
Phobias	Panic
Crying jags	Dependence, clinging
Disbelief	Desire for action
Repression	Desire for revenge
Laughing, joking	Disrupted sleep patterns
Guilt	Disrupted eating habits
Changes in sexual response	Skin reactions: hives, etc.
Fear	Feelings of going crazy
Shock	Compulsive actions
Frustration	Obsessive thoughts
Headaches	Apathy
Depression	Distrust

A reaction that is sometimes seen and needs explanation is the tendency to identify with the aggressor. This is particularly prevalent in cases that involve a long period of interaction between victim and offender, such as kidnapping or hostage taking. The victim, owing his or her life and physical safety to the caprice of the offender, is relieved and grateful to be alive. Most react with extreme passivity, and even come to feel sorry for the offender or to express positive emotions about him or her. Patricia Hearst's case fits this sort of reaction, commonly known as the "Stockholm Syndrome," a reference to a case in Sweden in which a woman held captive in a bank vault by robbers subsequently expressed feelings of love for the offender.

REFERENCES: Bard and Ellison, (1974); Ellison, (1975); Burgess and Holstrom, (1974); Sutherland and Scherl, (1970); Symonds, (1973); Holstrom and Burgess, (1978).

6. Accessibility, vulnerability, suggestibility: It is in times of crisis that the individual is most susceptible to change.

A further crucial aspect of crisis reactions is the potential for irrationality. In severe cases the disruption is such that a person in crisis *cannot be expected* to act and react rationally.[15] Soldiers and police officers have been known to "freeze" with gun in hand as shots are fired at them, and kidnapping victims often do not escape when the opportunity presents itself.

ACUTE CRISIS PHASE

In the acute crisis phase the needs of the victim include (1) regaining control over his or her life, (2) understanding what has happened and what is being done, to be able to give some meaning not only to the victimization but also to the subsequent psychological and investigative process, (3) being able to predict what will happen next, and in some cases (4) ventilating—getting it out of his or her system. One form of ventilation is talking about the experience in one's own way to someone who will listen without passing judgment, and thus can help the victim regain control, understand, and predict. (For a concrete example of how the first minutes of a police interview of a victim can begin to fulfill these needs, see Box 3.3.)

Experiences in the acute crisis phase are particularly important for beginning the process of healing and resolution of the crisis. It can set the stage for preserving or damaging the victim both as evidence—willingness to cooperate—and as a person. A recurring theme in the comments of victims is that the crime itself was minor compared to the trauma of the criminal justice process or, conversely, that the police officers were so helpful that the victim is willing to do almost anything to repay them for their kindness. But even under the best circumstances, with the most supportive family and authority figures, it takes time for the victim to resolve the crisis and return to prior, or improved, level of functioning. Indeed, it is safe to say that in cases involving threat to life, such as assault or rape, the victim will never be quite the same as he or she was before the incident. If nothing else, the sense of security, of vulnerability, of "that couldn't happen to me," is torn away. In severe cases, such as rape, it probably takes at least a year from the time of the last contact with the criminal justice system, even under the best circumstances, for the victim to feel recovered.

---

[15] Indeed, the purpose of training given to police officers, medical and military personnel, and others who face potentially stressful situations constantly is to lessen the unpredictability and therefore the crisis impact, increasing the chances of appropriate responses.

BOX 3.3

THE INITIAL POLICE INTERVIEW: PROTECTING EVIDENCE AND PERSON

Below is an excerpt from the initial police interview with a rape victim. It illustrates ways of getting information while keeping in mind the needs of the victim for psychological support. This is, of course, not the only acceptable format; *in interviewing there are no exact formulas.*

Officers Jackson and Fisher have received a radio call to respond to the scene of a rape that has occurred within the last ten minutes at the home of the victim, Sara Mills. They arrive at the home and knock on the door. A woman opens it. She is disheveled and looks as if she has been crying.

COMMENTS

FISHER: Ms. Mills?

Use of surname defines relationship as professional, helps moderate tendency to regress.

I'm Officer Fisher, this is my partner, Officer Jackson. We got a call that you needed help.

Expression of concern for victim's well-being, not only interest in offender.

May we come in?

Allows victim control. In cases such as this, forceful approach may put officer in same relation as offender: someone who forced victim to do something.

Are you all right? Can we get you anything?

MILLS: I think I'm all right.

They go inside and sit down in the living room. Mills appears very calm now, and tightly controlled. Jackson takes out a pad on which to write details. He will do most of the necessary evidence collection, while Fisher concentrates on the interview process.

FISHER: Do you feel able to talk   Control.
  to us now?
MILLS: Yes, I guess so.

Box 3.3 (*Continued*)

	COMMENTS
JACKSON: You've had a horrible experience, but you're safe now. We know it's sometimes hard to talk about it so soon after an attack, but we got the information from the dispatcher that this just happened—is that right? (Mills nods), so we need to get a description of this person right away so we can put it out on the police radio and have other officers start looking for him.	Acknowledges trauma of the experience. Reassurance. "Attack" indicates officer is prepared to believe that this was a violent assault, not an act involving consensual sex. Checks out information. Explains procedure. Lets victim know something will be done.
FISHER: Can you tell us what he looked like?	Somewhat ambiguous request leaves room for victim to start with things she found most salient.
MILLS: Well, I don't know, er, he was just sort of ordinary.	
FISHER: Would it be easier if I asked you questions? (Mills nods.) What color, what race was he?	Allows victim control over process (but not over what is done).
MILLS: White, his skin was very pale, like he never got out in the sun. I did notice he was wearing a wedding ring. And his hair was dark.	Details sometimes come out in "odd" sequences.
JACKSON: Was it long? short? How did he wear it.	While one officer often does the bulk of the interview, the other need not be silent.
MILLS: I didn't really notice.	

Officers continue until they get a sketchy description. Jackson goes out to the car to put the report over the radio. Fisher continues interview.

| FISHER: Are you sure I can't get you anything? Glass of water? Cigarette? (He sits in chair about two feet from the victim's, leaning forward, a hand on his knee held so that if she wants to she may grasp it.) | Reaffirmation of concern.

Nonverbal messages are crucial. This assures interest, confidentiality, willingness for physical contact if she feels the need. She controls that. |

	COMMENTS
MILLS: No, I'm all right. (Begins to shake and rock back and forth.)	
FISHER: If you'd feel better if you cried, go right ahead.	Permission.
MILLS: No. (and breaks into tears. Fisher waits quietly until she is finished.) I'm okay now.	
FISHER: Good. If you need to stop again, let me know. Now I'm going to have to ask you some questions that may not be easy to answer, but they are important so we can find this guy and prosecute him. When I get to a question that some people find difficult, I'll warn you. Okay?	Control. Reaffirms police mission. Predict. He does not give the option of not doing the task.
I want you to start at the beginning and tell me what happened here tonight.	Gives some structure to task, but not so much as to be suggestive.

As the interview continues, Jackson leaves from time to time to collect evidence that Mills mentions: sheets, clothing, and so on. When the officers have gotten a brief description of the event, sufficient to allow identification and protection of the "crime scene," they discuss with her the necessity of an immediate medical examination, and take her to the hospital.

RESOLUTION AND SECONDARY CRISIS PHASE

Within a few hours or days of the attack, most victims of serious crimes slip into a period of false recovery. In this stage the victim denies the impact of the event: "I'm all right now, everything is the same as it was before." He or she does not want to talk or think about the crime and may be reluctant to cooperate with criminal justice personnel. The timing of this period is extremely variable; in some victims it lasts only a few hours, in others it lasts weeks. Typically, it is followed by a secondary crisis reaction, a sort of "flashback," in which some of the symptoms of the acute crisis phase, particularly phobias and disturbances in eating and sleeping, return. The secondary crisis phase may be precipitated by events concerned with the investigation, such as court procedures, seeing the suspect again in a lineup or photospread, follow-up hospital examinations, and the like. In many cases, however, there is no obvious reason for its onset. The secondary crisis phase may last for hours, or days, and then will be followed by another "quiet" period. Often these periods alternate for months, with the recovery periods becoming longer and, if appropriate support is given, resolution of feelings about the event finally taking place.

The needs of the victim in these stages generally are the same as those of the acute crisis phase, with control being particularly salient. The victim needs to be warned of the possibility of the "flashbacks," so that if they occur he or she does not despair of going crazy and of never recovering. The victim also needs to be helped to understand something about the resolution periods, especially that, although it may be difficult, he or she may be called on for certain tasks connected with the investigation, and cooperation is crucial.

The Family in Crisis

Just as the victim of a crime is in crisis, so also family members and others in his or her social network usually are thrown into crisis by a violent crime. Family members tend to feel guilty that they were unable to prevent the crime. Sometimes they respond to this guilt by projecting blame on the victim: "I told you if you hung around people like that, stayed out till all hours, etc., something like this would happen." Because it is too painful for them to hear of the incident, they often attempt to cut off the ventilation process and to persuade the victim to "forget the whole thing" and refuse to cooperate in the criminal justice process. The crisis may be so severe for family members that they reject the victim: Rape victims sometimes are deserted by husbands or lovers.

Intervention techniques for family members include assuaging their guilt and giving them a role to play both in helping the victim recover and in the criminal justice process. These two birds may be killed with the stone of a statement such as

> sometimes family members feel guilt at a time like this, that they didn't do enough to protect [victim]. This is a natural feeling, but we want to reassure you that there is no evidence that either you or [victim] did anything wrong. But there is something you can do now to help him and us. Later he may want to talk about the attack. Don't force him, but do let him talk about it when and if he wants. This will be hard for you, we know, but it will help him if he can get it out of his system.
>
> Also there is something you can do for us. If, while he's talking, you hear any new information, write it down, and give us a call. . . .

This latter task is aimed at overcoming family members' feelings of helplessness and making them feel important.

In summary, crime victimization represents a potential crisis for both victims and their significant others. [As mentioned earlier, over 50 percent of the victims in one survey reported mental or emotional suffering (Viano et al., 1977.)]. Although emphasis has been placed on the maladaptive consequences of victimization (Burgess & Holstrom, 1974; Symonds, 1973; Bard & Sangrey, 1979), in part because people with problems are more likely to come to the attention of helping professionals than those who are coping well, many people cope well (Holstrom & Burgess, 1978; Ziegenhagen, 1976). The extent of that crisis and its resolution depend on factors such as the severity of the crime as perceived by the individual, his or her prior coping history, and the reactions of others to whom he or she turns for support.

A frequently overlooked caveat must be inserted here. Workers from the helping professions are often quick to assume that people in crisis need professional help to overcome it. Whereas some victims benefit from professional crisis intervention or from long-term therapy, many have adequate coping skills and support from their social networks and neither need nor want professional intervention (see Ziegenhagen, 1976). To assume automatically that victims need professional help may even be to start a self-fulfilling prophecy: The person constantly assured that she or he cannot cope alone begins to question her or his ability and, indeed, to cope less successfully. Also, the fact that many victims cope very well with the crime does not excuse thoughtlessness, rude, or accusatory behavior on the part of people in the criminal justice system with whom they interact.

APPLICATIONS OF THE KNOWLEDGE ABOUT VICTIMS TO CRIMINAL JUSTICE

As already noted, both sociological studies of victim characteristics and psychological work on crisis intervention have applications for honing crime prevention strategies. The work on attitudes about victims often is used on a basis for jury selection work. These are elaborated elsewhere in this volume. Information gathered from all sources is used in training courses for criminal justice personnel. These courses help investigators develop interview techniques that are consistent with both obtaining the maximum of accurate information and cooperation and providing crisis intervention as part of the service function of law enforcement.

Victim-Witness Programs

A recent development in criminal justice that builds heavily on the work of social scientists is the establishment of victim–witness programs. Victim–witness programs, funded by private foundations or government agencies, are usually units of the court or prosecutor's office. Their stated aims are to aid the victim both as evidence and as person: At their best they attempt to cut the number of cases lost due to unwillingness or inability of the victim to follow the case through, and to provide a variety of services (Viano et al., 1977; McDonald, 1976).

The kind of services provided by a victim–witness program may be seen in an examination of the work of one of the pioneering projects, the Victim/Witness Assistance Project for Brooklyn, New York, a cooperative venture of the Vera Institute of Justice, the New York City Police Department, the New York City Courts, and the King's County District Attorney's Office. The project was federally funded.[16]

The first action taken by the project was to replace the cumbersome and inadequate subpoena system with a computerized telephone alert system. Each potential witness including police officers completes a form indicating his or her potential availability; this information is stored in the computer that coordinates schedules for use in setting trial dates. Instead of reporting to court on the day set for trial and waiting hours only to have the case postponed, witnesses who so choose may be placed on standby alert: They must stay near a telephone and be able to get to court within one hour. In addition to the advantage to victims, this system means that police officers may continue their regular duties instead of sitting in court corridors. Brooklyn District Attorney Eugene Gold estimates that available police manpower is increased by 15 percent by this system, and the city saved nearly two million dollars a year in lost time, compensatory time, and overtime for officers.

The project also operates a reception center in the Criminal Court building, staffed by a trained counselor. Victims and prosecution witnesses for cases in different courts check into this central location and may wait in the lounge until their cases are called. This avoids the potential for contact and harassment with the defendant and his or her family or other defense witnesses. It also provides a nursery for the children of victims, witnesses, and defendants, staffed by a professional teacher, and provides meals.

Other services provided to victims are a bilingual hot line that provides emergency crisis counseling or which can inform a victim of the status of the case. A van is on 24-hour call to provide emergency service to fix broken locks and secure homes and businesses where

[16] This case study is drawn largely from Stern and Sullivan (1976).

break-ins have occurred. Another van provides transportation for elderly and disabled witnesses.[17]

Although such programs are useful in making the criminal justice procedure more palatable for those victims who wish to cooperate, they are not without their problems. McDonald (1976) reminds us that "some projects that are billed as 'assisting victims' are more accurately described as assisting the criminal justice system and extending government control over victims" (p. 35). Their prime concern remains to encourage and preserve the victim in his or her role as evidence. When their programs are within a prosecutor's office, and funding is from that source, humanitarian aims may take second place to practical considerations of the cost/benefit analysis variety. As DuBow and Becker (1976) put it, "[w]here programs are designed and administered by police or prosecutorial personnel it is understandable that they would encourage modes of citizen participation that would not interject new and potentially conflicting interests and perspectives" (p. 151).

"Advocacy" programs, at the extreme, may aim at restoring the victim to the role of prosecutor which now in criminal cases is taken by the state (DuBow & Becker, 1976), a position fraught with danger from both practical and constitutional viewpoints. It raises the specter of a return to justice by private vengence, a privilege that would soon be dominated by the rich. Poor victims, often lost in the process as it is, could lose what little hope of justice they presently hold.

Another related trend is the emergence of programs of restitution for victims as part of the sentencing of offenders. In theory, these programs will not only help recompense victims for their financial and emotional loss but will also help offenders realize that they have caused not just an impersonal damage to the system, but also a very personal damage to an individual.[18] These programs, too, have the potential of deteriorating into personal vendettas. A final sort of program for victims involves the existence of victim compensation boards. Although noble in purpose, most have been rendered ineffective by staggering amounts of red tape and small budgets (Geis, 1976).

SUMMARY

Emphasis on the victim is a dramatic change in focus for the criminal justice system. At the same time that this system has been considering

---

[17] For a more complete analysis of victim–witness programs, see Cannavale and Falcon (1976) and McDonald (1976).

[18] For further information on restitution, see Hudson and Galaway (1977).

the needs of victims to preserve them as evidence (the law enforcement role of police and prosecutor) and, it is to be hoped, as person (the service role), social scientists also have become increasingly interested in the victim of crime, both for a model of the attributions people make about cause and from a perspective that sees crime as an interactive system in which offender, victim, and society play complex roles. This chapter has explored some of the facets of the victim's role as evidence, as culprit, and as person. It is to be hoped that the focus on the victim will in no way abridge the right of the accused but will, perhaps, take another look at where his or her nose ends (to use the old metaphor) and the victim's begins.

PSYCHOLOGY AND THE POLICE

Ask most citizens (and some police officers) what the function of the police is, and the answer is likely to be some variation on a theme of "to catch criminals" or "to enforce the law." Although the focus of the police in recent years has, indeed, been on law enforcement (Wilson, 1968), and the police do investigate reports of crimes and apprehend suspects, the function and goals of policing are much broader and more complex than just law enforcement (Stotland & Berberich, 1979). Many police departments have acknowledged their multiple roles in the mottoes stenciled on patrol cars and shoulder patches: "To Protect and Serve."

The goals of police departments have been classified into three categories (Wilson, 1968; Skolnick, 1965: Bittner, 1970). The first, law enforcement, includes investigation of complaints, arrest and prosecution of suspects, and efforts at crime prevention. A second function is maintaining order: intervening in and arbitrating family and neighborhood disputes and keeping traffic moving, noise levels down, rowdy adolescents off the streets, and disturbances of the peace at a minimum. A third role involves providing services, such as assistance in medical and psychological emergencies, finding missing persons, checking on elderly people whose mail has not been collected, helping the motorists who locked themselves out of their cars, and the like.[1] Although departments differ in the emphasis they place on these functions, it has been estimated that between 66 and 90 percent of police time is given over to duties other than those involving law enforcement (Cumming, Cumming & Edel, 1965; President's Commission on Law Enforcement and Administration of Justice, 1967).

As policing has become increasingly complex, and as the public has demanded that police become more involved in skills that require sophistication in interpersonal relations, police administrators have looked for guidance to social scientists and social science theories. Psychologists and other social scientists now work with law enforcement agencies in many areas. Some of this work involves helping police in the fulfillment of their public roles: law enforcement, order maintenance, and service. Other interaction involves the bringing to bear of psychological principles on internal management strategies: strategies designed to select better candidates, to ameliorate the stress of the job, and to produce a more efficiently running organization.

Other chapters in this volume deal with the interaction between psychologists and police in the law enforcement function; these are the areas of eyewitness testimony, lineups, and dealing with crime victims. This chapter will emphasize the input of psychologists into the service and order maintenance functions and the internal management strategies of departments. It will attempt to highlight some of the pioneering programs and discuss some of the successes and pitfalls of efforts at collaboration between police and social scientists.

The interaction between psychologists and police is not a one-way street: psychologists imparting knowledge, police receiving. Psychologists and other social scientists have found work with police a fertile field for testing hypotheses and honing theories about the nature of human interaction in the "real world" (Bard, 1974).

POLICE/PSYCHOLOGIST INTERACTIONS IN THE POLICE FUNCTIONS OF MAINTAINING ORDER AND PROVIDING SERVICES

Police are in the business of resolving conflicts (Silberman, 1978). Much of the input of psychological insight into the police goals of

---

[1] Of course, any one incident can contain elements of all three. Thus working on a family fight may involve maintaining order by calming noisy disputants, preventing the crime of assault, and supplying referrals to service agencies, as well as arbitrating and mediating.

maintaining order and providing services has revolved around augmenting the skills of the police as crisis intervention agents.[2]

Psychologist Morton Bard, one of the pioneers in working with police in crisis intervention, suggests that police are uniquely well suited to be agents of such intervention. They have the advantages of immediacy—as Bittner (1970) puts it, they are the only ones in American society who make house calls without prior appointment—and they have authority: "the legal and symbolic power to 'do something'" (Bard, 1973). The 24-hour response capability insures that the police can be present at the time of the acute crisis phase, when people are especially open and accessible to change, and their authority increases the chances that people will listen and follow directions (Bard & Ellison, 1974). This suitability for crisis work has advantages for the police as well as for the people with whom they work: Crisis theory holds that appropriate intervention at these times will not only resolve that crisis situation but will also teach people new coping skills that will generalize to other situations, thus reducing the incidence of events that would call for police response in the future.

Crisis intervention work by psychologists with police has included training in the handling of people whose behavior is disruptive or deviant without being illegal: the kind of behavior often labeled "abnormal" or "mental illness," including suicide attempts. Many of these strategies have been rather simplistic attempts to generalize what works in the mental health practitioner's office to the streets. Not all the "experts" who counsel police in such matters have a firm grasp of the ways in which police interaction with citizens in their homes and on the streets differs from the interaction of mental health professionals in their offices with people who come to them for help.

Handling Domestic Disputes: Bard's Crisis Intervention Project

One outstanding example of a collaborative interaction between police and psychologists that did involve testing psychological hypotheses in the "real world" was Bard's (1969, 1970, 1971, 1972) work in training police to handle crisis intervention with families. Domestic disputes, as they are called, are of concern to police not only because they involve potential breaches of the peace, and, at times, violent, criminal assaults of citizens on one another, but also because "a significant proportion of injuries and fatalities suffered by police occur in the highly volatile family conflict situation" (Bard, Zacker, & Rutter, 1972). Over 20 percent of all police deaths and 40 percent of injuries incurred

---

[2] For an overview of crisis theory, review Chapter 3.

in the line of duty come during the course of intervening in family disputes (Bard, 1971).

The purpose of Bard's project was twofold: to "modify family assaults and family homicides . . . as well as to reduce personal danger to police officers in such situations" (Bard, Zacker, & Rutter, 1972).

A group of nine white and nine black officers (8 percent of the precinct complement) was selected from volunteers for the demonstration project. All had at least three years' service and "gave evidence of motivation and aptitude for family crisis specialization" (Bard, Zacker, & Rutter, 1972). Their "beat" was a New York City precinct serving "about 85,000 largely lower-class people" (Bard, Zacker, & Rutter, 1972). The officers functioned as "generalist-specialists": They performed routine patrol duties but were called out of their sectors, if necessary, and dispatched to all family disputes in the precinct.

The two-year project was divided into three stages. In the two-month "preparatory phase" officers were selected and given an intensive, 160-hour training course, which included lectures and readings, field trips, group discussions, and extensive use of "practice" through role playing. These practice sessions were reviewed and discussed by the officers and the advanced graduate students in clinical psychology who worked with them. Human relations workshops, designed to make the officers aware of their own values, attitudes, and responses, were also part of the training.

In contrast to previous tendencies of officers called on in family fights to advise individuals of their legal rights and to make arrests if the complaining party were willing to sign a complaint, these officers were trained to emphasize mediation of immediate disputes and referral to community agencies for solutions to chronic problems. Their aim was to divert people from the legal system wherever possible.[3]

During the 18-month "operational phase" the officers returned to patrol duty, but "responded to all complaints or requests for assistance that could be predetermined as involving a 'family disturbance'" (Bard, Zacker, & Rutter, 1972). During this phase, officers met frequently with each other and with group leaders who were familiar with the work of police officers to share experiences and to reconsider the actions they had taken. In addition to the group work, each officer met for at least an hour a week with a graduate student consultant.

In the last four months of the project, work continued, but an "evaluation phase" was added. Data that had been collected over the course of the demonstration were analyzed, "with an emphasis on

---

[3] This view is an important statement about the primacy of the police role as service deliverers over that of law enforcement.

simple tabulation in order to assess changes over time in a number of variables" (Bard, Zacker, & Rutter, 1972).

Evaluation of this and similar projects (Driscoll, Meyer, & Schanie, 1973) has been difficult because of the complexity of factors involved. The goal of reducing hazard to officers seems to have been met, and trained officers report more satisfaction with their work. There is some evidence that trained officers gave more satisfaction to the recipients of their services, but the data about recurrence of problems are unclear. Further, the Bard model has required a greater committment of training time, and therefore more money than most departments feel is justified. However, most police academies today include some training in handling domestic disputes in their curricula.

Psychologists, too, have benefited from the work of police in crisis intervention. It is providing them with data on the dynamics of family quarrels that are different from those data that can be obtained when the family members come into a therapist's office for counseling. Bard's project found, for example, that, contrary to the beliefs of social scientists and police that "family disputes are likely to involve assaultiveness and that such behavior is typically caused by alcohol use" (Bard & Zacker, 1974), assaults usually did not precede the arrival of police. Rather, the police often seemed to be called to serve as mediators before things went too far. Also, although one or more parties in a dispute may have had a drink or two (in 30 to 56 percent of the cases), in only 10 percent did the complainant allege that the other party was drunk—a conclusion supported by the officers in less than half of those incidents. Finally, when alcohol was used, assaults were less common than when there had been no drinking.

Recently, criticism of family crisis intervention strategies by police that follow the Bard model has come from advocates for battered women (Roy, 1977; Fields, 1978). These groups insist that the "law enforcement function of police work must take precedence in all assault cases and in verbal disturbances when threat of assault is indicated by past assault" (Dierking, 1978). They believe that police reluctance to arrest deprives women as a class of their civil rights and gives evidence of rampant sexism among police.

A "Training Key" (#245) issued by the International Association of Chiefs of Police (IACP) suggests that each strategy has merit, given the circumstances of the case. It reminds us that " 'family disturbances' and 'wife beatings' should not be viewed synonymously."[4]

[4] As already noted, studies of family violence (Steinmetz, 1977; Bard, 1971) show that in many calls to police from families no actual violence was involved. When there was violence, wives and husbands were about equally likely to use violence to try to resolve marital differences. Husbands, however, do far more physical

It further acknowledges that

> frustrated by the pattern of victim uncooperativeness, some police
> officers have developed an indifferent attitude toward arresting assaul-
> tive husbands. Battered wives in turn point to this attitude as one
> reason why they fail to proceed legally against their spouses. The two
> conflicting views produce a "chicken-versus-the-egg" controversy that
> is useless to pursue. A more constructive view is to find an approach
> that will accomplish the police mission in such cases and provide the
> victim with the best possible service. . . .

The solution, then, depends on both objective evidence of what
has occurred and the requests of the disputants. Often these requests
are for arbitration and mediation, not arrest. When the evidence of
assault is clear, the IACP believes, "an assault cannot be ignored."

Finally, in the defense of Bard and others, it must be pointed out
that even those departments that have provided some training for
officers in family crisis intervention have not always been consistent in
the amount of time spent in such training (typically a day or two in
recruit training), or in the support of officers who handle disputes in
the prescribed manner. Officers have complained to the authors that
even when they know the correct techniques, they may not be given
sufficient time with the family to complete a satisfactory intervention.

Although more work undoubtedly is needed, both in training and
evaluation of police handling of domestic disputes, the work thus far
gives evidence of the possibilities and problems in psychologist–police
interaction aimed at increasing police effectiveness.

Hostage Taking

Another form of crisis intervention that has grown out of interaction
between police and psychologists has been a spectacular and unqualified success. This area is hostage taking. Instances of hostage taking
have increased dramatically in recent years: from 120 in New York
City in 1970 to 300 in 1973 (Virzera, 1974). In the past, police typically
would rush to the scene where hostages had been taken, weapons
blazing. Hostages as well as hostage takers were likely to be killed.[5]

A change in orientation began with the taking of Israeli athletes
as hostages by Arab terrorists at the Munich Summer Olympics in

---

damage to their spouses than do wives. "Family calls" also include disputes between parents and children, including children battering aged parents, and among
siblings.

[5] Hostage taking refers to situations in which the location of offenders and victims,
and often their identities, are known. Kidnapping involves a known victim, but
unknown offenders and location.

1972.[6] In response to this event, Inspector Simon Eisdorfer of the New York City Police Department began a program of study and training in the dynamics of hostage situations. Consulting on the psychological aspects—motivation of hostage takers and appropriate negotiating tactics—was department psychologist Harvey Schlosberg (Gelb, 1977). The concepts developed by this group were first tested in January of 1973 (before the training was officially complete) at the siege of a sporting goods store in Brooklyn. There, four "Muslim" gunmen, interrupted in a robbery, held customers and employees hostage for three days. The siege finally came to an end when the hostages were able to escape. All the hostage takers were taken into custody unharmed.

Schlosberg and others (Kobetz, 1975; Hassel, 1975; Culley, 1974) analyzed a number of hostage-taking situations and divided them into four, sometimes overlapping, groups according to motivation. "Political ideologists and terrorist groups seize hostages in order to overthrow, disrupt, or exert pressure upon the existing government; obtain the release of so-called political prisoners; obtain money to advance their revolutionary aims; and obtain converts to their revolutionary cause" (Kobetz, 1975). Because they are motivated by ideology rather than personal gain, they tend to be the most difficult to deal with; many are willing to die for their cause. Other hostage takers are robbers or other felons, caught during the commission of a crime, who take hostages to secure their own release.[7] Similar motives are found in the hostage-taking incidents that occur in prisons. A final category of hostage taker is the psychotic or otherwise "disturbed individual, motivated by desire for recognition or to avenge real or imagined wrongs (Gelb, 1977; Kobetz, 1975).

The goal of the police in all hostage-taking situations is the preservation of the lives of hostages, police, *and* hostage takers (Virzera, 1974). In contrast to the older policy of action, the new policy emphasizes containment, patience, and negotiation. The approach has been remarkably successful. Since its inception, the New York City Police Department's hostage negotiation team has not "lost" a single life, either of hostage, officer, or hostage taker (Bolz, 1975).

Psychologists participate in hostage negotiations in a variety of ways. They help train negotiators. Although the negotiator usually is a police officer rather than a civilian psychologist, psychologists serve as consultants during a siege, gathering evidence from the negotiating

---

[6] Inadequate intelligence information about the number of terrorists involved was a factor in the subsequent failure of this operation.
[7] These "barricaded felons" will occasionally claim political motivations, as did the Brooklyn group (Cawley, 1974).

process and from background checks on the hostage taker to try to gain insight into their motives. This information is fed to the negotiator to give him clues for tactics that may sway the particular individual with whom he is working. Finally, psychologists work with law enforcement personnel to analyze hostage-taking situations "to develop profiles of both perpetrator and victims in order to assist with police planning and protection for high risk [potential] victims" (Kobetz, 1975) and to perfect negotiating techniques.[8]

The major role of psychologists working with police to enhance their performance of service delivery and order maintenance tasks, then, has been in training and evaluation. Although these efforts have not always met with unqualified success, they have shown promise and deserve continued consideration and refinement.

PSYCHOLOGISTS AND POLICE MANAGEMENT
Personnel Selection

Much of the involvement of psychologists with police has come at the level of internal management strategies. This involvement begins at the level of personnel selection.[9]

Perhaps the most common use of psychologists and psychiatrists in this realm has been for screening out "emotionally unfit" recruits through the use of clinical interviews and traditional psychological tests (Murphy, 1972).[10] Although the reports arising from these procedures may contain "rich descriptive accounts of typical personality and mental functioning . . . they are often devoid of data other than the clinician's personal impressions" (Lefkowitz, 1977). In policing, as in other fields, the crucial questions are whether the measuring instruments have predictive validity: Whether they serve as accurate predictors of future performance on selected tasks, known as criteria, and, as important but far more difficult to judge, whether the criteria

[8] An interesting sidelight of the analysis of the behavior of victims has been the discovery that many victims react to being taken hostage with extreme passivity and even come to identify with the hostage taker (Bolz, 1975). This so-called "Stockholm syndrome" (after an incident in Sweden where female hostages fell in love with male offenders) may have influenced the behavior of Patty Hearst. An awareness of the probability of such behavior keeps police from relying on hostages for help.

[9] This process has become particularly complex recently in light of pressures to implement Equal Employment Opportunity regulations. In some cases, it has necessitated major reassessments of the job of policing and the critical qualifications (Spielberger, 1979).

[10] Some of these testers have been "in-house": employed by the department. More frequently, they work in local agencies or are in private practice and perform evaluations for police departments on a part-time basis.

are appropriate indices of the police mandate. (For example, even if we were able to predict with precision which officers would be involved in shoot-outs with suspects, the question of the acceptability of "shooting it out" with suspects would remain.)[11] These questions are seldom considered (Lefkowitz, 1977).

Studies that have been conducted seem to show that psychological tests and psychiatric interviews have not demonstrated much predictive validity for police work (Levy, 1967). Levy (1967, 1973) has criticized the screening approach on the grounds that an individual who is not exhibiting "pathological qualities" at the time of the screening may develop them later, and, more important, that we have not determined what constitutes "emotional suitability" for law enforcement. On this last point, Rhead and his colleagues (1968) have noted that "certain traits ordinarily considered to be 'pathological' are essential ingredients of the personality structure of the 'normal' police officer."

In contrast to "screening" techniques based on personal impressions or global theories of the appropriate police personality are the procedures developed by organizational psychologists that attempt to establish meaningful, objective criteria for a job.[12] Although this kind of work has not been common—Lefkowitz (1977) found only ten examples in the literature—a few law enforcement agencies have realized the need for criterion-referenced measurements, and have undertaken programs of research and evaluation.

One such study is the massive effort of Dunnette and Motowidlo (1976). They first studied and attempted to define critical dimensions of job performance for each of four police jobs: general patrol officer, patrol sergeant, investigator/detective, and intermediate-level commander.

From a review of the literature, Dunnette and Motowidlo concluded that (1) much of the research on police selection procedures to that time had been "spotty and piecemeal" and (2) the focus of criterion research about the parameters of police effectiveness has been only weakly oriented toward actual dimensions of job performance." They elaborate on this last point:

> most studies have relied upon criteria such as existing departmental ratings or global measures (such as rankings) of overall effectiveness.

[11] That some departments believe shoot-outs are acceptable is seen from the number of medals given for such behavior (Bennett-Sandler & Ubell, 1977).
[12] As Lefkowitz (1977) has noted, this kind of establishment of predictive validity can include clinical instruments as well as "psychometric personnel methods." The difference between this and the uses already described is that clinical judgments are subjected to statistical analysis of their ability to predict successful policing.

In many studies, therefore, raters have been left free to use their own potentially biased definitions of what constitutes police officer effectiveness, with the result that the usual sources of rating error (leniency, halo, etc.) probably have been quite prevalent . . . (p. 1).

To address these problems, this work first assessed the critical dimensions of police performance, as defined by nine police psychologists (p. xvi) and used these to design new methods of rating job performance.[13] They then designed a series of "simulations and standardized situational tasks," such as role-playing exercises in areas believed to be representative of critical police tasks: domestic disputes, burglary investigations, "aided" case of a man injured at a hotel, and the like. Selection was done on the basis of performance on these tasks.

Although such programs are positive steps, they are not a panacea. Implementation of the suggestions would be expensive and involve major revisions of current practices. Practical barriers to such changes sometimes come from the civil service system, of which many departments are a part, and resistance may come from police organizations and unions. The crucial question of the definition of what exactly constitutes "good" police work—the goals and mandate of the institution —also remains. Such questions are matters of social policy and, of necessity, involve value judgments, which are not the psychologist's to make.

Emphasis on personality variables alone in selection, although important, may ignore the influence of organizational-structural determinants of police behavior. Much has been said in criminological, sociological, and psychological literature about the existence of a "modal police personality" (Lefkowitz, 1975). While, certainly, individual personality variables, such as those that may lead certain types of individuals to choose policing as a career, are present and important, they interact with organizational-structural variables to influence not only the sort of person the officer will become but also how well he or she can do his or her work. The interaction of individual and organizational variables is a major subject of concern for those who work in another subarea of policing in which psychologists and psychological theory are influential: police stress.

---

[13] These were used to measure concurrent validity. Concurrent validity is the relation between test scores and an external criterion supposed to measure the same thing. For concurrent validity, measurements are taken at the same time; for predictive validity, they are taken at different times, but on the same people. Concurrent validity tends to be used as a "quick and dirty" estimate of predictive validity (Anastasi, 1961).

Police Stress

Work in police stress involves interventions at both the individual and organizational level (Kroes, 1976; Kroes & Hurrell, 1975). The most common approach has been to attempt to identify officers who are exhibiting signs of distress (both physical and psychological) and to provide individual or small group counseling and other forms of psychotherapy. Many of the larger police departments throughout the country have psychological services units (Jacobi, 1975; Bennett-Sandler & Ubell, 1977; Schilling, 1978) that provide counseling for officers and sometimes for members of their families. Counseling may be on a voluntary basis, or it may be mandatory. Although these units undoubtedly are of assistance to some—70 percent of officers referred to the New York City Police Department's alcohol unit stay with the department (Bennett-Sandler & Ubell, 1977)—there are problems.

A first major problem is the stigma most officers, and many laypeople, attach to therapy.[14] Any admission of problems is seen as a sign of weakness, an insult to one's masculinity. ("Can you imagine John Wayne on a shrink's couch," one said.) A request for therapy is an admission of pathology.

Department-sponsored therapy has special problems, in addition to the problems inherent in any therapy for officers. Usually it is clear that the first loyalty of counselors hired by the department is to the department. This presents problems with confidentiality. For the sake of the department and the public, counselors feel obligated to report officers whose revelations indicate that they may be a menace to themselves and others.[15] Officers labeled as "problems" are relieved of their weapons and badges, the symbols of their unique position and authority, and placed in a limited duty assignment, commonly known to officers by the derogatory term, "bow and arrow squad." Under these conditions it is hardly surprising that few officers go for counseling willingly. Most wait until their problems are so severe and obvious that a superior forces them to seek help. This is hardly an ideal setting for a therapeutic relationship.

The use of counseling and other therapeutic services is primarily a curative approach. Another approach aims at prevention of the symptoms of stress. The primary techniques that have been employed

[14] The following discussion draws on unpublished interviews by the senior author.
[15] Many counselors prefer to err in the direction of false positives: If there is any indication that the officer might be dangerous, it is best to label him or her as such and not to take chances. Statistical and ethical problems with the prediction of dangerousness are discussed elsewhere in this volume.

emphasize the things that individuals can do, and concentrate on training. Officers are taught techniques such as biofeedback and meditation, which are believed to increase tolerance for stress (Benson, 1976; Maris & Maris, 1978). These approaches are relatively new; data on long-term effects are lacking.

A different approach assumes that although individual variables are important, even the "healthiest" individual in a high stress occupation needs supervisory and organizational support. Christina Maslach (1976) has used the terms "institutional dehumanization" and "burnout" to describe the process by which a person with original thought and creativity on the job is transformed into a mechanical, petty bureaucrat. She stresses the importance of a supportive supervisory and organizational structure, not only to allow the worker to function effectively with clients but also to prevent her from turning her frustrations inward, a process that can result in psychosomatic illnesses such as ulcers, hypertension, and heart problems, as well as symptoms of psychological disruption such as depression, suicide, family problems, and alcoholism.

Ellison and Genz (1978) have identified some situations and assignments in policing that are particularly stressful, and, like Maslach, have emphasized the importance of organizational support. Particularly hazardous assignments tend to be those that require the officer to combine a tough shell for his or her own protection with sensitivity to others: sex crimes investigations, crimes involving abused children and other juvenile work, undercover narcotics work, and the like. They suggest that the officer should be viewed as being in crisis (a view also taken by Kroes (1976) who refers to the police officer as "society's victim") and that his or her needs are similar to those of others under stress from chronic or accidental stressors. Their prescription includes the need for organizational changes that acknowledge and train for the enormous amount of discretion that officers are called on to exercise and encourages the use of strategies of participatory management that have been such a major factor in organizational theory in industry (see Hampton, Summer, & Webber, 1978).

Team Policing

A major shift in organizational structure in policing that has drawn heavily from theories from organizational and community psychology is the Neighborhood Police Team concept.[16] Team policing involves

---

[16] Team policing is consistent with management strategies such as McGregor's "Theory Y," "Management by Objectives," and "participative management." The reader who wishes a more thorough explanation of these concepts is referred to Hampton, Summer, and Webber (1978).

major restructuring of the traditional chains of police command.[17] Responsibility is shifted to much lower levels, primarily to the lieutenant and sergeant who serve as first-line supervisors. Many policy decisions are left to the team manager and the team. Each team is assigned regularly to a neighborhood and a shift and encouraged to get to know the special problems and resources of that neighborhood. Diversity of approach is encouraged, and patrol officers take over many of the prestigious and interesting investigative functions commonly assigned to detectives. Teams are encouraged to develop collaborative relationships with leaders of the community they serve and to work together to define problems and solutions for that community. Team policing, at its best, represents change at the institutional level, and reflects an understanding of modern management theory.

Evaluations of the success of team policing have varied. In some cities, such as Newark, crime decreased dramatically in the area served by the team, and officer morale was reported to be high.[18] In other cities, team policing was supported in theory, but the diffusion of responsibility crucial to its success was resisted by top police administrators. In some departments, "team policing" meant stenciling "Neighborhood Police Team" on several radio cars, or assigning officers to attend more meetings of community groups. It is hardly surprising that team policing was less than successful in the latter cases.

Psychological work aimed at increasing performance and job satisfaction that has focused on internal management strategies has taken a variety of paths, ranging from selection procedures to strategies involving organizational development and institutional change. As in other areas of endeavor, the success has been mixed, but the challenge is one that many psychologists and police administrators are accepting: to work together for the greater good of the institution and society at large.

GAINING ENTRY: THOUGHTS FOR PSYCHOLOGISTS

Police traditionally have displayed a certain tendency toward insularity and suspicion of "interference" from outsiders (Niederhoffer, 1967). In the case of social scientists, this reticence has not been wholly unjustified. Too frequently, social scientists have attempted to play

---

[17] Material for this discussion comes from Gay et al. (1975); Sherman et al. (1973); Murphy and Block (1970); and from interviews with Inspector John Cross, former commanding officer of the Neighborhood Police Unit of the Newark Police Department.

[18] It is a sad commentary on the fate of innovation in policing that this program, which succeeded on many levels, was dropped when federal funding ran out.

BOX 4.1

PROGRAM ASPECTS OF TEAM POLICING

ORGANIZATION & TEAM BUILDING ASPECTS

Elements	Activities
Team organization	Permanent assignment of officers to teams of 14–50 officers
	Permanent team assignment to shift or 24-hour responsibility for neighborhood
	Manpower allocation based on crime analysis, patrol workload
	Assignment of specialists and specialist responsibilities to teams
Enlarged job role of officer	Generalist/specialist officers
	Participation in team planning & decision making
Altered supervisory role and decentralization	Supervisor as planner/manager/leader
	Unified command structure
	Development of policy guidelines
	Participation & decentralized decision making
	Team meetings to plan operations
	Team information coordination

NEIGHBORHOOD OR COMMUNITY RELATIONS ASPECTS

Strategy	Activities
Stable geographic assignment	Officers work in defined neighborhood for extended period
Service orientation & increased citizen contact	Referral & "special" services
	Storefront headquarters
	Officer participation in community activities
	Walk & talk programs
	Foot & scooter patrol
	Nonaggressive patrol tactics
	Informal "blazer" uniforms
	Specially marked cars
Increased citizen participation in law enforcement	Citizen volunteer programs
	Crime prevention programs
	Citizen advisory councils
	Community meetings

REFERENCE: Brown, L. P., and Martin, E. E. Neighborhood team policing: a viable concept in Multnoma County. *The Police Chief*, May 1976, p. 85.

"all-knowing expert" and cast the officer in the role of "dumb cop." As mentioned earlier, they have assumed that the same skills and techniques that are appropriate in *their* setting and mandate will also work for the officer on the street. They have made the officer their handmaiden: someone to guide or force reluctant individuals into the "mental health" system. They have even, at times, tried to make the law subordinate to their understanding of human nature, so that they alone might be the determiners of who is guilty (or not guilty "by reason of insanity"), and what penalty should be inflicted.

A major concern for social scientists who wish to work with police, then, is an examination of their own motives, some degree of study of the organization, and a respect for the officers with whom they work as experts in areas about which they know very little. Such an approach stresses a recognition of respect for the officer's expertise and say, in effect, "Let us combine our separate areas of knowledge to create a new body of knowledge that will benefit us both."

We would strongly recommend that anyone wishing to work with police who has not had police experience try to arrange to spend time with officers, observing their work. Some departments are willing for "civilians" to ride along as observers; in lieu of this, informal conversations with officers, asking for their ideas and opinions, will provide surprising information and insight. We have usually found officers suspicious at first: They will test the psychologist's attitudes about policing and be defensive about the way they do their jobs. In this, they do not differ much from other workers who feel "under the gun." Once they find that the "outsider" is interested, has some knowledge, and is not quick to judge harshly, most will open up and, indeed, are anxious to talk about their work and its rewards and frustrations.

In addition to approval from "top brass," major opinion leaders in a police department are the first-line supervisors. One successful tactic when training police is to team teach with one of these officers.

A problem for psychologists who work with police is the temptation to become "co-opted": to come to identify too closely with the police view and to lose the objectivity that allows a fresh outlook. This problem is heightened manifold if the psychologist is employed by the department. Awareness of the problem and contact with members of one's own profession who are not involved in criminal justice help somewhat.

Policing is a difficult job. Although some officers respond inappropriately to the stresses, we have always been amazed and heartened that so many not only persevere under difficult circumstances but become "tolerant observers of the human comedy" (Niederhoffer, 1967), and even dedicated and successful agents for change.

5

PSYCHOLOGY AND
EYEWITNESS IDENTIFICATION

INTRODUCTION

The application of psychology to the problem of eyewitness identification in courts of law is an extension of ongoing basic research in human perception and memory, topics about which much is known but little is used in the legal establishments of the United States. This neglect stems from (1) the term "eyewitness" being overvalued as a sacred element of evidence in courts and (2) the tendency of basic researchers in perception and memory to stick to the narrow confines of the laboratory. In this chapter we attempt to bridge the gap between the laboratory and the real world in order to enhance the administration of justice.[1]

In hundreds of cases innocent men and women have been accused, tried, convicted, imprisoned, and even executed on the strength of confidently expressed eyewitness reports that have later been found to be erroneous. How many unchecked but false eyewitness reports

[1] Buckhout, R. Eyewitness testimony. *Scientific American,* 1974, *231* (6), 23–31. See also *Jurimetrics,* 1975, *15,* 171.

have played a role in convictions we will never know, but the problem is underscored by the fact that most psychologists agree that eyewitness identification can be very unreliable. Research on perception and memory suggests strongly that any eyewitness report should be evaluated cautiously and skeptically. Uncritical acceptance of eyewitness testimony seems to be based on the *fallacious* notion that the human observer is a perfect recording device of all that he or she sees or hears. Even the way questions are asked in court implies that the witness should have perfect recall. It may be asserted categorically that this is impossible; that human perception and memory function efficiently by being selective; that a human being has no usual need for perfect recall; that perception and memory are decision-making processes affected by the totality of a person's abilities, background, environment, attitudes, motives, and beliefs and the method of testing his or her recollection of people or events.[2]

The human observer is an active rather than a passive observer of the environment, motivated by (1) a desire to be accurate as he or she seeks meaning from the overabundance of information that affects his or her senses and (2) a desire to live up to the expectations of others and to stay in their good graces. These two factors make the eyes, ears, and other senses social as well as physical organs.[3]

In the psychologist's search for data on the physical capabilities of the eye and the ear, he or she speaks of an "ideal observer," a person who would cooperatively respond to lights and tones with unbiased ears and eyes, much like a machine. However, the ideal observer does not exist. Great effort and expense are put into a design of laboratories to provide an "ideal physical environment" free of distractions to enable the observer to concentrate. Such ideal environments can only be approached in a laboratory; in the real world they are seldom if ever found.

In a machine we expect that what comes out, the report, will be a direct function of what went in, the input or stimulus. But human perception has been characterized by some psychologists in terms of a slogan: The whole is greater than the sum of the parts. This slogan reflects on the ability of the human observer to select and summarize fragments of information and to reach conclusions based on his or her prior experience, familiarity, biases, expectancy, faith, and desire to appear certain.[4] Most human observers, for example, look at the moon and see a sphere despite their inability to check out the unseen side.

[2] Ibid.
[3] Ibid.
[4] Miller, G. A., & Buckhout, R. *Psychology: The Science of Mental Life.* New York: Harper & Row, 1973.

The conclusion is decision efficiently arrived at independent of the physical evidence which is incomplete.[5]

In the typical eyewitness situation, particularly involving criminal activities, the fallible human observer is ordinarily in a less than ideal environment. The situation is usually such that a person's ability to give a complete account of what took place or to identify the persons involved with complete accuracy is inherently limited by situational constraints. This strong inference is drawn by psychologists who have read and synthesized a long historical tradition of research on human perception, social psychology, cognition, learning, and memory.[6] In the legal tradition, there is a tendency for lawyers and legal scholars to decry the "vagaries of eyewitness testimony," while relying heavily on it in court. Finally, this is an area in which the wisdom of common sense—although often in conflict with both the scientific and legal traditions—is frequently relied on by all participants in the judicial process.

Common experience flows smoothly enough for most people if their basic perceptions of reality remain unchallenged. It takes a trip to a psychology lab or to San Francisco's Exploratorium for most people to experience the illusions, distortions, and nonsensory phenomena that were in the basic legacy of psychological research on perception in the 1930s.[7] By restricting our memory challenges to the remembering of familiar facts, faces, and events, we can avoid doubting our senses. But the legal and scientific processes both provide their own form of a challenge to basic perception. The lawyer can cross-examine in minute detail every statement a person makes about his or her memory of a past event and force a person to verbalize what he or she may have previously taken for granted. The perception researcher can conduct objective tests to measure the accuracy with which people remember. In recent years all three traditions have met on the common ground of the courtroom. We present the scientist's findings on the psychology of the eyewitness in the context of common sense and the law.

THE CRIME SITUATION

Simulating the basic elements of a crime, often staged before an audience of a classroom, has become one of those classic demonstra-

---

[5] Ibid.

[6] Marshall, J. *Law and Psychology in Conflict.* New York: Doubleday-Anchor, 1969. A classic early effort at integrating psychological and legal concepts into a practitioners guide for evaluating eyewitness testimony.

[7] Levine, F. J., & Tapp, J. The psychology of criminal identification: The gap from Wade to Kirby. *University of Pennsylvania Law Review,* 1973, *121,* 1079–1131. A comprehensive review of the research literature and a critical look at its use in legal settings.

tions that nearly always works. A professor lecturing a class is interrupted by an assailant who enters shouting; shots are fired, pushing and shoving erupt; all parties shout various words; the assailant exits; and research assistants appear with questionnaires to gather descriptions from the shaken audience members who are now called eyewitnesses. Whether this scenario is one staged in 1904 by Professor Hugo Muensterberg[8] or by Buckhout in 1974,[9] the results are remarkably similar. The eyewitness accounts of events differ drastically from one another, the ranges of physical descriptions are large and discrepant, clothing and physical objects are not agreed on, and the majority of the witnesses are unable to pick out the assailant from a lineup staged at a later time. The amount of faith in the repeatability of these findings was confirmed in the extreme by Buckhout who staged a simulated crime on a televised news broadcast and had the viewing audience phone in their choice of suspects from a lineup shown shortly after the crime.[10] Out of some 2145 viewer-witnesses who called in, only 14.7 percent correctly identified the "perpetrator" in the lineup—a figure that was roughly at the chance or guessing level.

The essential characteristics of the crime situation that lead to such a poor display of the memory process are speed and movement, stimulus overload, the fact that the perpetrator is a stranger to the witness, diversion of attention, excessive arousal, surprise, and limitations on the opportunity to observe the face. Most of these factors have been studied by researchers in memory and perception as separate *independent variables* that can negatively affect the initial processing of visual stimuli—which will, of course, lead to poorer memory in later testing.[11] Police authorities acknowledge that many of these characteristics are present in crimes that involve confrontation between a perpetrator and a victim or witness. Interviews with criminals themselves indicate that the "professional" robber is well aware of the need to use surprise to get control of the situation, instill fear, prevent the victim from staring at his or her face too long, and take a number of steps to ensure that he or she will not be identified at a

[8] Muensterberg, H. *On the Witness Stand.* New York: Doubleday, 1908.
[9] See Buckhout, op. cit.
[10] Buckhout, R. Nearly 2000 witnesses can be wrong. *Social Action and the Law,* 1975, 2, 3.
[11] Wells, G. L. Applied eyewitness-testimony research: System variables and estimator variables. *Journal of Personality and Social Psychology,* 1978, 36 (12), 1546–1557. Wells provides a useful dichotomy of estimator variables—factors affecting eyewitness reports that cannot be controlled, such as crime seriousness, complexity, familiarity, race, attractiveness, age, sex, and perceptual set; system variables include time delay until testing, suggestion, questioning, and lineup structure. The system variables can presumably be controlled to improve witness accuracy.

later time. Unfortunately, there are so-called impulsive criminals who, mistakenly believing that their features might leave an "indelible impression" on the witness, will kill or even blind a victim to ensure that "dead men tell no tales."[12]

Research on Situation Variables

INSIGNIFICANCE OF THE EVENTS OBSERVED

In placing the accused at or near the scene of a crime, witnesses are frequently asked to recall seeing the accused at a time when they were not *attaching importance* to the event. They saw the scene in passing or as a part of the normal routine of an ordinary day. Research on this type of situation dates at least back to 1895, when J. McKeen Cattell wrote about an experiment in which he asked students to describe the people, places, and events that they had encountered while walking to school over very familiar paths.[13] Such reports were incomplete and unreliable; some individuals were highly certain of details that had no basis in fact. Our interpretation is that insignificant events do not motivate the person to use fully the selective process of attention, making his or her memory less complete. An example might be the customer of a bank who is in line next to a man who quietly holds up the bank. Only later is she made aware of the significance— she is suddenly a "witness" who may not have been looking but is now expected to remember, because she was held for questioning by investigators.

A more recent and careful study of this variable was conducted by Leippe, Wells, and Ostrom (1978), in which a staged theft was performed in front of a group of witnesses.[14] The significance (or seriousness) of the theft was established by pointing out that the object stolen was either an electronic calculator or a pack of cigarettes. In addition, the researchers gave this information either before or after the theft. The dependent variable was the accuracy of identification of the perpetrator on a lineup of photographs. Consistent with

[12] Silberman, C. E. *Criminal Violence and Criminal Justice*. New York: Random House, 1978, p. 58. Reporting conversations with "professional" criminals, the author documents the robber's use of "front" or skill in handling people. The amateur, less experienced with manipulating people, may rely on the ancient mythology about photographic remembering which still has currency.

[13] Murphy, G. *Historical Introduction to Psychology*. New York: Appleton, 1949, pp. 244–245.

[14] Leippe, M. R., Wells, G. L., & Ostrom, T. M. Crime seriousness as a determinant of accuracy in eyewitness identification. *Journal of Applied Psychology*, 1978, *63* (3), 345–351. Prior knowledge of seriousness generally produced a higher number of identifications.

previous research, the highest percentage of correct identifications occurred in the high-significance-prior knowledge condition. The authors concluded that "perceived seriousness plays a role in motivating witnesses to make full use of selective attentional and encoding processes . . . greater depth of processing is characterized by attention to and examination of a greater number of facial features."[15, 16] Although the significance of an event serves to arouse and focus attention, we distinguish this moderate level of arousal from the kind of arousal common to stressful or life-threatening situations that have deleterious effects on attention and memory.

SHORTNESS OF THE PERIOD OF OBSERVATION

Research findings and common sense are in general agreement on the general effects of limited time periods in perception. As a general rule, the longer the exposure time of display of a face or an event, the more *opportunity* a witness will have to process and store that information in long-term memory.[17, 18] Whether that time is used efficiently by the witness is another matter which cannot be directly spoken about from the long tradition of perceptual research using the tachistoscope which times the presentation of visual targets to an observer.[19] In these laboratory studies the observer's head *cannot* move, making it possible to study duration effects (*if* eye movement remains restricted). The commonsense interpretation of the effects of time begins to founder

[15] Craik, F. I. M., & Lockhart, R. S. Levels of processing: A framework for memory research. *Journal of Verbal Learning and Verbal Behavior*, 1972, 11, 671–684.

[16] Bower, G. H., & Karlin, M. B. Depth of processing of faces and recognition memory. *Journal of Experimental Psychology*, 1974, *103*, 751–757. See also Strnad, B. N., & Mueller, J. H. Levels of processing in facial recognition memory. *Bulletin of the Psychonomic Society*, 1977, 9 (1), 17–18. Both studies show that deep processing under instructions enabled observers who were to evaluate honesty of likeableness to perform better on a later recognition test than observers who were asked to evaluate the gender of the target photo.

[17] Loftus, G. R. Eye fixations and recognition memory. *Cognitive Psychology*, 1972, 3, 525–557.

[18] Hintzman, D. L. Repetition and memory. In G. L. Bower (Ed.), *The Psychology of Learning and Motivation* (Vol. 10). New York: Academic Press, 1972. This and Loftus's study, op. cit., establish that *picture recognition* is a monotonically increasing function of prior exposure time.

[19] Faces are not perceived as concrete stimuli independent of context as they may be presented in a laboratory study. Researchers debate the process that enables most observers to be very good at remembering faces on which the eye has fixated. Given fixation, particularly with the fovea—the segment of the retina with the highest acuity—the debate is over whether an observer relies on summing up separate features or on forming a holistic impression or gestalt. The face is rich with information—a surplus that mandates selectivity in fixations over short or divided time periods.

somewhat when we consider the number of events or stimuli crowded into a given time period which may encroach on the "channel capacity" of the observer—a hypothetical limit on the amount of information that can be processed per unit time. Approaching this limit would presumably negate the positive effects of increasing the total time to observe.[20]

Another problem we have noted in our studies of eyewitnesses to crimes is marked tendency for virtually all eyewitnesses to exaggerate their estimates of the time elapsed in crime events.[21] Since witnesses are aware of the equation between time and memory, it is possible that they may lengthen their time estimates in an effort to bolster the validity of their descriptions.[22] However, the sheer complexity of crime events reminds us that earlier research on remembered time consistently showed that the more stimuli presented in a time interval the longer were the estimates of that time.[23, 24]

LESS THAN IDEAL OBSERVATION CONDITIONS

Crimes seldom occur in the well-controlled confines of the laboratory. The fast-moving, threatening, chaotic flow of events of a crime in progress conflict with the perceptual capability of the human observer. Often the presence of a crowd, distance, poor lighting, fast movements, and so on prevent the efficient workings of the attention process. Research into the limits of efficient functioning of the eye and other senses has established thresholds for those senses. As those limits are approached, eyewitness accounts become increasingly unreliable.[25]

[20] Complexity of a stimulus or event has a double-edged result. Although complexity can limit the processing of salient details and reduce the completeness of a description given in recalling an event, it may also serve as an effective aid to later recognition of a person when the observer is merely asked to make a yes or no decision on whether he or she has seen the person before. This is more likely to occur if the observer has an appreciable amount of time to process the information.

[21] See Buckhout, Eyewitness and Marshall, op. cit.

[22] Forensic experience confirms that the form of direct examination and cross-examination of eyewitnesses is directed at eliciting from the witness a confirmation that he or she "looked at the face constantly" or that he or she was distracted from looking directly for any length of time. Obviously, all parties are aware of the assumed positive relationship between exposure time and recognition and exploit the courtroom testimony to convey its relevance (to their interest) to the judge or jury.

[23] Block, R. A. Remembered duration: Effects of event and sequence complexity. *Memory and Cognition*, 1978, 6 (3), 320–326.

[24] Hicks, R. E., Miller, G. W., & Kinsbourne, M. Prospective and retrospective judgments of time as a function of amount of information processed. *American Journal of Psychology*, 1976, 89, 719–730.

[25] Stevens, S. S. *Handbook of Experimental Psychology*. New York: Wiley, 1950. An old standby representative of many sourcebooks on human sensory functions.

For a behavioral scientist to tell a lawyer or a juror that human beings cannot see in total darkness seems to represent the ultimate in pretentious overkill, but certain eyewitness situations require further study. Consider a murder case in which a police officer testifies that he saw the defendant shoot the victim whole both men stood in a poorly lit doorway in a building that was otherwise illuminated by high-intensity streetlights.[26] The witness, sitting 120 feet away inside a car was in a condition where his eyes were adapted to a generally high level of illumination. The eye adjusts the pupil to the average amount of light in the field of vision, not to dark spots in the center of the scene. Independent measures of the lighting in the doorway revealed that the light amounted to one-fifth of a candle, an amount that is well below the normal reading threshold. Buckhout (1974) presented these data to a jury during the trial without suggesting a conclusion. The jury in the case went to the scene of the crime and conducted an experiment of their own; placing a black member of the jury in the doorway. They found that they could not see the face of this familiar person and subsequently acquitted the defendant. These events suggested that the witness might have reached his conclusion from factors other than the events he perceived, that he might be suggesting a likely suspect to fit the prevalent theory of the crime, or that he might be lying.[27]

In yet another case in which the obvious might not be so apparent, a group of 50 high school students testified that they had seen the events leading to a midair collision of an airliner and a private aircraft while playing football nearby.[28] Included in their eyewitness reports were details about the numbers and lettering on the planes, reports of luggage and bodies falling out, and the alleged failure of the airliner to take evasive action to avoid a collision. Later analysis showed that the planes were in the clouds at the time of the collision, that the sound of the impact would have taken six or more seconds to reach the witnesses, and that the visual angle subtended by the size of the luggage and numbers at that distance was small enough to be below the usual threshold for the normal human observer. Because the witnesses later saw the crash and because they were familiar with the numbers on and the contents of airplanes, it was clear that they had constructed a plausible sequence of events that *should* have occurred in a midair collision; but as far as we know, it would be virtually impossible for them to have actually perceived (and stored in memory) the details that they enthusiastically testified to in the trial.

[26] See Buckhout, Eyewitness.
[27] Ibid.
[28] *Allegheny Airlines* v. *U.S. et al.*, U.S. Federal District Court, Indianapolis, Indiana.

Presumably, the late arriving sound of the midair impact alerted the witnesses to look up to see the planes crashing, and their testimony was based more on logical conjecture than their memory.

To summarize, the variables in the crime situation that may affect the memory of the eyewitness are numerous; research on the effects of stimulus characteristics on memory constitute a substantial portion of the (earlier) psychological research literature. Our belief is that most psychological researchers place greater emphasis on stimulus variables than on other sources of variability in explaining memory processes and that many of the findings are in substantial agreement with the general wisdom. The main argument will occur in the importance attached to stimulus as opposed to personal factors in evaluating eyewitness reports. Our analysis suggests that the conditions common to crimes (as well as accidents) place the eyewitness at a distinct disadvantage for taking in, processing, and remembering information of any kind. If crimes occurred in well-lighted stable areas, with substantial early warning, with lengthy time intervals, guided attention at a close distance, and one stimulus at a time, we would be remarking on how accurate the typical witness was. Reality (and the perpetrator) conspires to take advantage of the inherent vulnerabilities of the human perceiver.

Perception of the Face

The fact that a separate section on perception of the face is included in a section on the crime situation is due to the unique legal requirement (in most criminal cases) that a positive identification of the face of the defendant be made by a witness or victim if a criminal case is to proceed. A witness will be asked to give a detailed description including the face. In serious cases the witnesses may be asked to look at mug shots in a book of facial photographs, to contribute detailed information to an officer who might construct a composite drawing or photo of the suspect, to make an identification from an array of photos (usually of the face), and finally to made a formal identification of the suspect's face in court. Psychologists have treated the problem of face perception to a special kind of research because the face represents a very complex image whose storage in memory may involve different processes from those involved in remembering words, events, or sounds.

For many years researchers concentrated on studies of the perception of simpler visual images such as ambiguous shapes in which identifiable characteristics could be controlled. Subjects in this type of research would learn a number of the shapes and later be tested on their ability to recall and/or recognize them. This research paradigm has been carried over to testing of a person's ability to recall or recognize a previously seen face: usually involving a photograph or set of photographs that are shown once and then mixed in with a set of unfamiliar but similar face photographs for later recognition testing. The results of much of this type of research was the same: Hochberg and Galper, 1967, and Yin, 1969 found 90 to 96 percent accurate identifications;[29, 30] Shepard, 1967 and Nickerson, 1965, found up to 97 percent accurate identifications of previously seen pictures of scenes.[31, 32] High accuracy scores of this magnitude naturally spoke well of our ability to remember and recognize faces, but an examination of the laboratory procedures reveals an artifact that renders much of this research unsuitable for generalizing to the real world of the eyewitness to crime.

In most of these tests witnesses were tested for recognition using the *identical* face photographs that they had been exposed to previously—confronting the witness with a yes or no decision which may be far easier than the decision to be made by an eyewitness to an event in which the face was in motion, under a variety of changing lighting conditions and embedded in a rich context of other visual events and objects. In short, the real witness, in studying an ever-changing stimulus will usually be encoding the image of the face in a variety of ways whereas the typical research subject saw a fixed photograph. The research subject was usually tested with what amounts to an exact template of the original image seen—an uncommon and far easier memory task than that faced by the eyewitness. This artifact may account for the discrepancy between the high accuracy shown in many laboratory studies in face recognition and the much lower accuracy scores reported in recent eyewitness research studies. We assume that the poor conditions of observation typical of crime situations already described leave many eyewitnesses with fragmented images of the face as well as verbal and semantic labels in memory. The witness who is tested with face photographs must then form or construct a more concrete impression of what is in his or her memory in order to compare it to the photograph. The high expectation (by both witness

[29] Hochberg, J., & Galper, R. E. Recognition of faces: 1. An exploratory study. *Psychonomic Science*, 1967, 9, 619–620.
[30] Yin, R. K. Looking at upside-down faces. *Journal of Experimental Psychology*, 1969, 81, 141–145.
[31] Shepard, R. N. Recognition memory for words, sentences and pictures. *Journal of Verbal Learning and Verbal Behavior*, 1967, 6, 156–163.
[32] Nickerson, R. S. Short-term memory for complex meaningful visual configurations. *Canadian Journal of Psychology*, 1965, 19, 155–160.

and interrogator) that he or she has a clear image of a previously seen face stored in long-term memory can create a situation in which a witness is vulnerable to social pressure to identify or give a description even where his or her memory is quite poor.

A major issue in the psychological research literature is the difference between recall of the face—as given in a verbal description—and the ability of a witness to recognize a previously seen face in a test (e.g., a lineup or set of photos). As far as we can tell, researchers describe recall and recognition as two distinct activities. Goldstein, Johnson, and Chance (1977) state categorically that, "recognition memory for faces and perhaps other kinds of pictures is largely independent of the recall of details of the stimuli . . . recognition memory and reconstruction ability had little in common."[33] This opinion contrasts sharply with the opinion of people in law enforcement who rely on the fidelity of witness descriptions and the actual descriptions of the suspect.

Some researchers focus on the matchup of a list of specific features known (in Goldstein's case) as the Facial Feature Adjective List (FFAL). (See Table 5.1.) This list contains 23 separate items covering every conceivable physical feature of the human face and requires witnesses to recall degrees or colors of each item. Harmon (1973) used a similar approach in his development of an automatic facial feature selection program for a computer.[34] Harmon's computer program is the basis for commercially available computer-coded photographic mug shots of criminals which are used with witnesses who report facial features to an investigator in order to narrow down the number of photos to be viewed for identification. An essential reason for the development of these procedures is the hypothesis that the witness who demonstrates an extensive recall of facial features could predictably recognize the face at a later time.

Unfortunately, there is little if any empirical support for the hypothesis. Goldstein, Johnson, and Chance (1977) demonstrated that witnesses using the FFAL to describe a previously seen face from memory only seconds after viewing showed an average 51 percent agreement with the ratings of those faces that had been rated and standardized by a group of judges who had an unlimited amount of

[33] Goldstein, A. G., Johnson, K. S., & Chance, J. Face recognition and verbal description of faces from memory. Paper presented to the Psychonomic Society, Washington, D.C., November 1977. See also Goldstein, A. G. The fallibility of the eyewitness: Psychological evidence. In B. D. Sales (Ed.), *Psychology in the Legal Process.* New York: Spectrum, 1977.

[34] Harmon, L. D. The recognition of faces. *Scientific American,* 1973, 229 (5), 70–82. See also Goldstein, A. G., & Lesk, A. B. Man machine interaction in human face identification. *The Bell System Technical Journal,* 1972, 51 (2), 399–427.

Table 5.1 FACIAL FEATURE ADJECTIVE LIST

SHAPE OF FACE
Square   Round   Oval   V-Shaped

SHAPE OF FACE
Full   Thin   Average

LENGTH OF HAIR
Long   Short   Average

HAIR COLOR
Light   Dark

HAIR
Straight   Curly   Frizzy   Wavy

HAIR
Thick   Thin

NOSE
Large   Small   Average

NOSE
Sharp   Rounded   Average

BRIDGE OF NOSE
Wide   Narrow   Average

UPPER LIP OF MOUTH
Thick   Thin   Average

LOWER LIP OF MOUTH
Thick   Thin   Average

LIP LINE OF MOUTH
Well Defined   Not Well Defined   Average

HORIZONTAL WIDTH OF MOUTH
Wide   Small   Average

EYEBROWS
Slanted   Straight   Arched   Curved

EYEBROWS
Bushy   Thin   Average

EYEBROWS
Light   Dark

CHIN
V-shaped   Round   Square

FOREHEAD
High   Low   Average

EYES
Big   Small   Average

EYES
Slanted Up   Slanted Down   Average

EYES
Close Together   Far Apart   Average

COLOR OF IRIS
Light   Dark

SHAPE OF EYES
Almond   Round   Slitted   Average

time.[35] Correlations between descriptive accuracy and number of correct recognitions averaged around 0.15, a significant but practically meaningless level of association. It seems clear that the ability to provide detailed verbal descriptions of facial features may serve the needs of investigators who need to construct an image of what a witness perceived, but good describers do not necessarily make good recognizers.

If analysis of remembered features does not explain facial recognition, how is it that we remember faces at all? Clifford and Bull (1978), rely on the concept of the *perceptual gestalt*—where the whole of the face rather than the sum of the parts is acquired and stored in memory.[36] The authors point to a large number of studies that show that whole faces are remembered better than "scrambled" photos of faces; faces initially rated high in beauty are subsequently better recognized,[37] "pleasant" and "ugly" faces are memorized better than "medium" rated faces,[38] and, finally, that faces with certain expressions (e.g., smiling) are recognized better as well.[39] The point, of course, is that the face is such a rich source of information that few observers would have the time or motivation to perform a point-by-point analysis of every feature of the face. The marvelous efficiency of human memory is demonstrated by the fact that in ordinary life the observer does remember faces, although he or she may not be able to explain just how.

One of the factors that aids the observer in ordinary face recognition is the familiarity of the context. Obviously, if the observer encounters the same face a second time in the same place wearing the same clothing, recognition will be facilitated. Watkins, Ho, and Tulving (1976) demonstrated that when observers were tested with photos of faces that had been paired with verbal phrases, the recogni-

[35] Goldstein et al., op. cit. See also Goldstein, A. G., & Chance, J. Measuring psychological similarity of faces. *Bulletin of the Psychonomic Society*, 1976, 7, 407–408.

[36] Clifford, B. R., & Bull, R. *The Psychology of Person Identification*. London: Routledge & Kegan Paul, 1978. The authors provide the only coherent account of the unpublished research of Professor Goldstein and his colleagues. In addition, they provide a thorough review of all face perception research and carefully evaluate its legal significance.

[37] Cross, J., Cross, J., & Daly, J. Sex, race, age and beauty as factors in recognition of faces. *Perception and Psychophysics*, 1971, 10, 393–396.

[38] Peters, A. (1917) cited in H. Ellis, Recognizing faces. *British Journal of Psychology*, 1975, 66, 409–426.

[39] Galper, R., & Hochberg, H. Recognition memory for photographs of faces. *American Journal of Psychology*, 1971, 84, 351–354. See also Sorce, J. F., & Campos, J. J. The role of expression in the recognition of a face. *American Journal of Psychology*, 1974, 87 (1-2), 71–82.

tion performance was higher than that of observers whose test lacked the surrounding verbal context.[40] Similarly, Bassili (1978) found that movement of the surface of the face provides sufficient information for the perception of faces and for the discrimination of emotions.[41] In this very ingenious study, observers were presented with televised pictures of actors whose faces were painted black with white reflective spots so that only emotional movements and grimaces could be detected. The ability of observers to recognize these featureless faces tells us a great deal about the importance of nonverbal communication that an observer remembers but which he or she may not be able to verbalize. The feature information and the motion information are part of the perceptual gestalt that affect face recognition.

In the 1970s various researchers progressed along a line of investigation of how memory strength is affected by levels of processing of the original stimulus.

> If the stimulus is processed in terms of sensory (shallow) features, then the resultant memory trace will presumably be less durable than if the stimulus had been processed in terms of semantic (deep) features.[42]

Bower and Karlin (1974) showed pictures of faces to observers, requiring them to judge honesty, likableness, or gender of the face.[43] On a later recognition test, observers who made honesty or likableness decisions (deep processing) had a significantly greater number of recognitions than those who made a decision on the basis of sex of the face (shallow processing). Strnad and Mueller (1977) repeated this experiment with a set of more similar facial photos and got essentially the same results.[44, 45] These results imply that if an eyewitness to a crime endeavored to form a semantic or personality judgment rather than a point-by-point feature analysis, the time spent would lead to a

[40] Watkins, M. J., Ho, E., & Tulving, E. Context effects in recognition memory for faces. *Journal of Verbal Learning and Verbal Behavior*, 1976, *15*, 505–517.
[41] Bassili, J. Facial motion in the perception of faces and of emotional expression. *Journal of Experimental Psychology: Human Perception and Performance*, 1978, *4* (3), 373–379.
[42] Strnad, B. N., & Mueller, J. H. Levels of processing in facial recognition memory. *Bulletin of the Psychonomic Society*, 1977, *9* (1), 17–18. See also Craik, F. I. M., & Lockhart, R. S. Levels of processing a framework for memory research. *Journal of Verbal Learning and Verbal Behavior*, 1972, *11*, 671–684.
[43] Bower, G. H., & Karlin, M. B. Depth of processing pictures of faces and recognition memory. *Journal of Experimental Psychology*, 1974, *103*, 751–757.
[44] Strnad & Mueller, op. cit.; Craik & Lockhart, op. cit.
[45] Mueller, J. H., Carlomusto, M., & Goldstein, A. G. Orienting task and study time in facial recognition. *Bulletin of the Psychonomic Society*, 1978, *11* (5), 313–316. This study is more complex—involving a comparison between face feature processing and body (weight) processing (as well as "generosity"), but the results are the same.

more enduring perceptual gestalt which would probably aid in later tests of recognition.[46]

To summarize, we have learned a number of valuable lessons from traditional laboratory studies of face perception, with its more ideal conditions permitting a more refined study of memory processes. These lessons teach us that even where face recognition is at a high rate (from 50 to 95 percent), memory processes operate in ways that differ markedly from what is assumed by most crime investigators. Recall of a long list of specific facial features may aid an investigator but it plays a very minor role in aiding a witness to remember a face; and in fact may be a source of confusion and error. Eyewitnesses to crimes, who manifest a very low rate of face recognition (10 to 40 percent) do so for reasons that would disrupt any kind of memory processing.

Psychology of the Witness

STRESS

On no other issue is there more of a conflict between the layperson and the behavioral scientist than on just what happens to perception under stress. Where a crime victim may state emphatically that, "I will never forget that face!" the researcher rejoins with data that indicate that high levels of stress cause inaccuracies in perception. Violent crime, with its life-threatening aspects does give rise to stress reactions that have been so ably documented by Professor Hans Selye (1956, 1975).

> We suspected this adrenal response to play a useful part in a non-specific adaptive reaction, which we named the "alarm reaction." Subsequent studies showed that the alarm reaction is but the first stage of a much more prolonged general adaptation syndrome (GAS). The latter comprises three distinct stages, namely: (1) *the alarm reaction*, in which adaptation has not yet been acquired; (2) *the stage of resistance*, in which adaptation is optimal; (3) *the stage of exhaustion*, in which the acquired adaptation is lost again.[47]

[46] Yarmey, A. D. The effects of attractiveness, feature saliency, and liking on memory for faces. In M. Cook and G. Wilson (Eds.) *Love and Attraction: An International Conference.* Toronto: Pergamon Press, 1978, pp. 51–53. This study showed that high attractive females' and low attractive males' faces were more easily remembered and that the forgetting curves for deep processing and shallow processing (distinctive features) followed the same trend over 30 days.

[47] Selye, H. The stress concept: Its philosophical and psychosocial implications. *Bioscience Communications,* 1975, *1,* 131–145. See also Selye, H. *The Stress of Life.* New York: McGraw-Hill, 1956.

This universal pattern may prepare a person to run, fight, or bring an enormous amount of strength to bear on the situation, but the alarm reaction is not conducive to efficient observation, to storage into memory of small details, or to the formation of an enduring gestalt.

A person under stress is a less reliable witness than he or she would be normally. Research shows that observers are less capable of remembering details, less accurate in reading dials, and less certain in detecting signals when under stress.[48] They pay more attention to their own well-being and safety than to nonessential elements in the environment. Research with trained air force flight crew members confirms that even highly trained people become poorer observers when under stress. The crew members can never forget the stress and what hit them. The events, being highly significant at the time, can be remembered, but memory of details or the precise order of events is not so clear. Time estimates are especially exaggerated under stress.

Hugo Muensterberg, author of the classic work *On the Witness Stand*, stated in 1908 that although moderate stress might improve the accuracy of testimony, a great amount of stress (or very little) would hurt accuracy.[49] This hypothesis, confirmed in more recent research with fear, anxiety, and stress, can best be described as an inverted "U"-shaped function. At low levels of stress—where the attention value of the environment is insignificant—the witness does not pay much attention and thus has a selectively impoverished memory from which details can be retrieved. At moderate stress levels, as demonstrated in a 1978 study of crime seriousness by Leippe, Wells, and Ostrom, attention is more focused and memory is improved as indicated by higher recognition rates.[50] At high levels of stimulation and stress the attention processes become disrupted and less information is stored—hence leading to poorer memory and fewer correct recognitions. Kuehn (1974) in a study of police crime reports found that the more emotional or stress-provoking crimes (rape, assault) produced less complete descriptions from victims than did robberies; victims who were injured gave less complete descriptions than uninjured victims.[51] (See Table 5.2.)

In an experimental test of the effects of a relatively high degree of emotional arousal on eyewitness perception, Johnson and Scott (1976) staged a scene in which a man ran out of a laboratory after an argu-

[48] Buckhout, Eyewitness.
[49] Muensterberg, op. cit., cited in Levine & Tapp, op. cit.
[50] Leippe, Wells, & Ostrom, op. cit. Whether we call the phenomenon stress, anxiety, or arousal makes little difference to the theory.
[51] Kuehn, L. L. Looking down a gun barrel: Person perception and violent crime. *Perceptual and Motor Skills*, 1974, 39, 1159–1164.

Table 5.2 COMPLETENESS OF VICTIM'S DESCRIPTION OF
SUSPECT BY SELECTED VARIABLES

VARIABLES	% COMPLETE DESCRIPTIONS	N
TIME OF OFFENSE		
Daytime	64	39
Twilight	21*	14
Night	61	54
TYPE OF CRIME		
Robbery	61	61
Assault	33**	15
Rape	45	22
VICTIM INJURY		
Injured	40*	38
Not Injured	61	62
SEX OF VICTIM		
Male	66	52
Female	43†	44
RACE OF VICTIM		
White	58	74
Black	36†	11
INTERRACIAL CRIMES		
White victim, white suspect	83	18
White victim, black suspect	68	38
Black victim, black suspect	33**	6
Black victim, white suspect	none	none

*$p = .01$ **$p = .05$ †$p = .10$

SOURCE: Reprinted by permission of author and publisher from Kuehn, L. L., Looking down a gun barrel: Person perception and violent crime, *Perceptual and Motor Skills*, 1974, 39, 1159–1164. Table 2, p. 1162.

ment, clutching a letter opener in "blood-stained" hands.[52] This condition was contrasted with a scene in which the same man came out of the laboratory muttering about broken machines. The performance of witnesses in describing the assailant under the high arousal conditions was poorer, at least for the females. The remaining results of this study were complex and there has generally been little direct research on the perceptions of people caught in very high stress situations due to the obvious ethical problems involved. Our assumptions derived from a variety of studies, including those done with observations of the movements of the eye while viewing, suggest that high stress disrupts the normal smooth scanning of the field of vision

[52] Johnson, C. & Scott, B. Eyewitness testimony and suspect identification as a function of arousal, sex of witness and scheduling of interrogation. Paper presented at the American Psychological Association, Washington, D.C., September, 1976.

observed under low arousal conditions. Johnson and Scott reported that their witnesses tended to fixate on the blood and the weapon, giving better descriptions of the weapon than of the face.

This idea can be tested by asking a few people where they were when they first heard the emotion-provoking news of the assassination of President John F. Kennedy. They will probably recall vividly where they were and whom they were with. It is unlikely, however, that they will be able to describe what they or their companions were wearing.

Brown and Kulik (1977) made a study of the memories of persons at such critical points in their lives and found what they call "flashbulb memories."[53] However, they make the following distinctions between selective perception under stress and the mistaken notion that memory can act as a camera:

> An actual photograph, taken by flashbulb, preserves everything within its scope; it is altogether indiscriminate. Our flashbulb memories are not. The second authors' crying teacher had a hairdo and a dress that are missing from his memory. The first author faced a desk with many objects on it, and some kind of weather was visible through the window, but none of this is in his memory picture. In short, a flashbulb memory is only somewhat indiscriminate and is very far from complete. In these respects, it is unlike a photograph.[54]

Our final note about stress concerns the degree of confidence expressed by witnesses about their memory for details and their certainty in identifying someone. Buckhout (1976), Yarmey (1979), and others report that degree of confidence is not related to witness accuracy in remembering or recognizing someone.[55, 56] Both researchers record a confidence estimate along with measures of accuracy in recall and recognition. Eyewitnesses who do forget *that* face may still be 100 percent sure in a *mistaken* identification. Highly stressed witnesses under pressure of telling their story—especially those who are also victims—will never forget the fact that they were shot or mugged, but their statement about "never forgetting that face" does not gain much support from psychological research.[57]

---

[53] Brown, R., & Kulik, J. Flashbulb memories. *Cognition*, 1977, 5, 53–68, 73.

[54] Ibid., 74.

[55] Buckhout, R. Psychology and eyewitness identification. *Psychology and Law Review*, 1976, 2, 75–91.

[56] Yarmey, A. D. *The Psychology of Eyewitness Testimony.* New York: Free Press, 1979. Actually confidence is *not* correlated with witness accuracy.

[57] Marshall, Marquis, & Oskamp. Effects of Kind of Question and Atmosphere of Interrogation on Accuracy and Completeness of Testimony, *Harvard Law Review*, 1971, *84*, 1620. In *United States* v. *Amaral*, 488 F. 2d 1148 (9th Cir. 1973) the Court distorted information in a Center for Responsive Psychology report in order to defend cross-examination as the means for discovering eyewitness unreliability.

PHYSICAL CONDITION OF THE WITNESS

The human senses function much less efficiently when the body has become fatigued, ill, or injured, when the person is advanced in age, or when the person has subjected him or herself to overuse of alcohol, depressant or stimulant drugs, or hallucinogenic drugs.[58] Eyewitnesses have sometimes testified to details that they could not possibly have observed because of their physical condition. In one case a witness who was color blind testified to seeing shades of red, although it was physically impossible for him actually to see red. Color blindness, principally the inability to see red and green, is an inherited condition which affects approximately 5 to 10 percent of all men. If there is some doubt about the sensory capacity of an eyewitness, routine testing of eyes, ears, or any other sense organs can easily be obtained and made available to the court.[59] The sophistication of modern corrective medical techniques suggests the need for more detailed questioning of eyewitnesses by attorneys over matters such as eyeglasses, hearing loss, hearing aids, artificial pacemakers for the heart, and contact

---

The appellant sought relief from a denial by the trial judge allowing expert testimony on eyewitness credibility. Judge Turrentine, writing the opinion, rejected the plea, and stated criteria for accepting expert testimony: (1) a qualified expert, (2) proper subject, (3) conformity to a generally accepted explanatory theory, and (4) probative value compared to prejudicial effect. The Court excluded the expert testimony for its lack of probative value to the particular case, especially because it believed the jury was competent to judge the effects of stress on eyewitness testimony without expert help. In the opinion, Judge Turrentine lifted a phrase out of context from a Center for Responsive Psychology report and distorted research evidence on the effects of stress on perception to support the Court's conclusion that good cross-examination can bring out the witness's credibility for the jury to consider. Research demonstrates, however, that perception is made less reliable under stress and that assertions of certainty by stressed observers ("I'll never forget his face") are often ill founded. Cross-examination may tend to force the stressed observer to defend his or her perception, however unreliable, and encourage him or her to be more confident.

[58] The evidence of the effects of LSD and marijuana on human perception is not presently complete. The question of dosage levels, as in the case of alcohol, cannot be generalized because humans show wide individual differences in their ability to function with differing amounts of any intoxicant.

[59] These issues became paramount in *People* v. *Davis*, No. 52613 (Santa Clara Sup. Ct., Cal., May 27, 1972). A key eyewitness who influenced other witnesses and who purportedly saw Ms. Davis in a rented van used in the shoot-out at Marin County courthouse turned out to be color blind by his own admission. Yet he testified directly to seeing colors—notably red tinges in the hair. Assuming that the man was red-green color blind, the author of this article testified that the eyewitness's perceptions would be physically impossible, which raised doubts about the independence of the eyewitness's testimony. A rebuttal witness testified that the author was wrong: that in fact the witness was monochromatic, a rare condition of total color blindness. Thus much of the key witness's testimony was discredited.

lenses, all of which may affect the witness's physical ability to make a reliable eyewitness report. Yarmey (1979)[60] has written an especially useful review of vision, hearing, and memory factors affecting the very young and the very old witness.

However, there are physical conditions that affect all people and are of particular concern to the analysis of eyewitness reports. The intensity of light can affect color perception and, in turn, the accuracy of reporting.[61] Accurate color identification is particularly difficult at dusk or at night even though a person may have excellent vision. This loss of color discrimination is the result of chemical changes in the retina of the eye as it adjusts to night vision. By day, the *cones*—a structure in the retina—are most sensitive to light and permit color vision. As the intensity of light diminishes, the cones become less sensitive and night vision is achieved by another retina structure—*rods*—which require little light to permit vision but which are insensitive to color. With night vision the world might appear gray except for the fact that our experience tells us that cabs are yellow, stop signs are red, and so on. Statements about colors by witnesses from nighttime observations may be guesses rather than perceptions, particularly if the observation is based on seeing colors under mercury or sodium vapor lamps.

Dark adaptation is the product of a normal chemical change in sensitivity that takes approximately 20 to 25 minutes—as we go from a lighted area to a very dark one. Observations made during the dark adaptation period can be quite reduced in reliability. The time period for full dark adaptation is considerably longer in the aged.[62] These elements, familiar to most psychologists, are not so carefully considered by lawyers as they should be.

PRIOR CONDITIONING AND EXPERIENCE

Psychologists have done extensive research on how set, or expectancy, is used by the human observer to make judgments more efficiently. In a classic experiment by Bruner and Postman (1949) observers were shown a display of playing cards for a few seconds and asked to report the number of aces of spades in the display.[63] Most observers reported only three, although there were actually five. Two of the aces of spades were colored red instead of the more familiar black. The interpretation was given that because people were so familiar with black aces of spades, they did not waste time looking carefully at the

[60] Yarmey, op. cit.
[61] Ibid.
[62] Ibid.
[63] Bruner, J., & Postman, L. On the perception of incongruity: A paradigm. *Journal of Personality*, 1949, *18*, 206–223.

display. However, efficiency in this case led to the unreliable observations. In many criminal cases the prior conditioning of the witness may enable him or her to describe facts or events that were *not present* but should have been.

PERSONAL BIASES

Expectancy in its least palatable form can be found in the case of biases or prejudices held by a witness. A victim of a mugging may initially report being attacked by "niggers" and may, because of limited experience as well as prejudice, be unable to tell one black man from another. In a classic study of this phenomenon Allport and Postman's (1946), observers were asked to take a brief look at a picture of several people on a subway train.[64] In the picture a black man was seated and a white man was standing with a razor in his hand. When the story was passed on to others the final observer tended to report that the razor was in the hand of the black man (see Figure 5.1).

Prejudices may be racial or religious or based on physical characteristics such as long hair, dirty clothes, or status. All human beings have some *stereotypes* on which they make perceptual judgments; such stereotypes make decision making more efficient. A witness to an auto accident may save time by reporting his well-ingrained stereotype about "women drivers." But these shortcuts to thinking may be erroneously reported and expanded on by an eyewitness without his or her being aware that he or she is describing his or her stereotype rather than the events that actually took place. An experiment by Professor Elizabeth Loftus (1974) showed that witnesses to a filmed accident would give higher speed estimates when asked how fast the cars were going when they "smashed" as opposed to when they "hit" each other.[65] If the witnesses' biases are shared by an investigator taking a statement, the report may reflect their mutual biases rather than what was actually seen.

In some of our trial experience we have encountered eyewitnesses who were so biased in favor of the prosecutor's case that they were unwilling to acknowledge any doubt about their final identification of a suspect despite their uncertainty in the first identification. Some banks and airlines issue instructions to their employees to cooperate with police and prosecutors. Such cooperation is responsible citizenship, but it is also a potential source of bias, because those employees

[64] Allport, G. W., & Postman, L. The basic psychology of rumor. *Transcriptions of the New York Academy of Sciences, Series 11*, 1945, 8, 61–81.
[65] Loftus, E. F., & Palmer, J. C. Reconstruction of automobile destruction: An example of the interaction between language and memory. *Journal of Verbal Learning and Verbal Behavior*, 1974, 13, 585–589.

Figure 5.1   "Who had the razor?" After a brief look at a drawing such as this one, half of the observers report having seen the razor, a stereotyped symbol of violence in blacks, in the black man's hand. (Source: Adapted from Allport, G. W., and Postman, L. The basic psychology of rumour. *Transcriptions of the New York Academy of Sciences*, Series 11, 1945, 8, 147–149. Drawing from Buckhout, R. Eyewitness testimony. *Scientific American*, 1974, *231*, (6), 23–31.)

are aware of their company's strong interest in convicting the accused. The court is, of course, alert to some kinds of bias in witnesses—for example, warning juries to determine if any witness has an ulterior motive. Psychologists however are documenting biases that are normal to even the honest witness's attempt to perceive.

The International Association of Chiefs of Police in their Training Guide (1967) report the following actual example of a prejudiced witness:

A case in point was a middle-aged lady of European extraction who had her purse stolen containing her life savings of several thousand dollars. When she reported the theft to the police, she described the thief as an adolescent and gave the officer a description which identified the offender as definitely someone of latin extraction. At this particular time, Spanish speaking Americans were moving into this European ethnic community. The police subsequently arrested the offender, a blue-eyed, very light complected youth. However, due to the feeling of the victim towards these newcomers, the description she gave to the police was completely erroneous.[66]

[66] International Association of Chiefs of Police—Training Key #67, Witness Perception, 1967, available from 1319—18th St. N.W., Washington, D.C., 20036.

NEEDS AND MOTIVES: SEEING WHAT WE WANT TO SEE

The meaning of the phrase "need influences perception" has been demonstrated in numerous experiments in which people reported seeing certain things that in fact were not present. Levine, Chein, and Murphy (1942) asked volunteers to fast for 24 hours and then report what they "saw" in a series of blurred slides presented on a screen.[67] The longer the volunteers were deprived of food, the more frequently they reported seeing "food" in the blurred pictures. An analysis of the motives of the eyewitnesses at the time of the crime can be very valuable in determining whether the witness is reporting what he or she wanted to see rather than what was there.

DESIRE TO BE A PART OF HISTORY

A common behavior observed by journalists and psychologists is the tendency for people to claim that they were present when a significant historical event took place near their hometown or city, even though they were not physically present or active in the event. Such a story will make them sound interesting and is usually difficult or impossible to check. In one case a journalist fabricated a charming human interest story about a naked woman stuck to a newly painted toilet seat in a small town and published it through the newspaper wire services. He visited the town and interviewed citizens who claimed to have played a part in or witnessed this totally fictitious event. In criminal cases with publicity and a controversial defendant it is not uncommon for volunteer witnesses to come forward.[68]

In the case of *New York* v. *Gramaglia et al.* (1978) our analysis of the testimony of a very eager eyewitness to a murder revealed that he had volunteered himself repeatedly and positively identified most of the people whose pictures he was presented, people who were associates of the main defendants.[69] When some of the defendants confessed to the killing and other evidence emerged, it was established that some of the men identified were not even present at the scene of the crime. The witness gave newspaper interviews and made pronouncements about crime in the city. The need for society to write a history of major events produces witnesses to fill that need as the box about the Lincoln assassination suggests.

---

[67] Levine, R. I., Chein, I., & Murphy, G. The relation of the intensity of a need to the amount of perceptual distortion. *Journal of Psychology*, 1942, *13*, 283–293.
[68] Buckhout, Eyewitness.
[69] *People of the State of New York* v. *Gramaglia et al.*, 1978, Erie County Superior Court, Buffalo, N.Y.

Testing for Recall and Recognition: Identification

LENGTH OF TIME FROM EVENT TO TEST

One of the most stable findings of psychological research is that verbal information and pictorial information tend to be forgotten as time passes.[70] Passage of time without practice in recollection permits a witness to pay attention to more immediate matters. Perfect recall of information or faces is basically unnecessary and is rarely, if ever, found. The measurement of recall or the testing of recognition from a lineup or a set of photos will therefore generally be less reliable as the length of time from the event to the test increases. Not only is information forgotten but also the context in which it was first taken. That is, witnesses may remember a face but forget where they first saw it.[71]

One exception to these general research findings has been reported by Erdelyi et al. (1974, 1978) who found that memory for pictures got better over time.[72] This phenomenon is called *hypermnesia*—a sort of negative forgetting—which may be due to the form of questioning or relaxing (thinking) in between questioning sessions. Eugenio et al. (1979) found hypermnesia in recall in eyewitnesses to simulated crimes, but it was only early in the time period—30 minutes after it took place. Repeated questioning of accurate witnesses led to an increase in the reportings of plausible but erroneous memories of the crime.[73]

FILLING IN DETAILS THAT WERE NOT PRESENT

An efficient memory is characterized by certain techniques used to "store" information so that the essence of the information can be recalled (retrieved) when needed. *"Perceptual filling in"* is a name given to an act by an observer who takes an incomplete or fragmentary image and "cleans it up" when he or she is tested at a later time. In research on this phenomenon, subjects first drew an object they were shown and then were tested on their ability to reproduce the drawing (from memory) 30 days later and then three months later. One such object was an unclosed triangle. The observers first tended to make the

[70] Wickelgreen, W. A. *Learning and Memory*. Englewood Cliffs, N.J.: Prentice-Hall, 1977.

[71] Brown, E., Deffenbacher, K., & Sturgill, W. Memory for Faces and the Circumstances of Encounter. *Journal of Applied Psychology*, 1977, *62*, 311–318.

[72] Erdelyi, M. H., & Kleinbard, J. Has Ebbinghaus decayed with time? The growth of recall (hypermnesia) over days. *Journal of Experimental Psychology: Human Learning and Memory*, 1978, *4*, 275–289.

[73] Eugenio P., Kostes, S., Buckhout, R., & Ellison, K. W. *Hypermnesia and the Eyewitness to Crime*. Paper presented to the American Psychological Association Convention, New York City, September 1979.

EYEWITNESS REPORTS ON THE ASSASSINATION OF ABRAHAM LINCOLN

Bruce Catton

Few of the great events in American history have been described as often or in as much detail as the assassination of Abraham Lincoln. Here is one of the pivotal tragedies in our national story, and by now it is so completely familiar that the mere words "Ford's Theatre" or *Our American Cousin* immediately evoke the entire story for every American. If there is one chapter that we think we have by heart it is this one. . . .

The story always leads us, to be sure, to the same haunted, echoing mystery, and it leaves us with the same unwillingness to accept a cruel, seemingly meaningless twist of fate. But perhaps because of that very reluctance it is useful for us to hear the story, not as a tidy and well-arranged narrative but as a tale told by many voices whose conflicting testimony simply emphasizes the shock which the tragedy inflicted at the time.

Of necessity, history is selective. When it deals with an event like this it assembles the pertinent accounts and discards the irrelevant, carefully separates the probably true from the obviously false, pieces stray bits of testimony together, and presents us at last with a coherent story. This is the way history has to be, and if it were not told that way it would be unendurably confusing. Yet we may miss something when we read it that way, and what we miss can be important—the dreadful incoherence which the affair had at the time for the people who were involved in it. History's most compelling moments are not always as orderly as the books make them seem; sometimes they are in the highest degree disorderly, so bewildering that even people who lived through them may have only a shadowy idea of what they themselves saw. There is a confusion of tongues, which may indeed be a deep problem for the historian but which was after all part of the reality at the time. It is no wonder that history's tragedies give birth to myths and legends. Sometimes it seems marvelous that the real truth ever does take shape. . . .

This of course is where the story becomes interesting, because the people who left their stories did not see things the same way. Some of them, apparently, did not see at all what the others saw, so that the testimony is often at odds.

For instance, twenty-five different human beings asserted that they helped carry the body of Abraham Lincoln across the street from the theatre into the little house where he died. It is perfectly clear, to anyone who stops to think, that twenty-five people could not possibly get close enough to one man to join hands and carry him: yet they all said they did, and their stories vary enormously. One man solemnly testifies that the dying President was carried across the street on a shutter, wrenched from a theatre window by ardent onlookers; another man, with equal solemnity, says that the President was carried in the rocking chair he occupied when the fatal bullet was fired; to wind it up, eight different beings insist that they, individually, and unaided, held the President's head during the sad journey.

How about the house across the street, where the stricken man died? He was laid on a bed in a suffocating small room where four people would make a crowd. According to the testimony, no fewer than eighty-four people were in that room that night, at one time or another. After he died, coins the size of half dollars were laid on his eyelids to hold them down. Each one of three different men, all men of standing whose word there is little reason to doubt, asserts that he and he alone took two silver coins and laid them on those eyelids.

Then there was John Wilkes Booth, who pulled the trigger and, before a theatre full of people, leaped from the presidential box to the stage, shouted something only half-intelligible, then went to the wings and made his exit. How did he do all of this? According to one witness, he made a fifteen-foot leap, ran swiftly off-stage, and vanished. According to another, he slid down a flagpole (which did not actually exist), and more or less crept away. One witness saw him limping painfully across the stage moaning incoherently; another saw him stalking off calmly, dropping his "Sic semper tyrannis" as a good actor might; another saw him running furiously, saying nothing at all; still another remembered that he went off-stage on his hands and knees, making noises. . . . Apparently he got on-stage and then off, but the testimony about the way he did it is extremely varied.

Now what do we get out of all of this? We get, of course, the essential truth: that this crack-brained actor murdered Abraham Lincoln and then went away; and that this history of the United States thereafter was different from what it might have been if all of this had not happened—and perhaps that is really all we have to know. We have too many witnesses, and they tell too many different stories. Probably all of these people were honest enough; they just saw things differently when a terrible and unexpected catastrophe burst upon their vision. The historians have been working with all of this for generations, and by now they have pretty well agreed on what really happened, so that we have a tolerably clear story. But at the time the whole event was nothing but chaos.

Box 5.1 (Continued)

Apparently that is the way events usually are. Maybe eyewitnesses are sometimes the worst witnesses; maybe circumstantial evidence (highly derided in law courts and in mystery novels) is sometimes the only kind that is good. And maybe, too, it is good for us now and then to put ourselves back in the places of the people who had to live through these terrible moments, so that we can understand that history does not usually make real sense until long afterward. . . .

SOURCE: Foreword by Bruce Catton to *Twenty Days* by Dorothy Meserve Kunhardt and Philip B. Kunhardt, Jr. Copyright © 1965 by Dorothy Meserve Kunhardt and Philip B. Kunhardt, Jr. Reprinted with permission of Harper & Row, Publishers, Inc.

object more symmetrical, then almost closed the sides, and later filled it in to make a nice neat triangle. This finding was repeated with many objects, the tendency being for people to "improve" their memory by making what they remembered seem more logical. In an analysis of eyewitness reports in criminal cases it has been observed that the reports get more completed and less ambiguous as the witness moves from the initial police report, through a grand jury statement to actual testimony at a trial. The process of "filling" in is an efficient way to remember, but it can lead to unreliable recognition testing, because the witness may adjust his or her memory to fit the available suspects or pictures. If we rule out lying, it is possible that the witness may be unaware that he or she is distorting or constructing his or her memory. In an effort to be conscientious, he or she may confabulate parts of recall in order to make a chaotic memory seem more plausible to the questioners.

Loftus (1974) in her experiment demonstrated how the semantic value of the words used in asking questions about a filmed auto accident caused witnesses to distort their reports.[74] When witnesses were asked a question that used the word "smashed" as opposed to "hit" they were more likely to report having seen broken glass when, in fact, there had been none.

INTERROGATION: GETTING THE PICTURE

Research in the questioning of eyewitnesses—the "how?" and the usually poor results—dates back to the beginning of the twentieth century. Our present-day understanding of these problems has been

[74] Loftus, & Palmer, op. cit.

greatly aided by the fine systematic research conducted by Professor Elizabeth Loftus of the University of Washington.[75] In court, a witness cannot be asked leading questions as trial procedure is designed to minimize suggestions to allow the words to come from the witness's own recollection of events. But when police or other investigators first question a witness they need to construct their own image of what happened. Very often they will use leading questions, cues, and heavy probing to "squeeze out" information. Professor Loftus has synthesized the older research and her own to demonstrate how this form of interrogation leads to inaccurate and unreliable recall. As Hilgard and Loftus note:

> Eyewitness reports have been investigated in the psychological laboratory on and off ever since 1900. Specimen studies from the early period and from the last decade indicate that *free reports* are consistently more accurate but less complete than reports obtained through specifically directed inquiry. The optimal combination is free report followed by the asking of specific questions . . . the wording of questions put to a witness can distort the witness'[s] memory for the previously experienced event.[76]

We note that investigators (and the forms they are required to fill out) thrive on directed questions. Muscio (1915) showed that the use of objective questions—"Was *the* gun a revolver?" led to less reliable witness recall than the more subjective question—"Did you see *a* gun?"[77] Harris (1973) demonstrated that by simply changing one word in a question to viewers of a film, he got completely different average answers:[78]

QUESTION: "How *tall* was the basketball player?"
ANSWER: "79 inches."
QUESTION: "How *short* was the basketball player?"
ANSWER: "69 inches."

[75] Hilgard, E. R., & Loftus, E. F. Effective interrogation of the eyewitness. *International Journal of Clinical and Experimental Hypnosis*, 1979, in press.
[76] Ibid, See also Lipton, J. P. On the psychology of eyewitness testimony. *Journal of Applied Psychology*, 1977, 62, 90–95. Lipton found that free narrative subjects were 91 percent accurate but only 21 percent complete in describing a crime; interrogation (direct questions) yielded 75 percent completeness but only 56 percent accuracy.
[77] Muscio, B. The influence of the form of a question. *British Journal of Psychology*, 1915, 8, 351–389.
[78] Harris, R. Answering questions containing marked and unmarked adjectives and adverbs. *Journal of Experimental Psychology*, 1973, 97, 399–401.

Loftus and Zanni (1974)[79] tested witnesses to a filmed accident and found that using the article "the" in questions about a stop sign (there was none) produced more reports of stop signs and other nonexistent objects than did the same question worded subjectively as: "Did you see *a* stop sign?"

Loftus (1980) notes that questions that are designed to obtain information *from* a witness also supply information *to* a witness.[80] Leading questions that are suggestive thus can tamper with a witness's memory, leading to elaboration, distortions, simplifications, or complete reconstructions of events.[81] Laboratory research—where the true course of events and faces is checkable—is the psychologists tool for demonstrating this process. In one of the oldest studies, Cady (1924) tested witnesses to a "live" event by either asking for an open free report or by asking direct questions.[82] Clearly, the open free reports had fewer errors. Thus the investigator insists on asking detailed questions of eyewitnesses, he or she can expect more information but must be ready to sort out the errors by checking other sources of evidence.

SUGGESTIVITY IN THE TEST PROCEDURE

The lineup and the array of photographs used in testing the eyewitness's ability to identify a suspect can be analyzed as fair or unfair on the basis of criteria derived from multiple-choice testing on which most psychologists can agree.[83] A fair recognition test should be carefully designed to meet the following criteria:

1. All persons (or photos) should have an equal chance of being selected by a person who did not see the suspect.
2. All persons (or photos should be similar enough to each other and to the original description of the suspect to be confusing to a person who is merely guessing.
3. The test should be conducted without leading questions or suggestions from the test material or test giver.
4. The first test is the best test of memory—all later tests are affected by the first test.

[79] Loftus, E. F., & Zanni, G. Eyewitness testimony: The influence of the wording of a question. *Bulletin of the Psychonomic Society*, 1975, *5*, 86–88.
[80] Loftus, E. F. *Eyewitness Testimony*. Cambridge, Mass.: Harvard University Press, 1980.
[81] Bartlett, F. C. *Remembering*. Cambridge: Cambridge University Press, 1932.
[82] Cady, H. M. On the psychology of testimony. *American Journal of Psychology*, 1924, *35*, 110–112.
[83] Buckhout, R., Alper, A., Chern, S., Silverberg, G., & Slomovitz, M. Determinants of eyewitness performance on a lineup. *Bulletin of Psychonomic Society*, 1974, *4*, 191–192.

Too frequently, lineups or photograph arrays are carelessly assembled or even rigged in such a way as to make the eyewitness identification test completely unreliable.[84] If, for example, you present five pictures, the chance should be only one-fifth or 20 percent that any one picture will be chosen on the basis of guessing; but frequently, a single picture of a suspect may stand out. In *California* v. *Angela Davis*, (1972), the eyewitnesses were tested by the use of one set of nine pictures which included three photos showing the defendant Ms. Davis speaking at an outdoor rally, two mug shots of other women with different names, and one picture showing a 55-year-old woman.[85] It was so easy for a witness to rule out five pictures as ridiculous choices that the "test" was reduced to four pictures, including three of Ms. Davis. This meant that the odds were 75 percent that a witness would pick out a picture of Ms. Davis whether or not he had seen her. Such a "test" is meaningless to a psychologist and should be tainted as an item of evidence in court. However, in our experience, judges are not inclined to rule that biased tests change a witness's memory.[86]

Research on memory has also shown that if one item in the array of photos is uniquely different—in dress, race, height, sex, photographic quality—it is more likely to be picked out or attended to. Such an array is not *confusing* enough for it to be called a test. When a teacher makes up a multiple-choice test, he or she designs several answers that sound or look alike to make it difficult for a person who does not know the right answer to succeed. Police lineups and photo layouts are multiple-choice tests. If the rules for designing such tests are ignored by authorities, the tests become unreliable.

Biases can creep into testing unintentionally or through design. Doob and Kirschenbaum (1973) studied a real lineup in which a witness was tested for her ability to remember a face of a criminal she had described as "good looking."[87] The picture of the man she picked out and photos of all the other lineup participants was rated for attractiveness by a panel of judges who were not witnesses to the crime. The nonwitnesses rated the identified suspect's photo as the most good looking person pictured, indicating a major result of a biased test—even a person with no memory of the crime can pick out

---

[84] Buckhout, R., & Friere, V. Suggestivity in lineups and photospreads. *Center for Responsive Psychology Monograph* No. CR-5, New York: Brooklyn College, C.U.N.Y., 1975.

[85] *People* v. *Davis*. No. 52613, Santa Clara County Superior Court, California, May 27, 1972.

[86] Most suppression hearings in a trial result in a witness being allowed to make an identification.

[87] Doob, A. N., Kirschenbaum, H. M. Bias in police lineups—partial remembering. *Journal of Police Science and Administration*, 1973, *1*, 287–293.

the suspect. We would expect that the fair test would have nonwitnesses picking out any one of the photos equally because they should all look similar.

SUGGESTIVITY FROM THE TEST GIVER

No test with photographs or a lineup can be completely free of suggestion. When a witness is brought in by the police to be shown a set of photographs, he or she can safely assume that there is a reason for this and that the authorities have a suspect in mind (or in custody). The witness is thus under some pressure to pick someone, even if the officer showing the photographs is careful not to force the issue. The basic books in the field of eyewitness identification all recommend that no suggestions, hints, or pressure be transmitted to the witness by the test giver, but experience with criminal investigation reveals some abuses by zealous police officers.[88] Such abuse includes the police remarking on which pictures to skip, saying "Are you sure?" when the witness makes an error, the giving of hints, and the showing of enthusiasm when the "right" picture is selected. One variation, called the "Oklahoma lineup," has five police officers in line glancing obviously at the one real suspect. All such errors make us wonder if the identification is based on the witness's memory or on the test giver feeding on the witness's desire to please. This doubt clouds the reliability of the test.

Suggestions can be very subtle and the test giver may be unaware that he or she is biasing a test toward one person or photograph. Research by Fanselow (1975) has been done on tests where the test giver was instructed to smile and show approval *only* when a certain type of photograph or statement was picked.[89] Such social approval led to an increase in the rate of selecting that type of photograph, even though there was no "correct" answer. When a test is used that measures a need for social approval, it has been shown that people who need social approval, especially those who enthusiastically volunteer information, are even more influenced by suggestion and approval coming from the test giver. It is hard to say, "No, I don't recognize anyone," when social pressure to identify is on the person.

CONFORMITY

Are two eyewitnesses better than one? ten? seventeen? Certainly, the more agreement we find with others, the more confidence we have in our judgments of reality. But similarity of judgment is a two-edged

[88] Wall, P. *Eyewitness Identification in Criminal Cases.* New York: Thomas, 1965.
[89] Fanselow, M. How to bias an eyewitness. *Social Action and the Law*, 1975, *2* (3), 3–4.

sword—we can agree in error as easily as we agree in truth. Research on conformity has been a large factor in social psychology for decades —dominated by the work of Professor Solomon Asch (1956).[90] The results of this research indicate that an observer can be persuaded to conform to the majority opinion, even when the majority is wrong. In the typical Asch experiment, seven observers are shown three vertical lines and asked to tell which one is shorter. Six of the people are in the pay of the experimenter and only one person is actually being tested. The six employees of the researcher say that the objectively longer line is shorter. After hearing six people say this, a large percentage of the "innocent" subjects say that the longer line is shorter, despite the reality and despite the fact that if they were alone they probably would have no trouble giving the correct answer.

As a further test of eyewitness conformity, Alper et al. (1976) staged a "crime" in a classroom, asked for individual descriptions, and then put the witnesses into groups to produce composite verbal descriptions of the suspect.[91] The group descriptions were more complete than the individual reports, but there were significantly more errors of commission and an assortment of incorrect and stereotyped details. For example, the groups concluded incorrectly that the suspect was wearing the standard student uniform, blue dungarees. Thus conformity was achieved, but the description was in error.

INFLUENCE OF AUTHORITY FIGURES
The effects of suggestion on the reliability of identification can be greatly increased when figures in obvious authority are conducting the testing. In psychological research on suggestion, changing attitudes, and biased reports the effects are much greater when, for example, older, higher status, better dressed people, attractive women, or people in uniforms or white coats are used. In difficult or vague situations people do turn toward the leader, the father, or the person in authority. In some of our court experience we have found that people will misjudge distances and otherwise distort reality in efforts to follow their leader.

In many crime situations several witnesses who work together under a boss would find it difficult to disagree with their boss in public court room testimony or in picking out a photo from a mug book. The process of filling in details can be exaggerated when the boss and his or her employee share information and the employee feels obligated to

[90] Asch, S. E. Opinions and social pressure. *Scientific American*, 1955, *193* (5).
[91] Alper, A., Buckhout, R., Chern, S., Harwood, R., & Slomovits, M. Eyewitness identification: Accuracy of individual v. composite recollection of a crime. *Bulletin of the Psychonomic Society*, 1976, 8, 147–149.

back up the boss and remain in good graces. Legal history is replete with stories of witnesses who were rewarded by the authorities for "cooperating" by making an identification. One general conclusion of our research is that when we use pressure from authorities the frequency of attempted identifications, whether or not correct, increases.

PASSING ON A THEORY: THE SELF-FULFILLING PROPHECY

"If the data do not fit the theory, the data must be disposed of." This is a flip comment (known informally as Maier's law) made by psychologists about the powerful influence of a theory on observation.[92] In criminal investigations as in scientific investigations a theory can be a powerful tool for clarifying confusion, but it can also lead to distortion and unreliability as people cease to be open-minded about the real meaning of the facts. The eyewitness who sees "something" may be greatly influenced to shape his or her memory to fit a theory, especially a reasonable sounding and highly publicized theory.

Psychologists, in criticizing their own research, have conducted research in which people were supposed to pick out a "successful" face from a set of photos (Rosenthal, 1966). There was no correct answer, but the experimenter dropped hints to his test givers on what he thought the results should be.[93] Unconsciously, the test givers signaled the subjects on which photo to pick and produced results that supported their boss's" theory. These signals could be nonverbal, as, for example, where the test giver leaned toward and smiled at the person who was cooperating with his expectations. This seems to influence the person to be even more cooperative, regardless of the facts. Knowledge of the highly publicized theory of Angela Davis's involvement in the Marin County courtroom shoot-out was, in our opinion, a significant factor in producing questionable eyewitness identifications of the defendant in key locations.[94]

APPLIED PROBLEMS IN RECOGNITION TESTING

It is an old favorite for cartoons. The eyewitness confronts a lineup consisting of one black man, a refrigerator, a duck, a nun and a hatrack. Excitedly, she is pointing to the black man saying "He's the one." An exaggeration perhaps, but in our trial experience (Buckhout & Ellison, 1977) we have seen lineups or sets of photos with biases that approximate the cartoon conditions and affect the outcome of identi-

[92] Buckhout, Eyewitness.
[93] Rosenthal, R. *Experimenter Effects in Behavioral Research.* New York: Appleton, 1966.
[94] *People* v. *Davis,* op. cit.

fication (recognition) tests of witnesses to a crime.[95] Research on the psychology of the eyewitness suggests that the mishandling of recognition tests, in the unique setting of a criminal investigation, can lead to either false positive or mistaken identifications of an innocent person or false negative identifications—missing the guilty person entirely. Because these errors can compound injustices, some of our research has been directed toward those factors that determine good and bad recognition testing of the eyewitness of a crime—techniques that have been adapted from psychological laboratories by law enforcement agencies.[96]

If you ever see or become a victim of a serious crime, you may find yourself in great demand by the criminal justice system. The police investigation will be guided by your description of the features of the suspect and the details of his or her behavior (the m.o. or method of operation). The final identification of a suspect will require you to identify the suspect in court. The prosecutor will need your testimony. In turn, the jury will evaluate your identification testimony and, consistent with research reported by Professor Elizabeth Loftus,[97] will convict the suspect if jury members believe you. If you fail to identify the suspect, or if you identify the wrong person, it is highly likely that the prosecution of the routine criminal case will cease—so important is a positive identification in U.S. courts. Other forms of evidence, with the exception of fingerprints, are considered by many attorneys to be weak foundations for presenting a case to a jury. Gathering physical or circumstantial evidence is also a lot harder work which may be bypassed when an eyewitness is available.

Types of Errors

Yet, psychologists and court officers are wary of the known unreliability of eyewitness testimony. (See Table 5.3.) This point has been made repeatedly in scientific research and in the real-world experience of the court. Crimes rarely occur under ideal viewing conditions. The fast pace of events, poor lighting, divided attention, and the sheer trauma that affect both the spectator and the victim are factors that are known to contribute to selective and unreliable intake of perceptual information. The legal and psychological literature overflow with examples of fragmentary, stereotyping descriptions by witnesses that conflict both with the true facts (where available) and amongst

[95] Buckhout, R., & Ellison, K. W. The Lineup: A critical look. *Psychology Today*, 1977, *11* (1), 82–84, 88.
[96] *Model Rules: Eyewitness Identification*. Washington, D.C.: Police Foundation, 1974.
[97] Loftus, *Eyewitness*, op. cit.

Table 5.3 TYPES OF RECOGNITION ERRORS BY EYEWITNESSES

TYPE I	False positive identification of suspect in lineup—can only be rectified by other evidence, catching the true criminal or acquittal
TYPE II	False negative (Miss) witness—fails to recognize anyone in lineup including suspect on whom solid additional evidence of guilt exists.

the witnesses themselves. However unreliable the witness is, he or she may come to be needed as a piece of evidence to make the justice system work.

To illustrate the so-called Type I error, we can point to the testing of witnesses in the case of *United States* v. *Soliah,* where Steven Soliah (a friend of Patty Hearst) was identified by witnesses as having been one of four persons who robbed a bank in Sacramento in which a customer was shot to death.[98] Three of the gunmen wore ski masks; only one face was visible. Our background work with attorney Sheldon Otis showed that each witness had been tested with several groups of photographs of known bank robbers before Patty Hearst and her friends were picked up. Each of the witnesses made several identifications which were proved to be mistaken by FBI or state investigators. Finally, they were shown a set of photos depicting Steven Soliah (with his name attached) who was then in custody, plus several other known members of the then much publicized Symbionese Liberation Army.

This last set of photos was clearly biased—the witnesses could have picked anyone from the set and still have provided a welcome result to the investigators who finally had a solid theory as to who committed the crime. The point here is that an array of photos is a multiple-choice test, and if every answer is "right" in the judgment of the authorities, it cannot be considered a real test of the witness's memory. When Mr. Soliah was later displayed to witnesses in a physical lineup he stood out as a distinctive individual (in size and posture) and was identified.

On the strength of ths identification and his ties to a getaway car, Mr. Soliah was put on trial. The defense, believing that the defendant was *not* in the bank at all, found that a bank customer had been described as looking like Mr. Soliah by an FBI agent who interviewed him. He was brought into the courtroom—almost an exact look-alike—and told of having looked in at the robbery and then having ducked behind a counter. The defense argued that the witnesses had substituted this customer's face for that of one of the robbers and had then been led to a mistaken conclusion by the biased photo arrays and

[98] *U.S.* v. *Soliah,* Sacramento, Calif.: U.S. District Court, 1977.

lineup that emphasized the similar looking Mr. Soliah. The jury acquitted the defendant.

Any test for recognition should take into account the motivation of the witness as well as the adequacy of his or her memory for faces. Our research indicates a strong tendency for witnesses tested on a lineup in an experimental setting to say YES—up to 80 percent attempt an identification.[99] British sources report that over 60 percent of the witnesses in real lineups made an identification.[100] If the test (lineup or a group of photographs) is biased, this YES tendency may direct the witness to pick out the person who stands out because of the bias. This process can, of course, send an innocent person to jail or to the death chamber.

Biased Lineups

The types of biases that encourage attention to a particular person in a lineup or group of photos can come from the test procedure or from the test giver. The most biased lineup we have encountered was composed of five white men and one black man in an actual murder investigation in which a black suspect had been arrested (see Figure 5.2). The excuse given was that the police wanted to make the lineup representative of the town's population which had few black people! Another "justification" was that there were no other people in the building.[101]

But distinctiveness of a more subtle nature can result in an identification of a person who stands out even by people who never saw the crime. On occasion, we have tested the effects of bias in a lineup by administering a photo of the lineup to a large number of people who are given only a verbal description of the suspect provided by the actual witness. The lineup shown in Figure 5.3 was actually used to test the eyewitness to a holdup who described the gunman as a black male, 5'7", 160 lbs., 20 to 24 years old, with "braided" hair. The suspect (number 5 in the lineup) was picked by the eyewitness. When we asked a group of nonwitnesses to put themselves in the place of the eyewitness to the crime and pick the man who best fit the original

[99] Buckhout, R. Nearly 2000 Eyewitnesses Can Be Wrong. *Bulletin of the Psychomic Society*, 1980. In press.

[100] *Devlin Report*: Report to the secretary of state for the Home Department of the Departmental Committee on evidence of identification in criminal cases. House of Commons, Her Majesty's Stationary Office (Great Britain), April 26, 1975. A Parliament committee report that studied two mistaken identification cases in depth.

[101] *From Social Action and the Law*, 1975, 2 (2), cover page.

Figure 5.2   It's no joke: An actual police lineup used to test a witness to a murder in which the suspect was black. (Source: Attorney Ron Meshbesher, Minneapolis, Minnesota.)

description, over 52 percent picked number 5: a result that was significantly greater than chance.[102] Most said that they debated between number 2 and number 5 but that number 2 was too tall. They were all focusing on that unique feature of braided hair which means that few bothered to even look at the other persons in the lineup. These results were presented as part of expert testimony by Prof. Buckhout to the jury during the trial to support the defense argument that when a nonwitness can identify the accused criminal, the lineup is biased and the identification by the original witness may be attributable more to the bias than to the witness's memory. The jury acquitted the defendant.[103]

In our controlled research settings, where we have staged crimes and "created" witnesses, we have made a comparison of good and bad lineups with rather subtle biases to see if these biases will encourage Type I errors. In Figures 5.4 and 5.5 we show two versions of the same lineup of photographs where number 5's photograph is merely tilted and shows a different expression, as if it had been tossed

[102] *Florida* v. *Richard Campbell* (armed robbery), 74-2777, Circuit Court of Palm Beach County, April 1975.
[103] Buckhout, R., & Friere, V. Suggestivity in lineups and photo spreads: A casebook for lawyers. *Center for Responsive Psychology Monograph* No. CR-5, June 1975. The procedure used here was first suggested by Doob, A. and Kirschenbaum, (See Note 87). It involves having a group of non-witnesses attempt to identify a perpetrator from a lineup to see if it is biased.

in at the last minute. In an experiment, where we knew who the perpetrator was, we demonstrated that this biased photograph was picked more often than any other even where he was in fact the innocent man.

The effects of suggestiveness on the part of the person giving the test was anticipated by the research of Robert Rosenthal (1966) on the effects of experimenter bias.[104] Thus even when the person conducting the lineup is trying to give a fair test, he or she may unconsciously transmit cues or social approval to a cooperative witness whose memory for the face of the perpetrator is not very good. M. Fanselow, R. Buckhout (1976), and some of our students showed a film of a purse snatching in which the face of a young black attacker was visible for only a few seconds.[105] In the control condition the witnesses were shown six unbiased photographs, with the perpetrator's photo present among the six. Here only 25 percent of the witnesses correctly identified the suspect. In another condition we showed the witnesses six photos of *innocent* men and had the interviewer smile and nonverbally reinforce one particular photograph for each witness. We were simulating the real lineup situation in which the police officer

[104] Rosenthal, op. cit.
[105] Fanselow, M. S., & Buckhout, R. Nonverbal cueing as a source of biasing information in eyewitness identification testing. *Center for Responsive Psychology Monograph* No. CR-26, April 1976.

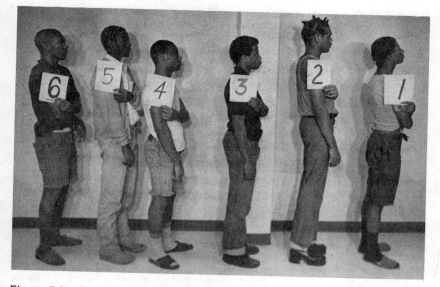

Figure 5.3   Actual police photo of lineup used to test witnesses in the case of *Florida* v. *Campbell*. (Source: Public Defender, West Palm Beach, Fla.)

Figure 5.4   An example of a reasonably balanced photospread lineup used in research by Buckhout, et al., (1975).

may believe that he has the man, but where in fact the man is innocent. Incredibly, 80 percent of these witnesses made an identification and a significant percentage (38 percent) chose the photograph that was reinforced. We thus demonstrated how the YES tendency plus nonverbal cueing—a form of bias—could encourage a large group of witnesses mistakenly to identify the wrong man.

In a murder case in New Hampshire, we reviewed a videotape recording of a lineup in which a witness identified a man as the killer after seeing a lineup in which the officer emphasized the suspect's lineup number by inadvertently repeating it.[106] In this case, too, the

[106] *New Hampshire* v. *William McKenney*, Superior Court, Stafford, SS, Dover, New Hampshire, March 1975. Actually, two young witnesses were tested. First they were prompted to come forward by another party who brought their attention to a newspaper photo of the defendant in handcuffs. One witness saw the lineup of five men with a perfect run through—each participant was referred to equally. This witness made no identification. The second witness was tested with the lineup officer saying, "Now I'll have all of the men turn around, for example— number 4. I'll say number 4 turn left, and so on. Number 4 was the defendant.

suspect was later acquitted by a jury when the defense attorney emphasized this point in his summation. More often, though, a solid positive identification expressed with certainty will stick and the accused will be convicted.

Are four witnesses' memories for recognition better than one? A common feature of criminal investigations is the creation of composite descriptions, drawings, or sketches of a perpetrator.[107] In the 1977 "Son of Sam" murder case in New York City, a series of composite sketches were provided by a number of eyewitnesses resulting in a final composite that appears to fit an idealized crazed killer more than the actual suspect (who was apprehended through a parking ticket). A number of people who resembled the composite drawing were detained for questioning. Although the *investigator* may gain more insight or perspective on the type of perpetrator, from a composite drawing, the price paid is the sacrificing of the independent memory

[107] Harmon, L. D. Recognition of faces. *Scientific American*, 1973, 229 (5), 70–82.

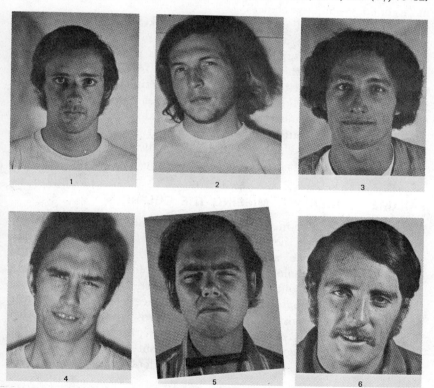

Figure 5.5   An example of a biased photospread lineup used in research by Buckhout et al., (1975).

of the witness. No longer can we depend on the witness speaking only of what he or she remembers about the crime—instead the witness is put in the position of comparing memories with other witnesses and the investigators. In one experimental study Arlene Rupp et al. (1977) staged a crime, collected an individual description from witnesses (recall), and then allowed the witnesses to collaborate as a group on producing a combined recall statement describing the crime and the perpetrator.[108] We found that the second description was more complete and more accurate than the original individual descriptions. However, when each of the witnesses was tested for recognition *individually* on a fair lineup, there were no significant differences in the number of correct identifications between witnesses who gave composite descriptions and those in the control group who were left alone. Despite the glibness and apparent verbal superiority of the witnesses in groups, there was no real improvement of the memory of these witnesses for the face of the perpetrator. Yet, the witnesses who were in groups were more likely to attempt identifications and expressed more confidence in their choices.

Our research and experience with mistaken identifications suggests that the lineup is a logical adaptation of a technique for testing the memory of a witness but that because it is a one-shot event, any mistakes or biases in the conduct of the lineup can interact with the motivation of the eyewitness to say YES and result in mistaken identifications. A way of dealing with this problem was hit on simultaneously by the junior author and by Professor Roy Malpass (Buckhout, 1980, Malpass, 1979). By cautioning the witness that the suspect might *not* be present, attempted identifications and mistakes were reduced, whereas the number of correct identifications was not affected.

FAILURE TO IDENTIFY: MISSING THE CULPRIT

As pointed out earlier in this book, in a criminal case the state is the plaintiff; the victim is merely evidence. Both defense and prosecution may use this "evidence" as they see fit to help their cases, even to the point of causing psychological or financial harm to the person involved. When identity of the offender is part of the evidence the victim gives, the defense often contends that this evidence constitutes a "false positive," a case of mistaken identity. The prosecution, on the other hand, is interested in avoiding "false negatives": the case in which the victim knows or recognizes a suspect, but out of fear or for other personal reasons refuses to make an official identification. It is always

---

[108] Rupp, A. et al. Making the blind see: Effects of discussion on eyewitness reports. *Center for Responsive Psychology Monograph* No. CR-19, 1977.

possible, of course, for a witness to be honestly stating genuine limits on his or her memory and choosing to say: "I don't recognize anyone."

Most of the scientific work on eyewitness identification has sought to test the reliability of this kind of evidence in controlled settings. Like the defense, these researchers have concentrated on the false positive, and the results of these studies have been used primarily by defense attorneys as evidence to support the defendant's claim of mistaken identity.

But a person watching a crime happen to someone else in a laboratory setting may react differently from a real crime victim, and recently investigators have begun to examine the experiences of real victims of crimes. This work was discussed in detail in Chapter 3; here we shall reiterate the issues crucial to the victim's role as eyewitness.[109]

As we noted, stress tends to lead to distortion in perception. The problem this presents for eyewitness identification is compounded if the interviewing officers treat the victim inappropriately, increasing the tendency to repress. The crisis is deepened. This person may respond in several ways, depending on the characteristics of the situation and his or her personality: He or she may become negativistic and uncooperative and refuse to continue in the court process, or may try to give the officers what they want, just to get rid of them, and identify anyone in the lineup as the offender. Although there is no hard evidence to indicate which tendency is most common, it is our impression from working with victims that it is the former.[110]

A victim who has been treated in positive, or even neutral fashion by the police, often will agree to cooperate. If a suspect is detained, and if the police give him or her clues that they are sure he or she is the one, and seem very anxious for a positive identification, the victim may wish to repay the officers who helped her by attempting to make an identification. For some this leads to the tendency to "finger" the most likely suspect (a process that may be unconscious.)

However, victims, too, watch Perry Mason. Competing with the desire to help or the desire for revenge is a fear of making a mistake and becoming the villain oneself by involving an innocent person in the criminal justice system. This process is sometimes encouraged by officers who "test how well the witness will stand up in court" by reminding him or her of the severity of the penalties and the consequences of making a mistake.) Such a person will treat the biased lineup as if it were a one-on-one situation, and say, "That fits the

[109] Bard, M., & Ellison, K. Crisis intervention and the investigation of forcible rape. *The Police Chief*, 1974, *41* (5), 68–73.

[110] Ellison, K. W. The victim in the criminal justice system. *Social Action and the Law*, 1976, 3 (2), 17.

description and is the only one it could possibly be, but still is not the right one."

Other problems arise that encourage some victims to say NO even though they recognize a suspect. Seeing the offender again must be difficult for a victim. For some, the fear of reprisal becomes overwhelming, and although they later tell a counselor they recognized one of the suspects, they fail to admit it to the police.

Once an identification has been made, the internal and external pressure is very strong for the victim to continue to affirm it. The need to maintain cognitive constancy becomes very important.[111] Still some victims become exasperated by the delay, which can run into months, and the time and money lost in numerous fruitless trips to court, and "disappear." (In some jurisdictions, the victim may have to make over a dozen appearances before he or she actually testifies at a trial).

Although Supreme Court decisions go back and forth in stressing or deemphasizing the identification process, there is an appreciation of the need to conduct fair identification tests—usually well-run lineups. Lineups have been found to be better tests of recognition memory then the more convenient photo spreads. Fair testing will go a long way toward reducing the probability of Type I errors. Establishing good rapport with witnesses and valuing their contribution to the process will help minimize errors arising from failure to identify. A "reliability of lineup" checklist[112] was designed to show the attorney or investigator the kinds of factors that produce bias or errors in the lineup testing phase. The set of notes with this chart documents what each problem can do to the reliability and/or validity of the test.

Our society, and particularly the criminal justice system, has failed to realize that every step in the criminal justice process is potentially traumatic not only for the accused but also for the victim. By failing to account for the multiple motivations of eyewitnesses, both Type I and Type II errors contribute to injustice and loss of respect for the system itself.

A CASE OF MISTAKEN IDENTITY

Perhaps the best way to illustrate how the factors previously enumerated apply to an actual criminal case is to present an analysis written by the senior author of a case in which seven eyewitnesses who identified an armed robber were proven to be mistaken. The case of

---

[111] Erikson, K. T. *Everything in its Path: Destruction of community in the Buffalo Creek Flood.* New York: Simon & Schuster, 1976.
[112] See Resource File Nos. 2 and 3.

the "Gentleman Bandit" in 1979 contained a number of the factors we have described and was one in which a research psychologist (Buckhout) had been engaged by the defense attorney to testify about these factors.[113]

CASE REPORT 5.1 *People of the State of Delaware v. Pagano*

Recently, we had an opportunity to see the unfolding of a set of events that puts into perspective the issues of eyewitness identification.

On January 11, 1979, the first of a series of robberies was committed near Wilmington, Delaware, by a bandit who was described as white, middle-aged, polite, wearing a dark full length coat, a walking hat, and carrying a small chrome plated pistol. The press quickly dubbed him the "Gentleman Bandit," because he frequently apologized as he walked off with the money from his robberies. At various times the newspapers carried a composite drawing prepared by the Delaware State Police. This drawing led anonymous individual(s) to report to the police that the composite looked very much like Father Bernard T. Pagano, the assistant pastor of St. Mary Refuge of Sinners Roman Catholic Church in Bethesda, Maryland.

Following some tentative identifications of Father Pagano by some of the robbery victims, the defendant was arrested. He engaged Dennis Spivak and Carl Schnee of the law firm of Schnee and Castle as his attorneys. In analyzing the procedures used to secure identifications, these attorneys became convinced that their client was an innocent victim of mistaken identification and that the state was proceeding with prosecution while taking no steps to check out the defendant's alibi. Based on defense counsel's information, we learned that various witnesses had had several opportunities to view Father Pagano or his picture prior to the in-court identification in which seven witnesses testified that they were absolutely sure that he was the "Gentleman Bandit." A very minor amount of physical and circumstantial evidence was presented by the state at the trial. What follows is a review of the steps in the identification process which led up to the in-court identification. (See Figure 5.6.)

THE COMPOSITES At least two composite drawings appeared in the newspapers, which depicted an older man wearing a hat.* The problem with composite drawings is that the process of reconstructing memories encourages stereotyped thinking by inducing the witnesses to verbalize and make decisions about types of noses, lip lines, eyes, and so on.

---

[113] *State of Delaware* v. *Bernard T. Pagano*, Superior Court, Wilmington, Delaware, August 1979. Reported in Buckhout, R. The Mistaken Seven. *Social Action and the Law*, 1979, *5* (3), 39–48.

* We have keyed the parts of Figure 5.6 with numbers that match the paragraph numbers.

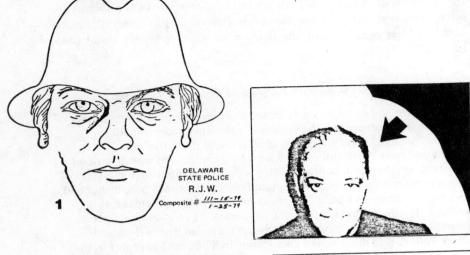

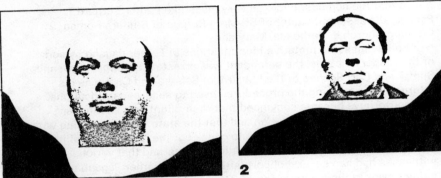

Figure 5.6 A chronology of events culminating in the identification of Father Pagano as the "Gentleman Bandit." The arrow points to the defendant and the numbers are keyed to subparagraphs in the text. (Source: Buckhout, R. The mistaken seven. *Criminal Defense*, 1980, (In press.)

Recent research has shown that composite drawings of people tend not to be reliably recognized by close friends of that individual.[114] The composite-making process (especially from identi-kit composites made from plastic overlays of face parts) is a general stereotyped face that can fit many people. If other witnesses see the composites, it can affect their attempts to reconstruct their own memory by causing them to become committed to the general set of features shown in the drawing. Although composites may play an important role in the investigation process, they are a potential source of bias and unreliability in that they

[114] Ellis, H. D., Shephert, J., & Davies, G. An investigation of the photo fit technique for recalling faces. *British Journal of Psychology*, 1975, *66*, 29–37.

3

Ronald Clouser   Father Pagano

6 1 2 3 8 4

125

may turn out to be more complete (due to pressure to fill in) than the memory from which they came.

SHOW-UP Prior to the arrest, police took two witnesses along while they staked out a physical fitness club frequented by the defendant. When the plan of viewing patrons leaving the club did not work, the police closed in and, accompanied by the witnesses, pursued Father Pagano in his car. The witnesses saw him alone at that time. The police thought the witnesses had signaled an identification, but the witnesses were not sure of their identification.

PHOTOSPREAD NUMBER 2 The police placed a ten-year-old snapshot of Father Pagano in an array of several other photos and obtained one tentative identification. The photos differed considerably in age, hair style, and photographic quality. A card covered the lower part of each photo (to hide the clerical collar), but only two photos, including the defendant's, showed dark clothing covering their shoulders. The background of Father Pagano's photo was very distinctive, making it stand out from the others.

NEWSPAPER PHOTOGRAPH The same photo of the defendant used in Photospread Number 2 appeared widely in the papers when he was arrested. All the witnesses admitted having seen it; some were interviewed that day on radio.

PHOTOSPREAD NUMBER 3 Armed with a recent photo of Father Pagano wearing a dark coat and a dark-colored hat with a light band, the police had officers pose wearing a dark coat and a hat with no band. The resulting photospread was shown to all witnesses, producing one more identification and an increase in certainty. Our analysis of this photospread led us to feel that it was a highly biased, unreliable test which unfairly focused on the defendant. He was the oldest man (53 years) in the array (none of the other men were older than 32); his hat and clothing were distinctively different; his picture was reverse printed, so that his photo was the only one to have the profile on the left. Further, because this was the second formal test, Father Pagano's face was the only one repeated from the first photospread, a tactic that has been shown in research by Brown and his colleagues (1977) to virtually guarantee an identification, whether the man is innocent or guilty.[115] In the display presented here, Pagano's photo is not included.

THE LINEUP The formal lineup, a redundant procedure which merely gave witnesses who "flunked" earlier tests a chance to take it again, was a reasonable test on the surface. The physical appearances and clothing of all participants were similar. It produced seven very positive

---

[115] Brown, Deffenbacher, & Sturgill, op. cit.

identifications. This was followed by the preliminary hearing, where the witnesses again identified Father Pagano in person, and his attorneys learned for the first time about all the preceding identification tests and show-ups. Even here it can be seen in the lineup that Father Pagano's body language—the folded hands—might give a clue to his priestly status. When attorney Spivak called us at this point, the case against Father Pagano looked overwhelming indeed. Complicating matters was the fact that the state polygrapher reported that the defendant had "flunked" the lie detector test.

Following a battle over admissibility, trial Judge Andrew Christie agreed to allow Dr. Buckhout to testify as an expert on eyewitness identification—a first in Delaware. We prepared to discuss the factors that affect the perception of eyewitnesses and the standards for reliable (and unreliable) testing of witness's memory for faces. The thrust of these comments on testing were to be that testing should be done only once in a nonbiased manner, because testing itself affects the witness's efforts to reconstruct memory. Seeing Father Pagano over and over again amounted to *practice*, where the witnesses had a better opportunity to observe *his* face than they did the face of the perpetrator. It is not surprising to us that the witnesses became more certain, because our own research indicates that certainty grows with each repeat identification (or near miss), whether or not the witness is correct. Certainty and accuracy appear not to be related at all.

On the day Dr. Buckhout was to testify, Ronald Clouser, a man in jail for similar robberies, appeared in court and, in true Perry Mason fashion, confessed to the crimes charged against Father Pagano. Although much younger (38 years old), he bore a striking resemblance to the defendant, and to the composite, especially when he was viewed wearing the hat. Shocked court officers and police conducted a rapid check of Clouser's story, confirming that he knew unpublished information about the crimes. When Clouser pleaded guilty to the robberies two days later, the charges against Father Pagano were dropped. However, the police still insist that he is guilty, a position that, as of this writing, remains unchanged.

The lesson we learn from this dramatic trial is just how far judicial errors can accumulate when total reliance is placed on eyewitness testimony. Here, as in many other cases, all investigative work by the police virtually stopped when an eyewitness made a tentative identification. The in-house use of lie detector testing, in spite of questions about its reliability and inadmissibility into evidence, probably contributed to lack of further effort, as did the controversial reputation of Father Pagano. The defendant was disliked by the local police, was seen as an unpriestlike maverick by gossipers, and was virtually abandoned by his church superiors: The bishop was alleged to have referred to him as a "known liar."

Forced to view Clouser in yet another lineup, four of the eyewitnesses testified that they could not make any identification. The pattern of hasty and biased testing resorted to in the beginning of the case had effectively denied them the opportunity to say "I don't know" and have that answer stand. Convinced that they had the right man, the police went on to violate every standard of good testing (for which they are well trained), and saw their case blown sky-high. Justice emerged primarily because of the fine investigative work of the defense attorneys, doing what the police should have done. The guilty conscience of the actual perpetrator and a lot of luck contributed to the happy outcome.

CONCLUSIONS

In the United Kingdom, the British court system is moving toward a policy in which the uncorroborated testimony of a lone eyewitness will require that a judge direct a verdict of acquittal except in unusual circumstances. This policy has emerged as a result of a parliamentary investigation that tended to confirm the unreliability of eyewitness testimony and the potential injustices that might emerge from over-reliance on it. In contrast, the earlier trend of U.S. Supreme Court decisions sparked by the *Wade* decision appears to have been over-taken by the *Mansen* v. *Breathwaite* (1977) decision that leaves the "independent basis" of a witness's memory intact no matter how sug-gestive the tests used were to try to test that memory. To this we can only express our profound disagreement with what at this time appears to be a step backward into the nineteenth-century view of the human perceiver as a camera. Clearly, modern research by psychologists has demonstrated that testing memory is a part of memory; where sugges-tive practices can lead a witness down the pathway to a mistaken identification. Conversely, the implementation of fair and reliable tests represent the *only* avenue for intervention and change by the justice system that can practically be undertaken. We can understand the witness at the point that the crime occurs, but there is little we can do about it.

SUMMARY

Research on the psychology of the eyewitness really began with the development of the first psychology laboratories in 1860. Even then, the essential facts about the limitations of human perception were being documented. In summary, eyewitness testimony, like physical or circumstantial evidence, is not any kind of magic pipeline to the truth. It is as subject to doubt and conjecture as any other kind of evidence.

Circumstantial evidence is tied together with a theory that must be subject to question. Eyewitness testimony is also based on a theory —constructed by a human being (with help from others)—about what reality was like in the past. Because that theory can be adjusted or changed due to the personality, the situation, or social pressure, it is unwise to accept such testimony without some question. We raise doubts about the eyewitness because we believe that he or she cannot, as a human being, live up to the popular myth that the brain indelibly records what it sees and hears. An eyewitness, seen in a more positive light, will behave as an *efficient* observer who *decides* what he or she saw. All people do this; thus all people have doubts about the absolute truth of what they saw. No expert can render a judgment about whether or not a witness was right, wrong, credible, accurate, or reliable. Once the observation is over, it is up to a jury to determine if the doubts about an eyewitness's testimony are reasonable enough to reject his or her testimony as *unlikely*. The psychological researcher as courtroom expert can only help by describing what happens to the thousands of witnesses who are tested under controlled conditions. We believe that jurors should be reminded that doubts exist about eyewitness testimony as they do about any evidence.

STUDYING THE JURY
AS A SOCIAL SYSTEM

> We who have served on juries have found it to be an
> experience which often makes us become strong defenders
> of this system of jurisprudence which allows a citizen to
> sit in judgment. We also became its greatest critics, and
> form a unique perspective. We became aware of the rights
> of jurors which can be reduced to a single simple right and
> need—the right to insist on an atmosphere in which a
> person can make a reasoned judgment.
>
> Mary Timothy, foreperson of the jury
> in *People* v. *Angela Davis*[1]

INTRODUCTION

When a lawyer wins a case for his or her client, confidence in his or
her ability to "psych" out a jury knows no limits. However, when a
lawyer loses, he or she may well attribute the jury's decision to the
capricious, unpredictable nature of people. The social scientist can
offer the findings of research on the effects of evidence or biographical
variables on the behavior of people, in general but has largely been
prevented from observing jurors directly. Yet, an understanding of how
jurors behave in the legal setting is of great interest to both the social
scientist and the attorney. Using the limited empirical data, the legal
observer's insights, and the testimonials of those citizens who have
actually served on juries, we propose to present a clearer picture of the
jury as a major subunit of the larger system of justice.

Some observers have aptly described the jury as the "flak catcher"
of the system:[2] a group of citizens hearing cases that have defied
lawyerly settlement on the civil side or cases that saw an avoidance

[1] Timothy, M. *Jury Woman*. Palo Alto, Calif.: EMTY Press, 1974.
[2] Mungham, G., & Bankowski, Z. The jury in the legal system. *Sociological Review Monograph*, 1977, (23), 202–225. This is a valuable overview of the socialization

of plea bargaining in the criminal court.[3] Because jury trials loom as expensive time-consuming affairs, all members and clients of the justice system are under pressure to avoid going to trial. An American citizen could conceivably have the matter of her parking ticket heard by a jury of her peers as a matter of constitutional right. But let her try it. The judge, the lawyer, the clerk, the costs, and ultimately her own common sense will prevail on her to accept the summary but brief mechanical justice offered by the judge or clerk. The gross estimate most agreed on by observers is that approximately 10 percent of all criminal defendants seek a trial by jury.[4] It is often said that were all defendants to exercise their right to a trial by jury, the system would probably break down completely.[5]

The complex filtering process which includes plea bargaining, dismissal of charges at any level, trials before judges, procedural delays, trading off time spent in jail for probable length of prison terms are maneuvers that are defended as necessary ways to prevent jury trials. The thrust of most change efforts is in the direction of improving efficiency. We observe a trend toward the use of smaller juries in a number of states,[6,7,8,9] cutting the number of jurors to six or eight in civil trials, misdemeanors, and lesser felonies. In recent

---

process in the English courtroom where, as in America, the crucial dimension is the judge. "The juror aids and abets the trial, but will always find it difficult to do much more, if this means running against the cues and indications laid down by the judge." The authors point out that jurors in the United Kingdom are never told of their powers or rights and in most cases can not ask questions during a trial.

[3] Goldman, P., & Holt, D. How Justice Works: *The People* v. *Donald Payne. Newsweek*, March 8, 1971, 20–37.

[4] These ball park estimates in the form of percentages are part of the legal *Zeitgeist* and are virtually uncheckable. A trial by jury is at the end of a long filtering process.

[5] This phrase is characteristic of the "opening the floodgates" or "Pandora's box" analysis periodically invoked in legal and judicial circles; often to moderate the advocates of change or outside critics. For a system that many feel is already broken down, the concern seems somewhat posthumous.

[6] *Williams* v. *Florida*, 399, U.S. 78C, 1970, pp. 78–113. The Supreme Court ruled that a six-person jury was not unconstitutional. See also *Colgrove* v. *Battin*, 413, U.S. 149, 1973; Fisher, H. R. The Seventh Amendment and the Common Law: No Magic in Numbers. *Federal Rules and Decisions*, 1973, 56, 507–534.

[7] Saks, M. *Jury Verdicts.* Lexington, Mass.: Lexington Books, 1977. A very thorough critique of research on jury size and decision rule.

[8] Rosenblatt, J. C. Should the size of the jury in criminal cases be reduced to six? An examination of the psychological evidence. *The Prosecutor*, 1972, 8 (4), 309–314. A good survey of the psychology of groups research literature, with a slanting of the evidence to support smaller juries.

[9] *Johnson* v. *Louisiana*, 406, U.S. 813, 1971, 356–403. See also *Apodaca et al.* v. *Oregon*, 406, U.S. 404, 1971, 404–415. These are the definitive cases on jury decision rule that permit less-than-unanimous verdicts.

decisions the Supreme Court has ruled in favor of smaller juries and the use of a less than unanimous verdict in state courts.[10] In many states steps are being taken to eliminate or minimize the length of pretrial (*voir dire*) examination of prospective jurors. Most of the reforms in the courts have been spotty; the jury system having been bypassed as other alternative means for rendering justice are pursued. The twelve-person jury of one's peers has had a sacrosanct image which may not prevail in the wake of the many changes taking place in the system as a whole. Still, with an estimated total of 150,000 jury trials occurring per year in the United States, this large subsystem touches a few average citizens in a very direct manner.

In the face of the evidence it is hard to refute charges that jury members are often *not* the peers of the accused, that racism and discrimination are brought to bear in decision making, the juries increase court costs and time delays, and that jurors may be more impressed by the antics of attorneys in the courtroom than would a presiding judge; but juries also bring *some* "average" citizens into the judicial process and add more of an element of uncertainty (in a positive sense) to the outcome of trials than would be the case if verdicts were rendered by professional tribunals or judges. What these strangers to the judicial process do in their deliberations can only be conjectured on because direct observation of jurors at work is forbidden by law. In this chapter we shall examine a sampling of research from the sociological, laboratory, survey, and field research methods which constitute a major research interest of social scientists who work on legal applications.

THE CHICAGO STUDIES: THE SOCIOLOGICAL TRADITION

Many sociologists, lawyers, and some psychologists spent some portion of their career time studying in the Jury Project at the University of Chicago (1950 to present) Law School under the guidance of Law Professor Harry Kalven or sociologist Hans Zeisel. Any researcher interested in juries will have to be influenced by the many products of this productive group.

Observing Jury Deliberations

The studies by Fred Strodtbeck and his colleagues (1957) of Chicago University have shown how factors such as social status, seating positions at the table, and sex-delineated roles affect jury deliberations. He used mock juries, the members of which were selected from actual

[10] Oelsner, Lesley. Smaller Juries Increase; Divided Verdicts Allowed. *New York Times*, July 21, 1975.

voter registration lists. The mock jurors listened to recorded civil trials, deliberated, and returned a verdict. During deliberations the interaction process among members was noted, scored, and analyzed. It was shown that a continuity of status transfers from the larger social system to the small group situation. Those persons highest on the socioeconomic scale tend to participate and influence more than those lower on the same scale. Strodtbeck also demonstrated how the seating positions at a jury table may influence deliberations.

His findings here concurred with those of Sommer (1969) who has also studied the effects of physical settings on attitudes and behavior. It was found that leaders (typically those from a higher economic class) tended to select the head position at a rectangular table more than would be expected by chance. In 1976 Nemeth reported, in a study on women in jury deliberations, that males were more likely to take one of the two head positions than were females. Strodtbeck found a striking trend for the person seated at one of the head positions to be elected foreperson. In view of the head chair's association with leadership, as well as the fact that people of higher status occupied the head chair, it was not surprising that people in the head chair participated in the discussion more than people at other positions. It would follow that those who participated more, influenced more than those who were less active. Subsequent ratings by all jury members showed that the people at the head chair were considered to have made the most significant contributions to the deliberations.

Strodtbeck further demonstrated a continuation in jury deliberations of sex role specialization observed in adult family behavior. For example, men typically initiated discussion directed at a solution of the problem whereas women tended more to react to the contributions of others. The trend for men to select a task emphasis and for women to select a social–emotional emphasis was reliably demonstrated using the *Bales Interaction Process Analysis* technique. In this method every vocal response during deliberations is coded in accordance with the source, to whom it is addressed, and which of 12 categories it fits. The 12 subcategories break down into two main categories: task orientation and socioemotional. Nemeth (1976), in a more tightly controlled study found similar differences between male and female jurors, but these differences in deliberation style had no impact on their tendencies to vote GUILTY or NOT GUILTY or to vote for plaintiff or defendant.

The American Jury

Outstanding among the many contributions of the Chicago group was Kalven and Zeisel's (1966) book, *The American Jury*—a major social science source on the subject of juries. Their approach involved the use of questionnaires sent to thousands of judges throughout the country. Judges were asked to describe briefly criminal trials over which they presided, giving the decision arrived at by the jury, and then telling how they would have disposed of that case had it been tried before them without a jury. The result was a systematic view of how often the jury disagrees with the judge, of the direction of the disagreement, and an assessment of the reasons for it. The study was very elaborate and extended over a period of years. Although many conclusions were drawn about how juries operate, we note that actual jury members were not used in the study. Of 3576 cases that were reviewed, in 85.4 percent the judge agreed with the jury verdict. (See Table 6.1.) Of the other 17 percent, where the judge disagreed, the reasons were generally due to the fact that juries tend to be slightly more lenient than judges; perhaps because they are allowed to take into account and respond to commonsense equities that the institutional constraints on judges does not permit. There were numerous methodological deficiencies in the research, but the overall study is a valuable resource—cited often by researchers and in all Supreme Court decisions that relate to jurors.

In terms of methodology it is not surprising that there are many weaknesses (acknowledged by the authors), most of which would prove particularly irksome to the social scientist. Fundamentally, one has no way of knowing whether the judges who claimed they would have rendered a particular decision would actually have done so. Furthermore, in attributing motives to jurors, the judges have relied on speculation rather than on direct knowledge of deliberation processes.

From a statistical point of view, we find that because some judges reported many more cases than others, specific biases may not have

Table 6.1 FROM THE AMERICAN JURY: VERDICT OF JURY AND JUDGE (IN PERCENT OF ALL 3576 TRIALS)

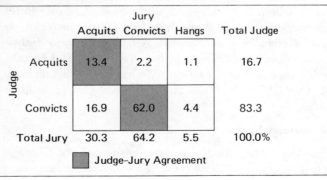

| | Jury | | | |
	Acquits	Convicts	Hangs	Total Judge
Judge Acquits	13.4	2.2	1.1	16.7
Judge Convicts	16.9	62.0	4.4	83.3
Total Jury	30.3	64.2	5.5	100.0%

■ Judge–Jury Agreement

been sufficiently counterbalanced; it must also be noted that the entire statistical treatment has been superficial, with specific analysis based on trends and percentage rather than on more exact statistical inference. Not a single statistical test was used in the entire book. However, although methodological weaknesses go uncorrected, they are freely noted and discussed by the authors. Furthermore, the qualifications one must impose on the conclusions drawn do not overshadow the value arising from the broad scope of the data collected nor the wit and wisdom displayed by the authors. *The American Jury* has its failings but remains a unique source of information, the value of which remains to be fully tested, hopefully by newer acquisitions of data.

Studying Juror Response to an Insanity Defense

Rita James Simon, (1969), (another Chicago researcher), studied the process by which juries reach their verdict in trials in which the defense is "insanity." For this, she set up a series of experimental trials, using over one thousand jurors chosen at random from the jury pools of Chicago, St. Louis, and Minneapolis.

Experimental jurors were drawn by lot from actual jury pools as part of their mandatory jury duty. They were then divided into individual juries and required to listen to a prerecorded staged trial. The first was on a charge of breaking and entering and the second trial was based on a charge of incest. Before the playing of the tape, the jurors were instructed by the judge to treat this trial with the same care and thought they would give in a real trial. Moreover, they were further divided into groups for additional instruction on which precise definition of "insanity" to use. Approximately one-third of the juries were told to use the traditional McNaughten definition [the defendant is excused only if he did not know what he was doing, or did not know that he was doing wrong], one-third were informed of the Durham version [a defendant is excused if his act was the product of a mental disease or defect], and the remainder were given no instruction.

The breaking and entering case dealt with a man who had a long history of psychotic disorders, institutional commitments, and attempted suicides. On the other hand, the defendant on the incest charge appeared to be a stable man with a steady job and high efficiency rating. The results seen in Table 6.2 show the differences in the number of NGI (not guilty by reason of insanity) decisions reached by each group. (Note that those given no instruction stayed more in line with the decisions reached by the Durham group.)

However, Simon failed somewhat in trying to draw any parallel between jurors' economic status, education, sympathies, and his pro-

Table 6.2 THE PERCENTAGE OF NOT GUILTY BY REASON OF INSANITY VERDICTS UNDER VARIOUS INSTRUCTIONS

	PERCENTAGE OF NGI DEPENDENT ON JURY INSTRUCTION ON INSANITY		
	CONTROL GROUP	MC NAUGHTON INSTRUCTION	DURHAM INSTRUCTION
TYPE OF CRIMINAL CASE			
Breaking & Entering	76	59	65
Incest	34	24	36

SOURCE: From Simon, *The Jury and the Defense of Insanity*, 1967.

pensity for accepting a NGI plea. In part, this was due to a failure to plan for and use the multivariate statistical analyses required. Perhaps the strongest asset of Professor Simon's book is its chapter showing the actual transcripts of the jury deliberations and the content analyses.

The Political Impact

A tragic and telling postscript to the efforts of Professors Strodtbeck and Kalven took place in a hearing before the Senate Committee on the Judiciary in 1955. Strodtbeck had designed a study with the co-operation of the courts, in which he planted tape recorders and microphones in order to record actual jury deliberations without the jurors' knowledge. An outraged reaction followed public discussion of this study, taking the form of criticisms of an "invasion of privacy," jury tampering, attempts to reverse verdicts, with the culmination of the Senate hearing chaired by Senator Eastland (Democrat, Arkansas).

Although Professor Strodtbeck, in his testimony, indicated that he had gone to great lengths to protect the identity of the jurors, it is evident that this research touched a number of societal nerves— images of "big brother," creating mistrust among jurors, and so on. McCarthyite members of the Judiciary Committee and its staff took the occasion to smear Strodtbeck and Kalven for alleged communist associations, thus tying together a research tactic and a manufactured American bugaboo. Laws passed after this event made it a felony to record jury deliberations.

One of the authors of *The American Jury*, Professor Hans Zeisel, served as an expert witness at the first Huey Newton trial in 1968. In this trial, defense attorney, Charles Garry, made use of the expert testimony of leading scholars to support motions challenging the adequacy of the system of jury selection in Alameda County, California. Six prominent social scientists provided research data and expert opinion in support of various aspects of these motions. The book entitled *Minimizing Racism in Jury Trials*, is a discussion and full transcript of the *voir dire* conducted by Charles Garry in the Huey Newton trial. The Newton *voir dire* was precedent shattering, because Garry questioned prospective jurors at some length about their general racial attitudes. Professor Robert Blauner, speaking on the topic of race relations, reported as a result of his observations, that concerned, knowledgeable, and politically active citizens had the worst chance of all to become a juror. The question and answer format in a *voir dire* makes it easy for the less active prospective juror to hide his or her opinions and protect him or herself by giving "acceptable" answers, or by feigning ignorance.

Zeisel testified to the fact of a simple positive correlation between the favoring of capital punishment and racist attitudes in voters who serve on juries. Procapital punishment jurors have clearly distinguishable personality characteristics that tend to be authoritarian. Sanford of the Wright Institute in Berkeley, Calif., coauthor of *Authoritarian Personality* (1950) testified that race and class prejudice are central to the authoritarian personality along with characteristics of rigidity and punitiveness. Thus members of the Chicago Jury Project have, in this and hundreds of capital punishment cases, coalesced the social science data with the concerns of attorneys to affect judicial decisions. In the 1980s, Professor Zeisel and his graduates continued to appear as experts in the courts on jury matters (especially in death penalty cases).

MOCK JURIES: THE LABORATORY APPROACH

We are going to be rather selective in reporting on laboratory research bearing on the jury system because (1) so much of the research has been competently reviewed elsewhere (Erlanger, 1970; Tapp, 1976; Brooks & Doob, 1976; Gerbasi, Zuckerman, & Reis, 1977); (2) some laboratory research will be reported on in connection with our discussion of the Supreme Court; and (3) so much of the laboratory work has been very poorly designed and executed as to have little applicability to the jury system. We are in agreement with most of the reviewers in that the ecological validity of much of what passes for "jury" studies is questionable because researchers have not always taken the time to use proper samples of subjects or have created very artificial simulations of jury trials. We tend to favor those studies that have required their mock jurors to observe the range of testimony common to a trial that had "jurors" actually deliberate as a group and vote on a group verdict, and in which a distinction is made between individual juror votes and group verdict before the results are generalized to jurors in the general population. Clearly, the enormous number of jury studies conducted during the 1970s has provided some valuable information that could not easily be gathered by sociological or field research methods.

Effects of Irrelevant Evidence on Verdicts

Researcher and lawyer alike can express an interest in how a single factor influences a jury. A number of researchers have studied the effects of varying the degree of attractiveness (based on either physical characteristics or social standing) of the defendant and/or the complainant in a trial (Griffit & Jackson, 1977; Kaplan & Kemmerick, 1974; Landy & Aronson, 1969; Sigall & Landy, 1972). That is, can research confirm or deny the common wisdom among trial attorneys that a physically attractive defendant will be treated more leniently by a jury than an unattractive defendant? Sigall and Ostrove (1975) created a mock jury trial situation for two crimes—robbery and swindling—while varying the attractiveness of the defendant by showing photographs of people whose degree of attractiveness had been rated by another group of judges. Thus for each crime the trial evidence was the same—only the face differed. Because the evidence pointed heavily toward the guilt of the defendant, the mock jurors were asked to give a recommended sentence as one index of how their thinking was swayed by the attractiveness factor. The authors report that the attractive defendant was treated more leniently *if* she was on trial for theft. In the case of the trial for swindling, the attractive defendant received a *longer* sentence.

The research answer for the psychologist was that the results support the existence of an interactive effect between attractiveness and type of crime. The answer given to a lawyer would be, "It depends." If attractiveness is related to the nature of the crime, such as swindling, the attractive swindler is likely to be perceived as using her attractiveness for illegal ends and is to be held more blameworthy by jurors. In the case of a theft, attractiveness is presumably unrelated to the nature of the crime, and a juror may surmise that such an attractive person is less likely to pull a holdup. Variables such as physical attractiveness should be irrelevant, of course, and jurors are typically warned by the judge to stick to the evidence—a warning that often goes unheeded. Research and common sense both agree that attractiveness can have an effect on a juror's thinking; presumably a prejudicial one. Being unattractive or neutral seems not to have any effect on juror attitudes.

The often-cited Landy and Aronson (1969) study, which reported more lenient sentences for medium and high status defendants, has been criticized as one example of the many attractiveness-type studies in which the variable of attractiveness (or status) may not be so simple as the researcher thinks. Elwork and Sales (1977) criticized the Landy and Aronson study for being founded on the naïve assumption that each defendant *should* receive the same sentence for the same crime. In other words, the researchers are brought to task for using the wrong basis of comparison (or null hypothesis) in their research. In most states, the *judge*, not the jury assigns a sentence; and he is legally required to use discretion based on the defendant's character, prior record, degree of dangerousness, and so on in sentencing. Elwork and Sales provide a useful analysis and critique of this study:

> By looking at the information given to the subject-jurors in the Landy & Aronson study (1969) we can infer that relevant factors entered into their decision-making. In the stories presented, the attractive defendant was described in such a way as to leave the impression that he was less of a threat to repeat a serious offense than the unattractive one. The attractive defendant was described as a respectable citizen who out of mourning and loneliness for his recently deceased wife, got drunk prior to his negligent automobile homicide. He had no previous criminal record and got himself injured as a result of the accident. Everything about the attractive defendant suggests that his crime was a one time occurrence with a low probability of being repeated. On the other hand, the unattractive defendant was described as a less than dependable person, who did have a previous criminal record, including a previous drug conviction. Since the negligent homicide was partially caused by drunken driving, the previous drug violation along with the rest of the description leads to a conclusion that this defendant did present a threat to society in the future. Thus, Landy & Aronson's subjects acted responsibly in assigning higher sentences to the less reliable defendant while holding both defendants equally guilty.

What emerges here is that the researchers were too heavy handed in setting up the level of attractiveness—as if they were comparing Charles Manson to Teddy Kennedy. Further, in putting their mock jurors in the real-world role of judges, their results are subject to alternative explanations other than the ones underlying the research. Landy and Aronson may have been right in their hunch that jurors are prejudiced by a defendant's background, but their research does not clearly support their hunch. A 1978 study by Bray, Struckman, Johnson, Osborne, McFarland, and Scott found no differences in verdict after deliberation over the fate of high- and low-status defendants.

More recent studies on the influence of "appearances" on jury behavior have employed videotape recordings of real or reenacted trials in order to test a given variable within a context which is richer and more realistic. Thus when Fontaine and Kiger (1978) set out to see if the defendant's status as a prisoner (as opposed to a person out on bail) would influence jurors, they had groups of jurors (students and voters) view a videotape of a murder trial that included still pictures of the defendant, actual audio excerpts from real trial testimony, and the legal instructions given by the judge. In addition to deciding on a verdict, the mock jurors gave a recommended sentence that, under Missouri state law, is an advisory process permitted by law. The independent variables were the appearance of the defendant in either prison garb or street clothing (dress) and the presence or absence of an armed guard. The results suggested that prison garb with no supervision and street clothing with supervision biased the jurors to recommend high sentences.

The major compromise to realistic simulation made by the investigators was their decision to forego jury deliberation; a sacrifice that eliminated the chance to see if the affects of the defendant's appearance would have been mitigated by healthy group discussion. In any event, there were minor differences in degree of guilt assigned to defendants in any condition. The authors made some useful suggestions about how to improve on realistic mock jury research designs. Field research results (Friedland, 1965) suggest that *anything* (including appearance) that conveys the impression that the defendant is already in custody or has a criminal record, results in his or her being seen as guilty and increases the likelihood that he or she will be found guilty and receive a more severe penalty.

As social psychologists have become more knowledgeable about legal problems, they have begun to adapt their experiments and underlying theories to provide tests of some of the assumptions that are already built into the law. As Doob (1976) points out, the court already has a mechanism for dealing with irrelevant information in a jury trial in the form of laws that exclude character evidence for the most part. In cases where character evidence gets before the jury (e.g., the defendant's prior criminal record) if and when the defendant testifies, jurors are instructed by the judge not to consider character in weighing the evidence. Concerned if these laws actually served a useful purpose, Doob and his colleagues conducted a very imaginative series of laboratory-based studies to test the effectiveness of these laws on juror attitudes. Briefly, Doob and Kirschenbaum (1972) found that the presence of evidence of a prior criminal record produced more guilty verdicts and the judge's instruction to limit the use of this information had no effect at all on the juror's behavior.

In a repeat version of their study that involved deliberation by mock jurors, Hans and Doob (1976) found that "40 percent of the juries that heard of an accused man's record arrived at guilty verdicts whereas none of the juries that heard nothing about the criminal record arrived at this verdict." Juries that knew about the man's record were more likely to discuss matters unfavorable to the accused and to overrate the weight of the prosecution's evidence. Any character evidence can completely change the tone of the jury deliberations and the types of testimony that jurors remember from the trial: a finding that has a parallel in the research of Owens, Bower, and Black (1979), who found that readers of a series of episodes were likely to remember the episodes and embellish them with fabricated information if they were supplied with a motive for the main character.

In concluding that existing laws are not effective in protecting the defendant from juror biases instilled by irrelevant information, Doob considers the two possibilities of absolute exclusion as opposed to a new policy of letting all character information be put before the jury in all cases. The latter policy would, of course, make the juror more like a judge (who has all this information anyway) and give him or her the power to convict a person for what kind of person he or she is rather than on the evidence in the case. As Doob puts it:

> The choice between these alternatives is not one that can easily be based on empirical evidence. It is a philosophical or ethical decision and the psychologist has no particular expertise to bring to bear on the decision. I favor the more or less complete exclusion of evidence of previous criminal activity. It would be deceptive of men, however, to suggest that this position follows directly from the results of the experiments that I have just described (p. 143).

FIELD RESEARCH ON JURIES

In spite of the obstacles, some researchers have brought their questionnaires and research designs into the field—the courtroom itself. In part, the aim was to improve on the ecological validity of the research. Another reason was to test some of the extra jurors—those not on a trial—who form a sample from which better generalizations can be made.

Buckhout et al. (1977) decided that one good way to study a jury would be at its own level, so with a group of trained participant observers they created a second jury inside the courtroom, made up of volunteer students. The second jury was referred to as a "parallel jury." Like its counterpart in the courtroom, the parallel jury sat in on the trial; viewed the entire case from jury selection to verdict. It, too, was instructed to come to a verdict, conforming to the same ground rules under which the real jury operated. That is, they were not to discuss the case with anyone until the deliberation period. Parenthetically, it should be noted that they often found that their "juries" were often the only public witnesses to the unpublicized criminal trials that grind on day after day in a superior court.

When the authors began, they had the cooperation of the trial judge in a California superior court who gave out invitations to each juror following the verdict (while still in the jury box), to join in a modified "encounter group" meeting between the two juries. The purpose of the meeting was to discuss the trial in a setting where 12 interested students, who know just as much about the case as the jurors, could ask questions that were germane to the juror's experience. All sessions were taped or recorded on television tape. The meetings were scheduled as soon as possible after the completion of the trial to maximize everybody's retention of information. The parallel jurors were encouraged to engage in a free, wide open discussion while keeping the lookout for seating arrangements, status dominance, and voting patterns recalled by the jurors. Discussions centered around the selection of the jury foreman, the reactions to the defendant and his appearance, evidence of prejudicial statements, differential reactions to authority figures, dominance or passivity of the individual personalities, and so on. A moderator probed both jury groups in order to bring out descriptive data to try to fill in the evident knowledge vacuum about the dynamics of juries. Student volunteers on parallel juries were asked to keep a journal.

The hope in developing these techniques was to describe and evaluate evidence of some of the group dynamics suggested in previous research in the laboratory in this complex field with the attendant reality of having to reach a verdict that counts.

The court in which the study was conducted was nothing like the Perry Mason image-of-justice myth that so many people cherish. This was an overcrowded court schedule, where many of the defendants were repeat offenders, where judges and lawyers were very jaded and overworked. In conversations with lawyers the authors were told that most defense lawyers believe that their clients are guilty of *something*, that much of the police work and evidence gathering in all but the major cases was incredibly sloppy, and that many court officers had a cynical attitude about the ability of the entire system to rehabilitate the people they judge.

CASE REPORT 6.1 *The State of California v. John Doe*

Table 6.3 presents the essentials of the case against John Doe whose trial was studied. The trial was held in the criminal division of the Alameda County California Superior Court before a jury. The defendant, a black man, was charged with a felony—assault with a deadly weapon. Specifically, the complainant charged that the defendant, while sitting in a car, threatened to kill him and subsequently fired two shots when the complainant approached. As is typical in cases like this, the accused was defended by a young assistant public defender and prosecuted by a

Table 6.3 THE STATE OF CALIFORNIA V. JOHN DOE

CHARGE
1. Assault with a deadly weapon.

COMPLAINANT: A BLACK LONGSHOREMAN
1. Charged that defendant shot two times at him while his car was stopped next to defendant's car.
2. Phoned police from closed gas station.
3. Did not know defendant.
4. Led police to where defendant worked.

DEFENDANT: A BLACK SERVICE STATION ATTENDANT
1. Just left complainant's ex-wife off.
2. Drove off at high speed when asked to stop by police.
3. Wrecked car, ran from scene of wreck and hid.
4. Was arrested across the street from his home in a park.
5. No weapon was found on him at the time of arrest.
6. Pleaded innocent to the charge.

POLICE
1. Two police departments involved.
2. A chrome .25 calibre automatic found in desk where defendant was employed with three rounds missing.
3. No test was performed to determine if weapon had been fired.
4. No test done to determine if defendant had fired a weapon recently.
5. No shell casing found at scene or in defendant's car.
6. No bullet holes in complainant's car.

young assistant district attorney. The defendant (an ex-felon) did not testify in his own behalf. The complaining witnesses included the arresting officers, the complainant, the defendant's employer who owned the gun available to him and the defendant, and the complainant's ex-wife who was used to attempt to impeach the testimony of the plaintiff. The trial lasted three days with the jury deliberating five hours before returning a verdict. The jury consisted of 11 caucasians and one black man. Four jurors were women. The average age of the group was 49; the average income of those who worked was approximately $12 to 14,000 per year. The jury was instructed to choose between three verdicts: guilty of the felony as charged; guilty of a misdemeanor (simple assault); or not guilty of a felony (acquittal). After the verdict was in, the judge described the research project and gave written invitations to the "encounter" meeting before dismissing the jurors.

The real jury found the defendant NOT GUILTY!

The parallel jury of students found the defendant NOT GUILTY! The main difference between the two juries was that the students reached their verdict in five minutes while the real jury took five hours; at one point requesting that the testimony of one of the witnesses be read back to them by the court clerk. Despite what might have been Buckhout's stereotypes of jurors, he found that most of the members of this real jury were quite conscientious. Seven out of the twelve jurors showed up for the encounter discussion meeting. The court officers were deliberately not invited to allow for a more unrestrained discussion. As the discussion evolved, the pattern of the actual deliberation became relatively clear.[11]

Anatomy of a Jury

The selection of the foreperson had gone according to the predictions of Sommer, in that a higher status man who just happened to sit at the head of the table was elected the foreman of the jury, by simply being asked if he had any objection to being foreman. They were an enthusiastic group of people who had established a surprising degree of rapport among themselves, considering the short time that they were together. Whereas the statistical averages of the data characterize this jury as upper middle class, there was enough diversity to include a steamfitter, a bank executive, and an engineer—distinguished, white haired and in possession of an ability to suppress other discussions while he talked, dominating much of the discussion. Although the foreman looked like the type who could lead, he tended to merely echo the sentiments of the engineer. Two jurors said very little and acknowledged that they participated only slightly in deliberations. Comic relief was a role taken on by a voluble Irishman with strong opinions and an ability to disarm the more serious-spoken types. The bank executive provided crisp summarizations of long periods of disconnected colloquy and tried to keep people on the track and on time. The steamfitter provided one of those rare insights that are seldom revealed on personality tests when he made the following statement: "When you see a black man in the courtroom, you automatically feel he's guilty, and you think, let them hang him; but once you become a juror you decide you have to be fair."[12]

If one had looked only at the external variables such as the judge, the lawyers, the evidence, or the trial record, one would have known very little about how this jury reached its verdict. First, it should be

[11] Buckhout, R. et al. A Jury Without Peers, in M. Reidel and P. Vales (Eds.) *Treating the Offender: Problems and Issues.* New York: Praeger, 1977.
[12] Balch, R. W., Griffiths, C. T., Hall, E. L., & Winfree, L. T. The socialization of jurors: The voir dire as a rite of passage. *Journal of Criminal Justice*, 1976, *4*, 271–283. The authors took special note of some of our anecdotal observations to buttress their point that an effective *voir dire* brings about changes in the juror's decision-making behavior. The authors seem to be overly impressed with the socialization that takes place; stating that this role training transcends the values and attitudes that the juror brings into the process. They view the *voir dire* as "a mechanism for easing the transition between the status of 'ordinary citizen' and membership in the courtroom social system." If this is so, we cannot help but wonder if this does not defeat the purpose for which the jury system was created.

mentioned that one of the more experienced jurors passed out slips to get a vote immediately. This device, which showed that most of the jurors were already in favor of acquittal, led to the quick identification of the holdouts against the majority and began a round of conformity pressures that continued until 4:57 P.M., when the verdict was reached in a final switch by the last holdout after it became evident that the judge might require the jury to return the next day. The central issue in the mind of the jurors was the credibility of the complaining witness, a factor that interacted with the persistent problem the jurors had in interpreting the concept of *reasonable doubt*[13] which was repeatedly explained by the judge and the public defender. The complaining witness was contradictory in his testimony and yet was the only witness to the alleged shooting. The arresting officers had done incredibly sloppy police work—failing to test whether the gun had been fired, failing to test the hands of the defendant for powder burns, and failing to search the car or the immediate area for expended shells.

The idea that developed during the juror's deliberation was that the case should never have come to trial as a felony charge for the state's factual evidence was so weak. That they had to discover this fact is interesting, because in conversations with the judge and the two attorneys the authors found that the case could have been tried as a misdemeanor on the charge of displaying a weapon. But the young assistant prosecutor had been assigned the case and was *told* to go for a felony conviction by the district attorney. The assistant prosecutor knew he had "lost" by the time the trial was over.

But the charade was carried out. The judge patiently explained points of law and logic—in the fashion of a freshman course in logic which moved one juror (the banker) to complain bitterly that he felt that the jury had been treated like children in a very patronizing manner. As Kadish and Kadish (1971) point out,[14] the judge officially

---

[13] Instructions on the concept of reasonable doubt are a feature of standardized instructions given by the judge to the jury in most jurisdictions. In fact, depending on the intellectual competence and judiciousness of the judge, the instructions are too often droned out as incomprehensible and implausible prose not unlike a poorly prepared philosophy lecture. The socialization goal is to get jurors to go against their better (especially if prejudiced) judgment that a person on trial is guilty of *something* and to acquit a defendant if the evidence leaves any "doubt in the mind of a reasonable person." Research on the attitudes of jurors who have completed service, indicates that the level of comprehension of formal instructions is low and that even experienced jurors retain attitudes that are skeptical or biased against an accused person. See Buckhout, R., & Baker, E. Surveying the attitudes of seated jurors. *Social Action and the Law*, 1977, *4* (6), 50–52.

[14] Kadish, M. R., & Kadish, S. H. The institutionalization of conflict: Jury acquittals. *Journal of Social Issues*, 1971, 27 (2), 199–218. This paper deals with

says "Follow my instructions" but *seems* to say, "use your judgment." Mr. Engineer thought the judge was just fine, and he and others expressed appreciation for the instructions that made their whole effort seem more worthwhile and a great exercise in civic responsibility. Resentment was expressed against the young public defender who had a tendency toward candor characterized by his description of the complainant as a "nut." The jurors were more impressed by the impeccable coolness of the D.A. and the kindliness of the judge. The essential point here is that all parties shared the same feeling about the complainant but differed only in their way of expressing it.

One of the key observations made by the parallel jury was the fact that despite the efforts to conceal the existence of prior convictions in the defendant's record (including armed assault and child molesting), the jurors had concluded that the defendant *did* indeed have a record. The defendant sat quietly and never looked at the jury. Various remarks by the jurors showed that they felt the defendant to be shifty-eyed or to be glowering. One thought that he saw the defendant wink at the woman in the case who was the wife of the complainant. Another contributing factor to this discovery by the jurors was the question asked by the D.A. which alluded to past misconduct, prompting the judge to make that time-honored legal admonition that guarantees perfect recall of information: "The jury will disregard that last remark and it will be stricken from the record."[15]

From the admonition in their instructions to judge the defendant to a "moral certainty," the deliberation moved toward the conversion of the holdouts. As 5 P.M. approached, the lone holdout for a guilty verdict was the single black juror, who, defying the logic of having a token black on a jury, wondered aloud how the white jurors could assume the defendant to be innocent. As the only member of the jury to have ever set foot in the area where the offense allegedly occurred, he saw the white jurors as people who bend over backwards to excuse a black man whose world they do not understand. The black juror was impressed by an incident in which the defendant ran when he saw a police car coming. This seemed to the juror to be clear evidence that the defendant had done *something* or else he would not have run. In

---

the ambiguous response of a listener to the formal content of the words and sentences. More recent research suggests a broad problem area in which the body language and speech style of the trial participants (especially the judge) can greatly affect the response and voting patterns of jurors in spite of the evidence. See Verdicts linked to speech style, *New York Times*, December 13, 1976.

[15] The earliest recorded psychological research on memory confirmed that any verbal material that is made to stand out (e.g., with color, size, or emphasis) gains in association value and tends to be remembered more readily than other material —a phenomenon known as the *Von Restorff* effect.

Garfinkel's terms, he was applying the common sense of his culture and not assuming the defendant to be a cultural "dope."[16] This is opposite to the demand of the court that he apply the rules of evidence that preclude reading a guilty motive into an independent act. The nonverbal communication picked up by the black juror in this instance and in the previous examples is indicative of the type of evidence that impresses jurors, lawyers, and judges alike—the jurors perhaps more so because they are nonverbal, passive listeners during the entire trial. There was a tendency to perceptually fill in details when the evidence was fragmentary or the concepts vague. Often this creativity took the form of distortions or confirmation of bias. Unfortunately, no regular procedure exists that might provide jurors and court officers alike with the feedback and sharing of information, which could be used to evaluate their joint efforts as would be the case in daily life.

In a way, the research project provided that opportunity; and, in a postmortem session with the public defender, the authors had a chance to compare our findings of how the jury deliberation performance matched up with the attorney's expectations when he helped select jurors in the pretrial *voir dire* hearing. The public defender learned of the jury's generally negative feeling toward him. In turn, the attorney gave a very candid account of the art of jury selection. In trying to get a jury that is sympathetic to his client, he tries to challenge members of fraternal groups, people with lots of kids, the blue-collar worker, Republicans, used car salesmen, uptight ladies who cross their legs (here employing the wisdom of the book *Body Language*), people who know police officers, and anybody who wears a suit with *white socks*. In turn, he saw his prosecutor opponent as having a similar disdain for Democrats, Peace and Freedom party members, long hairs, anyone from Berkeley, and (perhaps with some malice), people who appear to be too thoughtful.

With an air of resigned cynicism, the public defender told the authors that he had to assume that most of his clients were guilty, that he hardly had the time or the inclination to relate personally to the defendant, who incidentally, and not surprisingly, did not even bother to thank him when the not guilty verdict came in. Although the attorney positively supported the jury system as important to his client's welfare, the real business of the court is not so much in determining the question of guilt or innocence as it is in coping with the problem of processing the guilty into the prison system, for which he had no good words and no direct knowledge. He felt that the elaborate reading of the law to the jury by the judge was "just baloney": a

[16] Garfinkel, H. *Studies in Ethnomethodology.* Englewood Cliffs, N.J.: Prentice-Hall, 1967.

kind of window dressing to make the "game" seem plausible and meaningful to the juror. In the lawyer's opinion, jurors have gut reactions on guilt or innocence which they then rationalize in deference to the social pressures to be rational, logical, legal, and consistent. When asked about the contradiction of defending a client he knew to be guilty, he replied that it is virtually impossible to know the truth, and if the jury frees the man, "It's their decision." This diffusion of responsibility was also evident in the attitude of the prosecutor who felt that if the jury freed this known sex offender, "It's their community."[17]

Thus, in talking separately with all parties (except the defendant who remained in jail awaiting trial on other charges), Buckhout and his colleagues had an inkling of the dynamics of at least one jury trial. Psychological testing again revealed that the jurors tended to be very high in need for social approval;[18] experience showed that the jurors received a great amount of social approval from the court officers and tangentially from the research projects. The jury labored in a communication network in which both a spoken and an unspoken message were being expressed. The spoken message—coming through the mouth of the judge—is that the accused is innocent until proven guilty and that this must be proven by the evidence beyond a "reasonable doubt" and to a "moral certainty." The unspoken message was that the guy probably did something, that the case should never have come to trial, that the two young lawyers were out to enhance their experiences and their records, and that in the final analysis it did not really matter which verdict they came to as long as they got it in before 5 P.M. and that they were unanimous.

This jury got the message.

THE MORE THINGS CHANGE . . .

The authors were able to replicate the study with only one more jury trial. But at this point the research team relived the nightmare adventures of other investigators who have attempted to do research on the behavior of jurors. The district attorney, in conjunction with one of the judges in the superior court, raised questions about the research

---

[17] The *diffusion of responsibility* is a well-established theory used by social psychologists to explain the behavior of people in crowds. The words of the attorneys in this instance reaffirm the idea among legal professionals that jurors are the "flak catchers" to whom responsibility can be diffused.

[18] The need for social approval test measures the extent to which a person is willing to attribute value statements to him or herself, which are mere platitudes that do not have any discriminatory value. A strong need for social approval person is thought to be more compliant. See Crowne, D. P., & Marlowe, D. *The Approval Motive.* New York: Wiley, 1964.

that added up to an allegation that participation in a research study would somehow taint a juror who served in future juries. It is not uncommon for a person who serves once to serve again, because he or she obviously satisfies the selection criteria. The matter was brought up to the entire panel of judges where the district attorney threatened to challenge any juror who had been a subject; two judges worried about the adverse publicity; the jury commissioner worried about the discussion of the research among the ever-waiting jurors in the assembly room. And so, the official position of the court was a vote not to sanction the study officially. Cooperation from individual judges henceforth vanished. The authors had gotten too close but they had some data, a lot of insights into the jury, and rather thorough grounding in the *social ecology* of the courtroom.

The System in the Eyes of the Juror

In the California court system we studied, a person is called into the jury assembly room by subpoena along with hundreds of others. After a brief instructional speech by the jury commissioner he or she begins the process of hurrying up and waiting. Seated for long stretches of time in a day room, drably decorated in the plastic fashion of a Greyhound bus terminal, his or her first day may end up going home because most of the jury trials have been postponed by lawyers requesting a continuance. These "necessary" delays arise from the process of plea bargaining which will spare the jurors from involvement in some 85 to 90 percent of all criminal cases. Perhaps he or she will be bargaining him or herself with his or her employer to ensure receiving some salary that could not possibly be offset by the $5 per day (up to $20 per day in federal court) that he or she will receive for jury duty. In the city we studied, the juror remains on the panel for six weeks and may serve on one long trial, several short trials, or possibly no trials at all. When brought into a jury selection room with about 50 other people, he or she will see names drawn randomly out of a drum; people called forward and then questioned by both lawyers and the judge in the *voir dire* process.[19]

In the view of some of our jurors, the questioning during the *voir dire* is of the sort that only a saint could "pass" were he or she to be completely candid. In fact, candor is not the sort of thing that is ex-

[19] Despite the recent use of computers and automatic phone answering equipment, jury commissioners tend to err on the conservative side of calling in more jurors than would be needed in order to answer the call from a judge, who might want to start a trial on short notice. Our discussions with court clerks reminded us of the unchecked power of the judge in most courts and the tendency of some judges to bully the support personnel.

pected; the citizen is under pressure to appear to be a reasonable person and to deny biases that he or she may possess. Why do not the would-be jurors admit to prejudice in order to get out of jury duty? The fact is that they know that if they fail to serve on one jury, they will have to wait uncertainly; with their work and salary still subject to interruption. Thus the social pressure to elicit social approval from the court officers is very great. Privately, some jurors exhibit an air of resignation which reminds one somewhat painfully of those who are drafted; who, once selected, can only lament that they did not figure some way to avoid duty in the first place. Others, to be sure, sincerely look forward to serving on the jury as an enlightening and important facet of their responsibilities as citizens. For some, entrenched in boring civil service jobs or in retirement, jury duty is a relief from the tedium of their lives. But these attitudes are likely to be reflected in the high need for social approval scores we typically get from jurors.

Once selected to serve on a jury, the juror will sit silently through endless recitations of instructions from the judge and testimony from the principals in the case. In most cases she or he receives no written instructions, no explanation for delays, no training; is not encouraged to take notes; is not expected to ask questions during the trial; is not permitted to discuss the case with fellow jurors or family; and is not expected to follow media reports on the case. In an important case the juror may be sequestered in a hotel out of contact with anyone. The jurors are herded around together for meals, breaks, and recreation, causing many of them to draw the analogy between jury service and the army. As Garfinkle notes, the juror is being socialized into modifying his or her usual rules for making decisions and to adopt the official juror line. (e.g., "Between what is good and what is legal, the good juror does what is legal.) Indeed, the six to fourteen individuals will come to be referred to as *the jury*.[20]

Because a student of juries will probably never be allowed to serve on one, we have found that popular books written by former jurors can provide valuable insights; especially into the deliberation process. Mary Timothy, who served as foreperson of the jury in *People* v. *Angela Davis* wrote one of the best books of this genre— *Jury Woman*.[21] Ms. Timothy presents a well-documented diary of the searching mind of an intelligent layperson who expects so much from the expensive drama being staged to win her mind. In a more lucid manner than in most accounts, the author reveals that complex struggle between playing a role of being herself:

[20] Garfinkel, H., op. cit.
[21] Timothy, op. cit.

BOX 6.1

I WAS A JUROR

Wait a minute! True, I had a responsibility to do nothing that would in any way interfere with the trial. But did that really mean I couldn't be myself while I was functioning as a juror? There was no real reason I had to mimic all the other jurors and play the role as it was interpreted by the average person. I had been picked for this jury because I was myself, not because I would conform to someone's stereotype of a juror. I decided to be myself.

I went to my dressing table and picked up my "peace pin." It was a unique and beautiful pin. It had been designed by a medical student at Stanford during the Cambodia crisis in 1971. It incorporated the symbol of medicine (the winged staff) with the peace sign, blue on white. I wore it to court that morning.

It was a big decision for me: to quit pretending. Now I could laugh openly at the humorous episodes; I could show my irritation at the overt expressions of male chauvinism; I could even weep if I became overwhelmed with sorrow, despair. It was a big relief.

SOURCE: Mary Timothy, quoted from *Jury Woman*, Palo Alto, Calif.: EMTY Press, 1974.

The "Family"

In our research and trial experience we observed that most jurors take jury duty quite seriously; more seriously than the judge, the lawyers, or the defendant in many instances. As Kadish and Kadish (1971) imply,[22] the juror is the only person in the system of justice who does his or her work with no possibility of being challenged and who has no stake in preserving the system. The juror is not a part of the "family" which so aptly describes the social and professional inter-action of court officers in most courthouses. We even came to refer to the judge as the "godfather" who expects and receives obsequious deferrence from both young attorneys. Because a large majority of criminal cases involve a public defender (or a legal aid attorney in New York), as well as the district attorney's office, plea bargaining necessitates maintaining cordial relationships which has changed the shape of the older adversary system. In the few cases that do go to trial the young assistant public defenders and assistant district at-

[22] Kadish, & Kadish, op. cit.

torneys play a team track record game, in which individual performance of a cool, professional calibre may be rewarded by eventually being "rescued" through political favor or being hired by a prestigious private law firm.[23] Many young assistant D.A.s and public defenders end their brief stay in the system by becoming joint owners of law firms. The typical juror is tacitly unaware of the machinations behind the high-blown rhetoric they are exposed to. In essence, the "family" of court officers has passed the buck on cases that were not bargained (often because of the reluctance or innocence of the accused); diffusing the responsibility to that strangely unpredictable citizen.

To help reduce the uncertainty about the jurors, one courthouse we studied boasts a private intelligence service—a jury service—that constructs a biographical profile on most jurors on the panel. The service keeps track of the juror's party affiliation, race, age, and so on, and his or her voting record on previous trials. Often the fact sheet includes cryptic phrases such as "old lady in tennis shoes" or "uptight" or "long-haired, Berkeley type." These "data" are available for a fee to any lawyer, and the service is subscribed to regularly by the public defender's office and the district attorney, supplementing the hunches and biases that characterize lawyers attitudes toward jurors.

SUMMARY

Many commentators on the need for reform within the legal system will criticize juries as the fountainhead of irrational judgments, over-generous awards in civil cases, and a highly visible consumer of budget allocations. As British observers point out, there is a great deal of current concern about the unpredictability of jurors who might be recruited from a broader segment of society than before. It is clear that many within the legal profession are ambivalent or downright hostile toward any move toward a jury of one's peers because a predictable jury makes for a smoother running operation. Because the general trend in law has been toward proportionally fewer jury trials and increasing dependence on plea bargaining or negotiation, we expect to see even more criticism directed at those outsiders—members of the jury.

[23] Platt, A., & Pollock, R. Channeling Lawyers: The Careers of Public Defenders. In Bermant, G., Nemeth, C., and Vidmar, N. (Eds.), *Psychology and the Law.* Lexington, Mass.: D. C. Heath, 1976. The authors chronicle the socialization of the public defender, as this process contributes to the generally mediocre level of representation in many court districts. They studied the same county in which the trial cited in this chapter took place.

7

THE U.S. SUPREME COURT v. SOCIAL SCIENCE: THE JURY

It has become fashionable in scholarly legal writings for authors to pontificate on the impact—for good or evil—of the social sciences on the law. To some, the social sciences represent an untapped resource whose omission bespeaks of the naiveté or willful ignorance of the legally trained mind. To at least one, social science represents a severe threat, specifically in the area of jury selection—where the "stacking of juries" would be affected by the combination of social scientists and computers sold to the highest bidder.[1] In our opinion, what we are witnessing is a clash of two epistemologies: each of them quite distinct although the subject matter is identical. The U.S. Supreme Court has become the arena for the comparison of the two epistemologies and the perceptions generated by each concerning the jury. Although the Court has begun to hear arguments based on social science data, it remains a skeptical consumer, biased naturally toward the legal world view.

[1] Etzioni, A. Science: Threatening the jury trial. *Washington Post*, May 26, 1974.

JURY SIZE

Millions of people have served as jurors in the criminal justice system, leaving little or no trace of their individual presence on the system. In fact, jurors hear but a fraction of the cases heard in the system that negotiates or otherwise disposes of 90 percent or more of all cases through other forums.[2] In the view of many legal professionals jury trials are an expensive time-consuming element, motivating efforts to seek efficiency through reductions in jury size, relaxation of rules that demand a unanimous verdict, limitation of the length of preselection (*voir dire*) questioning, and so on. We shall examine the issue of jury size in depth as a model example of how the legal epistemology clashed with empirical findings from social science research in *Williams* v. *Florida* (1970).[3] Here is a sample of the Supreme Court's language in *Williams* v. *Florida*:

> When the unanimity requirement is retained, a jury of six as compared with one of twelve, (a) is as reliable a fact finder, (b) can exercise as much common sense judgment, and can ensure the same shared responsibility and community participation in the determination of guilt or innocence (see text in Resource File No. 16).

In holding that the size of a jury (*in other than federal cases*) is not constitutionally guaranteed, the Court referred only to *Law Review* articles that reported comparisons of nondifferent findings by large and small juries trying different cases,[4] plus the citation of *The American Jury* (1966) by Kalven and Zeisel,[5] which contains much confounded data that have never been statistically analyzed. In *Colgrove* v. *Battin* (1973) the Court extended the six-member jury

[2] Buckhout, R. Jury without peers. *Center Monograph* No. CR-2, 1973, Center for Responsive Psychology, Brooklyn, N.Y. An expanded version of paper published in Reidel, M., & Vales, P. (Eds.), *Treating the offender: Problems and issues*, New York: Praeger, 1977.
[3] *Williams* v. *Florida*, 399 U.S. 78, 1970.
[4] References cited in *Williams* v. *Florida* included: Wiehl, The six-man jury, *Gonzaga Law Review*, 1968, *4*, 35; Cronin, Six member juries tried in Massachusetts District Courts, *Journal of the American Judicial Society*, 1958, *42*, 136; New Jersey experiments with the six man jury. *Bulletin of the Section on Judicial Administration of the American Bar Association*, 1966, 9.
[5] Kalven, H., Jr., & Zeisel, H. *The American Jury*. Boston: Little, Brown, 1966. To some extent this book has something for everyone, but the data within suffer from uncorrected methodological weaknesses. It is a unique book, which has precedence for citation in many court decisions. But most of the data consist of reports by judges on their opinion versus the verdicts of juries. The bulk of data in this book was contributed by too few judges. Statistical significance tests were not possible because of the lack of independence of the data; a fact that is acknowledged by the authors.

prerogative to federal civil suits.[6] Justice Brennan, in the majority opinion, wrote that "much has been written about the six-member jury, but nothing that persuades us to depart from the conclusion reached in *Williams*" (p. 10). He carries this point further, noting that "four very recent studies have provided convincing empirical evidence at the correctness of the *Williams* conclusion that 'there is no discernible difference between the results reached by the two different sized juries'" (fn. 15, p. 11).[7]

The Court's reference to the convincing nature of the empirical evidence reviewed is especially disturbing. Three of the four studies noted were archival analyses, examining selected civil cases tried by six and twelve-member juries, in selected jurisdictions. With such references the Court stretches the social scientist's concept of what constitutes "empirical evidence."

Kalven and Zeisel (1966) pinpoint the nature and hazards of this type of study quite succinctly. In its optimal form, they explain,

> It can be viewed as simply a retrospective controlled experiment. The cases are grouped *after the fact* by the critical variable to see if the variable has produced a difference. . . . The logic is precisely the same as for the experiment, except for one important and in the end ineradicable difficulty; one can never be sure that the groups of cases to be compared are comparable in all respects other than the critical variable (pp. 89–90).[8]

The other study cited (Kessler, 1973), although experimental in nature, contained such extensive methodological weaknesses as to render it an impotent source of empirical data.[9] That single laboratory study that alleged to show no difference between six and twelve-person juries, was the target of a devastating reanalysis and critique

---

[6] *Colgrove* v. *Battin*, 413 U.S. 149, 1973. The court referred to the following four studies: Kessler, J. An empirical study of six and twelve-member jury decision-making processes. *University of Michigan Journal of Law Reform*, 1973, 6 (3), 671–711; Institute of judicial Administration. A comparison of six- and twelve-member juries in New Jersey Superior and County Court, 1972; Berman, G., & Coppock, R. Outcomes of six and twelve member jury trials: An analysis of 128 Civil cases in the State of Washington. *Washington Law Review*, 1973, 48, 593–596.

[7] Ibid.

[8] Kalven, & Zeisel, op. cit. As other social scientists have noted, the older comparisons of size six versus twelve-person jury outcomes neglect to recognize that cases were selected to fit small versus larger juries. Thus larger juries were used in more difficult cases—erasing a common basis for comparison.

[9] Kessler, J., op. cit. Much to her credit, Professor Kessler acknowledged the deficiencies in her research in a later article: Kessler, J. The social psychology of jury deliberations. In Simon, R. J. (Ed.), *The jury system in America*, Beverly Hills, Calif.: Sage, 1975.

by Diamond (1974) who noted that "distinctive features of the study make it illegitimate as a basis for conclusions about juries in general."[10] In brief, Diamond's critique made the following points:

1. The videotaped trial was so biased to the defendant that 80% of all jurors had a pre-verdict for the defendant. 10 of the 16 juries had a verdict prior to deliberation, thus providing only 6 juries over two conditions (6 vs. 12) to test the effects of size.
2. The sample size was two small—16 juries—to support any findings.[11]

Hans Zeisel[12] bitterly criticized the Supreme Court for its statistical ignorance of the fact that "the smaller the size of the sample, the larger the margin of error." Further, he notes that smaller juries mean less representativeness of the community in seated juries. Michael Saks noted that some of the studies cited in *Colgrove* actually reported data *opposite* to the interpretations made by the Courts.[13] His criticism, directed at both psychologists and lawyers was ably summed up as follows.

> The fact that reliable empirical evidence on these questions is lacking is largely the fault of social scientists who are insufficiently knowledgeable about the law to know what data the law needs. And the agents of the law are such strangers to empirical methods of understanding behavior they cannot tell that they have not been provided with the necessary empirical data.[14]

We have reviewed a number of other studies dealing mostly with the effects of group size in general and of jury size on verdicts, attitudes, and costs.[15] Attempts to show that time for a trial and related

---

[10] Diamond, Shari S. A jury experiment reanalyzed. *University of Michigan Journal of Law Reform*, 1974, 7 (2), 520–532.

[11] Ibid.

[12] Zeisel, H. Twelve is Just. *Trial*, 1974, *10* (6), 13–15. See also H. Zeisel, And then there were none: The dimunution of the federal jury. *University of Chicago Law Review*, 1971, 710 and Zeisel, H., "Six man juries, majority verdicts—What difference do they make?" Occasional papers from the University of Chicago Law School (available from the author).

[13] Saks, Michael, J. Ignorance of science is no excuse. *Trial*, 1974, *10* (6), 18–20.

[14] Ibid., 20.

[15] Fox, D., Lorge, I., Weltz, P., & Herrold, K. Comparison of decisions written by large and small groups. *American Psychologist*, 1953, *8*, 351; Gordon R. A study in forensic psychology: Petit jury verdicts as a function of the number of jury members. (Doctoral dissertation, University of Oklahoma); Ann Arbor, Mich.: University of Michigan Microfilms, 1968, No. 68-13250; Strodtbeck, F., James, R., & Hawkins, C. Social status in jury deliberations. *American Sociological Review*, 1957, *22*, 713–719; Thomas, E., & Fink, C. Effects of group size. *Psychological Bulletin*, 1963, *60*, 371–384; Rosenblatt, Julia C. Should the size of the jury in criminal cases be reduced to six? An examination of psychological evidence. *The Prosecutor: Journal of National District Attorney's Association*, 1972, 8 (4), 309–

costs would be reduced have not led to the expected results. The juror selection process continues on regardless of rule changes with the waste of resources coming primarily from unpredictable scheduling of litigants, judges, and trials. Unfortunately, the basic research literature does not contribute many relevant insights about the unique nature of the jury group, because the researchers had other, less formal, less proscribed groups in mind. One study was found that manipulated the six versus twelve-jury size and unanimous versus nonunanimous jury rule (Davis et al., 1975), but the authors lapsed into a lengthy analysis of individual verdict changes when the experimental manipulations yielded no significant differences in jury verdicts.

Considering that the goal of much jury research is to answer empirical questions about juries in actual trial settings, it is puzzling why so many studies avoid the essentials of jury decision making as a group. Foss[16] has reviewed some 23 jury simulation studies and presents the following pessimistic analysis:

A review of 23 jury simulation studies conducted since 1969 indicates several methodological and conceptual flaws. Nearly all studies reviewed lack any semblance of experimental realism, having relied totally on paper and pencil measures of individual judgements rendered after reading case descriptions. This alone probably accounts for several "sensational" findings. Furthermore, very few studies required group deliberations and decisions, thus ignoring the most important aspect of the jury process. Nor did many studies test explicit theoretical predictions, so while most were seemingly undertaken to illuminate juridical judgement processes, they were conducted in such a fashion as to prevent any generalization to actual juries. Thus, jury simulation research to date has produced little of practical or theoretical value.

Foss's critique was not of simulation per se, but of poor simulation highlighted by the tendency of many researchers to have mock

---

314; Davis, J. H., Kerr, N. L., Atkins, R. W., Holt, R., & Meek, D. The decision processes of 6 and 12-person mock juries assigned unanimous and ⅔ majority rules. *Journal of Personality and Social Psychology*, 1975, 32 (1), 1–14; Freidman, H. Trial by jury: Criteria for convictions, jury size and Type I and Type II errors. *The American Statistician*, 1972, 26, 21–23; Hare, A. P. Interaction and consensus in different sized groups. *American Sociological Review*, 1952, 17, 261–267; Pabst, W. R. What do six-member juries really save? *Judicature: Journal of the American Judicature Society*, 1973, 57 (1), 6–11.

[16] Foss, R. D. A critique of jury simulation research. Paper presented at the American Psychological Association Meeting, Chicago, Ill., September 1975. For reprints, contact the author at the Department of Sociology, Western Carolina University. Jurors are probably aware of how long a sentence is associated with each verdict in general terms, but the setting of the actual sentence is strictly up to the judge in most criminal cases.

jurors record "degree of guilt" or length of sentence. This tactic provides convenient continuous measures, to be sure, but is totally unrelated to the juror's role of saying guilty or not guilty to a set of alternative verdicts. Foss warns about using suggestive and misleading titles ("Jury Studies") for the many attribution theory studies that can easily be overgeneralized by courts not trained in interpreting the limitations of social psychological findings. To these caveats we would add the problem raised by Diamond and others[17] that good jury research is expensive. The unit of measure (the dependent variable) is a jury verdict by six to twelve people. Thus to get a respectable sample size in a two-condition experiment may require running hundreds of people for a minimum of two to three hours; a problem that has caused some researchers to look only at individual verdicts which, of course, *cannot* be generalized to final group verdicts.

One study that appeared at first to measure up to most of the criticisms was an experiment on six versus twelve-person jury size by Valenti and Dowling.[18] The authors presented a criminal case in two forms: proconviction and proacquittal—to six- and twelve-person juries. Where apparent guilt was low, the predeliberation verdict reported by jurors showed that about 60 percent in both six- and twelve-sized juries (see Table 7.1) were leaning toward acquittal. Deliberation by the six and twelve-person juries had no differential effect on the final verdicts with eight out of ten juries acquitting the defendant. However, in the prosecution-oriented case (with roughly 60 percent of all jurors leaning toward conviction), the jury size definitely affected the outcome of deliberation. Six-person juries were substantially more likely to convict than twelve-person juries. Thus the authors concluded that when there is a relatively strong prosecution case against the defendant, a twelve-person jury can and does produce some hung jury verdicts, whereas the six-person jury is more likely to convict in the face of the same evidence. Grofman,[19] in a reanalysis

[17] Diamond, S., op. cit. One procedure used by some authors is to cite a table in Kalven and Zeisel (1971, 77) where the direction of the preverdict vote is shown to be correlated with the outcome of the final vote. This is cited to support the researchers' belief that deliberation is unimportant. Such an assertion is nonsense because (1) data on deliberation shifts in real juries is not attainable and (2) all juries deliberate—a fact that any simulation must take into account.
[18] Valenti, A., & Dowling, L. Differential effects of jury size on verdicts following deliberation as a function of apparent guilt of the defendant. *Journal of Personality and Social Psychology*, 1975, 32, 655–663.
[19] Grofman, B. Communication: Differential effects of jury size revisited. *Social Action and the Law*, 1977, 4 (2), 5–9. Grofman correctly points out that because Valenti and Dowling were concerned with how jury size affected deliberation, it would be necessary for juries in each size condition to start off with the same predeliberation vote. In fact, they did not—the six-person juries were closer to a

Table 7.1 DATA ON SIX- VERSUS TWELVE-PERSON JURY
CONVICTIONS AND ACQUITTALS

	TWELVE-MEMBER		SIX-MEMBER	
	LOW APPARENT GUILT	HIGH APPARENT GUILT	LOW APPARENT GUILT	HIGH APPARENT GUILT
Acquittals	6	2	8	1
Hung Juries	2	6	0	0
Total Nonconvictions	(8)	(8)	(8)	(1)
Convictions	(2)	(2)	(2)	(9)

SOURCE: From Valenti and Dowling, 1975. From *Social Action and the Law*, 1976. Reprinted with permission of the Center for Responsive Psychology.

of the Valenti and Dowling data, demonstrated that the differences found were due largely to sampling error rather than to jury size.

In a comparison of six-person versus twelve-person juries hearing the same videotaped evidence in a murder trial and judge's charges, Buckhout et al.[20] found no significant difference in the overall number of verdicts, but the severity of verdicts (where juries could choose among first degree murder, second degree, and manslaughter) was greater in the six-person juries than in the twelve-person juries. An analysis of the mean jury verdicts showed that preverdicts became harsher as a result of deliberation by six-person juries and more lenient in twelve-person juries. The results came from one of the few studies done on real jurors in a jury assembly room although the number of juries tested was small.

A Brief for the Court

Professor Richard Lempert, in the most comprehensive article written on the problem of jury size,[21] gives an instructive analysis of the epistemological dilemma facing social scientists and the Court. Referring to the ideal experiment needed to test the size question,[22] Professor

---

decision than the twelve-person juries before they deliberated. See also, Gelfand, A. E. A statistical case for the twelve-member jury. *Trial*, 1977, *13* (2), 41–42.

[20] Buckhout, R., Weg, S., Reilly, V., & Frohboese, R. Jury verdicts: Comparison of six versus twelve person juries, unanimous versus majority decision in a murder trial. Center for Responsive Psychology Report No. CR-12, 1976. *Bulletin of the Psychonomic Society*, 1977, *10* (3), 175–178. See analysis of this study in Chapter 13.

[21] Lempert, R. O. Uncovering "nondiscernible" differences: Empirical research and the jury size cases. *Michigan Law Review*, 1975, *73* (4), 643–708.

[22] Zeisel, H., & Diamond, S. Convincing empirical evidence on the six member jury. *University of Chicago Law Review*, 1974, *41*, 281.

Lempert argues that large, significant or even discernible differences in percentages of guilty or not guilty (or plantiff v. Defendant) verdicts are not highly likely given the amount of verdict agreement between judge and jury documented in *The American Jury*. When we remember that it is *estimated*[23] that 66 to 90 percent of trial juries vote to convict, from a purely quantitative point of view, the amount of variability in actual jury outcomes is so small that Lempert's pessimism about finding differences is well founded. Lempert also makes a good point about the tendency of social scientists to use the most conservative form of statistical significance testing—Type I—in which the difference between two size conditions must be very large before one can reject the hypothesis of no difference. If we have, as we believe is the case, a situation where smaller differences in verdicts may affect the quality of justice, the conservative approach of the social scientists may lead to the overlooking of important differences in research results.

> The values of social science, however, are not the values of the law. When the Supreme Court rejects a constitutional attack on six-member juries partly on the ground that such a shift will not change trial results, surely the Court ought to be more concerned with Type II error, the possibility that available research has failed to reveal true differences between the verdicts rendered by different size juries, than with Type I error, the possibility that reported size effects do not in fact exist.[24]

The question of quality can only be speculated on at this time because there is really no tradition of quality control in the legal system; or is there much data analysis of trials, juries, or jurors. Our belief is that the trial court should develop a tradition as a research environment with routine data collection and analysis of the participants and results of trials. The jury is a unique kind of group, with the awesome pressure of making decisions that have serious consequences. The best a social scientist can do now is simulation, specula-

---

[23] These estimates are the typical ball park estimates of the judicial system; organized into 50 feudal state systems, the courts are only just entering the computer age and tend not to collect the kind of data on which social scientists can rely. But assuming the uniformity of results to be correct, there is not much variability within which to measure experimental error. Zeisel himself has published varying figures on how many juries are hung; yet, advocates on all sides of the jury size issue look on this parameter as a crucial indicator of the impact of procedural changes.

[24] Lampert, op. cit., 659. Type II error technically refers to the case where a researcher erroneously accepts a nondifference result as indicative of the underlying reality.

tion, and argument about the sheer mathematical consequences of changing the jury size.

Lempert ably demonstrates, for example, that jury decision making on the complex problems they face is likely to generate high levels of conformity and that reducing the jury size carries the risk of reducing the likelihood of there being minority group members or minority voices on a jury.

> While there is a danger that the presence of a single black would cause other jurors to defer too much to one who dishonestly or mistakenly purports to have cultural expertise, this danger is probably less than that of misunderstanding a peculiar feature of black culture. Furthermore, the potential danger of deference may well increase with smaller juries. The best counter to an unwarranted prima facie claim to expertise is the presence of another individual with a similar prima facie claim but with another viewpoint. The twelve-member jury is more likely than the six-member jury to have two or more blacks to correct or corroborate each other. Indeed, as long as black representation in the jury population is much above ten percent, the chances of finding one black on a jury are greater with six than with twelve.[25]

The Court Speaks

By 1977 the quantity and quality of revelant jury research had changed for the better and the time was ripe for the Supreme Court to engage in a fresh review of new empirical evidence concerning the issue of jury size. In *Ballew* v. *Georgia* (1978), the Court took advantage of that opportunity, with Justice Blackmun writing a majority opinion. This opinion includes a fine review of the social science literature on the topic of jury size, backing the Court's conclusion that, "a jury of less than six persons substantially threatens Sixth and Fourteenth amendment guarantees."[26]

The Court acknowledged that the earlier *Williams* v. *Florida* (1970) and *Colgrove* v. *Battin* (1973) decisions had generated a great deal of the new research on jury size. A further tribute to the activist nature of the psychologists and lawyers involved in pleading *Ballew* is the plaintive footnote in the text of the decision:

> Some of these studies have been pressed on us by the parties. . . . We have considered them carefully because they provide the only basis, besides judicial hunch, for a decision about whether smaller and smaller juries will be able to fulfill the purpose and function of the Sixth Amendment.[27]

[25] Ibid., 671.
[26] *Ballew* v. *Georgia*, U.S. 1978, 1–26.
[27] Ibid., Diamond, op. cit.

The Court relied heavily on the previous cited work by Lempert, a statistical modeling study by Nagel and Neef (1975), critical analyses of previous research by Zeisel (1971), and Zeisel and Diamond (1974), and the extensive presentation of empirical research and analyses by Michael Saks in his book, *Jury Verdicts* (1977).[28, 29, 30, 31] The Court concluded that "recent empirical data suggest that progressively smaller juries are less likely to foster effective group deliberation." Drawing on Lempert, the Court found that a review of the group dynamics literature supported the superiority of the group as opposed to individual decision making, particularly when it comes to interjecting the "common sense" of the community into the facts of a case.

Secondly, the Court concluded in *Ballew* that empirical data raise doubts about the accuracy of the results achieved by smaller and smaller juries. Combining the mathematical projections of Nagel and Neef—which suggest a jury size of six to eight persons to optimize risks of false conviction and failure to convict—with data from Saks's elegantly conducted mock jury trial research on juries of six versus twelve people, the Court reasoned that twelve-person juries are less likely to reach "extreme compromises" in verdicts than six-person juries. Saks had shown that his twelve-person juries were more likely to vote for the "correct" verdict than six-person juries. Correctness was assumed to be a verdict that fit a legal evaluation of the strength of the evidence presented at trial.

"Third, the data suggest that the verdicts of jury deliberations in criminal cases will vary as juries become smaller, and that the variance amounts to an imbalance to the detriment of one side, the defense."[32] The reasoning behind this finding is that the probability of the existence on a jury of a minority faction capable of arguing against the majority (enough to deadlock or "hang" the jury) will diminish as the jury size gets smaller. A smaller chance for a hung jury or a fighting minority faction can only hurt the defense in criminal trials where the general national trend is for the majority of juries to vote for conviction. The Court also expressed concern that the smaller juries would be less likely to include members of minority groups—directly affecting representation on the desired jury of one's peers. Justice Blackmun finally noted that even if the difference in verdicts between small and large juries occurred in 14 percent of the cases, this repre-

---

28 Nagel & Neef, Deductive modeling to determine an optimum jury size and fraction required to convict, *Washington University Law Quarterly*, 1975, 973–988.

29 Zeisel, Twelve, op. cit.; University of Chicago papers, op. cit.

30 Zeisel, & Diamond, op. cit.

31 Saks, M. J., *Jury Verdicts*. Lexington, Mass.: Lexington Books, 1977.

32 *Ballew v. Georgia*, op. cit.

sents an unacceptably large number of disparities on a national basis. Parenthetically, a number of studies, including Davis, et al. (1975) came under Court fire for methodological problems that minimized the generalizability of their findings.[33]

In general, although researchers may argue with some of the interpretations put on their research findings and with the Court's mixture of homilies with empiricism, the *Ballew* decision represents a landmark in the application of psychological research to the rendering of a Supreme Court decision that will directly affect policy in the courtrooms of the United States. The published decision, although merely setting a bottom line below which jury size may not drop, is a testimonial to the perspicacity and fine analysis of Lempert, who more than any other writer saw the ultimate decision in this area to be a matter of values.

> Current knowledge justifies the general conclusion that where the verdicts of six and twelve member juries diverge, the verdicts of twelve are likely to be of somewhat higher quality than the verdicts of six, and are likely to be superior with respect to other important values.[34]

VARIATIONS IN JURY DECISION-MAKING RULES: UNANIMOUS V. MAJORITY VERDICTS

As we observed in the preceding section, juries in the American judicial system can be described as conviction prone—whether or not one attributes this to the factual guilt of defendants or some systematic fact about juries. Because some 90 percent of juries convict the accused in criminal cases where a unanimous verdict is demanded, any change in decision rule would make most social scientists predict that a logical result would be an increase in the number of convictions. The Supreme Court has directly addressed the issue in *Johnson* v. *Louisiana* (1971)[35] and in *Apodaca* v. *Oregon*, 1971,[36] holding that a nine out of twelve vote by a criminal trial jury is sufficient to return either a guilty or nonguilty vote and does not deprive a defendant of due process or equal protection. The goal of some efficiency-minded jurists in this instance is to prevent "hung" juries which require either retrying or dismissing charges against an accused person. Some lawyers wonder

[33] Davis et al., op. cit.
[34] Lempert, op. cit., 698.
[35] *Johnson* v. *Louisiana*, 406 U.S. 813 (1971), 356–403. See text in Resource File No. 16.
[36] *Apodaca et al.* v. *Oregon*, 406 U.S. 404 (1971), 404–425.

Figure 7.1   Oliphant cartoon. (Source: © Pat Oliphant.)

whether, in a ten to two majority vote, the two minority jurors would ever have a chance to persuade the majority.

The particular hypothesis or statement of social fact that was crucial to the majority opinion in these cases was as follows:

> The ability of minority members of a jury to influence the majority members is not substantially affected by the right of the majority to reach a verdict without a requirement of unanimity; because majority members will be willing to give dissidents every opportunity to persuade them before shutting off debate. (*Johnson* v. *Louisiana*)

Justice White, writing for the majority, rests his case on the doctrine of the "conscientious juror" which appears to fly in the face of the thrust of most conformity research (as well as common sense) conducted by social scientists. As expressed by Justice Douglas in his dissent, the deliberative process would be cut off when a majority is reached, leading presumably to humoring but not really hearing the minority. "Yet human experience teaches that polite and academic conversation is no substitute for the earnest and robust argument necessary to reach unanimity."[37]

Although the text of the decision is largely a swapping of assertions, the ubiquitous *The American Jury*[38] is cited once again to sup-

---

[37] *Johnson* v. *Louisiana*, op cit.
[38] Kalven & Zeisel, op. cit. Again we warn that there are statistical problems with the data in *The American Jury*. We in fact do not have solid data on the frequency of hung juries.

port a contention that the majority rule would lead to a 45 percent reduction in hung juries. The particular source for this assertion was a comparison of 3512 cases in "unanimous" states versus 64 in non-unanimous states. Gelfand[39] notes that from 86 to 91 percent of verdicts are predicted by the direction of the majority vote on the first ballot. Obviously, if these data represent the situation, few real juries would have much convincing to do during deliberation.

But even if we accept these findings, can one view the reduction of hung juries as necessarily good? We have a value issue that catches both law and social science once again. Unlike the size issue, little published research existed in 1971 that would shed light on changes in verdict rules in juries. Therefore the Court seems to have voted its preference for the position that majority decisions by juries will save time and money.

The empirical evidence from the group dynamics literature shows a pattern that would predict considerable pressure on any minority coalition in a group;[40] even Kalven and Zeisel (1966) suggest that when juries are close to a decision, much of the deliberation time is spent pressuring the minority jury members. Curiously, there was little or no systematic research on the variation of decision rule as an independent variable in group decision making. Long after the Supreme Court acted in 1971, Davis et al. (1975) reported finding no significant differences in the verdicts reached (guilty or not guilty) by juries assigned unanimous or a two-thirds majority decision rule.[41] More hung juries were produced by the unanimous decision rule. Davis and his colleagues discuss their findings as being supportive of Justice Douglas's concerns, because the majority rule juries tended to deliberate for a much shorter time until they finally outvoted an unconvinced minority.

Buckhout et al. (1977) found that there was a large significant difference in verdict between unanimous and majority (10/12) decision rules in an experiment in which real jurors from a court-selected jury pool served as mock jurors witnessing a videotaped murder trial.[42] There were three times as many convictions under the majority rule as under the unanimous decision rule. If we can consider the unanimous verdict condition to be the control or standard against which to evaluate any procedural change, then it was clear in this study that the

[39] Grofman, op. cit.; Gelfand, op. cit.
[40] Kelley, H. H., & Thibaut, J. W. Group problem solving. In Lindzey, G. and Aronson, E. (Eds.), *The Handbook of Social Psychology*, Vol. 4 (2nd Ed.). Reading, Mass.: Addison-Wesley, 1969, 1–101.
[41] Davis et al., op. cit.
[42] Buckhout et al., Jury Verdicts, op. cit. See full text of this experiment in Chapter 13.

jurors under the different decision rules acted quite differently in the face of identical evidence. The author's experience with the particular trial and the conflicting evidence presented had shown that hung juries under unanimous decision rule were appropriate. Although there was no sentiment among the jurors for total acquittal of the accused, this was a case in which the prosecution was seeking a conviction of first degree murder. The deliberations were concerned with which of several lesser included verdicts (e.g., voluntary manslaughter) could be agreed on. The hung juries in the Buckhout et al. study reflect a certain wisdom and fairness in that, in the opinion of many attorneys, the evidence left a reasonable doubt that the *burden of proof* for a harsher verdict had been met. The stringent demand of a unanimous verdict rule appears to us to avoid a miscarriage of justice in those special instances where a relaxation of the rules could facilitate the reaching of a verdict in weak cases. Such a rule change could only result in a higher likelihood of convictions, given the fact that most juries (and most jurors) vote guilty. Privately, most judges recognize that the elaborate instructions on the presumption of innocence are designed to counter this basic attitudinal tendency on the part of jurors,[43] but they acknowledge doubts about the effectiveness of *any* instructions.

In a reanalysis of their data, Buckhout et al. note in Table 7.2 that the deliberations under the two different decision rules led to a significant difference in *concordance*, where concordance is defined as percent agreement with a legally correct verdict. That is, where jurors began with a lot of disagreement over which of five verdicts to vote for, the nonunanimous decision rule led to more shifts toward a compromise verdict and hence fewer hung juries than under the normal unanimous decision rule.

Unlike the conflict over the effects of jury size, the question of changing the verdict decision rule, even where there are fewer published empirical findings, produces a strong NO from the social scientist. Although we can see the importance of replicating this research with the different cases, evidence, and sizes, we are confident that the research will continue to show a large difference in the direction of more verdicts with a less than unanimous decision rule. The values of both the Court and the social scientists should be offended at the prospect.

[43] Schulman, J. Personal communication, 1976. Schulman describes the many surveys he had conducted on representative samples of potential jurors which show that 60 percent or more of the potential jurors have a presumption of guilt about any defendant. He has never found people who were strongly prodefendant, because it is clear that most citizens equate arrest or indictment as some evidence of guilt.

Table 7.2 ANALYSIS OF SHIFTS IN JUROR VERDICT PREFERENCES
UNDER UNANIMOUS AND NONUNANIMOUS DECISION RULES

PARAMETER	UNANIMOUS $(n = 90)$	NONUNANIMOUS $(N = 96)$
Average degree (probability) of initial concordance	0.488	0.433
Average degree of final concordance	0.758	0.933[a]
Number of juries shifting to different compromise verdict	1 out of 10 Juries	6 out of 10 Juries

[a] $p < 0.05$

"THE JURY WILL DISREGARD . . .": THE PREJUDICIAL EFFECTS OF INADMISSIBLE TESTIMONY

A fairly large number of cases have drifted up through appeals channels in the courts which claim that a defendant's right to due process were compromised by the entry into the trial record of testimony or characterizations that prejudice the defendant or his or her image. In the legal game of "protecting the record," a careful judge will issue cautionary instructions to the jury to ignore or disregard the offending (often violative of evidence law) testimony. In three Supreme Court cases, the appellants argued that such instructions were ineffective, in that a judge's instructions to disregard may serve to highlight the prejudicial information and make it more *salient* to a juror. Both the majority and dissenting opinion writers found something in *The American Jury* (1966) to back up their decision.

In this area of human behavior (attitude formation and change) an extensive body of research has existed for years, allowing us to rephrase the Supreme Court's language in the form of the hypotheses the Court might have relied on to deny the two of the appellant's claims in *Spencer* v. *the State of Texas* (1967).[44]

> Jurors are not significantly influenced in determining the guilt of a criminal defendant by the knowledge that he has committed other unrelated crimes, so long as they are instructed by the judge that such information should be ignored in determining guilt or innocence.

From *Frazier* v. *Cupp* (1969):

> Jurors cautioned by a judge to disregard all statements made by counsel not supported by evidence are not likely to have their judgement as to defendant's guilt influenced by a prosecutor's opening asserting that a co-conspirator would testify implicating the defendant in crime and

[44] *Spencer* v. *State of Texas*, 87 Supreme Court 648, 385 U.S. 567 (1967).

the subsequent refusal of the alleged co-conspirator to testify on grounds of self-incrimination when called to the witness stand.[45]

From *Bruton* v. *U.S.* (1968):

A judge's cautionary instructions to a jury cannot effectively erase or remove the effect of testimony the jurors are later told to disregard.[46]

The language of both *Spencer* v. *Texas* and *Frazier* v. *Cupp* speak of a stand taken by the Court on a model of how the human mind works and an operating theory of attitude change. The focus of trial adversaries and the judge on the written record implies to us that it is convenient to regard the juror as a *tabula rasa* on which the evidence in the case will be written (or from which the evidence will be erased). The *New Yorker* cartoon (Figure 7.2) illustrates the folly of a model which breeds such language by Supreme Court judges as the following:

It is hard for us to imagine that the minds of jurors would be so influenced by such incidental statements during this long trial that they would not appraise the evidence objectively and dispassionately.[47]

Indeed great pains are taken during a trial to "protect" the jury from nonevidence data through the techniques of sequestering, sidebar conferences, argument of legal points without the jury, the dressing of a jailed defendant in civilian clothes, and so on. Finally, the thrust of instructions by the judge is an effort to channel the perspective powers of the jury to matters considered to be relevant. When viewed in the manner of Ervin Goffman,[48] any trial court involves a staged managed "play," where court officers attempt to project the idea that the jury should consider the trial to be a purposeful analysis of a presumably innocent person who must be proven guilty.

Yet, the attorneys and the judge are people, too—who usually do not believe very strongly in the impressions that they are conveying verbally to the jury. The lawyer who "accidentally" slips in a bit of inadmissible testimony intuitively knows about the *Von Restorff* effect,[49] taught to generations of social scientists. Briefly, this phenomenon involves the superior retention of verbal material made distinctive (by a change in color or emphasis) in a list of otherwise similar material. The instructions by the judge can merely serve as an additional reinforcer to draw more attention to the offending testimony.

Of course, if one chooses to view the judge's instructions as an

[45] *Frazier* v. *Cupp*, 89 Supreme Court 1420, 394 U.S. 731 (1969).
[46] *Bruton* v. *United States*, 391 U.S. 123, 88 Supreme Court 1620 (1968).
[47] *Spencer* v. *State of Texas*, op. cit.
[48] Goffman, E. *The Presentation of Self in Everyday Life.* Garden City, N.Y.: Doubleday, 1959.
[49] Munn, N. M. *Psychology.* Harcourt Brace Jovanovich, 1952.

"The jury will disregard the witness's last remarks."

Figure 7.2   New Yorker cartoon. (Source: Drawing by Lorenz; © 1977, The *New Yorker Magazine*, Inc.)

isolated persuasion attempt, then one can indeed turn to the attitude literature to find support for the social fact that a highly credible source (the judge) will generally be a more effective producer of attitude change than the less credible attorneys.[50] But such an ostrichlike view of a trial ignores the fact that a judge may deliver his or her warning in a desultory fashion or one that conveys non-verbally to the jury that the judge knows that the defendant is really a crook but he or she "has to say this." Justice Warren in a dissent in the *Spencer* case acknowledged this analysis by quoting Justice Jackson:[51] "The naive assumption that prejudicial effects can be over-come by instructions to the jury . . . all practicing lawyers know to be unmitigated fictions."

Fictions have a way of becoming convenient and breed, in the case of a trial, a great potential for a two-tier communication system in which nonstated implications can be signaled to a jury by mandatory but meaningless warnings. The courtroom is not a well-controlled experiment in persuasion but a total phenomenological experience. Psychological research on the verbal aspects of communication have shown that some information has a sleeper effect causing attitude

[50] McGuire, W. J. The nature of attitudes and attitude change. In Lindzey, G., and Aronson, E., op. cit.
[51] *Spencer* v. *State of Texas*, op. cit.

change at a later time;[52] research on nonverbal communication suggests that the nonverbal portion of a communication may account for as much as 90 percent of the information transmitted.[53]

More recent research has been directed specifically toward the questions discussed in the preceding Supreme Court cases, and the trend seems clearly to support the alternate hypothesis that so-called irrelevant information is prejudicial to a defendant. Doob and Kirschenbaum (1972) report a jury simulation in which instructions to ignore a defendant's prior criminal record were futile.[54] "An accused person with previous criminal convictions stands a much greater chance of being convicted of a crime than does a person with no such history."[55] Sue (1973) found that inadmissible testimony *did* have an effect on simulated jurors' decisions.[56] Hendricks (1975) found that the effect of merely pleading the Fifth Amendment by either the defendant or a co-conspirator prejudiced the jury against the defendant.[57] Thus, at least in regard to the *Spencer* and *Frazier* cases, the evidence shows that the Supreme Court was just dead wrong. The language of the Court has been so consistently wrong and so fraught with wishful thinking on the issue of prejudicial testimony that we can see more the need for litigation or legislation than for research in this area. Indeed, in the *Bruton* case, the court accepted the alternative hypothesis that cautionary instructions cannot remove the effects of testimony that the jury is told to disregard.[58]

SUMMARY

In this chapter we have implied that the Supreme Court and the Community of Social Science are at odds. For the time being this is true since the common turf of both institutions is at stake when we consider the smaller but important institution called the jury. In the name of efficiency the criminal justice system has been proportionally reducing its reliance upon the jury system and referring more and

[52] McGuire, op. cit.

[53] Mehrabian, A. *Non-verbal Communication.* Englewood Cliffs, N.J.: Prentice-Hall, 1970.

[54] Doob, A. N., & Kirshenbaum, H. M. Some empirical evidence of the effect of S. 12 on the Canada Evidence Act on an accused. *Criminal Law Quarterly,* 1972, *15,* 88–96.

[55] Brooks, W. N., & Doob, A. N. Justice and the jury. *Journal of Applied Social Psychology,* 1975, *31* (3), 171–182.

[56] Sue, S. Effects of inadmissible evidence on the decision of simulated jurors—A moral dilemma. *Journal of Applied Social Psychology,* 1973, *3* (4), 345–353.

[57] Hendricks, C. Effects of pleading the fifth amendment on the perceptions of guilt and morality. *Bulletin of Psychonomic Society,* 1975, *6* (5), 300–304.

[58] *Bruton v. United States,* op. cit.

more cases to plea bargaining. The Supreme Court has been responsive to suggestions from prosecutors in the United States that major relaxations of the old rules of a twelve person unanimous jury be reconsidered also in the interest of efficiency. The work of the social scientists, founded on the fascinating simulation in the laboratory of the jury process, has largely been aimed at raising questions about the impact of changes in the jury system on verdict outcome. The so-called battle will continue and it appears that the Supreme Court is taking more account of what social scientists have to offer.[59]

[59] *Boulden* v. *Holman*, 394 U.S. 478, 89 Supreme Court 1138, 1969.

CASE STUDIES IN SCIENTIFIC
JURY SELECTION: AN INSIDE VIEW

In the 1970s a fair amount of speculation arose in the legal and social science literature about the specter of "scientific jury selection." Ostensibly, the proposition was that social scientists would offer to apply survey and measurement techniques to ascertain the demographic and attitudinal states of members of a jury pool and thus aid an attorney in selecting appropriate jurors for his or her cause. The technique first gained a round of favorable publicity followed in rapid succession by a period of skepticism and ethical concern and, ultimately, the publication of technical discussions accompanied by a period of benign neglect from the press. Noting that most of the writing about jury selection was offered by observers who were never personally involved, we thought that the reflective observations of some of the "co-conspirators" might make up for the fact that few of the people who originated "scientific jury selection" have taken the time to write about their experiences.[1]

[1] The "co-conspirators" included Richard Christie (Columbia University), Jay Shulman (private consultant, sociologist), Neal Bush (attorney, Detroit), and David Kairys (attorney, Philadelphia).

THE NATIONAL JURY PROJECT

The untold story of the scientific jury selection minimovement is centered around the growth and ultimate dissolution of a nonprofit corporation of legal workers, lawyers, social scientists, and concerned people who incorporated in 1975 under the name of the National Jury Project.[2] The inspiration and guiding spirit of the group was Jay Schulman, (see Figure 8.1) a man of energy, vision, and social concern, whose charisma in inspiring the efforts of members of both the legal and social science professions can never be underestimated. What brought this strange amalgam together was outrage: outrage at the political prosecutions of the Nixon era against those who protested U.S. policy in Vietnam. The particular trial was *U.S. v. Ahmed et al.*, in which the government indicted a large group of activists for violating federal conspiracy laws.[3] This case has been known popularly as the "Harrisburg 7."

The climate of the times in which the so-called "Harrisburg 7" trial took place is hard to imagine in a post-Watergate era. When some critics raise questions about the fairness of the application of scientific jury selection techniques to one side of an adversary process, we cannot forget that in 1970 the criminal justice system was being used as a political weapon against dissent by President Nixon, Attorney General John Mitchell, and FBI Director J. Edgar Hoover. In the face of what the defendants perceived to be political oppression, they enlisted the aid of concerned social scientists who offered to help in any way they could.

DEFENSE COMMITTEES

The social scientists inexorably found themselves drawn into that uniquely American institution, the defense committee.[4] The defense committee is an intense, ad hoc, short-lived phenomenon, a loosely

2 The National Jury Project was still in existence in 1981 as a nonprofit foundation and information center, with branches in six states.

3 Schulman, J., Shaver, P., Colman, R., Emrich, B., & Christie, R. Recipe for a Jury, *Psychology Today*, 1973, 6, 37–84, available as *Center Monograph No. CR-16*, Center for Responsive Psychology, Brooklyn College, Brooklyn, N.Y., 11210. This article is the most thorough account of the jury selection approach pioneered by Jay Schulman. See also Mossman, K. Jury Selection: An Expert's View. *Psychology Today*, 1973, 6, 78–79.

4 Although most defense committees have been rather loosely organized, they have frequently been the targets of infiltration by intelligence agents from the government, as has been documented in the so-called "Gainsville 8" and Attica trials. In the Gainsville trial FBI agents were literally found in a closet doing something to a phone used by the defense lawyers. An FBI agent was planted on the Attica Defense Committee in Erie County, N.Y. Of course, the advocacy system itself

organized group made up of the friends and lawyers of the accused. Defense committees are usually organized around the cause of an accused person who is a figure of some fame or notoriety. In history, famous cases such as the Sacco-Vanzetti case had a defense committee that included people of the stature of Felix Frankfurter—the same Frankfurter who was later to become the distinguished Justice of the U.S. Supreme Court. Committees make use of the American penchant for organization to raise money, send out "inside" news to supporters, and run errands for the lawyers who usually end up as committee leaders. The rewards to the individual committee members are usually nontangible—a rush of excitement at being a part of history, the comradery, a reaffirmation of their ideological beliefs. For the social scientists the defense committees offered an additional incentive—the relevant employment of their skills in a worthy effort. Although money is always in short supply—in research laboratories as well as on defense committees—there often is a surplus of bright, motivated volunteers who have made large-scale surveys possible.

The issue of money and resources is no small problem in planning a serious legal defense of an unpopular person.[5] When the government takes a strong interest in a case, it can apply almost unlimited financial and personnel resources to the investigation and the trial. In the matter of jury selection, the government has access to FBI, military, and Internal Revenue Service records, and it would be (and still is) naïve to assume that they would not use such information in spite of legal sanctions against invasion of privacy. Lawyers and social scientists at least share a degree of faith in the equation that states that the more background information available on a person, the more accurately one can predict a person's attitude toward a given case.

The gathering of information costs money, as defense committees learned when they tried to determine how jury members might react

---

encourages in all participants an "anything goes" attitude. In their zealous search for information defense committee investigators have been accused of jury tampering.

[5] It was estimated that the U.S. government spent over two million dollars to prosecute the Berrigan case, whereas the defense committee raised and spent several hundred thousand dollars. As court costs escalate, every little decision carries a price tag. The need for a transcript of a day's hearing can cost anywhere from $200 to $1200. A defense committee, involving private counsel for a defendant, has to petition the court for recovery of specific costs after the trial. Payment is up to the trial judge's discretion. The court clerk who must type up the transcript will often insist on cash in advance for a transcript. Lawyer's fees paid by the court to an appointed attorney vary greatly but are nearly always a fraction of the going rate for a privately retained attorney. In the Commonwealth of Virginia, a court appointed defense attorney receives $25 for a misdemeanor trial and $75 for a felony trial.

Figure 8.1   Social scientists Richard Christie and Jay Schulman, cofounders of the National Jury Project, at a strategy session. (Source: © from *Time*, January 28, 1974, p. 60)

toward their defendant or to the evidence. Under federal law a federal case may be tried in any federal district at the government's discretion, setting up a situation in which a defense committee might find itself far from home base trying to evaluate a jury pool that is unfamiliar to the attorneys. Such was the case in the Harrisburg trial where the government opted to try the case in a conservative area in Pennsylvania which even boasts an active Ku Klux Klan chapter.[6] The defense lawyers (Ramsey Clark, Paul O'Dwyer, Leonard Boudine) were New York City attorneys on foreign territory—just as attorney F. Lee Bailey found himself in a new state in the case of *U.S.* v. *Patty Hearst.*

GETTING INVOLVED: PSYCHOLOGISTS FOR THE DEFENSE

At this point, we would like to share with the reader the world view of the criminal defense attorney and his or her social science colleagues

---

[6] Schulman, J. A Systematic Approach to Successful Jury Selection. *Guild Notes*, 1973, *II*, (7), 13–20.

as it relates to their hope of finding favorable jurors anywhere. We begin with the bold fact that most defense attorneys in most criminal trials know that they are likely to lose. The statistics bear out the assertion that most trials result in conviction of the accused.[7] Secondly, it is usually acknowledged by court officers and confirmed in research that the vast majority of jurors who serve come to court with a *presumption of guilt* about the defendant.[8] In surveys conducted on jurors and former jurors a common finding is that the majority of jurors will endorse statements favoring the placing of the burden of proof on the defendant. In highly publicized cases we have generally found that the majority of potential jurors have already decided that the defendant is guilty before the trial begins. In fact, finding individuals in any community who are ecstatically in favor of *any* defendant in a criminal trial is a statistical rarity.[9] The fact that the judge and the defense attorney will spend a great deal of time coaching the prospective juror to accept an act on the "presumption of innocence" is a tribute to everybody's awareness that the juror is being asked to put aside his or her "better judgment;" a judgement that may not be wholly unreasonable. The defense lawyers and the social scientists would agree that the main goal of jury selection is to *avoid* those persons whose minds are so rigidly made up that they could not fairly evaluate evidence. Thus through *voir dire* and the careful exercise of

---

[7] A perusal of the administrative statistics for the year 1976 in the U.S. largest court system (New York City) reveals a 66 percent conviction rate overall; 96 percent in Bronx County's Major Offense Bureau, and it is estimated informally by attorneys that the conviction rate is close to 90 percent nationally. The "Chicago Studies" of juries reported an 83 percent conviction rate in a sampling of over 3500 criminal cases in the early 1960s. See Kalven, H. and Zeisel, H. *The American Jury*, Chicago, Ill.: University of Chicago Press, 1971.

[8] Buckhout, R., & Baker, E. Surveying the attitudes of seated jurors. *Social Action and the Law*, 1977, *4* (6) pp. 90–92. In a survey of jurors who had completed service in the U.S. Federal Court (Eastern District) it was found that even jurors who had been socialized by the system were still willing to endorse requirements that defendants prove their innocence, that defendants be required to take the witness stand, and that the taking of the Fifth Amendment implies that a person is hiding his or her guilt. Former jurors surveyed about a highly publicized case in a small county were found to have prejudged the guilt of the defendant; see Buckhout, R., Weg, S. & Cohen, R. Case Study of the Presumption of Guilt in Jurors. *Center Monograph No. CR-8*, Center for Responsive Psychology, 1975, Brooklyn College, Brooklyn, N.Y. 11210.

[9] Schulman, op. cit. As Schulman has pointed out, most people do not appreciate the stigma of a prior arrest. A presumption of innocence is a legal fiction, however convenient, that can only be willfully adopted by a person who is either open-minded to start with or is so authoritarian that he or she would follow a judge's instructions even where the judge is him or herself very even-handed about justice. See also Schulman, J. Strategies and issues in systematic jury selection. Unpublished paper, 1976.

Table 8.1   COMPARISON OF METHODS OF LAWYERS
AND SOCIAL SCIENTISTS IN JURY SELECTION

AREA	SOCIAL SCIENTISTS	LAWYERS
Jury panel characteristics	Surveys and demographic studies	Experience with previous jury pools
In-court observations	Systematic ratings	Intuition based on experience
Reputations of jury pool members	Information networks	Informal contact
Jury composition	Use of findings from small group research	Selection of key jurors
Follow-up	Systematic interviews of jurors and peremptory challenges	Informal feedback

SOURCE: Personal Communication from Professor Richard Christie, Columbia University.

challenges, the defense attorney will generally fight an uphill battle whereas his or her opponent on the state or government prosecution side is generally less dependent on the selection process.

Richard Christie, a social psychologist who has worked closely with Jay Schulman, points out that once he and other social scientists began assisting in jury selection the two different world views of the lawyer and the social scientist became apparent.[10] The more experienced lawyers (like the more experienced anybody) can reasonably argue that their intuition shaped by hundreds of jury selections enables them to discriminate among potentially "good" and "bad" jurors. Further, most experienced trial attorneys place a great deal of faith in their ability to persuade or educate the jury with either the use of emotion (a Freudian model of man) or logic (the "juror-as-a-rational-person" theory). Because specific feedback from jurors is rather informal and because a trial has so many elements that might "cause" victory or defeat, few attorney's assumptions have been subjected to the type of checking that would satisfy a social scientist. Christie summarizes some of the differences in approach in Table 8.1.

We are all consumers of survey results and lawyers are no exceptions. But the social scientist's use of surveys and/or demographic data provide a level of detail which bothers many lawyers who are more used to using intuition. One of the highlights of the jury survey work in the Harrisburg 7 trial was the wealth of counter-intuitive information generated. As Christie documents:

[10] Christie, R. Probability v. Precedence: The social psychology of jury selection. In G. Bermant, C. Nemeth, and N. Vidmar (Eds.), *Psychology and the Law*, Lexington, Mass.: D. C. Heath, 1976.

In Harrisburg, the expected finding that younger people would be more liberal did not emerge . . . the area was economically depressed . . . and there were no major liberal arts colleges in the area. Bright young high school graduates tended to leave the area for their higher education, and once they were gone there was little to bring them back. Those people who remained were the ones who fit comfortably into the conservative, predominantly fundamentalist Protestant, rural, small town ambience and thus were not different ideologically from the older people.[11]

This type of analysis does clash with some stereotypes held by defense attorneys who, as a rule, believe that the more educated person would make a more open-minded, hence a more acceptable, juror. The relative rarity of a young educated person in a U.S. jury pool until very recently, may have helped to support a seldom requited lust for any juror under the age of 45. Tate et al. (1974) ran down a list of stereotypes that they found to be common among trial attorneys.[12]

Generally they feel that persons of Latin descent are emotional while British, Germans and Scandanavians are conservative and will support the prosecution more than the defense. Blacks, Italians, Irishmen, Jews, Frenchmen and Spaniards are expected to support the defense more than the prosecution. Waitresses, bartenders, artists, actors, social scientists and persons with more experience in the world are thought to make better jurors than engineers and accountants. (p. 132)

In testing the preferences of a group of Canadian lawyers who were asked to choose jurors for a specific set of cases, Tate et al. found a strong preference for male jurors and a decided antipathy toward jurors who were dressed in a "rebellious" fashion. Tate et al. found in their data, and we find in our experience, that lawyers tend to have *general* stereotypes that they apply to the selection of jurors in all cases even though they certainly will vary trial techniques to fit the crime.

In an interesting manner the lawyers appear to have chosen one side of a major controversy in psychological theory: the argument over which is more important in predicting behavior—the personality traits of the subject or purely situation factors such as evidence.[13, 14] Social

---

[11] Ibid, p. 267.

[12] Tate, E., Hawrish, E., & Clark, S. Communication variables in jury selection. *Journal of Communication*, 1974, 24 (3), 130–139.

[13] Mischel, W. Toward a cognitive social learning reconceptualization of personality. *Psychological Review*, 1973, 80, 252–283.

[14] Saks, M. J. The limits of scientific jury selection: Ethical and empirical. *Jurimetrics Journal*, 1976, 17 (1), 3–22. See also Saks, M. Social scientists can't rig juries. *Psychology Today*, 1976, 9 (8), 48–57. Prof. Saks uses his critique of jury selection to make a sweeping attack on all personality theories: "The Freudian theory that we all have a core personality is either inadequate, trivial or wrong."

BOX 8.1
TEXAS JUSTICE
A JURY OF YOUR PEERS???

The following is an excerpt from a book titled Prosecution Course put out by the Dallas County District Attorney's office. The book was developed as part of a course for new prosecuting attorneys in this state. The section we quote is out of the chapter on "Jury Selection in a Criminal Case" by Jon Sparling, an assistant D.A. in Dallas. Sparling was the first Dallas prosecuter to get a 1,000 year sentence for a convicted felon: he is also known for his prosecution in the Guzman-Lopez case involving the killers of two Dallas County sheriff's deputies. . . . Who you select for the jury is, at best a calculated risk. Instincts about veniremen may be developed by experience, but even the young prosecutor may improve the odds by the use of certain guidelines—if you know what to look for.

The following outline contains very little substantive law because I presume that any prosecutor is as able to look it up as I. The outline does, however, contain one prosecutor's ideas on some things that need to be said to the panel, and some things to look for in a juror . . .

III. What to look for in a juror.
    A. Attitudes.
        1. You are not looking for a fair juror, but rather a strong, biased and sometimes hypocritical individual who believes that Defendants are different from them in kind, rather than degree.
        2. You are not looking for any member of a minority group which may subject him to oppression—they almost always empathize with the accused.
        3. You are not looking for the free thinkers and flower children.
    B. Observation is worthwhile.
        1. Look at the panel out in the hall before they are seated. You can often spot the show-offs and the liberals by how and to whom they are talking.
        2. Observe the veniremen as they walk into the courtroom.
            a. You can tell almost as much about a man by how he walks, as how he talks.
            b. Look for physical afflictions. These people usually sympathize with the accused.
        3. Dress.
            a. Conservatively, well dressed people are generally stable and good for the State.
            b. In many counties, the jury summons states that the appropriate dress is coat and tie. One who does not wear a coat and tie is often a non-conformist and therefore a bad State's juror.
        4. Women.
            a. I don't like women jurors because I can't trust them.
            b. They do, however, make the best jurors in cases involving crimes against children.
            c. It is possible that their "women's intuition" can help you if you can't win your case with the facts.
            d. Young women too often sympathize with the Defendant; old women wearing too much make-up are usually unstable, and therefore are bad State's jurors.

Reprinted in The Texas Observer, May 11, '73

psychologists were generally moving away from personality traits in the 1970s, whereas lawyers—with a traditional preference for the influence of situational factors—began to look more closely at personality. But the fact remains that the lawyer and the social scientist view the world and thus select jurors in a decidedly different way.

Our point is not that the social scientist's way is a better way but that we are all students of the same, very complex slice of life. The practitioners such as Jay Schulman who pioneered a new role for social scientists did so as skilled, imaginative consultants, not as purveyors of some strange new form of magic emanating from computers.[15] Much of the criticism that was generated by the publicity surrounding the political trials was addressed to scientific jury selection as technology running amok. Much of this concern, as we shall develop, was either misdirected or influenced by some rather naïve views of how the criminal justice system really works. Schulman and his colleagues have served as interdisciplinarians—aware of social science research which is relevant and able to convince legally trained people of its applicability to the system. The result of this pioneering effort was the bringing about of major social change in how the entire jury system functions as well as a remarkable string of acquittals in political trials in which the hard evidence was either flimsy or non-existent.[16] (See Figure 8.2)

SYSTEMATIC JURY SELECTION

As we have intimated, a systematic approach to any facet of the criminal justice system requires money and energy that are never in

[15] Etzioni, E. Science: Threatening the Jury Trial, *Washington Post*, Sunday, May 26, 1974. In this most naïve of critiques, the author lapses into believing that the threat from statistical approaches to jury selection is to the "lawyers on both sides (who) . . . were more or less equal in their ability to exercise this kind of homespun social psychology." An editor of *Science* noted in review that the inequities in the jury selection are in favor of the prosecution and the general lack of representativeness in jury pools makes the situation a stacked deck. Shapley, D. jury selection: Social scientists gamble in an already loaded game. *Science, 185,* 1974 (September 20), 1033–1071.

[16] Some of the soundest criticism of the methodological limitations of scientific jury selection has come from Professor Richard Berk (University of California, Santa Barbara) who has also had some experience in using the techniques in the civil trial following the murder of Black Panther Fred Hampton in Chicago (*Iberia, Hampton, administratrix, etc., et al.* v. *Edward Hanrahan, et al., No. 70c 1384 consolidated*). See Berk, R. A. Social science and jury selection: A case study of a civil suit. In G. Bermant, C. Nemeth, and Vidmar, N. (Eds.), *Psychology and the Law,* Lexington, Mass.: D. C. Heath, 1976; Berk, R. A., Hennessy, M., & Swan, J. The vagaries and vulgarities of "scientific" jury selection: A methodological evaluation. *Evaluation Quarterly,* 1977, 1 (1), 143–158.

Figure 8.2 The jury. (Source: The Bettman Archives, © 1974, The New York Times Company. Reprinted by permission.

surplus. When we were approached as the National Jury Project to consider a case, we emphasized that ideally a good defense in a jury trial (or a good prosecution) involved placing all factors into a holistic context. In the sections that follow, we shall review the different areas in which social science assistance was given by members of the National Jury Project and its associates.[17]

· *Securing a Change of Venue.* In 1977 the defense attorneys for the man accused as the ".44 calibre killer" (or "Son of Sam") sought unsuccessfully to have the trial moved out of Brooklyn, New York to an upstate county, on the grounds that the excessive publicity on the case had "poisoned the well," so that a fair trial was impossible. Such motions are often filed in criminal cases but are often denied because the assertions of prior bias by potential jurors can easily be offset by assertions that (1) most jurors are conscientious, (2) the judge can socialize the jurors into putting aside their prejudices and pay atten-

[17] Kairys, D., Schulman, J., & Harring, S. *The Jury System: New Methods for Reducing Prejudice,* National Jury Project and the National Lawyers Guild, 1975. This is a basic "how-to do it" manual produced by members of the National Jury Project on the basis of experience.

BOX 8.2

THOUGHTS ON SERVING
IN A SEAT OF JUDGMENT

By Daniel Schorr*

WASHINGTON—The Juror's Manual of the United States District Court says that jury service is "perhaps the most vital duty next to fighting in defense of one's country." Yet it seemed hilarious to almost everyone who heard about it when Judge John J. Sirica, whose Watergate trial and other man-of-the-year-making activities I had covered, summoned me by form letter for two months of jury duty.

Colleagues took off on rollicking fantasies of my sitting in judgment on the Ehrlichmans, Haldemans and Colsons I had so long staked out, broadcasting exclusives from hidden microphones in the jury room.

I suppose that there is something intrinsically funny about being suddenly translated from the free press to the fair trial corner of the ring. But it also seemed absurd to many that someone as busy and recognizable as a television newsman should be asked to spend his time this way. The impression has somehow got around that this "most vital duty" is meant for the idle and for the anonymous.

Judge Sirica, himself amused at what random selection had wrought, offered to excuse me. I held that it was up to my employer, C.B.S. News, to say whether my services were deemed indispensable. C.B.S., which is anxious to make the point that it seeks no privilege for its personnel save First Amendment privilege, has a rigid rule against asking exemption from jury service. So, I served.

When I arrived in the jury lounge to join the new contingent of some 200, there was a ripple of double-takes. From the jury-lounge staff there was much deference, coffee and offers to excuse me on any day when I might have something more momentous to do. It was nice, they said, that I was willing to serve. But, alas, I would probably spend most of my time in the lounge. For experience indicated that a well-known newsman would probably never make it through the preemptory challenges to the jury box.

That prediction was supported by every judge and lawyer of my acquaintanceship. The general theory was that trial lawyers don't like to take risks and that anyone recognizable is perceived as an undefined risk, someone on whom a losing client might focus in criticizing his counsel.

The conventional wisdom proved spectacularly wrong. I was called for four criminal cases—three narcotics, one armed robbery—and was not challenged in any. The Government, apparently as a policy matter, challenged no one. All of the four defendants were black, and defense challenges, applied generously, reflected a pattern of eliminating the elderly, the stern-looking, and whites. But they always left one white man and one white woman. I became the token white man in these cases.

The race- and class-consciousness evoked in the jury selection pursued us silently into the jury room. Three times, as though carrying out the decision of some secret caucus, the jurors selected me as foreman. The fourth time, when I demurred, they selected the other white. But if management was left to whites, discussion was not. Younger blacks displayed expressiveness, vehemence and sensitivity about being listened to that often seemed less connected with current proceedings than prior conditions of discrimination.

The sense of minority was dramatically displayed by one angry young black woman, holding out against the rest of us. I asked her to make her argument. She said that for all she cared we could just go ahead and report a verdict without her. When I reminded her of the requirement for a unanimous verdict, she said: "You're eleven to one against me. Isn't that unanimous enough?"

And then there was the juror who exercised his freedom of choice by saying he would join us to make the verdict unanimous but might just change his mind if polled in the courtroom. It took us another hour to get his assurance that he would stick to his vote.

The greatest problem in the jury room is focusing on the evidence. Inexplicably, note-taking by jurors in the courtroom is prohibited, leaving jurors to rely later on often conflicting recollections of testimony. There is also considerable theorizing and sheer conjecture, based less on evidence than personal grievance and personal experience. And preciseness of deliberation appears to suffer from leniency in excusing busy professionals, leaving juries weighed with the marginally employed, who welcome the $20 daily fee, the retired, and others out of the mainstream. Jury service has tended to become an activity for those whose regular activities are not valued by society.

But, in the end, though lacking much common language and common experience, we in the jury room found common ground. In my four cases we brought out verdicts—two guilty, two not guilty—that my conscience can live with. Let me, though, reveal the jury-room secret that despite judges' instructions to the contrary we engaged in a certain amount of "jury revisionism" of the law.

We were more inclined to find reasonable doubt in the case of a young man accused of selling his own clinic dose of methadone to a soliciting undercover policeman than a man accused of heroin-pushing.

In the end, Judge Sirica got from me a requested memorandum with observations about the jury system in practice. I got from him a personally signed certificate of service. I also got an experience that should be shared by more "busy" people, if this "vital duty" is really to rest on a peer relationship.

SOURCE: © 1974 by The New York Times Company. Reprinted by permission. From the *New York Times*, April 25, 1974.
* Daniel Schorr was an investigative reporter for C.B.S. News in Washington who had specialized for a year and a half on Watergate.

tion to the evidence, and (3) effective screening in the *voir dire* can eliminate the most prejudiced jurors. The social scientist's answer is that any or all of those assertions might be true, but the way to determine whether or not the "well has been poisoned" is to measure attitudes. In the cases worked on by members of the National Jury

Project, the key consideration was the presentation of statistical survey data during an evidentiary hearing on the motion for a change of venue.[18]

Professor John McConahay (Duke University) described an example of this process as it was used in *North Carolina* v. *Joan Little*.[19] A survey was conducted on a random sample of registered voters (the source of jurors) in the county where the crime took place and several adjacent counties. The key questions were (1) measurement of how much the person had heard about the case, (2) preconception of guilt, and (3) racism (e.g., "Do you believe that black women have lower morals than white women?"). The results showed a statistically significantly higher degree of case knowledge, preconception of guilt, *and* racism among potential jurors in the county of the crime than in the adjacent and more urban counties. The defense team, armed with these data, asked for a change of venue. The evidence presentation included the statistical results of the survey, newspaper clippings, affidavits from people in the community, and expert testimony from sociologists who specialized in research on the effects of publicity on attitudes. The judge, convinced that racism would hamper a fair trial, ordered the trial moved from Beaufort County to the more urban Wake County.[20] The text of the written motions and the format of the evidentiary hearing (supplemented by the appropriate local survey data) have been used by the National Jury project

---

[18] Although the effects of pretrial publicity on jurors has been a subject of legal concern (*Sheppard* v. *Maxwell*, 384 U.S. 333, 1966), the research literature has been far from convincing. Some evidence shows that while biases can be created by publicity, they can be mitigated by good selective screening during the *voir dire*, assuming that the respective attorneys for each side ask the right questions. Even if this is true, the existence of a high level of bias in the community means that a really effective screening of jurors will require more time and money, the lack of which can reduce the possibility of a fair trial. See Padawer-Singer, A., & Barton, A. H. The impact of pretrial publicity on jurors' verdicts. In R. J. Simon (Ed.), *The Jury System in America*, Beverly Hills, Calif.: Sage Publications, 1975, pp. 123–142 and Zanzola, L. The role of pretrial publicity in the trial process and jury deliberations, unpublished master's thesis, Northern Illinois University, 1977.
[19] McConahay, J. B., Mullin, C. J., & Fredrick, J. The uses of social science in trials with political and racial overtones: The trial of Joan Little. *Law and Contemporary Problems*, 1977, *41* (1).
[20] Many observers were convinced that the granting of a change of venue was the main reason for the ultimate acquittal of Joan Little because everybody knew everybody in Beaufort County, N.C., and relatives of the deceased man in the case served on the grand jury that brought in the indictment. Efforts to quash the indictment had been unsuccessful. Clearly, in real-world cases, excessive publicity can create an enormous burden for either side. In some states, jurors are "imported" from nearby communities to reduce the possibility of their being "contaminated" by pretrial publicity.

BOX 8.3

A CASE IN POINT[21]

One of the most difficult consulting roles ever undertaken by the National Jury Project was *Commonwealth* v. *Schwartz*, a murder case in a rural county in Pennsylvania in which the son of the richest man in the area was accused of hiring someone to kill a rival suitor. The charges of "contract murder" were brought in an atmosphere of excessive publicity which played up several stigmatizing categories in which the accused could be placed. He was young, Jewish (in a conservative Protestant county), a dwarf, rich and possessed of a "bad reputation." In the survey conducted for purposes of seeking a change of venue, over 90 percent of a random sample of registered voters knew the defendant's name and the case. Over 75 percent of that group acknowledged that they already had formed an opinion that the defendant was guilty and offered negative commentary about the character of the defendant and his family. With an election looming, it was no surprise that the district attorney argued that the defendant could receive a fair trial and that the judge denied the motion to move the trial.

When the *voir dire* took place, hundreds of jurors were screened as the negative attitudes predicted by the survey manifested themselves. The local newspaper even printed a handy guide to the prospective juror on how to get off the jury by tailoring the answers to their questions to provoke a challenge for cause. In one bizarre instance, a prospective juror admitted to having been a member of the Hitler Youth organization as a teenager in Germany. He denied having any anti-Semitic feelings on the grounds that the Hitler Youth was a "boy scout organization."

---

to aid change of venue motions in a number of cases in South Dakota where local prejudice against Native Americans hampered jury selection in trials stemming from the Wounded Knee incidents in the early 1970s. The attitudinal surveys in these cases documented those unique situations where the prejudice was so internalized into the culture that a fair trial would be impossible.[21]

In the more rural sections of South Dakota the population base is so small that jurors are called to serve for as long as six months, with many individuals serving for multiple terms. Contrary to the spirit of

[21] (See Box No. 8.3) In this case example we have altered the name and locale to preserve the anonymity of the parties to a legal matter that still had further hearings to go in 1978.

the laws regarding the composition of juries, some people literally become professional jurors if they have a lot of spare time. As one observer notes, "Jury service has tended to become an activity for those whose regular activities are not valued by society."[22] Because jurors are of a type, their attitudes can be understood from surveys and predicted with a fair degree of accuracy.

· *Challenging Jury Composition.* The principle of a trial by jury of one's peers remains just that—a principle. The typical jury in the United States is composed of white males in their mid-forties, with above average incomes, families, and establishment-oriented attitudes. As Van Dyke notes:

> Despite recent gains, in most courts in the U.S. significant segments of the population are still not included on juries as often as they would be in a completely random system aimed at impaneling a representative cross-section. Blue-collar workers, non-whites, the young, the elderly and women are the groups most widely underrepresented on juries. . . . This is a picture of juries that are more homogeneous than the population at large.[23]

Summarizing considerable research on the question, we can state that the typical juror is more prestigeful, older, and most often from another socioeconomic class than the typical accused person in a criminal trial. Further, it is known from psychological research that jurors are more punitive toward a person of a lower socioeconomic background or to whom they cannot sympathize.[24] Professor Freda Adler reports that the greater the gulf between the average "prestige" score of the defendant and the average prestige score of the criminal trial jury the more likely the defendant was to be convicted.[25] Similar findings with civil court jurors reveal a tendency for jurors to decide in favor of the plaintiff in their own occupational group.[26] Thus the

---

[22] Schorr, D., see Box 8.2.

[23] Van Dyke, J. M. *Jury Selection Procedures: Our Uncertain Commitment to Representative Panels*, Cambridge, Mass.: Ballinger, 1977, pp. 24–25. The definitive book on the procedures, administrative and legal, for selecting jurors in the United States. It is also a thoughtful critique with a wealth of specific suggestions for improving the representativeness and impartiality of jury panels. See also Alker, H. R., Hosticka, C., & Mitchell, M. Jury selection as a biased process. *Law and Society Review*, 1976, *11* (1), 9–41.

[24] Gerbasi, K. C., Zuckerman, M., & Reis, H. T. Justice needs a new blindfold: A review of mock jury research. *Psychological Bulletin*, 1977, *84* (2), 323–345.

[25] Adler, F. Socioeconomic factors influencing jury verdicts. *New York University Review of Law and Social Change*, (Winter 1973), *3*, 1.

[26] Jury Verdict Research, Inc., *Personal Injury Valuation Handbooks, Vol. VIII, Psychological Factors Affecting Verdicts-Jurors*, Cleveland, J. V. R., Inc. 1969.

consequences of a nonrepresentative jury panel can be to jeopardize a fair trial as well as to violate a constitutional principle.

We point out that we are referring to the entire jury panel rather than to the individual jury when looking into the problem of representation. A trial jury represents the summed judgment of the attorneys and the court, selections made from the available jury panel or "pool." The representativeness of the jury pool can be tested against the proportions of various categories of people in the latest available census data on the area from which the jury panel is selected. With the aid of some relatively simple statistics,[27] the proportions of women, for example, in the population and in the jury pool can be compared. Social scientists attached to the National Jury Project frequently found themselves testifying in pretrial evidentiary hearings concerning the "goodness of fit" between the population data and the data on a jury pool.[28] (See Figure 8.3.) The argument presented in this case was that the jury pool that had only 16.8 percent women significantly underrepresented the proportion of women in the Erie (New York) County population of registered voters which officially showed 53 percent women.

The statistical argument is that any sample of people randomly drawn from such a population would have a similar (not necessarily equal) proportion of women *if* the sample were drawn in an unbiased manner. Assuming that the county selected a jury pool of 1000 people, several times a year, the statistician would expect that each jury pool would have an average of somewhere around 530 women. The probability of coming up with a jury pool with only 168 women is a statistical rarity. Just how rare can be easily calculated; in this case it is a one in one billion shot.[29] This means that it *could* occur, but when

---

These expensive compilations of data are known largely to litigation attorneys and are very tantalizing collections of data that were never analyzed statistically. Thus minor differences in verdict trends as a function of race, sex, and so on are lumped together in a confusing manner.

[27] Any standard statistics book will do; we use Hays, W. L. *Statistics for Psychologists*, New York: Holt, Rinehart and Winston, 1963.

[28] The trial of the Attica Brothers involved the National Jury Project for a number of years. The citation for the example in Figure 8.3 is *People v. Attica Brothers: Ernest Bixby, et al.*, Superior Court of New York, Erie County (July 2, 1974). Graph cited in Kairys, D. et al., op. cit. See also Levine, A. G., & Schweber-Koren, C. Jury selection in Erie County: Changing a sexist system. *Law and Society Review*, 1976, *11* (1), 43–55.

[29] For those who have statistical training, here is the computation. Assuming an n of 1000 for a typical pool of jurors in a particular month, we had a sample $p = 0.168$ and a $q = 0.832$, compared to the census proportions of $p = 0.53$ and $q = 0.47$. p is the proportion of women; q the proportion of men. Figuring the standard deviation of the sample as $\sigma p = \sqrt{pq/n}$, then $\sigma p = 0.0118194$.

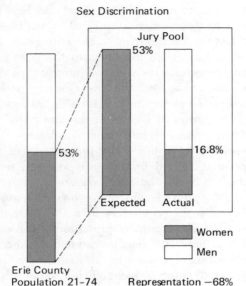

Figure 8.3 Contrasting census data with actual jury demographics. (Source: Exhibits from the Attica Composition Challenge, New York State Supreme Court, Erie County, Buffalo, N.Y., 1976.)

this proportion comes up repeatedly, the social scientist would conclude that the sample was *biased* in some manner. In the Erie County case that involved the prosecution of inmates in the Attica uprising in 1972, the evidentiary hearing included testimony that highlighted the discriminatory methods used by jury commissioners (who deliberately failed to call women) which could reasonably explain the overwhelming bias against women and blacks in the jury pools. The courts ordered a complete change in the methods of jury selection to ensure more representative jury pools. By June 1976, 58 percent of the jury pool members were women.

It is safe to say that representative jury panels are rare in any part of the United States. The systems in the various jurisdictions serve to filter the population so that any attempt at representativeness in the jury pools is defeated. The basis of most selection is the registered voter list, a notoriously biased sample in itself which automatically excludes from 30 to 50 percent of those eligible for jury duty. More

---

We used the z test of significance of a difference in proportions where $z = (p(\text{population}) - p(\text{sample}))/\sigma$ p, $z = 30.673$, a score that is significant beyond the 0.0000001 level of significance which is the limit of our tables. Hence we conservatively estimated the one in a billion figure in the text.

minority group members are missed because of low minority voter registration. Although it has been suggested that social security numbers be used, objections to an invasion of privacy have stalled this attempted reform.

Next in the filtering process is the mailing out of notices or summonses to jury duty. If the mail gets through (despite out of date addresses), many prospective jurors will ignore the summons, knowing that the courts will never follow through on the threats to arrest them for failing to report.[30] Finally, the maintaining of a so-called "wheel" from which jurors can be called requires updating, replacement, and supplementation to maintain representativeness which is at best spotty. The result is that a substantial segment of the population is never touched by the possibility of jury duty.

The next major stage for filtering the jury pool is the request for excuses from jury duty. In a study of some 1346 citizens called for jury duty in New Jersey, Richert (1976) found that 49.8 percent wrote to the court in an effort to be excused from serving.[31] Of these excuses, 55.7 percent were for medical or personal hardship, 23.4 percent were work or financial hardships, and 5.6 percent for religious or philosophical conflict with the system of justice. Certain classes of people— clergy, police officers, doctors, and so on—can exercise an exemption from jury duty. Aliens, ex-felons, and the illiterate are usually disqualified. In general, excuses are easy to obtain and are rarely checked for their validity. In New Hampshire, jurors are selected by a screening panel that adjusts the schedules to suit people they know who have the time. The result is often a type of discretion in granting excuses that contributes a bias and nonrepresentativeness to the jury pool. Such biasing procedures have been successfully challenged during pretrial proceedings by the National Jury Project, with the result that changes in selection procedures were ordered by the court.

In the course of these suits an increasingly larger number of demographic variables have come in to use as tests for ensuring representativeness of the jury pool, the classification coming to be known as "cognizable classes."[32] A cognizable class has been variously defined as "economic, social, religious, racial, political and geographical classes of the community . . ." or as a category that distinguishes in jurors a different outlook on justice or juror's responsibility.

Although the courts have accepted race and sex as cognizable classes, there has been a tendency to react to any other basis for

[30] Van Dyke, J. op. cit.
[31] Richert, J. P. Jurors' attitudes toward jury service. *The Justice System Journal*, 1977, *38*, 233–45.
[32] Kairys, D. et al., op. cit., p. 10.

challenging the composition of juries by demanding proof that the legal attitudes of jurors differ significantly within that class. For example, one National Jury Project case involved a challenge to the makeup of the Grand Jury in Queens County, New York, where the critical problem of nonrepresentativeness was in the age of the grand jurors.[33] Only 5 percent of the grand jurors were under the age of 30 as compared to 27 percent of the general population in the county; 51 percent were over 60 years old as compared to the population's 19 percent. The petitioners had to collect data and prove (which they did) that older people and younger people have different attitudes about justice! This evidentiary battle involved extensive testimony by social scientists who were qualified to conduct and interpret the attitude studies. Because the courts are sensitive to attacks on the administrative procedures, social scientists are frequently challenged on the technical merits of the statistical arguments they make regarding jury composition.[34]

· *The Attitude Survey for Prediction.* Critics of systematic jury selection have pointed to the conduct of an attitude survey as an expensive and questionable undertaking, fraught with enormous logistical problems, doubts about generalizability, and patchwork tactics.[35] We agree. But this is true of any survey, and although a professional marketing survey firm could conduct a very sophisticated survey at very high cost, the real question remains about whether any effort of this magnitude is worthwhile. We would suggest that a well-conducted attitudinal survey on the population from which jurors are likely to be drawn can be a worthwhile investment when it is limited to a specific court district and focuses on general attitudes that are related to the juror's role.

It is quite true that many of the surveys conducted by members of the National Jury Project in political trials contained specific references to the trial at hand, but the bulk of the questions were repeated

[33] Faust, R., & Carlson, J. The impact of age and other stratification variables on attitudes toward justice, *Center Monograph No. CR-32,* 1977, Center for Responsive Psychology, Brooklyn College, Brooklyn, N.Y. 11210.

[34] For an extended and valuable discussion of the statistical problems involved in jury composition challenges, see DeCani, J. S. Statistical evidence in jury discrimination cases. *The Journal of Criminal Law & Criminology,* 1974, 65 (2), 234–238. For a cogent account of jury panel challenges on racial grounds in the deep south, see Farmer, M. C. Jury composition challenges. *Law and Psychology Review,* 1976, 2, 45–74.

[35] Bermant, J., & Sales, B. D. A critical evaluation of the systematic approach to jury selection, paper presented to the American Psychological Association, Washington, D.C., 1976.

from one trial to the next. Underlying the need to learn about the attitudes of potential jurors is the idea that people have a relatively stable theory of justice at any given point in their lives and that it can be evaluated by their answers to standard questions. Central to our conceptualization of this theory of justice is a measure of the degree of *authoritarianism*; a personality variable that has been studied by social psychologists since 1950.[36] The high authoritarian is not necessarily a Nazi storm trooper. In fact, authoritarianism is a personality syndrome or collection of traits that affect the way a person perceives the world. The common textbook definition includes the following: "rigid adherence to conventional values, concern for power and toughness in interpersonal relationships, and a tendency to shift responsibility for events with negative consequences away from the self and to project their causes onto forces beyond individual control."[37] Jurors as a group generally score moderately high on scales that measure authoritarianism and researchers have related high authoritarianism to punitiveness both in sentencing and verdict severity.[38] In our opinion, some degree of authoritarianism is a common syndrome in U.S. citizens and is a factor in the types of legal judgments that jurors will be asked to make.[39]

The National Jury Project empirically developed and checked the reliability of an authoritarianism scale that dwells on common beliefs about the law (Resource File No. 7). The combined score on this measure has proven to be one of the best predictors of conviction proneness we have encountered.[40] Research on the relationship between authoritarianism and punitiveness in sentencing and in voting

[36] Adorno, T. W., Frenkel-Brunswik, E., Levinson, D. J., & Sanford, R. N. *The Authoritarian Personality*, New York: Harper & Row, 1950.

[37] Shaver, K. G. *Principles of Social Psychology*, Cambridge, Mass.: Winthrop, 1977, p. 136.

[38] Rokeach, M., & Vidmar, N. Testimony concerning possible jury bias in a Black Panther murder trial. Unpublished Manuscript, 1973.

[39] Buckhout, R., et al. Jury without peers. In M. Reidel, and P. Vales (Eds.), *Treating the Offender: Problems and Issues*, New York: Praeger, 1977. Available as *Center Monograph No. CR-2*, 1973, Center for Responsive Psychology, Brooklyn College, Brooklyn, N.Y. 11210.

[40] Buckhout, R., & Baker, E., op. cit. In a study of the attitudes of seated jurors in the Supreme Court of Kings County, N.Y., the score derived from the authoritarianism score in Table 8.2 was significantly correlated with age ($r = 0.42$, $p < 0.001$ and negatively correlated with education ($r = -0.32$, $p < 0.01$). Those favoring the death penalty had significantly higher authoritarianism scores and supported statements against the Fifth Amendment and in favor of forcing defendants to take the witness stand. See also Mills, C. J. & Bohannon, W. E. Character structure and jury behavior, *Journal of Personality and Social Psychology*, 1980, 38, 662–667.

guilty is very consistent, highlighted by the tendency for highly authoritarian people to be strongly in favor of the death penalty.[41] We note also that authoritarianism tends to increase with age and to decrease as a person acquires more education.[42] This finding is exacerbated by the homogeneous nature of people in the jury pool who tend to be older and to average something less than a complete college education. As these more established people judge defendants who tend to be younger and poorer, there is evidence that the high authoritarians are more likely to dwell on the character and personality of the defendant rather than on the evidence.[43]

A useful jury selection questionnaire will thus consist of (1) items designed to measure authoritarianism, (2) attitude items that may be related to the type of cases, (3) extensive demographic questions going beyond those allowed in court,[44] and (4) some measure of conviction proneness. The last part poses a problem that several critics have noted because it suggests that a survey be made prior to every trial. They have in mind the example of the Joan Little trial,[45] where prospective jurors were asked directly if they believed that the defendant was guilty. A more realistic approach is to ask general questions about the guilt of those arrested in different classes of crimes. (e.g., "How likely is it—on a scale from one to ten—that a person arrested for selling drugs is guilty?"). Because answers vary in the *degree of guilt*, the social scientist can show statistically who in the sample group tended to be high or low in conviction proneness and provide a profile of the ideal defense or prosecution juror. The mechanics of this process can be seen in the following case study.

CASE REPORT 8.1 U.S. v. Swinton: Selecting the Jury[46]

Patricia Swinton was another fugitive, in the year 1975, in deep trouble as the defendant in a case of conspiracy and bombing buildings which caused injuries. The bombings were touted as a political act by a friend (Jane Alpert) and by her former boyfriend, who had confessed to the same crimes and had served time in jail. As excerpts from the publicity material suggest, Pat Swinton had been a mere cog in a complex case,

---

[41] Ibid. Because of the statistical complexity, we have placed the details of test development in Resource File 7.

[42] Ibid.

[43] Berg, K., & Vidmar, N. Authoritarianism and recall of evidence about criminal behavior. *Journal of Research in Personality*, 1975, 9, 147–157.

[44] A full text of a typical jury selection questionnaire can be found in Resources File No. 6. It may be copied for use in research or education.

[45] McConahay et al., op. cit. Most of the surveys conducted in the early phases to support motions to quash the grand jury and to change venue of necessity were specific to the case. The data were then used as the basis for shaping *voir dire* questions and for determining priorities in the exercise of challenges.

but by making loud public statements she became a public figure of some note in the New York area. Behind the scene in the courtroom was a lineup of activists who formed a defense committee to raise money for Pat Swinton's defense—renaming her SHOSHANA. Arrayed against this group were U.S. attorneys and a federal judge (Justice Seymour Pollack), who had been involved in previous cases and who had to answer to public opinion about who was to be punished for bombing buildings. Although this trial did not attract the national publicity of *U.S.* v. *Daniel Ellsberg,* all participants felt very much like they were in the spotlight of newspapers and television networks.

Members of the "SHOSHANA" defense committee approached the National Jury Project, asking us to apply the techniques of scientific jury selection during the trial which was slated for the U.S. Federal Court, Southern District of New York encompassing Manhattan, the Bronx, Westchester, and Putnam County. Working with limited resources we put together a survey instrument and selected a sample of home telephone numbers from the relevant directories.[47] Consultation with the defense attorneys and the members of the committee convinced us to structure the survey in the following way.

Part I consisted of eight items of an *authoritarianism* scale which we had previously developed and found to be useful in predicting verdict tendencies in jurors. Part II consisted of items seeking the degree of endorsement of various forms of political protest from writing to congressmen and women to bombing buildings. We called the factor *political expediency.* Part III consisted of various questions measuring conviction proneness including an item requesting a "degree of guilt" response to the prison inmates in the Attica case. Part IV consisted of an elaborate set of demographic questions similar to the common types of questions used in a *voir dire.* The purpose of the survey was to measure the strength of the first two attitude factors

[46] Buckhout, R. *U.S.* v. *Swinton*: A case history of jury selection. *Social Action and the Law*, 1978, *4* (4), 27–29. The case was tried in the U.S. Federal Court, Southern District of New York, in October 1976. The account of the Swinton trial can be compared with the very fine documentary account of jury selection in the case of former Attorney General John Mitchell which was conducted in the same court district. See Zeisel, H., & Diamond, S. S. The jury selection in the Mitchell-Stans conspiracy trial. *American Bar Foundation Research Journal*, 1976, *1* (1), 151–174.

[47] Ideally, a survey researcher would seek a random sample of the population and, again ideally, a fully randomized list of in-service phone numbers would be one of the best ways to assure an unbiased sample. However, phone numbers in Manhattan pose problems in the form of ever-changing business listings, phone machines, not-at-home, and so on. Trained interviewers made calls on a random basis, asking for the registered voter according to a plan that took age and sex into account.

among voters (potential jurors) in the Eastern District and to produce a profile of the most desirable and least desirable juror to aid in the use of challenges by the defense attorneys. The complex statistical analysis included factor analysis, multiple regression, and automatic interaction detection analysis.[48] The resulting profile told us that the worst possible juror would be Catholic, over 40, white collar, and a reader of the *New York Daily News*. The best would be a nonreligious, under 40, educated male from Manhattan who read the *Times* (none in this category appeared for jury duty).

In most federal courtrooms the judge asks all the questions of the jurors. Information comes in fast and it is up to the attorneys to determine quickly whom they do *not* want. That is, both sides have a fixed number of peremptory challenges that can be exercised to strike jurors from the panel. If any evidence of prejudice emerges during questioning, a challenge for cause can be brought which is ruled on by the judge. The survey data and resulting profiles were used to set up a priority list of jurors whose demographic profiles made them clearly unsuitable and worth challenging. A second group was declared suspect and was made the subject of further scrutiny or challenges for cause.

On the day set for jury selection we assembled a team of observers armed with checklists (see Resource File No. 8) set up for each factor. As information came in from questioning (done by the judge), the observer would check the sheet and assign a score for the political expediency factor and another person would calculate the score for the authoritarianism factor. One psychologist, using his subjective judgment based on appearance, body language, and social interactions with other jurors, assigned a numerical score to each juror independently from the other two factor scores. A brief conference permitted the addition of the three scores and the ultimate ranking of each juror according to his or her favorability. The trial attorneys made the final choices armed with the data from the team, which is summarized in Table 8.2. High positive scores were favorable to the defense.

[48] The statistical analysis was done by formatting and programming the data for SPSS and OSIRIS analysis. A principle components factor analysis was performed which yielded two main factors. Factor one—"political expediency"—had an eigenvalue of 3.59. Respondents who scored high on this factor were unfavorable jurors to the defense because they showed strong disagreement with the tactics of political protest. Factor two with an eigenvalue of 1.95 was authoritarianism. The factors were rotated to achieve simple structure (varimax criterion). Factor scores were computed for each person and then analyzed on the AID (Automatic Interaction Detection) analysis program. The resulting maps showing demographic breakdowns of both factor scores are presented in Resource File No. 7. See also Brams, S. J., & Davis, M. D. A game-theory approach to jury selection. *Trial*, 1976, *14*, (December), 47–49.

Table 8.2 SUMMARY OF IN-COURT SCORES[a] AND
DISPOSITION OF JURORS IN *U.S.* v. *SWINTON*

SOURCE	POLITICAL SCORE	AUTHORITARIAN SCORE	SUBJECT EVALUATION	TOTAL
Selected jurors	−0.33	0	+0.92	+0.20
Alternate jurors	−1.75	−2.00	−1.75	−1.83
Removed by U.S.	+0.57	+0.43	+1.57	+0.85
Removed by defense	−1.59	−0.36	−0.54	−0.83
Total jury panel (Average)	−3.10	−1.94	+0.20	−1.63

[a] Scores range from −3 to +3

Naturally, even though we looked for low authoritarians and people who were not offended by political expediency, few highly favorable jurors even showed up at the courthouse. The average scores for the jury pool were the low (unfavorable) end, meaning that they all tended to look alike. The numerical ratings became useful and proved to be reliable in that the selected jurors had "better" scores than those jurors who were left over, excused, or challenged by the defense. For the most part we chose jurors or exercised challenges in keeping with our factor scores, except for one juror chosen on the basis of subjective ratings. In the absence of ideal jurors our detailed profiles from the computer analysis gave us a range of second best, third best alternatives, and so on. These are, of course, *inferences* about the juror's factor scores predicted from the known demographic data.

The trial of Patricia Swinton took five days followed by 11 hours of deliberation by the jury. Then, to the cheers of a partisan audience, the jury returned a verdict of NOT GUILTY. As a final postscript, some of the jurors showed up at a loud victory party staged by friends of the defendant and filled in some of the details for us. They confirmed that at least two of the jurors who had the highest authoritarian scores were the two who held out for conviction. After they were persuaded to vote with the majority for acquittal, the jurors engaged in an act that vindicated our feeling that we had selected a fairly open-minded group of people. After sealing the verdict that indicated their agreement that the government had not met the burden of proof of guilt, the jurors voted informally about how they *really* felt about the defendant. The informal vote was 10 to 2 favoring the idea that the defendant had done *something*.

CONDUCT OF THE VOIR DIRE

In those courtrooms where the attorneys conduct the *voir dire* on prospective jurors, the ultimate screening and selecting of jurors takes place. The trend in court administration is to shorten the *voir dire* process—usually to save time by having the judge ask standard questions. The experience of the National Jury Project was that the social scientist could aid the attorney in conducting a *voir dire* to yield the kind of meaningful information that could facilitate the use of challenges. As a general rule, we argued for an expanded *voir dire* and an increase in the number of challenges. The requests would run counter to those who saw the *voir dire* mainly as a mechanism for socializing or presensitizing the prospective juror to the case.

Clearly, the *voir dire* is the phase of the trial when all efforts expended in systematic jury selection can finally be put to work. Our main role as social scientists has been to rate each prospective juror on the main factors and to provide a numerical rating of favorability (or rank order) to the attorney. Two examples of the in-court rating forms are shown in the Resource File No. 8. We have found that multiple observers are better—each rating a certain number of jurors on a single factor. This maximizes reliability and prevents the social scientists from trying to play lawyer. Although some writers have described the attempts to include systematically ratings of the body language of the jurors, the approach has some very real limitations.

Most of quality research on non-verbal behavior has been done in a setting where through the use of film records and/or multiple observers, carefully timed observations of posture, clothing, movements, facial expressions, and vocal tone could be analyzed in reference to the context of the events and other people in the setting.[49] It is indeed tempting when we think of the strong pressures on the juror to respond to the strong social demands of speaking about him or herself and his or her beliefs in the formal, public setting of a courtroom. Research and experience convince us that a person will be less candid—will try to project a socially worthwhile image. If the prospective juror is lying, we can presumably detect "leakages" of his or her true feelings which, according to some researchers, can be seen in certain gestures. But the *voir dire* hearing moves very fast and we know that success at doing a "cold reading" of a stranger requires experience. It is very doubtful that inexperienced social scientists can add much to the ability of experienced trial attorneys to "read" jurors. They are in the position of having left their tools at home. On the other hand, when

[49] Alker, H. R., Hosticka, C., & Mitchell, M., Jury selection as a biased social process. *Law & Society Review*, 1976, *11* (1), 9–41; Alker, H. R., & Barnard, J. J. Procedural and social biases in the jury selection process. *The Justice System Journal*, 1978, *3* (3), 220–241. The last article is a very useful guide to the researcher in how to test for and report on goodness-of-fit problems in comparing ideal to real representativeness in jury pools.

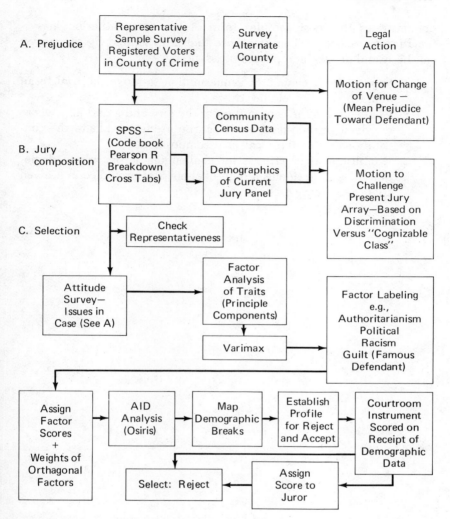

Figure 8.4   Data flow in Scientific Jury Selection.

the *voir dire* is conducted rapidly by the judge, the numerical ratings provided by social scientists can be of some value.

SUMMARY

To summarize, we find that the unique contribution of the social scientists attached to the National Jury Project has been in developing and using sampling surveys to ascertain the law-related attitudes of potential jurors in the community in which they work. Figure 8.4

demonstrates the most complex form of the data gathering in systematic jury selection. The data base that is generated by the survey can be useful at all three phases of advocacy.

1. Support for a change of venue motion to move the trial to an area where less prejudice exists.
2. Challenges to the composition of the jury and grand jury where the demographic data alone can be used to evaluate the constitutionality of the local jury composition.
3. Establishment of criteria for challenging jurors whose demographic profile signals a high likelihood of prejudice in a given trial (See Figure 8.4).

THE SOCIAL SCIENTIST AS EXPERT
ADVISOR IN THE LEGAL SETTING

"They are everywhere!" "They're everywhere!" To hear some lawyers tell it, social scientists are showing up in virtually all areas affected by the law. Welcomed by some and scorned by others, the social scientist more often than not is going to function as advisor or consultant rather than having any direct responsibility. Those social scientists who do consult are transitional persons, creating roles for themselves and establishing cross-disciplinary links with the legal and judicial professions in an increasing variety of areas. In this section we shall examine the role of the social scientist as an expert witness in court. To focus on this role will permit the closer study of two key questions— (1) What are the ground rules (ethically and scientifically) to which social scientists should adhere in offering their expertise? (2) What can a social scientist really add that is different, valuable, or worth listening to.

LOOKING INWARD

To answer the first question the psychological profession addresses itself to the issue in a long in-house memorandum in 1978 in an effort to recommend modifications to the ethical standards of the profession, reflecting the increasing involvement of psychologists in the criminal justice system.[1] The scope of the committee's concern can be ascertained from the following excerpt from the introduction to their findings.

> Psychologists are involved in virtually every facet of the criminal justice system. When a person is arrested, it may well be by a police officer who was screened by a psychologist before being hired, and trained by other psychologists in ways of handling such potentially hazardous situations as an arrest. Should the police officer use undue force or poor judgment in effecting the arrest, the officer may be sent to the department's psychologist for treatment.
>
> The defendant then may be evaluated by a psychologist to determine if he or she is competent to stand trial before a jury that other psychologists are in the process of selecting. If competent, the defendant may be examined by a psychologist to determine whether he or she was insane at the time of the offense and so should be sent to a mental hospital for psychological treatment. At the trial, eyewitnesses to the crime may have their perception and memory challenged by a psychological expert. If judged guilty, the fate of the convicted offender may rest in part on what a psychologist recommends to the judge in a pre-sentence evaluation.
>
> Should the offender be sent to prison, he or she may be classified by one psychologist for the purpose of being treated by another, and the treatment may not end until a third psychologist predicts that the offender can be released into society without risk of recidivism. Remaining free on parole may be contingent upon attendance at outpatient psychotherapy.[2]

Such involvement creates an ethical quandary in which psychologists with their skills and values may find themselves at odds with the values and ethical standards of the organization with which they are consulting or even working in. Should they be disloyal to the agency (e.g., a police force) and inform the world of some easily documented racist practice or should they protect the agency on the grounds of confidentiality? Should psychologists (or indeed can they) guarantee confidentiality to an individual client in the total institutions that are common in the criminal justice system? If psychologists get too close in to the criminal justice agency, is it inevitable that they will be co-opted? Does this risk of co-optation, excessive identification, and outright advocacy invariably mean that social scientists will cease to be trusted objective scientists (or clinicians) by their own profession? The

---

[1] Monahan, J. (Ed.), Report of the task force on the role of psychology in the criminal justice system. American Psychological Association, February 1978 (In-House Memorandum). See also, Monahan, J., (Ed.), *Who is the Client?*, Washington, D.C.: American Psychological Association, 1980.

[2] Ibid, p. 1.

attempts by the psychological task force to answer these and other questions led to a set of recommendations that are summarized in the Resources File.[3]

The anguish displayed by the writers of the report reflect the fact that the legal setting will encounter at least two basically different types of social science trained individuals. The older group, made up of those who are employed full time in the corrections, psychiatric hospital, and social welfare agency fields have a track record already established for both professional input and ethics. If history is any guide, anyone employed and paid full time by a criminal justice agency has already been co-opted and has come to grips with the dilemmas of loyalty and values. Our focus in this section will be instead on those psychologists who are basically tied to academic or research institutions and who have been loaning their skills and expertise to the legal profession or are contemplating doing so in an ever-increasing variety of areas. The clash of values and even basic styles of thinking is inevitable. The results of the clash can be frustrating and rewarding, as both authors of this book have had the opportunity to discover.

THE LANGUAGE BARRIER

We acknowledge at the outset that few of the many thousands of trained social scientists in the United States have received the kind of relevant training that would suit them for work in the applied setting such as the criminal justice system. The lawyer learns one language; the social scientist learns another. The topic may be the same—the behavior of people; but the two-discipline approach the topic from different perspectives. Professor Paul Meehl, a distinguished clinical psychologist, refers to the lawyer's brand of psychology as "fireside induction."

> by fireside inductions, I mean those commonsense empirical generalizations about human behavior that we accept on the culture's authority plus introspection plus anecdotal evidence from ordinary life . . . designating what people believe about human conduct, about how it is to be described, explained, predicted and controlled.[4]

We have also encountered other versions of this "theory" in what psychologists refer to as "naïve psychology" or even as *paleologic*.[5]

[3] See Law and Psychology Resources File No. 9.
[4] Meehl, P. E. Law and the fireside induction. In J. L. Tapp, and F. J. Levine (Eds.), *Law Justice and the Individual in Society*. New York: Holt, Rinehart and Winston, 1977, pp. 10–28. See also Meehl, P. E. Psychology and the criminal law. *University of Richmond Law Review*, 1970, 5, 1–30.
[5] See the discussion of naïve psychology in Chapter 1. See also a description of paleologic in Chapter 12 in the discussion of capital punishment.

Professor Meehl is, of course, skeptical of fireside inductions, preferring as a matter of his own training to lean on quantitative documentary research or systematic experimentation to test out generalizations about human behavior. But as one of the social scientists who has crossed the line to work effectively with lawyers and the courts, he has become aware of the limitations of both approaches as well as their strengths.

Social scientists favor the experimental approach, where the variables are under the control of the experimenter and extraneous influences can be controlled. Such conditions favor the *reliability* of a statement of causality because, at least in theory, if the exact conditions are duplicated somewhere else, the same outcome of the experiment can be reasonably expected. Scientists share a common socialization into the world of methodology and implicitly trust the published statements of their colleagues unless other evidence dictates a cessation of that trust. Thus a published laboratory study tends to carry a great deal of weight among scientists and may be relied on by the social scientist who is asked for his or her opinion in court or by a legislative committee. The expert imparts his or her knowledge of the details of that published experiment which may be a highly sophisticated statistical research design producing many qualifying statements about the meaning of the results.

Of course, even a brilliantly conducted experiment may cover such a narrow range of human behavior that a gap develops between the results of the experiment and the real-life problem for which questions are being directed toward the social scientist. For example, much of what social scientists know about the effects of punishment on behavior has been accumulated from thousands of studies conducted on rats. How much of these findings can be generalized to the human condition? This may sound like a hostile question to the social scientist, but it is in fact a very fair question as the lawyer seeks to question, debate, and possibly undermine the logical basis of the proposition being put forward by the expert. The social scientist who cannot cope with that question has failed to come to grips with the fundamental problems of *validity* which is relevant to any kind of research method.

THE RELIGIOUS STRUGGLE

Professor B. F. Skinner once stated, as a basic law for research, that any gain in control is paid for by a loss of flexibility.[6] What this means is that a good researcher who seeks to narrow down his or her experiment to the point where only one variable is causally related to

---

[6] Skinner, B. F. *The Cumulative Record*. New York: Appleton, Crofts, 1960.

another (e.g., amount of electric shock influences amount of aggressive behavior) may produce elegant data that cannot be generalized to the real world. Although such studies contribute a great deal to the development of theory within the discipline, the demand for validity is that the experimental results have something to say about violent behavior in human beings. However, most basic researchers are not motivated to meet the validity demands of the real world, preferring to sharpen up on techniques, theory, and methodology in an attempt to produce reliable results. Hence the expert is constrained to qualify the presentation of results by carefully stating the limitations of the data from the original research. Thus in an area such as research on violent behavior, the social science expert must qualify his or her testimony with some or all of the following.

1. Theories of violent behavior depend heavily on animal research, justified on the grounds of some anatomical and evolutionary relationships to people.
2. Experiments with humans have involved the behavior of children or college students with the liberal use of deception and simulation.
3. Ethical constraints have prohibited social scientists from doing experimental research on the levels of violence encountered by victims of crime.
4. Several theories exist of what causes violent behavior among people; my research and experience lead me to lean toward theory "X."

Compare this to the fireside induction among some law enforcement officials who argue that violent behavior comes from bad people. As Professor Meehl points out, the psychologist tends to look at the research on punishment and conclude that it is not an effective technique for controlling behavior, whereas the fireside induction is stating that of course punishment works.[7] The clash ostensibly has common sense pitted against hard data from the laboratory. In reality it is a clash of *faith*. The social scientist cannot duplicate the world of crime in a laboratory; the lawyer has no special access to proving his or her assertion. Yet major decisions affecting laws, judge and jury decisions, and the building of prisons to punish criminals, rest on conclusions about violent human behavior. We must recognize that fireside inductions have been around a lot longer than psychologists and have been the basis for social policy decisions affecting the control of criminal and/or violent behavior. The social scientist is a newcomer and must be ready to prove to a skeptical audience that his or her unusual perspective is, at least in some instances, better than common wisdom.

[7] Meehl, P., op. cit.

The two types of thinking most often clash when there is confusion over whether you are talking about statistical norms in society or about the individual. The social scientist may be convinced that the data say that the threat of punishment will not deter crime.[8] Lawyers or police officers, relying on common sense, would not want to abandon their belief that the threat of swift and certain retaliation would cause any would-be killer to hesitate. Arguments such as this could do with a little more understanding by the social scientist as Professor Meehl illustrates:

> (Drug) Peddlers have a solid conviction, amounting to a subjective certainty, that if, they are known or strongly suspected to have turned stool pigeon, they will be killed by the organized narcotics underworld. Why as a psychologist should I dismiss this kind of evidence as worthless because it is not "scientific" but merely anecdotal?[9]

The data-oriented approach of the social scientist can help in areas that are immune to fireside inductions or where the commonsense approach has clearly failed. The vision of some social scientists such as Campbell[10] is to have institutions themselves conducting social experiments and collecting data. In this way, truly relevant data might supplant the speculations of both the expert social scientist and the more anecdotal attorney.

THE PSYCHIATRIC CONNECTION

Before discussing the role of psychologists in the giving of expert testimony, we should note that the only reason psychologists have ever been permitted to testify was due to efforts by the American Psychiatric Association to exclude psychologists from the courtroom.[11] Prior to 1962 the legal status of psychologists in the courtroom was very uncertain; sociologists and other social scientists were seldom seen except as they might be quoted in cases argued before the appellate

[8] In this case the ideal never exists. The social scientist looks at fragmentary data that only support the null hypothesis—for example, the rate of executions is not related to the murder rate. The cop works in a system where the probability of being caught, convicted, or punished is low.

[9] Meehl, P., op. cit.

[10] Campbell, D. T. Legal reforms as experiments. *Journal of Legal Education*, 1971, *23*, 217–239.

[11] Perlin, M. L. The legal status of the psychologist in the courtroom. Paper presented to the American Psychological Association Meetings, Washington, D.C., September 1976; Ennis, B. J., & Litwack, T. R. Psychiatry and the presumption of expertise: Flipping coins in the courtroom. *California Law Review*, 1974, *62* (3), 693–752; Bazelon, D. L. Psychiatrists and the adversary process. *Scientific American*, 1974, *230* (6), 18–23; Bartholomew, A. A., Badger, P., & Milte, K. L. The psychologist as expert witness in the criminal courts. *Australian Psychologist*, 1977, *12* (2), 133–150; Moskowitz, M. J. Hugo Munsterberg: A study in the history of applied psychology. *American Psychologist*, 1977, *32* (10), 824–842.

courts. In the landmark case, *Jenkins* v. *United States*, the Court of Appeals (under Judge David L. Bazelon) ruled that the trial judge was in error in excluding a psychologist's testimony when the judge stated that a psychologist was not qualified to give a "medical" opinion as to a medical disease or defect.[12]

The American Psychiatric Association, reflecting the guild mentality common to many professions, had argued in an *amicus curiae* brief to the court that, in contrast to the medically trained psychiatrists, a psychologist was a mere layman; a test giver who is ancillary to medical doctors. Judge Bazelon, writing for the majority, ruled that "*some* psychologists are qualified to render expert testimony in the field of mental disorder."[13] Some judges noted that psychiatrists already depend on the results of tests given by psychologists to base their own diagnosis. The *Jenkins* decision opened the door for psychologists to testify by removing legal obstacles, but the language of the dissenters and the psychiatrists lingers on to this day. Justice Burger (Chief Justice of the Supreme Court in 1977) reacted to the *Jenkins* decision with an all too familiar litany:

> psychology is at best an infant science . . . psychiatry and psychology cannot claim to be truly scientific and that some psychiatrists and psychologists may be claiming too much in relation to what they really understood about the human personality and human behavior.[14]

Subsequent decisions affirmed the place of a psychologist in court but the controversy over the status of psychology as a science still produces sharp reactions from some judges and lawyers. In light of more recent attacks on the general lack of reliability and validity in the predictions of psychiatrists, any social science scientist can expect a rough time as an expert witness in court.[15]

EXPERT TESTIMONY BY SOCIAL SCIENTISTS

Whereas the psychiatrist and the clinical psychologist have been accepted in the courts of the United States, it is a rarer event for the social scientist to give testimony in criminal trials. The social scientist

[12] *Jenkins* v. *United States,* 307 F. 2d 637, 651, 652 (D.C. Cir. 1961) (Bastian, J. dissenting). See also *U.S.* v. *Green,* 373 F. Supp. 149 158 (E.D. pa. 1974); *Blunt* v. *U.S.,* 389 F. 2d 545, 547 (D.C. Cir. 1967); *People* v. *Lyles,* 526 P. 2d 1332, 1334–1335 (Colo. Supp. Ct. 1974). For extended case discussion see Pacht, et al. The current status of the psychologist as an expert witness. *Professional Psychology,* 1973, 4, 409.

[13] *Jenkins* v. *United States,* op. cit.

[14] Burger, W. Psychiatrists, lawyers and the courts. 28 *Federal Probation,* 1967, 3, 7.

[15] Ennis, B. J., & Litwack, T. R. Psychiatry and the presumption of expertise: Flipping coins in the courtroom. *California Law Review,* 1974, 62 (3), 693–752.

will be called on to give testimony about research, experience, writings and readings in his or her special area. Although the social scientist may offer general conclusions of his or her research, he or she is usually not asked to give a specific opinion on the main issue before the judge or jury. Rather, he or she is asked to give the type of background information based on his or her research that will *aid* the trier of fact in reaching a decision.

Professor Marvin Wolfgang, perhaps the leading criminologist in the United States, made this distinction clearly in an article he wrote about his experiences as an expert witness, presenting his research data to courts in the South, where the main issue was whether or not there existed a pattern of discrimination in the administration of the death penalty in rape cases.[16] As an objective scientist, Wolfgang faced the dilemma of being asked by one side of the adversary process to testify. Fortunately, the dilemma was moderated by the fact that the conclusions of the elegantly designed surveys had yielded data that his employer (the NAACP Legal Defense Fund) felt supported their legal position and their values. Briefly, Professor Wolfgang had demonstrated that "Black defendants whose (rape) victims were white were sentenced to death eighteen times more frequently than defendants in any other racial combination of defendant or victim." Although Professor Wolfgang shared the social goals of the Legal Defense Fund, he writes that he still had to assert his own standards of scientific caution on what he testified to lest he compromise his own credibility and merely be perceived in the court as an advocate with an ideological axe to grind.

> It is my belief then and it is my continued belief, that by exercising scientific caution in the style of expressing research findings, the social scientist retains his integrity as a scientist, and, at the same time, can produce compelling, persuasive, convincing and rigorous testimony as an expert witness.[17]

Professor Wolfgang goes on to describe in realistic terms just what the language gap can produce between lawyers and social scientists. As an expert witness (usually before a judge) he is providing the research information in which statistically significant *differences* become evidence for the court to consider in rendering a legal, social, or

---

[16] Wolfgang, M. E. The social scientist in court. *The Journal of Criminal Law and Criminology*, 1974, 65 (2), 239–247. See also Meltsner, M. *Cruel and Unusual: The Supreme Court and Capital Punishment.* New York: Morrow Paperback, 1973; Remer, L. Criminologist for the defense. *Human Behavior*, December 1977, 57–59. Woocher, F. D. Did your eyes deceive you? Expert psychological testimony on the unreliability of eyewitness identifications. *Stanford Law Review*, 1977, 29 (5), 969–1030.

[17] Wolfgang, M. E., op. cit.

political decision. The probalistic interpretation of data that is the stock in trade of the social scientist cannot be compromised under pressure from the court which might prefer to hear a more direct expression of opinion on the political decision. The differences in sentencing blacks to death for rape existed; but the critical leap to deciding whether this difference resulted from discriminatory practices in the courts or by juries would remain a political or legal decision. Although it might be vexing for social scientists to have to resort to statistics to buttress an obvious conclusion, statistical analysis remains their strongest claim to expertise whereas legal conclusions are beyond their competence—as expert witnesses in court.

In much of the article Wolfgang describes the vital process of rehearsing the expert witness for his or her presentation of testimony. Consistent with a growing body of literature on the topic,[18,19] the coaching of the social scientist is crucial for both the scientist and the lawyers who will ask the questions. Because the two professions speak different languages about the same subject matter, the social scientist has to be prepared for an attack in cross-examination which will probably be directed at (1) any hint of personal bias, (2) the expert witness fee, (3) his or her ego, (4) the immaturity or vagueness of the discipline, and (5) serious questions about the reliability and validity of the conclusions. The junior author, testifying about survey research in the (to him) strange state of South Dakota, was asked to give the mileage distances between cities in the state. Social scientists have to be trained to respond cooly to the attack style of cross-examination— which in the rules of the game of adversary proceedings is designed to minimize the impact of any testimony or to denigrate the witness who presents it. Any statement that has been previously published or uttered in court by the expert may be introduced by opposing counsel in an effort to impeach his or her testimony. Numerous articles have been written on how to prepare an expert witness as well as how to demolish one on the stand.[20] Wolfgang's research contributions became the basis for the successful attack on the use of the death penalty in rape cases thanks to his effective performance as an expert witness, which greatly aided the fine litigation work of the NAACP Legal Defense Fund.[21]

[18] Jackson, T. P. Presenting expert testimony. *Trial*, Winter 1975, 41–44.
[19] Brodsky, S. I. The mental health professional on the witness stand: A survival guide. In B. D. Sales (Ed.), *Psychology in the legal process*. New York: Spectrum, 1977.
[20] Ziskin, J. *Coping with Psychiatric and Psychological Testimony*, 2d ed., Beverly Hills, Calif.: Law and Psychology Press, 1975.
[21] See a more specific discussion of social science inputs to death penalty trials in Chapter 12.

PRESENTING A SOCIAL SCIENCE PERSPECTIVE

Although there are numerous occasions in court where specific research data from the social sciences are appropriate, there are also issues where both the law and the research have not yet come to grips with an agreed on answer. In many respects the input of the social scientists to the landmark Supreme Court decision in *Brown* v. *Board of Education* (1954) was more of the social science perspective rather than hard data.[22] Building from specific experiments, generalizing to the institutions in which inequalities exist, the social scientists described what in their view a segregated education could do to children. In a similar vein Professor Michael Saks, finding himself on a legislative subcommittee dealing with the issue of policies affecting organ and tissue transplants, found that as a social psychologist he was able to contribute a perspective about the decision making and education of potential donors from a research perspective which had never occurred to the other legal and medically oriented members.[23]

The senior author, serving as a consultant to the defense committee of the celebrated case of *People of the State of North Carolina* v. *Joan Little*, found herself in a similar role when the lawyers tried to present a different perspective on the basic facts of the case.[24] The basic fact pattern concerned the incident in which the defendant was allegedly forced to commit oral sodomy on a guard while she was in jail. She subsequently grabbed an ice pick and stabbed the jailer repeatedly and escaped. Ellison's account of her role as an expert is excerpted below. In essence, her task became one of educating the defense lawyers and then the court on a social scientist's perspective of how the behavior of the defendant might be interpreted in the context of what is known about a total institution.

In Court re Joan Little

Racism and sexism were the themes of the fund-raising campaign, but, with the exception of the jury selection project, the defense strategy in the Joan Little case differed very little from that of any other murder case. The social issues were being largely ignored. So when my name was suggested to the defense team as a psychologist knowledgeable about rape, the first idea was to use me in traditional ways: to testify about the "mental state" of the defendant. But I am not a clinician;

22 *Brown* v. *Board of Education of Topeka et al.*, 349 U.S. (1954). See text in Resource File No. 16.
23 Saks, M. Social psychological contributions to a legislative subcommittee on organ and tissue transplants. *American Psychologist*, 1978, 33 (7), 680–690.
24 Ellison, K. W. Psychologist in court: Testimony on rape in the Joan Little trial. *Social Action and the Law*, 1975, 2 (6), 5.

even if I were, I have seen too many cases where defense and prosecution have "experts" in behavior presenting contradictory findings (and, too often, alas, making fools of themselves) to feel this was a viable role for me.

Rather, I saw as my most important potential contribution the education of the defense team, and, we hoped, the court, about the relevance of some of the social issues. As I talked with attorney Karen Galloway, we came to define the primary issue within my sphere of expertise as the question of control.

Control is the vital factor which differentiates consensual sex from rape, as giving money away gladly is differentiated from robbery. The purpose of a total institution, such as a prison, is to deprive the inmate of control and vest it in the staff. Society has recognized the dangers inherent in some such situations of unequal power, and considered any sexual relations within them to be statutory rape. Using the same rationale, any sex between staff and inmates in a total institution must be seen as rape; indeed, some states include such situations in the definition of statutory rape. Free, informed consent is impossible. The inmate subjected to sex with a staff member, then, can be expected to display the crisis reactions found in all victims of forcible rape.

Given this introduction, the majority of the hypothetical questions Galloway prepared for my testimony were to address the findings of my work and that of others in the field that a person in crisis cannot be expected to act rationally or to perceive veridically. In this light, Joan Little's testimony about her behavior when confronted with a demand for sex was not inconsistent with the behavior of a rape victim.

Expert testimony, however, can be a two-edged sword. I warned Galloway that, under astute cross-examination, I would have to testify that the dead guard was not the "typical" rapist, nor could I testify that Little could not have been lying. The problem, however, never arose. Shortly after I began to testify, the prosecution objected, the jury was excused, a *voir dire* conducted, and the judge ruled that "this is a relatively new field" and he "[knew] of no North Carolina law admitting it into evidence." I was excused.

Was my appearance totally useless? I think not. The testimony was heard by the court, the spectators, and through the press, some of it reached the public. The judge incorporated some of my analysis in his charge to the jury. Perhaps to some extent the stage has been set, and the next judge will feel less need for caution. (I had presented similar testimony which was accepted in a military court martial earlier in the year, the first time anyone could find that an expert witness had been used in this way.) Finally, Karen Galloway, in the summation called the best of the trial by the press, dealt in vivid detail with the larger political issues, one of which involved the responsibility of authority in situations of unequal power and control.

And so Joan Little was acquitted. The decision was made, however, not on the political issues, but on the technicality of a poor investigation by the state. The decision freed the defendant, but made no statement about the rights of other prisoners, or blacks or women.

PRESENTING SCIENTIFIC TESTIMONY ON HUMAN PERCEPTION

This section reflects to a great extent the personal experiences of the junior author in acting as an expert witness on the psychology of eyewitness testimony.[25] Let us face it, psychologists do threaten. Merely to take the results of modern-day perception research seriously is to threaten the very basic nature of one's beliefs in a stable world. When our work remains buried in the laboratories and journals it offends no one—threatens no institution. When any psychologist stands up before a jury to tell its members that eyewitness testimony may be unreliable, that psychologist may threaten the juror's way of perceiving the world. When the psychologist previews this testimony for a judge, the thrust of that perception research threatens a basic philosophical premise on which evidence is presented in a courtroom.

That philosophical premise, usually referred to as "common sense" by a judge, is an epistemology that depends on convincing yourself that the brain is a tape recorder or copying machine. This is a comfortable modern metaphor based on fireside induction which leads to a largely erroneous model of how memory works.

Every piece of information that has been experienced by the senses is thought to be stored somewhere inside the copying machine. The faltering witness who cannot remember, simply has a "defective copying machine." The glib witness who tells a very complete story is thought to be possessed with a superior copying machine. The psychologist comes in and says that most human beings have perceptual limits in a crime situation. He or she rejects the copying machine theory. He may go on to say that if the conditions that prevailed in the crime before the court were tested, most witnesses would not be able to remember much of anything or be able later to identify anybody who was at the crime scene. Any psychologist who tells it like it is from his or her scientific point of view can expect to run into trouble, because comfortable metaphors abound in legal institutions.

Any psychologist who goes into court expecting to be loved will be disappointed. Like any other expert, he or she can be characterized as an enemy of common sense. Medical doctors have a license to be an enemy of common sense; to question our logic, to challenge our habits and beliefs, and to call us fools if, in their opinion, we are

[25] Buckhout, R. Nobody likes a smartass: Expert testimony by psychologists. *Social Action and the Law*, 1976, 3 (4), 41–50.

taking liberties with our own health. Accordingly, experts with an M.D. in front of their names usually have no trouble being qualified as experts in the courtroom. Psychologists—would-be experts in human behavior which, of course, everybody studies for a living—in nearly all cases will have to prove themselves. A simple case in point is attribution research.[26] Many of the attribution studies in the literature use examples from the courtroom. Courts and their officers and juries have been making attributions for centuries. A psychologist who comes in as a scientist to explain attribution to a court, will have a hard time proving that his research is any better or more scientific than the accumulated experience (common sense) of the people in court.

In 1977 the spectacle of the testimony of the psychologists and psychiatrists in the Patty Hearst trial created a new horror story in legal circles to bedevil any psychologist who wishes to testify in the future. Thanks to an overly permissive judge and several ego-tripping professionals, the entire country witnessed the worst kind of expert testimony—the doctor as God syndrome—highlighted by two experts who claimed to be truth or lie detectors. Whatever may be the merits of their testimony, these analysts of Patty Hearst's veracity seriously damaged the reputation of psychologists among legal people. A psychological expert offering scientific data in order to aid the jury in evaluating eyewitness identifications may well have to explain how he or she is different from the "experts" who dominated the Hearst trial.

Role of a Psychologist in Court

An effective role of a psychologist (especially a research scientist) as an expert is really rather limited, but may include:

1. Giving assistance to an attorney in analyzing the identification process to search for sources of unreliability.
2. Preparation of written affidavits presenting an expert opinion for the record, the judge or the appeals court.
3. Conducting a brief case—specific experiment designed to test
   (a) factors in the environment at the time the witness viewed the crime or
   (b) testing the degree of bias in lineups or photo arrays as pioneered by Doob and Kirschenbaum (1973).
4. Presenting testimony before the jury to aid them in evaluating identification testimony by presenting research findings from the memory/perception literature.

[26] See *Social Action and the Law*, April 1976, 3 (3), for an attribution analysis of the Patty Hearst case.

An example of the first role (see Resources File No. 4 for text)[27] would be for the psychologist to examine all the materials available on the nature of how the suspect in the case was identified. Typically this would include the first description given by a witness when memory is still fresh, a complete physical description of the accused, photographs and statements pertaining to the conduct of all physical lineups, and/or arrays of photographs used to test the witness's ability to recognize the perpetrator—later statements by witnesses from court hearings or depositions. The psychologist would then review the materials to see if factors that contribute to the unreliability of perception were present. In a case that hinges primarily on eyewitness testimony the psychologist can aid in the shaping of the strategy for defending the accused person at trial. The conduct of an after-the-fact experiment is a rare but possible contribution by a psychologist which is described in Chapter 7.[28]

Of course, the testimony before the jury is the main point of contention. Too many cases in criminal court are prosecuted on the weight of eyewitness testimony—sometimes a single eyewitness—with other physical or circumstantial evidence weak or nonexistent.[29, 30] When any psychologist is brought in to testify for the defense the usual purpose is to raise doubts about the accuracy or reliability of the eyewitness testimony. The judge and the lawyers may share the belief of most psychologists that eyewitness testimony tends to be unreliable, but many prosecutors and a large percentage of judges simply do not want the jury to hear scientific evidence—from an outsider yet—that might negate the main evidence on which the trial has proceeded.

The Discretionary Power of the Judge

The trial judge has the authority to rule on whether any expert witness should be allowed to testify, and this discretionary power has generally been upheld in the appeals courts. We have heard reactions from judges following the offer of testimony by psychologists which ran the gamut from, "Everybody knows that," through "Why didn't you bring

[27] The text of a case analysis is given in the Resource File No. 4.
[28] Doob, A. N., & Kirschenbaum, H. M. Bias in police lineups—partial remembering. *Journal of Police Science and Administration*, 1973, *1* (3).
[29] Buckhout, R. Eyewitness testimony. *Scientific American*, 1974 *213* (6), 23–31. *See also Jurimetrics*, American Bar Association, Spring 1975,
[30] Grano, J. D. Kirby, Biggers and Ash: Do any constitutional safeguards remain against the danger of convicting the innocent. *Michigan Law Review*, 1974, *72* (4), 56–90. The author analyzes the "revolution" in eyewitness-related decisions of the Supreme Court, finding that serious challenges to eyewitness testimony may be found in only about 15 percent of criminal cases, where the witnesses and suspects are strangers.

the witness to your hospital and test him," to "the testimony of the expert would be prejudicial because it would invade the province of the jury as finder of fact."

For the scientist trying to testify the expectation that he or she might examine an eyewitness to a past event, runs very counter to his or her research habits but reveals the kind of expectations that have been created by medical doctors and psychiatrists who might base their testimony on such an examination. As scientists we are limited in our testimony in court to presenting general conclusions about the effects of certain variables on visual perception in an effort to aid the jury in sorting through the specific factors present in the case before them.

In two cases heard before the U.S. Court of Appeals for the Ninth Circuit,[31, 32] the Court upheld the trial judge's decision to exclude the expert testimony of a psychologist concerning eyewitness identification.[33] The grounds for both decisions were that the judge showed proper discretion in ruling that such testimony would invade the province of the jury. The language of these decisions has, of course, become the precedent for upholding the exclusion of psychologist's testimony in other courts, notably in New York[34] and in Washington, D.C.[35] Appeals decisions emanate from convictions, and it is ironic that in cases where psychologists *have* been permitted to testify, an acquittal of the defendant meant that a record of the judge's positive reaction to the testimony does not exist in the legal literature.[36] Only

---

[31] *U.S.* v. *Amaral*, 488 F 2d 1148 (CA 9, 1973).

[32] *U.S.* v. *Brown*, 501 F 2d 146 (CA 9, 1974).

[33] In *U.S.* v. *Brown, Swain and Nobels* the case went to the U.S. Supreme Court on another issue raised by the appellant (see U.S. Supreme Court No. 74-634). Dr. Buckhout was the psychologist excluded, although he never personally appeared. Appellants' briefs may be obtained from the Office of the Federal Public Defender, Los Angeles, Calif. See also *People* v. *Guzman*, 47 (CA 3d 380 1975) for another state case in which the judge's discretion in excluding expert testimony was upheld. The operative language as usual is that identification is "something everyone knows about" (p. 385).

[34] *People* v. *Valentine, Brown, Young and Petty*, 6 AD 1, F $17, 287 (New York Appellate Division 1976).

[35] *U.S.* v. *Jackson*, District of Columbia Superior Court, Cr. No. 16158-74 (1975). Copies of the transcript of Dr. Buckhout's testimony are available from the Center for Responsive Psychology for $4.00.

[36] For the record, as of July 1, 1978, Dr. Buckhout had testified in the following cases. (a) *People* v. *Chavez* (Rape-robbery), Superior Court, Alameda County Calif., July 15, 1970; (b) *People* v. *Richardson and Williams* (Armed robbery), Superior Court, Alameda County, California, October 29, 1971; (c) *People* v. *Angela Y. Davis* (Murder), Superior Court, Santa Clara County, California, May 23, 1972; (d) *People* v. *Pratt* (Murder), Superior Court, Los Angeles, June 27, 1972; (e) *People* v. *Castle* (Armed robbery), Superior Court, Contra Costa

when the defendant loses and appeals his or her case is a record likely to be made. Unlike the testimony of a clinical psychologist concerning competence or insanity, the offering of scientific expert testimony has been met by determined resistance. Buckhout (1976) describes one such episode which took place in the Queens County Supreme Court in New York.

> One of the trials in which I was not permitted to testify is an instructive case in how legal and scientific attitudes clash. The case was one in which a young man was accused of the armed robbery of a store run by a blind Vietnam veteran and his family. The main witness was the store owner's wife, who, by her own declaration was legally blind. The judge, incensed at the nature of the crime and prejudiced against the lower class black defendant (who had no prior record) refused to allow the defense attorney to arrange to have the witness receive an eye examination. Further, he permitted the woman to "correct" her in-court identification when she mistakenly picked out the brother of the defendant. When I was offered as an expert witness, the judge joined with the prosecutor in a free-wheeling attack on intellectuals in general and psychology in particular (because, they claimed it lacks the exactness of mathematics), berated the defense attorney for bringing me in, gleefully threw me out in a hail of invectives, and got back to the business of sending to jail for 7-14 years a kid whose guilt had not been proven. Note: This conviction was later reversed on appeal

---

County, California, April 1, 1974; (f) *People* v. *Kincy, et al.* (Assault with deadly weapon), Superior Court San Bernardino County, California, on April 3, 8, 1974; (g) *People* v. *Richard Boldon* (Attempted murder), No. 3180-74, Queens County Supreme Court, New York, April 8, 1975; (h) *Florida* v. *Richard Campbell* (Armed robbery), 74-2777, Circuit Court of Palm Beach County, Florida, April 24, 1975. (*Wade* hearing and trial); (i) *People* v. *Ernest Montgomery, R. Woods, and L. Whitehead* (Attempted murder), Bronx County Supreme Court, New York; (j) *People* v. *Eugene Duncan* (Murder), No. 71-112, County Court, Tomkins County, Ithaca, New York, June 19, 1975; (k) *State* v. *Chaisson* (Fraud, grand larceny), Douglas County Court, Omaha, Nebraska, June 5, 1975; (l) *People* v. *Milton Rucker* (Armed robbery), New York County Supreme Court, September 19, 1975; (m) *People* v. *Kenneth Wilson* (Armed robbery), Queens County Supreme Court, New York, October 6, 1975; (n) *State* v. *Leo McGill and John Hall* (Murder), Ingham County District Court, Lansing, Michigan, October 8, 1975; (o) *People* v. *Moulterie* (Rape, Kings County Supreme Court, New York, July 1976; (p) *People* v. *Edward Stevens* (Rape), Orange County Court, Goshen, New York, March 15, 1976; (q) *U.S.* v. *Soliah* (Robbery), U.S. District Court, Eastern District of California, Sacramento, California, April 1976; (r) *U.S.* v. *Roszoryk* (Extortion), U.S. District Court, Western Michigan, Grand Rapids, Michigan, June 1, 1976; (s) *U.S.* v. *Jarvik* (Robbery), U.S. District Court, Eastern District, Brooklyn, N.Y. July 19, 1976; and (t) *U.S.* v. *Richard Coleman Smith* (Armed robbery), Central District of California, Case No. 10171-HP-CD, August 30, 1972.

due to prejudicial remarks by the judge and prosecutor. While I have occasionally been thrown out with more sincerity and style (with a written opinion), the tendency of appeals courts to support a judge's discretion includes the tendency to support judges who neither know the law nor care about it. I should note that getting thrown out by a judge may not be a total loss, since it is still possible for an expert to get his/her testimony on the record either for the purpose of appealing the case (e.g., where there is clear evidence of a suggestive lineup) or for educating a judge who might be open-minded on everything but the legal admissibility of an expert's testimony. I am convinced that this possibility argues that some form of the expert's testimony should be written up in the form of an affidavit in advance of a courtroom appearance.[37]

In one case the battle over the admissibility of expert testimony on identification produced a courtroom fight in which the maturity and value of the field of psychology was the main issue.[38] The judge (who published his opinion in a journal,[39] supported the government's assertion that the existence of so few titles in the research literature under the heading "human identification and misidentification of other human beings," bespoke a field that was not sufficiently established to have general acceptance—one of the requirements for admissibility of expert testimony. The catch here was that the U.S. attorney had cleverly ordered a computer search of titles in the psychological literature using key words from the official taxonomy which had the effect of narrowing down the research titles to those that fit a highly specific area which is a subfield of human visual perception. Most psychologists are taught that a specific application such as human identification of faces is not the way most of the literature in the field of perception is classified. The broader classification of human visual perception (and perhaps feature or picture recognition) would produce thousands of relevant titles from the published literature. In spite of the defense's counterpresentation of thousands of titles in perception and memory, the judge felt that "even though jurors may have less skill than doctors of psychology, nevertheless, they should be able to draw their own conclusions."[40] Here we believe that the judge was trying to protect common sense from the encroachment of experts. In a companion article in the same journal, Clifford Wilson, an attorney,

[37] *People* v. *Daniel Woodbery*, Queens County Supreme Court, New York (Q520577/75), June 1976 (Quoted from case notes by Prof. Robert Buckhout).
[38] *U.S.* v. *Jackson*, op. cit.
[39] Goodrich, G. A. Should experts be allowed to testify concerning eyewitness testimony in criminal cases? *The Judges Journal*, 1975, *14* (4), 70–71.
[40] Ibid.

countered the judge on his failure to cover the *specifics* of research in perception, memory, *or* eyewitness testimony;[41] and then went on to a point-by-point dissection of the legal basis for admissibility. Citing from the federal rules of evidence (Rule 702) he points out these new rules require merely that the expert testimony be *helpful* to the jury.

> If scientific, technical, or other specialized knowledge will assist the trier of fact to *understand* the evidence or to determine a fact in issue, a witness qualified as an expert by knowledge, skill, experience, training, or education, may testify thereto in the form of an opinion or otherwise.

The author, in pointing out that an eyewitness expert should not always be allowed to testify (e.g., where the eyewitness testimony is of little weight in the evidence), concludes that:

> Without such insight (expert testimony) the trier of fact must rely on cross-examination of the eyewitness to judge the credibility of such testimony. Cross-examination may be a powerful tool in exposing a witness who is lying to or misleading the trier of fact, but it is less effective in exposing the psychological factors leading the eyewitness to his or her testimony. The expert is not concerned with truth and veracity but with the ability of the eyewitness to perceive and remember accurately.[42]

Admissability of Expert Testimony:
A Psychologist's Reaction

Our reaction to these arguments for and against allowing psychological expert testimony suggest to us that we as psychologists are perceived as stepping on the turf of the court officers rather than being seen as an invader of the jury's province. The judge, for example, generally has usually already ruled on the constitutionality of the lineups, photos, or face-to-face identifications by the time the expert is introduced. The expert's role is usually to respond to the defense attorney's attempt to argue identification matters to the jury to which the judge would never agree. Further, his testimony which centers on the broad range of scientific findings about perception may conflict with the instructions that the judge is required by law to give to the jury regarding identification. For the most part the recommended instructions for judges to give to juries are relatively simplistic, very contradictory, and totally devoid of any reference to scientific find-

[41] Wilson, C. R. Psychological opinions on the accuracy of expert testimony. *The Judges Journal*, 1975, *14* (4), 72–74.
[42] *Ibid.* Many appeals of convictions fail because the eyewitness testimony may have been a minor part of the totality of evidence supporting a finding of guilt.

ings.[43] The legal decisions to date do not question the value of expert testimony by psychologists but support the trial judge's role in determining its admissibility. Thus in any trial, a judge who is not close-minded or threatened may allow a psychologist to testify on the problems in eyewitness identification, provided that the psychologist is qualified and that the testimony is relevant.

Of course, in some cases, expert testimony on the vagaries of eyewitness testimony might not be relevant at all, or it might serve to detract attention from the details of a complex case in which other evidence is more salient. In one such instance the junior author was presented to the trial court as a potential expert witness in the trial of the Croatian hijackers who hijacked an aircraft and had planted a bomb that later killed a police officer (*U.S.* v. *Busic* et al., 1977).[44] After hearing the proposed testimony in a traditional *offer of proof*, the trial judge did not permit it to be presented to the jury because the relevance of the testimony was clear only in the case of one of the many defendants who claimed to be the victim of mistaken identity. The judge felt that an overall criticism of eyewitness testimony would be prejudicial in that it might raise doubts about other testimony and other matters for which other solid evidence existed. Instead, the judge incorporated parts of Professor Buckhout's testimony into his instructions to the jury to aid them in focusing their attention on what was essentially two separate matters. The main charge of hijacking did not depend on eyewitness testimony whereas the charge of placing a bomb in a locker did. Following the judge's instructions, the jury returned a split verdict, deciding that the alleged bomb assembler was in fact innocent of that specific charge, although all were guilty of hijacking.

A BRIEF FOR A COURT FACING A PSYCHOLOGIST

The final case we would like to bring to your attention is a murder case in Lansing, Michigan, in which the judge *did* allow the psychologist (Buckhout) to testify.[45] We shall be quoting from a motion

---

[43] In *U.S.* v. *Telfaire*, 469 F 2d 552 (1972), a set of model instructions to jurors was recommended but not implemented. These are not bad on the vagaries of initial perception, but they neglect the problems of testing recognition such as in lineups and contain no reference to data.

[44] *U.S.* v. *Busic* et al., U.S. Federal Court, Eastern District, Brooklyn, N.Y., June, 1977. An offer of proof is a shortened form of the proposed testimony presented to the judge for a ruling outside of the presence of a jury.

[45] *Michigan* v. *Hall and McGill*, Circuit Court, County of Ingham, No. 75-25859-FY, October 8, 1975. Copies of the transcript of Dr. Buckhout's testimony are available from the Center for Responsive Psychology Brooklyn College, C.U.N.Y., Brooklyn, N.Y. 11210, for $4.00.

Table 9.1 FACTORS AFFECTING THE UNRELIABILITY
OF EYEWITNESS IDENTIFICATION

THE ORIGINAL SITUATION
 1. Insignificance of events
 2. Shortness of period of observation
 3. Less than ideal observation conditions

THE WITNESS
 4. Stress
 5. Physical condition of the witness
 6. Prior conditioning and experience
 7. Personal biases
 8. Needs and motives—seeing what we want to see
 9. Desire to be a part of history

TESTING FOR IDENTIFICATION
 10. Length of time from event to test
 11. Filling in details that were not there
 12. Suggestions from the test procedure (lineup, photo array)
 13. Suggestions from test giver
 14. Conformity
 15. Relation to authority figures
 16. Passing on a theory: the self-fulfilling prophecy

to qualify as an expert which has been used in this and other cases.[46]
Such a motion is written in advance of the *voir dire* examination of
any expert; usually as a joint project of the attorney and the psychologist. In the Michigan case, three men from a card game were
murdered in a shoot-out in which one survivor identified one of the
defendants from a highly biased photo array from his hospital bed.
Professor Buckhout had been brought in to testify first as to the
general set of factors that affect the unreliability of eyewitness perception and memory and finally to give his opinion as to the fairness of
the photo-array test from a technical point of view (see Table 9.1).[47]
This model deposition has evolved from a series of cases in which
judges insisted on an advance presentation of what the expert was
going to say.

Following the legal exposition of relevant case law, in the given
state, Professor Buckhout added the foregoing information in a
deposition:

> In general outline my testimony covers the scientific contributions of
> psychologists to the understanding of human visual perception with
> special emphasis on the social and perceptual factors in eyewitness

[46] *U.S.* v. *Soliah*, Memorandum on admissibility of expert testimony on eyewitness
identification. Center for Responsive Psychology Monograph No. CR-6, April 16,
1976.
[47] Buckhout, R. Psychology and eyewitness identification. *Law and Psychology
Review*, 1976, 2, 75–91.

identification. The main points of my testimony are outlined in Table 9.1—"Factors Affecting the Unreliability of Eyewitness Identification." The list was developed in answer to a basic question about the eyewitness to a crime: If we conceive of an ideal observer as a hypothetical possibility (perfect recall of the events seen plus perfect ability to recognize a face from a good lineup at a much later date) what factors cause an eyewitness to a crime to deviate from the ideal of a "perfect witness?" The sixteen factors cited are backed up by specific experimental research by experimental psychologists, dating back to as far as 1895, and a subject of continued research today. Published research on visual perception, from which I draw these findings and upon which I base these opinions, amounts to about 450 articles per year, including some articles published by me.[48]

A key question asked of me is what contribution a scientific study of the perceptual abilities of eyewitnesses can add to the common experience of the average person (juror) who witnesses all the time and can apply common-sense analysis to possible witnessing errors. My answer is that our scientific contribution comes from our use of previously checked filmed crimes to test *hundreds* of eyewitnesses with the *same* crime where we can *check* the accuracy against a true record of the events. We learn much about the *typical* response of *average* normal witnesses under unique conditions inherent in viewing a crime. Such test films shown under controlled conditions (chiefly involving surprising the witness) permit giving an accuracy score to each person so that they can be classified as highly observant, somewhat observant or "blind." All witnesses are tested with carefully constructed lineups and/or photo-spreads under different conditions. I have conducted tests on over 8,000 eyewitnesses using this approach; other psychologists have tested many thousands more. All of these findings combine to permit an expert to provide the court and the jury [with] a more complete understanding of the eyewitness in the scientific literature— sources of data which are not commonly read by laymen. Laymen who compare their own experiences are rarely able to check *their* eyewitness accounts against an objective standard for accuracy. As such, while both experts and laymen may agree on some points about eyewitness reports, on many they do not. In my opinion, laymen also rely on certain myths which, while convenient to everyday life, *may* introduce distortions into the way eyewitness reports are evaluated. In the area of testing eyewitnesses with photo-spreads or lineups, the layman has *little or no experience* with what has become a highly technical area (for both psychologists and lawyers).

Because the Michigan case resulted in an acquittal, no record existed of the judge's favorable ruling allowing the testimony. Therefore, the

[48] Levine, F. J., & Tapp, J. L. The psychology of criminal identification: The gap from *Wade* to *Kirby, University of Pennsylvania Law Review,* May 1973, *121* (5), 1079–1134.

memorandum continued with excerpts from Professor Buckhout's recollection of the points made by the judge.[49]

1. I, the witness, was a *qualified expert* in the social and perceptual factors in eyewitness identification;

As Perlin points out, the possession of a Ph.D. in psychology would normally be enough to qualify anyone to testify according to precedents established in *Jenkins* v. *U.S.*[50] However, direct experience (not just teaching) in the research to be discussed is vital if the testimony is to be seen as credible.

2. That the testimony was a *proper subject* on the basis of its relevance to the murder case where eyewitness testimony constituted a proportionately heavy weight of the evidence against the accused;
3. That the expert testimony covered material which was in *conformity to a generally accepted explanatory theory* in the field of psychology on the strength of an offer of proof which cited the long listing of the research on human perception, citation of findings in standard reference works and signs of continued research through hundreds of research references. I would note that my research on eyewitness testimony is frequently cited in general psychology textbooks as a model for how research in perception is to be conducted. Legal reference works of psychologists abound in Wigmore, law reviews, and in all Supreme Court decisions;

Judges have a natural fear that the adversary system may produce a battle of the experts—particularly in the social sciences—where unresolved disputes will be argued out before the jury. Because many judges *do not accept* the findings of perception research, preferring to lean on fireside inductions, they will not infrequently rule out psychological testimony on perception because it is "too new," or "too controversial" because the field is "too young." This conclusion is erroneous; perception and memory research has evolved as a central focus of psychology since the beginning.

4. That the *probative value* of the expert testimony outweighed any potential prejudicial effect it might have on the jury;
5. That the *time* to be taken up by direct examination of the expert witness was less than one hour and thus did not appear to consume too much trial time in relation to its probative value;
6. That he felt that the expert testimony *did not invade the province of the jury* as finders of fact but would be educative and helpful to them in evaluating the eyewitness testimony since the offer of proof stated specifically the defense intention to solicit general research

---

[49] Buckhout, R. Psychology . . . ,
[50] Perlin, op. cit.

findings from the witness. In fact, I stated during *voir dire* my own
standard—that I will never characterize or give an opinion on the
credibility or reliability of a named witness in a trial since I believe
that this is properly the province of the jury. My role is to present
scientific findings of a general nature and to be responsive to hypothetical questions posed by counsel or the court. My opinions will
always be limited to opinions on how a *typical* observer responds as
a witness to certain conditions on which research evidence is
available;

This is a severe limitation on the expert testimony of a scientist but
it is a vital one. Many judges and lawyers recall an old story about
the Alger Hiss case in which the psychiatrist who observed the witness
(Whitaker Chambers) on the stand—later testified that he concluded
that Chambers was a liar! This is the kind of nonsensical posturing by
an expert who claims more power (because of his training) than any
human being can have to determine truth.

  7. That the scope of the expert testimony covered the topic of eye-
     witness identification to such a depth and in reference to scientific
     research and publications which were clearly *beyond the ken* of
     laymen who become jurors.

Unfortunately, the cult of the expert still lives and the role of the
expert must always be separated from that of the layperson if he or
she is to be able to play a unique role in a courtroom.

  Although this kind of presentation has been moderately successful
in moving judges to permit psychologists to testify on eyewitness
testimony, the problem remains a fundamental clash of two distinct
outlooks. The thrust of a psychologist who testifies about probabilities
rather than certainties is that he or she complicates things. Eyewitness
testimony after all is a convenient fiction on which matters can proceed
normally in a court of law. Introduction of a "new" type of expert
testimony carries with it the threat of reform, and we believe it is fair
to say that reform in the criminal justice system will always be resisted.
The judicial establishment of Great Britain has already tackled this
problem, and in a particularly outstanding report by Lord Devlin
reached a conclusion that would bring shudders to many jurists in the
United States.[51] In a summary recommendation after a fine case,
practice and evidence presentation, Lord Devlin's committee made the
following recommendation:

[51] "Devlin Report." Report to the secretary of state for the Home Department of
the Departmental Committee on Evidence of Identification in Criminal Cases,
House of Commons, April 26, 1976, Chairman: Rt. Hon. Lord Devlin, London:
Her Majesty's Stationery Office.

We do however wish to insure that in ordinary cases prosecutions are not brought on eyewitness evidence only and that, if brought, they will fail. We think that they ought to fail, since in our opinion it is only in exceptional cases that identification evidence is by itself sufficiently reliable to exclude a reasonable doubt about guilt. We recommend that the trial judge should be required by statute

1. to direct the jury that it is not safe to convict upon eyewitness evidence unless the circumstances of the identification are exceptional or the eyewitness evidence is supported by substantial evidence of another sort; and
2. to indicate to the jury that the circumstances, if any, which they might regard as exceptional and the evidence, if any, which they might regard as supporting the identification; and
3. if he is unable to indicate either such circumstances or such evidence to direct the jury to return a verdict of not guilty.[52]

The Devlin report acknowledges from trial practice the lesson that Professor Elizabeth Loftus found in her research showing that jurors tend to overrate the importance of eyewitness testimony.[53] Lord Devlin's commission also acknowledged that what we are really dealing with here is not willful lying by eyewitnesses but the problem of honest but mistaken identifications that can lead to miscarriages of justice. In Great Britain the percentage of cases involving pure identification testimony by a single witness is very low. The thrust of the report is that the relative rarity of these events permits more careful analysis of the exceptional circumstances of the identification, a process that would be aided by the type of expert testimony we have been discussing.

In contrast, in the United States we do not even know how many cases would be affected by a more careful evaluation of eyewitness testimony. If it is the case, as so many court officers claim, that challenges to eyewitness testimony would destroy a large number of cases, then perhaps we are merely dealing with sloppy evidence gathering and incompetent prosecution. Our experience has been that psychologists are called rather rarely into cases where identification testimony is usually weak, where it is the only evidence, or where everybody involved in the case may have some doubts about the correct identification of the perpetrator. We seriously doubt that we will ever see the courts overrun with psychologists. On the other hand, if some reform is needed in the courts in the United States to minimize prosecutions with eyewitness testimony alone, then we think it is about time that

[52] Ibid.
[53] Loftus, E. R. Reconstruction of memory: The incredible eyewitness. *Jurimetrics Journal*, 1975, *15* (3), 188–193.

the courts caught up with the British system which after all is only belatedly catching up itself with Mosaic law which also proscribed against the use of a single eyewitness as decisive evidence.

As psychologists, our main contribution has been and should continue to be the publication of solid empirical research findings that will aid in the understanding of how any observer perceives, remembers, and later recognizes the details of complex events in which he or she found him or herself a witness. A relatively small number of us may find a place testifying as experts in the courtrooms in our own home states. But the battle over the admissibility of experts on eyewitness testimony is but a microcosmic version of the battle psychologists have always had in establishing their credibility as scientists who meddle in the most basic of human affairs. Although we think psychologists have a great deal to contribute to certain trial proceedings, we do not expect the battle of empirical data versus common sense to be won in the courtroom. Although not too many people in the courts may like us, they will respect us if we are willing to step up and say the things that ought to be said within the limits of our discipline.[54]

> judges should be open to the possibility that expert testimony may indeed be helpful to jurors in cases where the dangers of identification are not readily apparent to the layperson.[55]

[54] Opton, E. M. How to witness expertly. *Newsletter of the Society for the Psychological Study of Social Issues,* Fall 1973. Professor Opton really had the best advice for how to behave on the expert witness stand at a very practical level:

> This situation presents a temptation to show your opposition, the scientific contempt they so richly deserve, a contempt they merit all the more because they are Wrong and you are Right. Do not take this ego-trip. *Nobody loves a smart-ass,* and the judge and jury may identify more with the side that does not understand the situation than with you. An effective expert witness will show respect for the opposition even as he demonstrates how they are mistaken.

[55] Sobel, N. *Eyewitness identification.* New York: Boardman, 1976, supplement, p. 87.

10

PSYCHOLOGICAL TESTING
AND THE LAW

We begin for a change, with a conclusion: that the time has come to abandon the I.Q. test.[1] We know that this unabashed statement would provoke Stanford Professor Leon Cronbach to shout "antiintellectualism,"[2] but we propose to address the profession with the facts, acknowledged even by Cronbach, that I.Q. tests do *not* measure innate ability, that they *do* discriminate against minority people, and that the profession is in debate over the abuses of tests by the gatekeepers of society. Faced with these facts, we ask what the profession proposes to do about cleaning its own house before the courts or legislatures do it for them.

[1] Based on a contribution to a symposium on "I.Q. Testing Today," the meetings of the American Orthopsychiatric Association, Washington, D.C., March 23, 1975. See *Social Action and the Law*, June 1974, *1* (6), entire issue.

[2] Cronbach, Lee J. Five decades of public controversy over mental testing. *American Psychologist*, 1975, *30* (1), 1–14. "The Social scientist is trained to think that he does not know all the answers. The social scientist is not trained to realize that he does not know all of the questions. And that is why his social influence is not unfailingly constructive." From a position statement by a leading pioneer in the testing establishment.

TESTS ON TRIAL

The point is that regardless of the heat and intensity of nature–nurture debates within the social science professions, the legal status of all psychological tests and their consequences is being questioned in the not too friendly environment of the courtroom as individuals and groups challenge the racial and class discrimination which undeniably results from nearly all testing programs. The focus here is on I.Q. tests because of their social importance—and the fact that psychologists have created a numerical legacy that gave the stamp of scientific legitimacy to the age-old myth of easily quantifiable innate differences in intelligence and that the profession then sat by while the public and many scientists settled on the absurd notion that intelligence is what I.Q. tests measure.[3] Psychologists may hold different, qualified views about the nature of intellectual functioning, but the general public, most teachers, most journalists, and most students have formed an equation made up of the myth plus the convenient fiction of a test score.

Brains = I.Q.   and   I.Q. = Brains

Convenient fictions are hardly new. From the psychologists structuring of behaviorism on the "reflex" to the government's measurement of quality with the Gross National Product (GNP), ordinary language itself is replete with concepts that "Everyone . . . has a notion of . . . sufficiently correct—for common purposes."[4] But unlike some myths, the I.Q. has assumed a place in the law as well as in the language. The I.Q. score has a life or death meaning for millions of citizens who can be institutionalized, sterilized, denied all civil rights, channeled into or out of educational opportunities, stigmatized, drafted, or finally committed on the basis of this magic number. Prof. Cronbach in 1975 lamented the spilling over of academic debates into the public arena because of the damage that could be wrought by "our innocence,"[5] a curiously ostrichlike posture for an academician whose university— like all universities—has been pouring out press releases since its beginning. We submit that citizens do have a vital stake in observing and evaluating professional debates—their confusions, their certainties

---

[3] Jensen, A. R. How much can we boost I.Q. and scholastic achievement. *Harvard Educational Review*, 1969, 39 (1), 1–123. The now famous but largely unread statement of the hereditary argument on the causes of I.Q. score differences among racial groups. This is a very complex area which draws in divided opinions from the psychological profession.

[4] Wechsler, D. Intelligence defined and undefined: A relativistic appraisal. *American Psychologist*, 1975, 30 (2), 135–139. A position statement by a leading developer of I.Q. tests.

[5] Cronbach, op. cit.

and even their damned fools. The public and the courts are now awake to the testing establishment, its size, its impact on lives, its costs, its conflicts, its historic lack of accountability. Those critics who now advocate reform go before the public to try to undo years of un-challenged access to the public ear by the testing establishment. The days of minor unnoticed nature–nurture debates are over and we might as well get used to it.

A "LAWSUIT"

How would the psychological testing profession fare in a court of law? Not too well if we look at recent cases. Imagine if you will the type of evidence that could be assembled by a group of plaintiffs suing the state, the Psychological Corporation, the Educational Testing Service (ETS), various school psychologists and psychometricians, and com-panies or schools that act on the basis of the available tests that allegedly measure intelligence. The premise in Law might well be Title VII of the 1964 Civil Rights Act. Let us assume a group of plaintiffs that might include the following.

> A 6-year-old chicano boy placed, along with some of his fellow chicano students, into a class for mentally retarded children,[6] whose attorney argues that the test used was in English and was "anglocentric"—and therefore unsuitable for testing him and his fellow students.[7]
> A Class action by a large group of black children labeled mentally retarded, who note that 50 percent of all children in their "special education" class are black, despite the fact that only 25 percent of the total school population is black: They sue for relabeling and punitive damages on the grounds that the test results reveal the inadequacy of the Stanford-Binet I.Q. test.[8] One plaintiff sues because his score was based on a test given by a student doing her first test for a Stanford-Binet class.

[6] Based on an actual challenge brought by a group of psychologists in San Francisco, California, and Martin Glick of the California Rural Legal Assistance. The suit charged that 25 percent of all Chicano school children in the district were placed in special education classes for the mentally retarded. A U.S. District Court ordered that 30,000 children be retested with a Spanish language test. The results showed that 45 percent of the students had been misclassified and that the group average I.Q. was 17 points too low. The school district had previously refused to reclassify the children because they stood to lose a subsidy of $550 per child given by the state for the special education classes. See Miller, G. A. & Buckhout, R. *Psychology: The Science of Mental Life*, New York: Harper & Row, 1973, pp. 165–170. See also Baker, L. Concern over I.Q. testing. *San Francisco Chronicle,*

These amateur testers' scores are used as a legal basis for institutionalization of a child in New York State and elsewhere.

A poor white man denied a job because he scored low on a "group" type I.Q. scale seeks relief in the form of retesting and punitive damages on the grounds that the I.Q. test score (1) has no proven validity in predicting the criterion behavior of job performance[9] and (2) the claim for validity of the test is based on a high correlation with the Stanford-Binet I.Q. scale which some experts feel should be withdrawn from use because of its age.

A "C-Tracker" in a high school tracking system seeks damages from the school for stigmatizing him for life as a "dull-normal" by assigning him to a low-noncollege track on the basis of a low I.Q. score which subjected him to low expectations by his teachers, lowering of his own aspiration and self-esteem, and caused him to live down to these prophecies.[10] He is joined in the suit by an "A-Track" student who seeks recovery of psychiatric fees spent in accommodating to having been labeled "gifted" by the same test.

A black university professor seeks to have his I.Q. score of 75 removed from his school, military, and other records so as to change his legal status as a mental defective, which (technically) demands that he not be allowed to vote and that he be sterilized before he is issued a marriage license. He is joined in the suit by his cousin who seeks lost wages for the time spent as a drafted infantryman in Vietnam on the strength of a national exam score from a test correlated with the Stanford-Binet instrument.

March 5, 1970 and *Larry P. v. Riles*, U.S. District Court, San Francisco, filed October 16, 1979.

[7] *Newsweek*, September 20, 1970. Tests that destroy. See also editorial: Wrong results from I.Q. tests. *San Francisco Chronicle*, January 27, 1970.

[8] Williams, Robert L. Scientific racism and I.Q.: The silent mugging of the black community. *Psychology Today*, May 1974, *8*, 32. Too often, professional psychologists who teach testing methods, turn over actual cases to poorly trained students. The test results computed by the inexperienced student are then reported to the agency as if the psychologist had personally administered the test.

[9] Burns, W. C. Personnel testing and the courts. Presentation to the American Psychology-Law Society, San Francisco, California, June 1974. The author points out that many tests used in industrial settings are only used to screen new employees and have rarely been validated on the appropriate reference group, namely, the people in the company or in the region where the job applicant seeks to work. It would be similar to the situation where a company uses polygraph or lie detector

This may sound fanciful, but the legal precedent for most of these actions is well established in civil law. These grievances symbolize the human costs endured by people who have become victims of a mere test—a well-intentioned tool that has become a means of quantifying and streamlining oppression as well as business as usual.[11] The I.Q. score epitomizes the always popular business of classifying people with a single number, a procedure that seems highly dubious in any setting. Just as physicists had to face demands for accountability for atomic energy research, it seems to us that psychologists will have to account for the typical social consequences of their once sacred cow—the I.Q. test. Like the Christian Scientist with appendicitis, the environmentally conscious psychologist may have to explain why he or she teaches, uses, and sells a product that is believed by the consumer to be an infallible index of inherited intelligence. Legislatures and courts are already hearing arguments about IQ tests and in many instances are deciding in favor of "victim" and seeking to ban the use of the I.Q. scales by decree.[12] Even those who vehemently denounce Berkeley Professor Arthur Jensen have failed to recognize that the I.Q. score does damage and yet it continues to be patched up, used, and justified by a vast network of schools, test manufacturers, and school psychologists on students who depend on the I.Q. test as a "bread and butter" item eagerly consumed by a poorly informed public.[13]

Many of the arguments massed by the critics of Professor Jensen,[14] are potential evidence to support the hypothetical plaintiffs in their

---

tests on all job applicants but never checks the baseline level of "lying" among the people who currently hold the jobs.

[10] Kagan, J. The magical aura of the I.Q. *Saturday Review*, December 4, 1971, pp. 92–93. The impact of the concept I.Q. on parents cannot be exaggerated. Most parents of school age children are keenly aware of the tests but have an awe of the I.Q. score as if it predestined their children to greatness or obscurity. The social damage of the uncritical acceptance of I.Q. scores as in index of intelligence is hard to estimate. I.Q. is as much a part of the English language regarding "brains" as XEROX is a generic term for photocopying.

[11] "I.Q." *Science for the People*, 1974, 6, 2–entire issue.

[12] In late 1977 testimony began in U.S. District Court, Northern District of California in the matter of *Larry P.* v. *Riles*, in which the plaintiffs sought to stop the State of California Board of Education from using I.Q. tests to select students for "special" classes—a euphemism for classes for the mentally retarded. Witnesses testifying on behalf of the plaintiff included Professors Leon Kamin, Jane Mercer, and George Albee, all of whom are cited in this article. See *APA Monitor*, 1977, 8, p. 3 (*11*, p. 3–4, *12*); p. 3, 1978, 9 (1) p. 3–5 for excellent coverage of the detailed testimony in this case. In 1979, the court ruled in favor of the plaintiffs.

[13] Scarr-Salaptek, S. Race, social class and I.Q. *Science*, 1971, *174* (4015) 1223–1228.

[14] Jensen, A. R. The differences are real. *Psychology Today*, 6, December 1973, 7, 80–84.

lawsuit, which might seek to establish that an I.Q. score should not have a sole legal basis for decision making that can determine a person's life.[15]

THE IQ IS NOT AN IQ

It seems clear that I.Q. tests do not in fact measure what "everybody" thinks of as intelligence. As Professor Tuddenham (1963) pointed out in his excellent article, Binet's I.Q. scale "was a pragmatic tool designed to meet a specific, if limited, social objective—to screen from the school population those children unable to profit by regular instruction."[16] In short, the entire I.Q. testing enterprise began as an administrative effort to predict success in the schools that teach, however badly, the distillation of what a society thinks is important. As Professor Leon Kamin notes, the British and American psychologists who embraced and refined the Binet tests were primarily eugenicists (or in some cases racists) who saw the mental measurement as a means for identifying and sorting out the hereditarily fit from those who were not.[17] The point is that the inventions (tests) of these men were put to use in World War I to select soldiers *before* any data were gathered to check basic assumptions. Binet's modest I.Q. measure rode along for free on the wave of the eugenicist's enthusiastic pushing of hereditary intelligence measurement as a cure for society's "ills" such as the immigration of "undesirables," the existence of mental defectives, and so on. Notorious publicists such as Henry Goddard preached that it was "possible to restate practically all of our social problems in terms of mental level . . ."[18] As Professor Tuddenham notes:

> There were few who noticed the logical flaw behind the eloquence— that the hereditary, biological intelligence that Goddard postulated and the intelligence which the tests in fact measure were *not* the same thing.[19]

Such lapses in logic may not pass unnoticed by courts that must ultimately decide if an I.Q. score should continue to have the force of law. A product that is marketed as or is believed to be a measure of

---

[15] Rice, B. The high cost of thinking the unthinkable. *Psychology Today*, December 1973, *6*, 89–93.
[16] Tuddenham, Read D. The nature and measurement of intelligence. In L. Postman (Ed.), *Psychology in the Making*, New York: Knopf, 1963. (See also Topoff, H. Genes, intelligence and race. In E. Tobach, et al.), *The Four Horsemen: Racism, Sexism, Militarism and Social Darwinism*, New York: Behavioral Publications, 1974.
[17] Kamin, Leon, *The Science and Politics of I.Q.*, Potomac, Md.: Erlbaum, 1974.
[18] Ibid.
[19] Tuddenham, op. cit.

innate intelligence but that is in fact a measure of verbal ability to master school-taught skills, is, in a close reading of the law, a case of fraudulent advertising or mere quackery. Time has seen little change, as newer I.Q. tests are validated against previous ones that all relate back to the Stanford-Binet I.Q. test. The "chutzpah" of test builders claims should be dropped from use, especially by professionals in the testing business who know better.

Even the term "intelligence" has come to be meaningless, due to the disagreements among professionals about what they mean—one or 120 factors that may or may not be underlying intellectual behavior.[20] The confusion evident in Professor David Wechsler's 1975 attempt to define intelligence reveals the following probable picture of the pragmatism of the professionals. "To hell with the theory, we've got the numbers to solve problems with, so keep the faith!" But the faith is not even being kept by the professionals, some of whom would have been excellent witnesses for the plaintiff, like Professor David McClelland.

> Psychologists used to say as a kind of "in" joke that intelligence is what the intelligence tests measure. That seems to be uncomfortably near the whole truth and nothing but the truth. But what's funny about it, when the public took us more seriously than we did ourselves and used the tests to screen people out of opportunities for education and high-status jobs? And why call excellence at these test games intelligence? (p. 2)[21]

IQ VERSUS THE CIVIL RIGHTS ACT

The writings of Arthur Jensen and Richard Herrnstein (among many others) contain evidence that the end result of I.Q. testing is a pattern of discrimination on the basis of race—a condition that on its face violates the 1964 Civil Rights Act. The U.S. Supreme Court has interpreted the act in *Grings* v. *Duke Power Company* (1971) to mean that an employer cannot require a high school education or the passing of a

> standard intelligence test as a condition of employment in or transfer to jobs, where neither standard was shown to be significantly related to successful job performance (or that) both requirements operated to disqualify negroes at a substantially higher rate than white applicants.[22]

---

[20] Bane, M. J., & Jencks, C. Five myths about your I.Q. *Harpers*, February 1973, 28–40. Theories on the nature of intelligence range from the "single-factor" theory (sometimes referred to as "g" or general factor) which is very popular to a statistically complex model with as many as 120 "capacities" identified as important in functioning at an intellectual level.

[21] McClelland, D. C. Testing for competence rather than for "intelligence." *American Psychologist*, 1973, 28 (1), 1–4.

[22] Rogosin, H. R. *The Grings v. Duke Power Case.* Conference paper—available

Thus if you ignore Professor Richard Herrnstein's (1971) failure to acknowledge the problem of how to interpret causality in correlation data, you find that he provides evidence of how minorities and poor people in general are systematically excluded from certain high status jobs and happen to have lower I.Q. scores—a violation of the law.[23] And considering the evidence that overall the I.Q. score does not generally correlate with *success* in real life, real jobs, you have another piece of evidence that suggests that I.Q. tests may violate the law. This is interpretable by examining the distribution of scores. The fact that black people score an average 15 points lower than whites on most I.Q. tests will be seen as evidence of insufficient intelligence by Professor Arthur Jensen; but a judge is just as likely to see a *prima facie* case of discrimination in the test results.

If test producers retained social responsibility for their tests as they once did, they might regard the evidence of racial discrimination as a weakness of the test itself and correct it; as they once did to "correct" for sex differences. Terman and other pioneers went to great lengths to discard subtests that favored boys or girls, but no such efforts were made on racial differences.[24] The scores were changed because it was assumed that basically males *could not* differ in intelligence, and any test that did show a difference was an *invalid* test. But the Supreme Court was quite careful in pointing to the language of the Civil Rights law which only permits agencies to

> give and act upon the results of any professionally developed ability test provided that such tests . . . are *not designed, intended, or used* to discriminate because of race, color, religion, sex or national origin . . . (p. 427)[25]

---

from The Community Relations Education Federation, 4034 Buckingham Road, Los Angeles, California 90008.

[23] Herrnstein, R., I.Q. *Atlantic,* 1971, *228* (3), 43–64. Professor Herrnstein supports many of the arguments raised by Arthur Jensen to the effect that he regards intelligence as a trait that is largely inherited. Based on a statistical argument that has many opponents, Jensen and Herrnstein believe that intelligence is 80 percent inherited. Herrnstein goes on to argue in his article that the I.Q. deficiencies in minority members determines an occupational caste system in which "tendency to be unemployed may run in the genes of the family about as certainly as bad teeth do now." In our judgment both authors mistake a correlation between occupation and I.Q. test score for a causal relationship.

[24] The techniques for standardizing tests to satisfy statistical criteria for reliability and validity are stringent. For example, if a test for giving definitions of words (part of an intelligence test) had been found repeatedly to favor boys rather than girls, Terman and his colleagues would revise the test to make sure that boys and girls had the same average score. Any other result *did not fit the theory* that all boys and girls are alike.

[25] *Grings* v. *Duke Power,* 945 U.S. 849, 1971. This decision has been cited as

This broad language has alarmed some professionals who forsee the door open to lawsuits on grounds ranging from malpractice to attacks on the basic tests themselves on the grounds of intent to discriminate, that final point being in fact provable by the racist published statements of the early pioneers of testing.

We are indebted to Professor Ted Goertzel (1970) for his incisive analysis of "The myth of the Normal Curve" which clearly shows how true believers in hereditary intelligence misapply the normal curve—designed to fit data with random errors—to I.Q. scores which were acknowledged from the beginning to have errors influenced by sociocultural factors, for example, education and opportunity.[26] But if assumptions are ignored, normal curves can be plotted over any distribution of *any* kind of errors. The normal curve is, of course, used or, rather, misused to adjust and justify *all tests*—and in many ways is regarded by some professionals as a natural law in and of itelf. To accuse black people or poor people of suffering from "skewed distributions" is the height of blind worship of a convenient myth and is, in our opinion, the height of irresponsibility.

RECOMMENDATIONS

The first recommendation that occurs to us for the psychological profession is to do nothing at all and allow the natural forces of society —court decrees, malpractice judgments, and class action suits—slowly but surely to eliminate or whittle down the now profligate use of I.Q. tests (and other aptitude tests) in the United States. But that will never happen; there are jobs, reputations, and egos at stake and the published explanations and apologies from the living giants of the testing establishment indicate that we are going to see a battle. Because we do not expect Professor David Wechsler or any other psychologist to go on the Johnny Carson show and say "We blew it," we shall address ourselves to the steps that socially conscious professionals might take to work with the courts in responding to lawsuits that seem to us to be inevitable. People who see themselves as victims of test abuse are well advised to seek relief from the courts rather than to expect the testing establishment to let go of one of their pet tools.

---

precedence in *Chance* v. *Board of Examiners*, 458, F. 2d 1167 (2d Cir., 1972) and others.

[26] Goertzel, Ted. The myth of the normal curve. Unpublished paper, 1970. Available from the author, Department of Sociology, Rutgers University, Camden, New Jersey 08102. The argument is quite technical, but his point is that the curve was meant to fit data from a simple, well defined source, not from a source as complex as intellectual performance.

1. *Testify.* Advocates of test reform should be heard from as expert witnesses or through *amicus briefs* to aid jurors and judges in wading through the statistical overkill brought on by the testing professionals.[27] Sorry, but people still do not understand validity, reliability, or I.Q. scores that well; in the adversary system, a poor person with a legitimate complaint about test discrimination can easily lose to the well-financed experts and legal talent of testing companies or schools. Note also that cases may crop up in every state whose legal systems still do not have diplomatic relations with one another. Thus the basis of litigation will differ from state to state. Social scientists will especially need to know the local precedents in their home communities.

2. *Review and Comment.* The testing establishment suffers from an inbreeding of test users, test makers, and test reviewers who think alike but rarely have an impact on test abuses until long after the social damage has been done. We desperately need an independent review service or even one that is unashamedly critical of most tests to replace the highly respected second volume *Mental Measurements Yearbook*, whose primary function seems to be to grow larger.[28] General rhetorical attacks on test abuse may raise consciousness, but they fall on deaf ears in courts that must decide on the technical merits of a single test. For example, an up-to-date critique of the Stanford-Binet test would be very useful, but it will be contrasted with material from the yearbook. It must be noted that Boros had this to say about the Stanford-Binet:

> The Stanford-Binet Intelligence Scale is an old, old vehicle. It has led a distinguished life as a pioneer in a bootstrap operation that is the assessment enterprise. It's time is just about over. *Requiescat in pace.*

Any critical technical review of tests had better be empirical and of high quality. Testing mythology cannot be effectively countered in court with eloquent outrage or sloppy methodology. As recent lawsuits indicate, the technical level of discussion is high and the standards of discourse are improving.

3. *Collect Impact Data; Publish it, Replicate it.* The thrust of the attacks on test abuse as a violation of the Civil Rights Act requires empirical data to document the abuses. So far, this work has been done by concerned legal groups—ACLU (American Civil Liberties Union), the NAACP Legal Defense Fund, and so on—who have a chronic shortage of financial resources. Lawyers often need statistical help to

[27] See Gianutsos, R., Wither Intelligence. *Social Action*, 1974, 7 (3) 1, 7–9, for an excellent discussion of how to wade through statistical myths.
[28] Boros, D. F. (Ed.) *The Seventh Mental Measurements Yearbook*, Vols. I and II, Princeton, N.J. Gryphon Press, 1972.

234 PSYCHOLOGICAL TESTING AND THE LAW

describe the discrimination evident in such situations as the new suburban ghettos, for example, high schools in which up to half of the largely black school population is classified as mentally retarded. Repeated statistical studies are needed to document such abuses.

4. *Truth in Testing*. The analogy between tests used to classify and drugs used in therapy breaks down when we realize that the citizen consumer is told little or nothing about the tests he or she is often coerced to take. It is possible that test makers could be required to provide understandable data (labels) with I.Q. tests explaining what they can or cannot do. Presently most tests are wrapped in mystery, security, and copyright laws so that only professionals can evaluate them. Reform-minded psychologists could provide a valuable service by designing the appropriate labels, defining reliability, dosage, when to take the test (if ever), and warnings about side effects (e.g., discrimination).

The 1980 "Truth in Testing" law in New York State is an exemplary step which required that students taking the SAT, LSAT, etc. be given copies of their answers, the questions and the correct answers. Despite the outcries from testing companies about the cost involved, less than 7 percent of the students requested such information. Many students ran to adjoining states to take the tests which were so important to their careers. The ability to examine the basis of one's scores may help students to seek specific coaching in areas of weakness. Despite test company claims, test performance *can* be improved with *knowledgeable* coaching.

5. *Developing Alternatives*. The testing establishment has one compelling argument in its favor—the convenience of simplified classification of people which has precedence—a principle that is highly regarded in the law. If certain I.Q. tests are banned from use, decisions must and, of course, will be made and we must acknowledge that discrimination existed in the U.S. long before the advent of tests. This means the development of genuinely valid tests that are based on worthwhile criteria or the frank admission in some areas that tests can never do the job. We certainly feel that this is the case with intelligence testing; a concept that should be abandoned along with the I.Q. test. The logical direction would be the development of multiple criteria or profiles reflecting both the complexities of people and the highly limited role that tests can play. Professor Jane Mercer[29] has

[29] Mercer, J. R. I.Q. the lethal label. *Psychology Today*, 1972, 6 (9) 44–47, 95–97. Professor Mercer, testifying in *Larry P.* v. *Riles*, op. cit. summarized the goals of the test reformers with the following quote from the play *Raisin in the Sun*: "When you start measuring somebody, measure him right, child, measure him right. Make sure you done taken into account what hills and valleys he come through before he got to where he is." See also "N.Y. Law . . . ," *The Chronicle of Higher Education*, 1980, *20* (22), p. 3.

suggested that we take pluralistic assessment in the classification of the mentally retarded based on (1) an index of a child's social and ethnic milieu, (2) a measure of adaptive behavior, (3) a test of school readiness, and (4) the same test interpreted within the child's ethnic norms. Defenders of the I.Q. test ultimately justify its validity by arguing that it is vital to use the test in identifying mental defectives. But it can also be argued that a severely retarded person will fail *any* test. The real damage is done by the labeling of EMRs or TMRs (65–85 I.Q.); stigmatized by a legally required test that, as argued here, does not measure intelligence.[30]

6. *Recall.* When the auto manufacturers are caught with a dangerous defect showing, they are required by law to recall the vehicle. We like the approach and suggest that some entity—the government or the various professional organizations—evaluate and then order a recall of those tests from the market, which (1) discriminate against racial or ethnic groups or (2) have no demonstrable validity in the settings in which they are used. (It seems likely that the Stanford-Binet, the WISC, and a number of the cheaper group I.Q. tests would be prime candidates for recall.) Such an entity could enforce remedies such as proper standardization of the test against representative samples, changing its name to fit its actual function, changes in subtests, validation, reliability testing, and so on.

7. *Repeal.* In our opinion, laws now on the books that mandate labeling a person mentally retarded or defective on the basis of low I.Q. scores should be abolished, the social science and helping professional organizations should take the lead in lobbying for their repeal. The case against the I.Q. test score as a convenient myth has been made, and the law should reflect the judgment of professionals that I.Q. does *not* in fact equal brains.[31]

SUMMARY

We realize that attacks on psychological testing in the courts cuts very close to home.[32] Many psychologists learn how to give the Wechsler Adult Intelligence Scale (WAIS) or Stanford-Binet Intelligence in the ritual "test and measurement" course; many professionals in school

---

[30] Beeghley, L., & Butler, E. W. The consequences of intelligence testing in the public schools before and after segregation. *Social Problems*, 1974, *21* (5), 740–754. "EMR's" is a code for "Educable Mentally Retarded; TMR means Trainable Mentally Retarded.

[31] Garcia, J., I.Q.: the conspiracy. *Psychology Today*, September 1972, 5, 40–43, 94.

[32] Aptitude tests, particularly those administered by the Educational Testing Service for admission to college, graduate school and law school have come under increasing attacks on the grounds of their questionable validity. By this we mean that although the tests do predict school grades rather well (as they should

psychology or counseling use these tests diagnostically as well as to meet legal requirements. But it is the legal use of the I.Q. that hurts people, and it behooves professionals to clean their own houses and to take action to prevent test abuse. The testing industry has acknowledged, within its ranks, the pure fiction of the I.Q., but has done virtually nothing to prevent abuses or to educate the public on the uncertainties that plague psychologists concerning just what intelligence is. Professor Cronbach lamented the sordid public airing of dirty laundry but overlooked the fact that the testing industry has not decisively corrected the built-in racial bias of the I.Q. test nor has it thought the unthinkable: the possibility of abandoning I.Q. testing in favor of more careful skills testing. We ourselves must be ready to admit that innate intelligence is impossible to measure, that the I.Q. test is a museum piece whose use should be curtailed. And we should begin close to home by revising our education programs that still function as if I.Q. testing were one of the psychologist's main contributions to hard science.

Occasionally, for a variety of reasons, society does end up throwing the baby out with the bath water. It does not do so easily, as any student of recent national politics and U.S. foreign policy can attest. But the logical comeback from that dilemma seems fairly obvious:

Have another baby.

---

because they determine who gets into school), there is little or no evidence relating a score on the tests to any good measure of performance in the ultimate activity of a person who takes them—their performance on a job or in any sphere of real life.

BOX 10.1

I.Q. TESTS ON TRIAL

By George W. Albee*

BURLINGTON, Vt.—Intelligence-quotient tests, better known as I.Q. tests, have been around since the turn of this century. The first I.Q. test was developed in France by a psychologist, Alfred Binet, whose name still is attached to the most widely used child test.

The number of different I.Q. tests is enormous. Some are administered individually and others are given in groups. Where once the I.Q. was obtained by dividing a child's mental age by his or her chronological age, this practice is no longer universally followed. It only worked for children between the ages of 3 and 13 anyway, because mental development begins to slow down at age 13 and to level off in the mid-20's. The speed (but not the power) of mental processes actually begins a long slow decline after age 30.

Obviously, dividing mental age by the steadily increasing chronological age would give the same individual declining I.Q. scores over time. Sophisticated statistical techniques have been developed that compare each person with his or her own age group. As a result, the I.Q. is a measure that compares the person tested with a large number of other persons of the same age.

The problem that has led to recent criticisms of the I.Q. tests is one of bias. The tests were developed originally to identify which French school-children would not profit from public education in regular classes. The tests are still used largely to predict school performance. But our schools are staffed by teachers and principals drawn from the middle class. The content of our school curriculum is highly verbal and quantitative. Schools teach the things that the dominant establishment in a society wants children to learn.

We live in an industrial society in which consumption of manufactured goods is required of everyone. Our consuming society relies heavily on verbal communication and on arithmetic. We must be able to read to understand advertising and we must be able to handle money and use installment credit.

As a result, our tests are loaded with verbal and quantitative (mathematical) questions. Persons being tested are asked to use and define words and to manipulate symbols. They are also asked to handle numbers. Because these tasks are an important part of the school program, intelligence tests predict school performance with a fair degree of accuracy for middle-class children. The tests also require attention, strong efforts, desire to succeed and attention to detail. All are middle-class personality characteristics.

Most intelligence tests have been standardized on a "random"

* George W. Albee is a professor of psychology at the University of Vermont and past president of the American Psychological Association.
Answers to the questions: (1) Cadillac, (2) Buick Electra 225, (3) white man, (4) Bill Robinson (a dancer), (5) hog intestines that, when cooked, are edible.

Box 10.1 (*Continued*)

sample of the white population. The two most popular individual child tests, the Stanford-Binet and the Wechsler Intelligence Scale for Children, were standardized on a cross-section of the white population. Appropriate numbers of families from each social class were drawn and the children in them were tested.

But the definition of the child's social class was based on the father's occupation. Clearly the standardization sample is biased in favor of white, urban, intact families (using the father's occupation meant that there was a father present).

Recently a class-action suit was brought in the United States District Court in San Francisco against the California Board of Education. The plaintiffs were a group of black children who had been placed in special classes for the educable mentally retarded on the basis of their I.Q. test scores. The plaintiffs argued that answers to questions given by inner-city black children were marked wrong because they did not agree with the white norms.

For example, what is the correct response to the question, "What would you do if another child grabbed your hat and ran with it?" Middle-class children respond by saying they would report the culprit to the teacher or to the parents. Black ghetto children often responded that they would chase the culprit and fight for their hat. Black psychologists point out that neither answer is absolutely correct for all children and that the black child's answer should be scored correct.

In classes for the educable mentally retarded in California there are three times as many children with Spanish surnames and four times as many black children, proportionately, as there are white English-speaking children. Either we believe that black and Chicano children are basically inferior intellectually, or the tests do not deal fairly with these minority children. The issue is before the court.

Are intelligence tests unfair to children in Vermont? Probably, to some extent. David Weschler, who developed the Weschler Intelligence Scale for Children, spent most of his professional life at Bellevue Hospital in New York City. The standardization sample for his, and for most intelligence tests, is heavily weighted with city children. It is not unreasonable to assume that children reared on farms and in the country might have more difficulty with words that are familiar to city children.

Such words as subway, delicatessen, smog, litter would naturally be more familiar to urban than to rural children. An exception might be "litter." But if "litter" is defined as a pig's babies, this answer may not satisfy the scoring key on the test, and the Vermont farm child could be penalized in a way very much like the black child or Chicano child is penalized for giving an answer that does not agree with the white, urban majority.

Robert Williams, a black psychologist, has illustrated the point by developing an I.Q. test that asks questions familiar to any ghetto child but unfamiliar to the middle-class white majority. How many of the following questions can you answer?
1. What kind of a car is called "Hog"?
2. What kind of a car is called a "Deuce and a Quarter"?
3. Who is Mr. Charlie?
4. Who was Bojangles?
5. What does the word "chittlin" mean? (The answers are below.)
Clearly, I.Q. tests can be biased in a variety of ways. Efforts at

developing "culture-fair" or "culture-free" tests have been largely unsuccessful. Even tests that do not require talking have been found to be highly affected by culture.

One psychologist, Wayne Dennis, tested children in 56 different societies around the world with a simple test called "Draw-a-Man." (This task is a good measure of the child's I.Q. in that it correlates highly with scores on verbal I.Q. tests among American middle-class children.) But on this nonverbal test Bedouin children averaged 58 I.Q. and Hopi and Zuni Indian children averaged about 125.

Are the Indian children really superior to middle-class school children? Are Bedouin children really so retarded? Further investigation revealed that the Arab children lived in a culture that forbade drawing or the making of images. On the other hand, the Indian children lived in a culture that emphasized and rewarded drawings and decoration. Even this nonverbal I.Q. test was highly sensitive to practice and experience.

Should I.Q. tests be abandoned? The California lawsuit does not demand that they be abolished. It simply asks that they no longer be used as the basis for placing minority children in special classes. There are several reasons for opposing the use of I.Q. tests as the exclusive basis for making decisions about school placement of children.

They can lead to what the President's Commission on Mental Retardation has called the "six-hour retarded child." These are children who adapt perfectly well to their communities, neighborhoods and home environments, but who do poorly in school. They often become behavior problems in school. Teachers refer them for testing in order to get them out of regular classes and into special classes for slow learners.

This placement leads to the stigma of being called mentally retarded. Other children make fun of the "retards," and the effect on the children is devastating. Rarely do they "get out" of the special classes. Opportunities for further education and for skilled employment are reduced. The children develop negative attitudes toward themselves. Often this situation leads to a self-fulfilling prophecy where the children begin to act in the way that the teachers, schools and peers expect them to act.

What is the solution? It is frequently suggested that an intelligence test should not be used without at the same time having a thorough study of the adaptive skills of the child. Certainly some children are unable to profit from regular instruction in all school subjects. But not all of these low scorers are actually retarded children—some of them simply need additional help in developing learning skills and work habits. Others need to be placed in mainstream courses, and careful tailoring of curriculum to their own level of ability in other courses. They do not need to be labeled "retarded."

Whatever the outcome of the California suit, the I.Q. test is no longer going to be the sole determinant of a child's long-term future. The trial has held tests up to the light so that their strengths and weaknesses can be assessed. They have been shown to have no magical properties. Rather they are only one of many ways of studying the child. They are more a measure of past achievement and of social class experience than they are of some mysterious abstraction called intelligence.

SOURCE: © 1978 by the New York Times Company. Reprinted by permission. This article appeared February 12, 1978).

11

SOCIAL SCIENCE AND
THE PRISON SYSTEM

"The prison is the place where the process of incarceration takes place at the order of the court."[1] This very apt description is not found in modern textbooks on penology which might dwell on what appear to be higher purposes. But the prison is an institution with a legal purpose, a budget, a staff, a profession, a client population, rules and a place in society—where society commits incarceration. As such, it is accountable to society and has often been found wanting; in fact, the prison system is thought of by most of society to be a colossal failure as an institution. The prison system may succeed at incarcerating people, but it has consistently failed the higher purposes imputed to it by an ignorant public and by its more ardent spokespeople. Still, although a failure, no one seems to care all that much. In fact, to some extent failure is its own reward, at least in the world of prisons.

[1] Conrad, J. P. Citizens and Criminals. *Law and Psychology Review*, 1977, 3, 14–23.

BACKGROUND

As Conrad[2] points out, the historical role of the prison was custodial, where the primary measures were to assure security and to treat the prisoner as if he or she were civilly dead. Society was once content to view the prison as a rug under which to sweep deviants as long as they would not remind society of its seamier side. "The fault resides in the offender."[3] But modern times have changed that focus from the warehouse of society's garbage to an institution dedicated to changing human behavior in some profound if unspecified way. Under the aegis of rehabilitation and even prison reform, the prison *business* has become big business and is getting bigger. Even if the pendulum is swinging back to conceiving of the prison as a warehouse, more warehouses will be needed to house a growing population of prisoners.

In New York State in 1978 the high crime rate became a topic in the elections as the candidates debated death penalty bills and mandatory prison sentences. In a state system that processes over 200,000 arrests per year, there is a finite number of state prison "beds" (6000–8000) that open up each year, unless public money can be found to expand the system. Accommodations in the form of plea bargaining, dismissal of charges, and failure to enforce laws have been and will continue as all participants in the system are aware of limited prison space. The public is understandably not thrilled with the prospect of raising taxes to pay for new prisons. However, there is not a shred of scientific evidence that would tell society whether more or fewer prisons would have any effect on overall crime rates.[4] Although faith in the deterrent effects of prison persists, hard evidence to back this faith does not exist.

Recidivism

The prison, like many other legal and judicial subdivisions, has a hard time knowing just what it is doing. Research is a low priority item in the budget and planning in a system that is overwhelmed.[5] Thus the numbers represent a statistical nightmare as each of the 50 separate

[2] Ibid, p. 14.
[3] Miller, J. G. The abandonment of rehabilitation in corrections: Some thoughts and dilemmas. *Law and Psychology Review*, 1977, 3, 25–30.
[4] Nagel, W. G. A statement on behalf of a moratorium on prison construction. *Law and Psychology Review*, 1977, 3, 31–51.
[5] Kaplan, J. *Criminal Justice*, 2d ed. Mineola, N.Y.: Foundation Press, 1978, pp. 570–571. Washington State, which has the best records on parolees, reports that after 2½ years, 62 percent of parolees had no penal action, 13 percent were convicted again, 7 percent were back in prison for technical violations, and 28 percent were wanted for breaking parole.

state and the federal government prison systems provide separate numerical accounts. Most prison systems use the *recidivism* rate as the common yardstick to measure "success," yet the definition varies from state to state and record keeping is a major problem. Although the definition has one stable element—the percentage of former inmates who return to prison—the published ranges of the statistic (25 to 75 percent) make one suspicious of the reliability of the data. On the low end of recidivism data the problem may come from the fact that the more seasoned criminal does not get caught again or burns out. But the calculation of recidivism rates depends on the adequacy of archival files in prisons and precincts—a source noted more for chaos than careful compilation. Still the recidivism rate is the one number that is shared and understood by the prison professionals, social scientists, and to some extent by the public. Statistical studies aimed at finding predictors of recidivism may themselves be unreliable because of the unreliability of these basic data.

Recidivism has a magic to it that permits the prison reformer to point with pride to a low recidivism rate as proof of the efficacy of the new changes being made in penology. The more cynical prison professional can gain solace from a *high* recidivism rate by asserting that the "right people" are in prison and that the inevitable return to prison fulfills the prophecy that crime is the product of bad character. With this wide net of interpretation of the most widely used measure of effectiveness, it is no wonder that the prison system in the United States has been aptly described as wallowing in a "model muddle."[6]

> Corrections employees, judges, police, legislators and inmates all have diverse vague and often conflicting ideas of what prisons are supposed to accomplish. As a prominent corrections official put it, we are trying to operate the prison to be both a junkyard and a salvage yard. This has produced jarring discrepancies in the lengths of sentences, the time of counselling and vocational programs. . . . A successful revision of sentencing practices requires a consensus as to the objectives of punishment. We cannot continue a situation in which some judges see a prison sentence as retribution while others see it as re-education. (pp. 17–18)[7]

The Paleological Argument

As Professor Robert Sommer (University of California, Riverside) points out,[8] this does not exhaust the list of models. We have evolved a

---

[6] Sommer, R. *The End of Imprisonment*. New York: Oxford University Press, 1976. A wise and compassionate treatise reflecting the Goffman tradition of analysis. Professor Sommer favors detention as a social policy alternative.
[7] Ibid.
[8] Ibid.

system of penitentiaries (intended to exact penance from those who stray) that probably best fit the *retribution* and *incapacitation* models. No one inside the prisons (except perhaps the inmates) likes to talk about retribution or vengeance but quite clearly prisons serve this function. The ordinary citizen has transferred the power of revenge to the state, where the application of the "eye for an eye" principle results in punishing the offender and ignoring the individual victim. When retribution is discussed, rational analysis is overwhelmed by what Professor Sommer refers to as *paleologic*—patterns of thinking that are primitive, emotionally laden and outside ordinary rational constraints.[9] What an individual calls "common sense" does not need data, evidence, or experience of first-hand knowledge. As we discuss in Chapter 12, belief in capital punishment as effective retribution is paleological. A stand against capital punishment based on the sanctity of human life is equally paleological.

> Knowing this can help us understand the terrible acrimony and frustration accompanying discussion of serious correctional issues. The model muddle can account for the confusion, but understanding the acrimony requires us to attend to paleologic. (p. 38)[10]

The problem with the paleologic argument is that a person can invoke scenarios that seem airtight, for example, instant incarceration would not only be just revenge but the criminal would be off the streets. Translating these verities into pragmatic social policy complicates matters considerably.

Incapacitation and Other Models

The incapacitation model advocated by Wilson[11] and others has been interpreted as detaining and even aging the criminal by its supporters and as a return to warehousing by its critics. The model is based on the assumption that repeat criminals sooner or later get arrested and that a mandatory prison term (even for a first offense) has a statistically greater chance of detaining some criminals and hence preventing some crimes. The problem with this model is a certain vagueness about just what the period of incapacitation would be like. Prison does injury. When the inmate is freed after a short mandatory sentence, what is he or she going to do to society? Where would the increased prison population be housed?

Other models that permeate the corrections system include *deterrence, reform, restitution, reeducation, integration* (retaining and

[9] Ibid.
[10] Ibid.
[11] Wilson, J. Q. *Thinking About Crime.* New York: Basic Books, 1975.

244 SOCIAL SCIENCE AND THE PRISON SYSTEM

developing community ties) and that ever-present *rehabilitation*. Although it is true that correctional institutions will work with various combinations of these models, there are inherent logical contradictions among the models that can only serve to confuse. The biggest contradiction comes with rehabilitation, the twentieth century buzz word that has been used by the current generation of prison administrators to describe what modern prisons are all about.

REHABILITATION—ACCORDING TO MENNINGER

Despite the tide of opinion against rehabilitation in prisons, the foremost proponent of rehabilitation in 1978 was still Dr. Karl Menninger, author of the now classic *The Crime of Punishment*.[12] A passionate humanist and psychiatrist, Dr. Menninger helped to create the prison reform movement—that criminals were capable of changing with decent humane prisons. It is his belief that punishment aggravates crime; he noted as a result of his clinical interviews with inmates that a high percentage of those interviewed claimed to have been beaten as a child.

Menninger asserts, with reasonably good authority, that 98 percent of all criminal acts do not result in imprisonment. In other words, for most criminals crime pays and does not involve a very high risk of capture or confinement. Thus the criminals in prison are a drop in the bucket, a group that far too many other experts dwell on as if they were mainly responsible for the problem of crime.[13] If you could imagine some 1000 criminals sitting around at a "perpetrator?" convention, the discussion about deterrence or possible imprisonment would probably be as remote a topic as death itself. (only 20 or so may ever serve time). Those who get caught would be regarded as stupid. Although the proponents for all models for correction agree on the need for swift and certain sanctions against crime, the fact is that there is no such thing in the United States. Punishment is therefore a mere expression of a feeling of vengeance designed to injure and thus is cruel and a mark against the values of those who administer it. Further, in Menninger's view, punishment backfires in the high recidivism rates and the anger it produces in most inmates.

> There's a conservation of violence like there's conservation of energy. If a child lives after being severely beaten, do you think he'll forget it? . . . Everything we call crime is a rather stupid, mismanaged, pitiful struggle by beaten and angry kids to get revenge in the most evil way they can.[14]

[12] Menninger, K. *The Crime of Punishment*. New York: Viking Press, 1966.
[13] Goleman, D. Proud to be a bleeding heart, *Psychology Today*, 1978, *12* (1), 80.
[14] Ibid.

Menninger was instrumental in creating the Kansas Reception Center, a facility that processes all state prisoners for a few weeks of observation and testing. There, a group of psychiatrists and psychologists are responsible for the all important task of prisoner classification —recommending level of control required (custody) and treatment and rehabilitation programs for each inmate on an individual basis. They can and often do influence the downgrading of sentences by requesting the sentencing judge to consider their clinical findings. Unlike the Patuxent, Maryland "psychiatric prison," the diagnostic center is not involved directly in carrying out the sentences.

Menninger and his colleagues have always dismissed the notion of a "criminal mind" as the product of stereotyping, prejudice, and pseudo-psychology.

> Wickedness describes conduct not people. . . . Viewing people as wicked or having a criminal mind justifies their mistreatment. It confirms stereotypes and prejudice. This kind of stereotype has been used against Blacks, Jews, Indians and now against lawbreakers. In each case it has excused brutality and injustice in the name of good.[15]

The recent wave of books that exasperatedly look at the repeat offenders as hopeless and unchangeable have not caused Menninger to change his views about rehabilitation. Convinced that if you treat people like animals they will act like animals, Menninger is a supporter of the parole system. With the exception of serious, violent crimes, he argues that the parole system is a cheaper and more effective way of dealing with a large number of criminals. Further, the man on parole if working is better able to rehabilitate, to support his family and even to make restitution for his crimes.

The practical impact of Menninger's views on the prison system has been enormous as other states have copied the Kansas model. But it is the spirit of prison reform and Menninger's compassion for the human beings caught up in crime and corrections that have made him an important voice in this area. Rehabilitation of inmates has been centered mainly in the large prisons where the model muddle is most readily apparent. Legislating humaneness to a bureaucracy has been every bit as difficult as legislating morality to an individual.

There is a fundamental problem in placing psychiatrists and psychologists into an ongoing prison system. If mental health professionals see the criminal as sick, their counterpart on the corrections staff (perhaps even the warden) may see the same criminal as depraved and beyond redemption. The compromise of playing a role in determining how dangerous the inmate may be co-opts mental health

[15] Ibid.

professionals. If they receive their salary from the prison system, they will be seen as part of that system by the inmate—even though the mental health professional promises confidentiality. Mental health professionals will always be outnumbered and are highly dependent on information coming from prison staff members to base their judgments realistically. Even mental health professionals must be protected by the guards so that another dependency restricts their range of independence. We note also that mental health professionals become the butt of jokes of both inmate and staff as they bring a very different perspective of crime and its causes to the prison. At a deeper level, mental health professionals' loyalty is divided between the institution and the client. Although Menninger and his disciples have had an immense impact on the creation of rehabilitation programs and even on the language of the corrections field, history has tended to regard the reform experiment as a policy disaster and, unfortunately, to attempt to rewrite itself by repudiating not only Menninger's specific proposals but even to reject Dr. Menninger's exalted view of human beings.

REHABILITATION—IN PRACTICE

The rehabilitation cycle in most prisons involves the declaration that the inmate is to be rehabilitated, reformed, or cured while he is in prison. The dictionary definition of rehabilitation deal with returning something to its original state. The absurdity of making rehabilitation the reason for a prison sentence is highlighted by the fact that the original state of the typical inmate is that of a crook or a full-fledged member of a violent subculture. The imprisonment of the Watergate conspirators in the 1970s opened up a dialogue that brought anti-rehabilitation sentiments out of the closet in the world of law enforcement. But acknowledging the myth is one thing; the changes are still being debated. The public was satisfied to see retribution take its course in the imprisonment of ex-presidential aide Charles Colson or former Attorney General John Mitchell, but the rhetoric of rehabilitation still permeates the system and directly affects the ordinary inmate in "Catch-22" fashion.

The inmate who has been processed through a plea-bargained sentence (85 to 90 percent of all criminals are) comes to prison having admitted little about his or her crime and is forced into a system where the only way out is to provide continuous proof to the authorities (especially the parole board) that he or she is on the road to reform. Even in the most repressive maximum security prisons most prisoners can avail themselves of educational opportunities, Alcoholics Anonymous, group therapy, counseling, religious services, and so on.

Each of these "brownie points" become markers to present to a parole board which is looking for some sign that the inmate has learned his or her lesson. In states such as California where the notion of an indeterminate sentence was originally built into the law, the parole board became the determining factor in sentence length. As a result, California ended up with inmates serving longer sentences than any others in the United States.

As is the case in most total institutions, the *form* of compliance to the legislative mandate for rehabilitation came to replace the substance. As inmates realized, because genuine rehabilitation is impossible in a prison, the whole line is to be viewed as patently false and if they do not succeed at "conning" the parole board, they could conceivably stay in prison forever. It should not be surprising to learn that books on psychology and short courses in how to present oneself to the parole board became part of a cottage industry in the California system.[16]

The myth becomes the working reality at all levels of interaction within the prison system. A man is thrown into solitary confinement (the hole) in part as punishment for an infraction of the rules and also so that he will learn a lesson and perhaps repent and become "self-reliant." In an effort to sound more civilized, the hole may be euphemistically relabeled the adjustment center. As George Jackson[17] and other inmate writers have pointed out, the adjustment centers became the dumping ground for the rebellious, the politically active, and the crazies. The hole serves the institutional function of isolating potential trouble makers or leaders from the main prison population. Placing these individuals under 24-hour direct surveillance gave rise to a number of ill-advised schemes for "rehabilitating" these hard core candidates for change. To some professionals in the total institution the challenge to intervene and bring about change in a difficult person is always present. In distorting the guidelines for therapeutic treatment, prison professionals can and do coerce the recalcitrant prisoner into rehabilitative programs and thus further deny his or her freedom under the name of a benign purpose. Psychologists generally feel that any treatment service in prison should be voluntary.

When we examine the research literature to relate the amount of participation in rehabilitative programs to recidivism, the findings are grim indeed. The now famous Martinson (1974) review[18] of some 231

[16] Mitford, J. *Kind and Usual Punishment*. New York: Knopf, 1973.

[17] Jackson, G. *Soledad Brothers. The Prison Letters of George Jackson*, New York: Dell, 1971.

[18] Martinson, R. What works?—Questions and answers about prison reform. *The Public Interest,* 1974, 35, 22–54. See also a review of earlier studies by Bailey, W. C. An evaluation of one hundred reports. In L. Radzinowicz and M. E.

published studies on the treatment of juvenile and adult criminals led the reviewer to conclude that rehabilitative efforts have *no effect* at all on rates of recidivism. Jacobson and Wirt (1969) reported on a longitudinal study of the effects of group psychotherapy on 446 inmates.[19] Comparing the treated inmates to an untreated matching control group, the authors found that the control inmates actually made a *better* adjustment to parole. Similarly, a study in California showed that inmates who participated in counseling treatment were just as likely to become repeat offenders as those in the untreated control condition.[20] Rappaport (1977), a community psychologist, attributes these failures to the general failure of psychotherapy as a method of treating lower socioeconomic class clients.[21] Whether these failures are principally due to the basic weaknesses of treatment techniques or to their half-hearted, underfinanced use in the prison system, the case for the expansion of ineffective rehabilitative techniques is not supportable by data, save for the isolated individual case.

NOTES ON THE TOTAL INSTITUTION

One of the hallmarks of social science research in the 1960s was an explosion of literature on the destructive nature of institutions and the oppressive role that institutions play against the individual. Much of the best of that research and theory building can be traced to Erving Goffman,[22] whose writing we admire as an example of the kind of common language we have tried to stress throughout the book. Although no correctional officer or warden would have trouble describing a prison, we turn to an observer of people interacting in a variety of multiple-person settings to get a good conceptual grasp of the nature of the *total* institution—a category in which all prisons fit.

> A basic social arrangement in modern society is that the individual tends to sleep, play and work in different places, with different co-participants, under different authorities and without an over-all rational plan. The central feature of total institutions can be described as a breakdown of the barriers ordinarily separating these three spheres of life. First, all aspects of life are conducted in the same place and under the same

Wolfgang (Eds.), *The Criminal in Confinement*, Vol. III. New York: Basic Books, 1971.

[19] Jacobson, J. L., & Wirt, R. D. MMPI profiles associated with outcomes of group psychotherapy with prisoners. In J. N. Butcher (Ed.), *MMPI: Research Developments and Clinical Applications*. New York: McGraw-Hill, 1969.

[20] Kassenbaum, G., Ward, D., & Wilner, D. *Prison Treatment and Parole Survival: An Empirical Assessment*. New York: Wiley, 1971.

[21] Rappaport, J. *Community Psychology: Values, Research and Action*. New York: Holt, Rinehart and Winston, 1977.

[22] Goffman, E. *Asylums*. New York: Doubleday (Anchor), 1961.

single authority. Second, each phase of the member's daily activity is carried on in the immediate company of a large batch of others all of whom are treated alike and required to do the same thing together. Third, all phases of the day's activities are tightly scheduled, with one activity leading at a prearranged time into the next, the whole sequence of activities being imposed from above by a system of explicit formal rulings and a body of officials. Finally, the various enforced activities are brought together into a single rational plan purportedly designed to fill the aims of the institution. (p. 6)[23]

The prison, the monastery, the army boot camp and the mental hospital function as total institutions with a common set of characteristics which Goffman writes about in a number of books.

The effect on the individual is a process aptly described as the *mortification of self*. Through the uniform issue of clothing, the haircutting, the stripping away of civil rights, the open walled cells with bars—even the bathroom stalls that are open—the inmate is deprived of his or her personal means of self-identification. Every manifestation of a personal nature come under the scrutiny of the guards or staff who may, in their obsession with social control, regard as trivial a behavior as teeth brushing (the right way) to be a key to good or bad character and hence an opportunity to force the process of reeducation and rehabilitation. The inmate will live in constant fear of violating a set of rules that seem at first to encompass every facet of living; but in reality are subsumed under an outward show of unquestioning submission to authority which can be accomplished in a variety of ways. Privileges are granted to those who learn the code and "go along."

The theme of dehumanization of the inmate and the lower echelon guards is in no way exaggerated by the literature of the total institution. They are locked into a master–slave relationship with only a relatively small authentic difference in power. If the situation gets out of control, the guard is every bit as vulnerable and subject to punitive measures as the inmate. In some states such as Mississippi, this relationship is further blurred by the fact that prisoner trusties once acted as guards and were empowered to carry and use guns to maintain order. If an inmate was killed by another inmate, it mattered little.[24] Among professional guards, the incidence of "burnout" due to stress is very high and results from the same pattern of social distancing and dulling of feelings described elsewhere in this text.[25]

[23] Ibid.
[24] Murton, T. One year of prison reform. *The Nation, 22*, January 12, 1970, 12–17. This article was the basis for the 1980 movie "Brubaker," which starred Robert Redford.
[25] See Ellison, K. W., & Genz, J. L. The police officer as burned out samaritan. *FBI Law Enforcement Bulletin*, March 1978, 47 (3), 1–7.

Increasingly, as the prisons become more and more overcrowded, the total institution breeds a subculture that is made up of the inmates who may run the prison for all practical day-to-day purposes. The available firsthand accounts of this process (Smith, 1978) are largely journalistic but they tend to confirm the process among prisoners as one mimicking the total institution in each crowded sleeping area.[26]

SIMULATING THE TOTAL INSTITUTION: PRISON CREATION IN SIX DAYS

In recent years many social scientists have come to place great emphasis on the importance of the individual's environment in attempts to understand personality and behavior (or behavior pathology, as the case may be). As a result of work done by researchers such as Professor Stanley Milgram of the City University of New York, we are just now beginning to grasp the overwhelming impact of "setting" on the shaping of character, and therefore the uselessness of an analysis of the individual without regard for the social context in which the individual operates.[27]

An awareness of this order is especially pertinent in the United States, where the dehumanizing aspects of an increasingly institutionalized society are continually resulting in more and more people unknowingly being forced to forsake individuality and true self-expression in exchange for lifetime occupations as cultural actors, playing out their lives in a variety of strict social roles. Occasionally, caught up in the "moment" and having lost both a sense of self-awareness and perspective over the situation as a result of this role playing, many develop ego-alien patterns of behavior and thought, although most are rarely aware of this co-optation of self by role.

On another level, particularly maladaptive behavior within the framework of an institutional setting may then be traced back to the institution itself; in the case of America's penal system, perhaps we should no longer be content with fixing the blame for its failure on deficiencies in the character of those who populate this environment.[28] Have observers wrongly attributed the violence and degradation of prison life to sadistic personality traits of the guards or to the anti-social life-styles of the prisoners?

[26] See "A New Way for Jailers: An Inmate's View," by Edgar Smith, convicted murderer, reprinted in Resource File No. 10.
[27] Milgram, S. *The Individual in a social world.* Reading, Mass.: Addison-Wesley, 1977.
[28] Toch, H. *Living in Prison: The Ecology of Survival.* New York: The Free Press, 1977.

The Prison in the Psychology Department

In the summer of 1971 Philip Zimbardo, Craig Haney, and Curt Banks constructed a mock prison environment in the basement of a Stanford University Psychology Department building for the purpose of studying the behavioral and psychological consequences of imprisonment—specifically, the subtle changes that might take place over time in a man who is introduced into a prisonlike environment.[29] "Stanford County Prison" was replete with iron-barred cells, a prison "yard," and various video and recording devices, and a "prison populace" was secured by placing an ad in a local paper promising $15.00 a day for volunteers to participate in a "psychological study of prison life." Seventy-five students responded but intensive psychological batteries designed to screen out the least emotionally stable brought the final number down to 20. Half of those were then randomly designated as "guards," whereas the other ten were to be the "prisoners." Neither group was given any specific instructions on how to perform the various functions their roles might require. And because all were paid equally (regardless of what actually occurred), there were no tangible incentives for them to behave in one specific way or another.

On the first day of the planned two-week experiment, the volunteer prisoners were "arrested" at their homes by cooperating officers of the Palo Alto Police Department, "booked," and delivered to the Stanford Prison where they were stripped, skin-searched, deloused, issued a uniform, towel, and soap, and assigned to one of the three adjoining jail cells. The "guards," supplied with khakis, silver reflector sunglasses, long billy clubs, and whistles were then put in charge of the operation.

Despite preliminary fears on the part of the researchers that the subjects might fail to take any part of the simulation seriously, it soon became painfully clear that *all* involved were beginning to inextricably merge reality with the illusion of imprisonment, readily giving up their own identities to allow the assigned roles and social dynamics of the situation to guide, shape, and eventually control freedom of thought and action. The guards enjoyed their new power, and delighted in harassing and degrading the prisoners. As the study progressed harassment escalated to more extreme levels, with guards often going out of their way to actually increasing their own workload just to create additional opportunities for themselves to humiliate the prisoners. The most

[29] Zimbardo, P. G. Haney, C., Banks, C., & Jaffe, D. The mind is a formidable jailer: A pirandellian prison. *New York Times Magazine*, April 8, 1973. See also a critique of this research by Banuazizi, A., & Movahedi, S. Interpersonal dynamics in a simulated prison: A methodological analysis. *American Psychologist,* 1975, *30* (2), 152–160.

sadistic behavior, however, was saved for moments when they were alone with the prisoners, out of sight of the experimenters who were considered "soft." The prisoners themselves were mildly rebellious at the start of the experiment, yet became quite passive and obedient after a day or two, effecting a submissive demeanor of lowered heads, glassy stares, and blank expressions and mumbling almost inaudibly when spoken to. So enmeshed had they become in their roles as prisoners, that analysis of their "private" (secretly recorded) in-cell conversation revealed that a full 90 percent of their talk related directly to prison matters and less than 10 percent to the outside world and nonprison topics. For all intents and purposes, the subjects were no longer college students partaking in a research project, but were actual members of a prison society.

Only 36 hours into the study the experimenters were forced to release their first prisoner, who was visibly suffering from acute depression, disorganized thinking, uncontrollable fits of rage, and crying. At first they doubted his sincerity for it seemed inconceivable at the time that anyone could have been so profoundly disturbed by the mock prison in so short a time. Yet on each succeeding day they were forced to release one additional prisoner, each of whom evidenced some form of emotional breakdown.

It was not until the sixth day, with the five remaining prisoners obviously shaken by the experience and appearing on the verge of collapse, that the experimenters were able to remove themselves from the situation enough to realize that the "simulation" should be terminated.

A series of encounter and debriefing sessions among prisoners, guards, and experimenters followed, which allowed for the release of pent-up emotions and discussion of the profound moral and social implications of the study. Charges of unethical conduct on the part of the experimenters were made, as a result of the extreme duress subjects were submitted to. Yet subsequent tests on subjects showed no signs of psychological impairment, and all participants in the experiment agreed that they had benefited from their experiences in terms of heightened self-awareness and insight and greater understanding of the necessity for immediate prison reform.

More urgent, however, are the perplexing problems that the research by Haney and Zimbardo (1977) present.[30] The careful screening process and random role assignment of the subjects cancel out any possibility of a predilection among them toward the elicited behavior,

---

[30] Haney, C., & Zimbardo, P. G. The socialization into criminality—on becoming a prisoner and a guard. In J. L. Tapp and F. J. Levine (Eds.), *Law Justice and the Individual in Society*. New York: Holt, Rinehart and Winston, 1977.

leaving only the obviously pathological qualities inherent in the structure of the prison environment as the determining factors. From this, a genuinely terrifying thought emerges: within an astonishingly brief period of time, within the most benign of prisons free from racism, involuntary homosexuality, and physical brutality, and within the context of a maximum two-week "sentence," the *simulation* produced sadism in men who were not sadistic, emotional breakdown in people chosen for their stability, and loss of objectivity in men whose professional training should have prevented it.

The Stanford Prison study added a social psychological dimension to the study of the total institution. Psychologists have tended to praise these findings as indicative of the process in a real prison. Corrections officials dismiss the study as biased and naïve. Ethical reasons had limited the simulation by not bringing in racism, sadism, sexual threat, violence, and other *degradation rituals* that are common in prison. But the lesson was clear—even decent people can become dehumanized by a total institution.

BARS FELL ON ALABAMA

It is not uncommon for people with some psychological training to be involved in prison work as corrections psychologists or as aides to the process of classifying inmates. The classification process—in which an inmate is labeled according to the degree of security required to keep him or her in custody and the type of "treatment" he or she needs is at the heart of the prison system. It is, of course, an intensely political process as the existence of facilities, personnel, and careers may be enhanced or obviated by any major changes in classification schemes. For example, if a larger percentage of inmates is classified as nondangerous and eligible for placement in a community work release program, this will reduce the population at the maximum security prison.

Beyond the political consequences, the decision is a difficult one for either the trained psychologist or the corrections classification officer. The custody decision involves the determination as to the level of danger that a given inmate represents to the community or to him or herself. Critics point out a general tendency for corrections personnel to be overconservative—overclassifying inmates into the maximum security prisons and thus exacerbating the population crush in those older, fortresslike facilities.

In 1976 U.S. District Judge Frank Johnson handed down a decision that indicted the Alabama prison system for a level of overcrowding, filth, and lack of services in the prison system that was unconstitutional. He further ordered that the state develop a plan to offer adequate medical and mental health services, tying the plan into the staff of the Center for Correctional Psychology at the University of Alabama.[31] This center, which involved psychologist Stanley Brodsky and others, had done extensive studies of the prison system and was prepared with rather specific recommendations. In later rulings by Judge Johnson the state was ordered to cease accepting new prisoners until the population at each existing institution was reduced to design capacity, and the state was ordered to contract with the Center for Correctional Psychology to develop a plan of inmate classification. We believe this is the first time that an outside group of social scientists was ever allowed to dictate to or review the policy of an in-prison agency.

Cast into an adversary role at first with the prison staff, Professor Brodsky and his group worked as effective social change agents to implement a plan to reclassify all inmates in the prison (3500) as a basis for restructuring the prison system.[32] Looking into the existing classification system they encountered the chaos of the agency file that combines fact, conjecture, opinions, hearsay, and wordy pseudo-psychology mixed in with anecdotes. The files were useless except as they had guided the earlier custody classification process to overpredict dangerousness. Professor John Monahan (University of Virginia) reviewed the general tendency toward overprediction of dangerousness in light of the national statistics which indicate a violent crime rate of 187 per 100,000 population.[33] As Table 11.1 illustrates, in a series of studies the percent of true positives was always topped by the rate of false positives. In one illustrative example, 86 percent of the inmates identified as violent did not in fact commit a violent act while on parole. Monahan also convincingly shows that prior violence in the record of the inmate did not predict violent acts and would probably lead to 19 false positives out of every 20 predictions. The point is that violence occurs too infrequently in a single individual's lifetime to be precisely predicted by any technique now at our disposal.

The results of the reclassification showed that whereas previously 40 percent of the prison population had been classified as maximum security offenders, the new level was 3 percent. Twenty-five percent were identified as being nondangerous and eligible for community placement. A working relationship for reform of the educational, medical, and mental health of inmates who need that service was created as a result of the joint reclassification effort. Regrettably, the

[31] Brodsky, S. L. Psychology at the interface of law and corrections. *Law and Psychology Review*, 1977, 3, 1–14.

[32] Brodsky, S. L. Prison notes. *APA Monitor*, 6, September/October, 1976, 24.

[33] Monahan, J. The prevention of violence. In J. Monahan (Ed.), *Community Mental Health and the Criminal Justice System*. New York: Pergamon Press, 1976.

Table 11.1 THE PREDICTION OF VIOLENCE

STUDY	PERCENT TRUE POSITIVES	PERCENT FALSE POSITIVES	N PREDICTED VIOLENT	FOLLOW-UP YEARS
Wenk et al. (1972) Study 1	14.0	86.0	?	?
Wenk et al. (1972) Study 2	0.3	99.7	1630	1
Wenk et al. (1972) Study 3	6.2	93.8	104	1
Steadman (1973)	20.0	80.0	967	4
Kozol et al. (1972)	34.7	65.3	49	5
State of Maryland (1973)	46.0	54.0	221	3
Thornberry and Jacoby (1974)	14.0	86.0	438	4

SOURCE: From Monahan, J. (Ed.), *Community Mental Health and the Criminal Justice System*, Pergamon Press, 1976. Reprinted with permission.

overcrowding that was cured in the state prisons was passed on to the city and county jails.[34]

WHEN PSYCHIATRISTS RAN A PRISON—PATUXENT

In 1975 the Maryland State Legislature voted to abolish the Patuxent Institution, a prison that earned the reputation as the therapeutic prison with a psychiatrist for a warden.[35] Within the standard maximum security design for prisons, 400 or more "defective delinquents" were treated by a large staff of psychiatrists and psychologists in a program which lasted over 20 years. The operating principle was that crime is a symptom of mental illness and that the defective delinquent is, under Maryland law, one who shows "persistent, aggravated antisocial or criminal behavior . . . and who is found to have either such intellectual deficiency or emotional unbalance or both, as to clearly demonstrate an actual danger to society." All inmates were given *indeterminate* sentences and "encouraged" to participate in therapy programs. Of course, the inmates quickly learned that one *had* to participate in order to convince the psychiatrist that they were on the road to recovery. To rebel meant they might never leave Patuxent, because the psychiatrist's analysis was the only factor determining an inmate's release date.

[34] Brodsky, S. L., *Supra*, Note 32.
[35] Trotter, S. Patuxent: Therapeutic prison faces test. *APA Monitor*, May 1975, *6* (5), p. 1.

The Patuxent program was a mixture of two major trends in psychiatry—the *psychodynamic* and *behavior modification* approaches —a mix found in many mental hospitals. The traditional psychodynamic analysis of a person's problems (a long term process grounded in Freudian theory) was combined with behavior modification based on psychological learning theory. Processing, testing, and classifying could take as long as a year, with a showing of 53 percent of those tested ultimately committed to Patuxent. The treatment scheme was described in official pamphlets as "taken from psychological learning theory . . . to assist the *patient* (italics added) in developing behavioral controls using increased rewards as a motivator." This is a legalistic translation of behavior modification which was visible in the prison as the Graded Tier System. The four different cell areas were graded according to the amount of privileges available. If an inmate could demonstrate good behavior and impulse control, he would move up to the better cell areas. Of course, he could also move down—as low as a solitary cell that was as filthy and degrading at Patuxent as in any prison. In fact, it took a class action suit (*McCray* v. *Maryland*) to get the Patuxent administration finally to put a 15-day limit on sentences to the hole that were running for months.

In the running of the prison the psychiatrists substituted for the normal parole board function, conditioning a man's release on whether he was cured as opposed to whether he was rehabilitated. As was the case in California, the actual time served by inmates in Patuxent was higher than it would have been in other prisons. Although the recidivism rate was reportedly low, the data was affected by the fact that many prisoners were kept there long enough to be incapacitated by age.

Critics of the Patuxent experiment in therapy point out that from the beginning there were distortions of the aims of psychology, therapy, and even behavior modifications. Opton (1975) was especially outraged at members of the psychological profession who tried to rationalize the use of behavior modification in prisons by standing on a kind of ethical neutrality.[36] For Opton its use in any total institution is a fraud and a sham.

> Although institutional behavior modification programs may be ineffective in changing real-world behavior, the more extreme forms effectively produce institutional docility. . . . Behavior modification in total institutions is largely a sham, a verbal facade which conceals maneuvering in the ceaseless struggle for power between keepers and the caged. The

[36] Opton, E. M. Institutional behavior modification as a fraud and a sham. *Arizona Law Review*, 1975, *17* (1), 20–28. Opton, E. M. When psychiatry goes to prison, law is the loser. *Social Action and the Law*, 1975, *2* (5), 7–8.

most important weapon available to administrators of total institutions is the power to mete out rewards and punishments. By rewarding conformity with privileges and punishing self-assertion with progressively more severe deprivations of human contact, the outnumbered men who run total institutions are able to maintain power over the inmates.[37]

In the institution's search for euphemisms the language of behavior modification was ideal because there is not even a word for punishment —only negative reinforcement.[38, 39] In the welter of lawsuits and hearings that welled up around the "therapy" prison, the negative reinforcement came to be seen as cruel and unusual punishment. The defensive quotes of the psychiatrists (e.g., indeterminate sentences are a necessary part of treatment) reveal the level of co-optation that can overtake the well-intentioned mental health professional or physician who tries to practice therapy on the inmates who are housed within a sick institution. Most psychological observers have concluded that the prison is no place to try to cure illnesses brought on by the institution itself.

MODERN NIHILISM

In the late 1970s the pendulum of change was shifting in full gear to the right. We say to the right because some of the more conservative observers and scholars whose lifetime specialty was corrections had been saying all along that prisons are not the place to try to rehabilitate. However, the significant change that occurred during this time was that scholars from the center joined in with the more conservative scholars in one of the fastest transformations of opinion ever seen in the academic world. Stunned by rising crime rates, stunned by the carefully documented papers that had shown the failure of the prison system in graphic detail, and stunned by some personal experiences with crime scholars seem to be reaching a consensus that the prison system needed to be changed. Although details differ, most of the scholars were moving toward the direction of emphasis on the

---

[37] Ibid.

[38] Gaylin, W., & Blatte, H. Behavior modification in prisons. *The American Criminal Law Review*, 1975, *13* (11), 11–35. See also Wexler, D. Behavior modification and the legal developments. *American Behavioral Scientist*, 1975, *18* (5), 679–684.

[39] Silber, D. E. The place of behavior therapy in correction. *Crime and Delinquency*, April 1976, *6*, 211–217. The author presents the details of positive and aversive conditioning techniques (as they should be done) and sees some value for their use in prisons. Essentially an apology for behavior modification. He even manages to glide over the horrendous use of anectine in California—a drug that causes momentary paralysis—in a "therapeutic" technique that was in fact punishment.

prison as a place to punish, to exact retribution, and to incapacitate an offender for a known period of time.[40] Another facet of the program was some degree of modification of the way in which sentences were handed out. Most of the criticism of sentencing in the United States has centered on the utter chaos in its administration. Sentencing is seen as the victim of too much discretion so that the new look at the new prison would call for either a mandatory minimum sentence for virtually all offenders on an assured basis or some mandatory maximum sentence with no chance for parole.[41]

Essential to the thinking of most of the scholars was the proposition that parole boards had to go. Once again, the literature had indicted the parole boards on two counts. As the agents of release, parole boards were found at fault, so frequently releasing prisoners who later returned or releasing particularly dangerous people who committed mayhem before they returned to the prison. On the other extreme, the second count of the indictment documented by many a reformer showed that parole boards, operating within the confines of rules governing indeterminate sentences, had produced a situation in which the sentences and time served by a prisoner were longer than ever before. Mid-seventies thinking had it that society would best be served by some system of known sentence lengths given to virtually all offenders with a minimization of the amount of discretion which characterizes the entire criminal justice system.

One of the leading proponents of the new look is Professor Norval Morris of the University of Chicago.[42] His views, which were very influential among corrections people as well as among scholars, could be summarized in a quick phrase that he once gave about the definition of prison. "Prisons exist because we do not know what to do with serious offenders." Professor Morris was not paraphrasing a popular folk song but, rather, was looking realistically at the continued existence and likely continued existence of prisons in the United States. His concern is what happens there and what happens now. Few scholars have so strongly advocated the replacement of the rehabilitation model. Professor Morris believes that rehabilitation facilities should be retained in the prison to be used by prisoners who *want* them. He is convinced that many of the people who come to prison (remembering that only 2 percent of outstanding criminals do) come to the prison as losers, recalcitrants, ill educated, vocationally untrained, addicted,

[40] Boland, B. and Wilson, J. Q. Age, crime and punishment. *The Public Interest,* 1978, *51,* 22–34.
[41] Wilson J. Q. op. cit.
[42] *U.S. News and World Report,* June 20, 1977, interview with Norval Morris, Dean University of Chicago Law School.

socially isolated, and in need of many kinds of help. However, he does not feel the prison is the proper place to *mandate* a cure as a condition for release.

The purpose of prisons, as he sees it, is to incapacitate certain classes of serious offenders. As Professor James Q. Wilson and some of his colleagues point out in an article on age, crime, and punishment,[43] "young males commit more crimes than older males . . . a well-established criminological fact. The thrust of this research and a previous piece of research by Petersilia[44] showed a clear trend downward in the number of crimes committed as the person got older. Thus the period of incapacitation is seen as a mechanism basically for *aging* a criminal, provided that he is caught at an early stage in his career. This type of thinking runs counter to the thinking of many professional police officers whose energies are devoted to catching up with the seasoned career criminal offender. The solution, of course, carries a price and some difficulty for other agencies. Implicit in the Morris and Wilson views is the idea that the arrest and conviction and incarceration of juvenile offenders and young adult male offenders must be increased if a serious dent is to be made in the crime wave. The problems created for the police, the juvenile courts, and the corrections facilities should be obvious by now. The United States already has one of the largest prisoner populations in the world."

A MODEL PRISON

In 1970 a model federal prison was opened in the rolling countryside of Butner, North Carolina.[45] The purpose of the prison beyond its usual role was to test out ideas for the "new prison system." The particular theory being tested at Butner might be thought of as directly guided by Professor Norval Morris's ideas.[46] The designers of the prison, incorporating some of the more modern notions of architecture, created a medium security facility that, on the inside, looks like a

[43] Boland, et al., op. cit.
[44] Petersilia, J. Developing programs for the habitual offender: New directions in research. In R. C. Huff (Ed.), *Contemporary Corrections*. Beverly Hills, Calif.: Sage, 1977.
[45] Holden, C. Butner: Experimental U.S. prison holds promise, stirs trepidation. *Science*, 1974, *185*, 423–427.
[46] Morris, N. Who should go to prison. In B. D. Sales (Ed.), *Perspectives in Law and Psychology, Vol. I: The Criminal Justice System*. New York: Plenum Press, 1977, pp. 151–160; Carrol, J. S., & Payne, J. W. Judgments about crime and the criminal: A model and method for investigating parole decisions. In B. D. Sales (Ed.), *Perspectives in Law and Psychology, Vol. I: The Criminal Justice System*. New York: Plenum Press, 1977, pp. 191–239; Fighting federal prisons. *Jericho— Newsletter of the National Moratorium on Prison Construction*, 1978, *1* (13), 6–7.

dormitory. The living units on the grounds contained only 50 to 75 inmates each of whom had originally a private room with their own key in order to maintain privacy. The theory here was that imprisonment is punishment enough. Further, it was the intention to make the inmate feel safe from such dangers as assault, rape, and robbery which officials in the prison believe should not be a part of any man's sentence. Typical of the Morris approach, the intention at Butner was to set a firm release date which the inmate would know from the start and to provide opportunities for nonmandatory participation in rehabilitation programs. The physical facilities, the size of the staff, and the planned general "plushness" of the prison make it seem superficially attractive to critics. As is the criticism of much of the federal prison system, the Butner facility was marked for criticism as being too much of a luxury site and less like the ordinary prison.

However, the frustrating history of attempting experimentally to change things is running into the same pattern at Butner. As of 1977, the facility was already overcrowded as more than one prisoner was jammed into what had been intended to be a single room. In addition, many of the promises for known release dates and for rehabilitation facilities had never been fulfilled. However, the design of the prison is being copied in the building of many other prisons throughout the United States and will undoubtedly be looked to as a proving ground for the new look in prisons.[47]

IS THERE HOPE?

We have been painting a rather bleak picture of the prison system in the United States. Psychologists and other social scientists have been involved in many aspects of the prison system, but the match is not a good one. With or without psychologists, prisons will continue to exist; in fact, more are being built each year. New experimental prisons inspired by the reformers and by enlightened penologists coexist with fortresslike dungeons which continue to be used because of the inmate population explosion. Even a move toward *decarceration*—having inmates placed in the community—has not stemmed the overcrowding as newer laws mandate more prison sentences and reduce the chances for parole.[48]

The idea behind decarceration or community treatment is a noble and sound one. Taking a page from the critics of total institutions, the advocates of community corrections argue that for the vast majority of

[47] On January 1, 1978, 294,896 inmates were in prison in the United States.
[48] Scull, A. T. *Decarceration.* Englewood Cliffs, N. J.: Prentice-Hall, 1977. See also Deinstitutionalization, *Corrections Magazine*, 1975, 2 (2), 3–28.

inmates, rehabilitation is a costly failure on the inside. Why not bring the inmate back to the community under supervision where he can see and support his family and have the advantage of seeing non-deviant people. It is a moderate proposal to stand somewhere between the two existing methods: imprisonment in a total institution or doing nothing. But the model for conducting such a program comes to society from a very similar move which has been taking place in the large mental hospitals. It is all too plain that the move to save patients from the deleterious effects of institutionalization led to their abandonment in the ill-prepared community. Responsibility passed from overworked hospital staff members to landlords of fleabag hotels and to the overworked staffs of welfare offices that had to finance the new venture. The former patients wandered the streets, unable to care for themselves and generally annoyed the people in the communities in which they wandered. Research at Harvard's Center for Criminal Justice (Scull, 1977) indicated that one of the most ambitious community-based corrections systems in the United States showed no difference in recidivism rate from the old system; although admittedly there were data problems with the research.[49]

Smith (1978) describes the start of a long-term process of reform of the indeterminate sentence program in the national leader of trends —California.[50] The new look was given the usual acronym—DSL— standing for the *Determinate Sentencing Law*. The legislature enacted the sweeping reform legislation after rejecting the usual request for more funds for more prison beds. The aim of the DSL is that prisoners should be punished on a "same-crime, same punishment basis, effectively removing sentence discretion from the hands of judges except in cases with unusual mitigating circumstances. Rehabilitation has been made optional and the prisons no longer discuss rehabilitation as a goal. The purpose is to punish and ultimately to reduce the prison population that had grown to unmanageable proportions as a result of the policy of indeterminate sentencing.

Wolfgang (1978), writing a sweeping overview of the criminal justice system, sees the new look in corrections as a "triumph of the public mind" because he believes that the general public never really endorsed the reform and rehabilitation era.

> Neoclassicism was born from the popular culture and is now nourished by sophisticated research. Deterrence, retribution, and punishment never really abandoned by the populace, have once again become acceptable to those "with power to enforce their beliefs." Reformation,

---

[49] Deinstitutionalization Ibid.
[50] Smith, E. A new way for jailers, *Bergen Record*, July 23, 1978, p. B-5. Written by a "lifer" at San Quentin prison. See the entire text in Resource File No. 10.

262 SOCIAL SCIENCE AND THE PRISON SYSTEM

although still accepted as desirable, is dethroned from its position of dominance and is subordinated within a more retributive penology.

Wolfgang, evidently endorsing the new look, sees more hope in this revival than we do. It is fitting that he should have the final word.

The public, the police, the judiciary and legislators are now joined by many social scientists in an ethical stance that requests retribution not revenge, as the definition of justice, that requires an emphasis on stability rather than law and order, that looks to certainty rather than severity of punishment.[51]

[51] Wolfgang, M. E. Real and perceived changes of crime and punishment. *Daedalus*, 1978, *107* (1), 143–157.

12

ON CAPITAL PUNISHMENT

The death penalty is an emotional topic with very little common meeting ground between its supporters and opponents. Although there has been a rapid decline in administration of the death penalty worldwide, the clamor in Western countries (notably the United States) has been for the resumption of executions.[1] Advocates for the death penalty, supported by debatable percentages of public opinion, argued in the late 1970s much as was argued in ancient Greece: "punish them as they deserve and teach your allies by a striking example that the penalty of rebellion is death."[2] The counterargument then as now is that deterrence does not succeed in restraining human nature from doing what it has once set its mind on. Utilitarian arguments, however, carry little weight when marshaled against what social psychologist Daryl Bem (1970) refers to as primitive beliefs based on external authority.[3]

[1] Jayewardene, C. H. S. *The Penalty of Death: The Canadian Experiment*, Lexington, Mass.: Heath, 1977.
[2] Ibid, p. xi. Cited as the justification for killing the defeated Mitylenian rebels given by Cleon of Athens, in the foreword to the book by Professor Thorsten Sellin.
[3] Bem, D. J. *Beliefs, Attitudes and Human Affairs*, Belmont, Calif.: Brooks/Cole, 1970.

Few human beings ever have the direct experience of having to fight off another human being; fewer still will ever find themselves in a "kill or be killed" situation. Yet as human beings they contemplate such situations and rely on the axioms taught to them by their family or culture on how to cope with this hypothetical situation. Our assertion is that most human beings hear the same axiom, to the effect that one's survival will depend on how effectively one communicates a counterthreat to kill against the would-be killer. Hence a *deterrence* theory begins as a primitive belief element which is later integrated into "higher-order beliefs."[4] The strength of primitive beliefs is formidable because they are such a vital part of being human. As Bem expresses it, "emphasis upon the innocence of childhood should not obscure the fact that we all hold primitive beliefs. It is an epistemological and psychological necessity, not a flaw of intellect or a surplus of naivete."[5] Nor, we might add, do we see the belief in the death penalty as a deterrent to be the result of some evil or pathological thinking. When we ask someone how he feels about the death penalty we place him in the position of making abstract generalizations. Small wonder that so many people will report the voices of their primitive beliefs which speak in less chaotic or less statistical terms. In 1979 public opinion surveys showed that more than 65 percent of the American people supported the general concept of the death penalty.[6]

Social scientists do not report their opinions in the form of polls but if we count the published conclusions of those who have studied the relationship between the death penalty and the crime rate, we conclude that the overwhelming weight of the social science data argues against the so-called deterrent value of the death penalty.[7] We suspect that the vigor of the stand taken by these social scientists is shaped by the fact that their own primitive beliefs have undergone a basic change. They have become advocates even though the working role models in the sciences are usually held up as models of dispassionate objectivity. As we shall develop, even with objectivity on their side, the social scientists find themselves in a clash of primitive

[4] Ibid, p. 10.
[5] Ibid, p. 7.
[6] The Harris survey reported in 1977 that 67 percent of the American people favored the death penalty. Other details are presented in Box 12.1. Cited in *Social Action & the Law*, 1977, *4* (1), 74.
[7] Bedau, H. A., & Pierce, C. M. (Eds.) *Capital Punishment in the United States*, New York: AMS Press, 1976. "The object of this volume is . . . to bring together in one place as much as possible of the best social science research on capital punishment . . . that has appeared since the Supreme Court's ruling . . . in *Furman* v. *Georgia*." This book is virtually the trial manual for evidentiary hearings on challenges to the death penalty.

beliefs—most directly with the political leaders of society—but indirectly with the members of the general public who would rather see *their* primitive beliefs prevail.[8] Life would be simpler if . . .

We shall examine the research background, first presenting an overview of the deterrence literature and then some recent studies of the complexity of public opinion about the death penalty.

BACKGROUND

The forces opposing capital punishment believed they had won a decisive victory in June 1972 when the U.S. Supreme Court ruled in *Furman* v. *Georgia*[9] and two related cases that the death penalty was unconstitutional as it was in violation of the Eighth Amendment which forbade "cruel and unusual punishments." After a long struggle the reformers behind the movement were gratified finally to see the Court reversing death sentences in some 120 cases encompassing a wide variety of crimes, statutes, and fact situations. By the end of 1972, because of the *Furman* decision, nearly two dozen states overturned their death penalty statutes and ordered the resentencing of prisoners awaiting execution.

However, this victory was short lived as legislative movements calling for the restoration of the death penalty were almost immediately initiated. They might perhaps have been anticipated as the Court decision was a close one, decided by a five to four verdict; and as the justices failed to reach any clear consensus, nine separate opinions were written. Furthermore, it was evident that their chief objection was not to the death penalty per se but to the arbitrary capricious manner in which it was imposed.

Since *Furman*, legislators have labored to design a "correctly" framed death penalty statute that might be found acceptable by the Supreme Court; that is, one that makes the death penalty mandatory for specified crimes. Accordingly, President Nixon sent to Congress in March 1973 a proposal that would authorize the reinstatement of capital punishment under fairly clear standards for certain federal offenses (e.g., war-related treason, sabotage and espionage, and particular crimes that result in death). Simultaneously, more than four-fifths of the state legislatures have made some effort to reinstate the death penalty by either specifying the offenses for which a death

---

[8] We are indebted to Attorney James Kakoulis who collaborated with us on the research, writing, and analysis for this section.

[9] *Furman* v. *Georgia*, 408 U.S. 238, (1972). The Supreme Court ruled on a confusing analysis of the concept of cruel and unusual punishment in light of the relative infrequency of executions in a system marked by endless levels of discretion that proved to be discriminatory.

sentence might be imposed or by reducing judicial discretion in imposing death sentences.

Much of the drive behind the movement to restore capital punishment is drawn from public opinion as public support for the death penalty is currently at its highest point in two decades. Supporters of capital punishment are a growing majority as a 1974 poll showed a loss of 15 percent among those opposing the death penalty since 1966, the year when public opposition was strongest.[10] Thus those opposing capital punishment have seen their efforts become distorted, rather than abolishing the death penalty, the Supreme Court decision has focused attention on the possibility of finding acceptable forms of the death penalty. As of December 1976, 444 people were sitting on death row, with the numbers growing every year. The Supreme Court decision may well have "rescued" capital punishment from the slow withering away of its use in recent decades.[11]

THE DETERRENCE ARGUMENT

The deterrent model of punishment, which evolved in the eighteenth and nineteenth centuries, was basically utilitarian in nature.[12] Following Jeremy Bentham's example, punishment was a part of the scheme that would lead to the achievement of the greatest happiness for the greatest number. Seeing humans as essentially pleasure-seeking and pain-avoiding creatures, advocates of punishment argued that we must deal with the criminal in such a way as to serve notice of the consequences of potential offenders. Deterrence theory argues that potential criminals will refrain from committing offenses because the pleasure they might receive from the act is more than offset by the risk of great unpleasantness from legal sanctions. Supporters of this theory can therefore point to the fact that the fear of death may well be the strongest motivation in humans and can then claim the death penalty to be a uniquely powerful means of protecting the community.

Deterrence theory is the argument we like to present to justify capital punishment because then it does not appear to be wrathful and vengeful behavior but, rather, it appears as a humane and civilized sacrifice toward the common safety. This rationale is used throughout

[10] Kakoulis, J. The Myths of Capital Punishment. *Center Monograph No. CR-13*, June 1974, Center for Responsive Psychology, Brooklyn College, Brooklyn, N.Y. 11210.

[11] *Capital Punishment 1976*, National Prisoner Statistics Bulletin SD-NPS-CP-5, November 1977, Law Enforcement Assistance Administration, National Criminal Justice Information and Statistics Service.

[12] Ibid. Deterrence is also used by the U.S. government as "the effects of formal, governmentally generated sanctions to control crime."

the official literature of the criminal justice system and the correctional systems. In 1977 a government bulletin soliciting research proposals described the theory in the following words.

> Simply stated, the theory of general deterrence proposes that increasing the levels of sanctions against criminal activities will have as one result a decline in the levels of those activities by people other than the sanctioned offender. The entire population is presumed to have opportunities for and highly variable prior inclinations toward the commission of criminal acts. Each individual in the population is assumed to weigh the likely risks and potential rewards from criminal acts against the costs and benefits of pursuing his personal goals through legal alternatives. The levels of criminal activity (crime rates) observed are therefore the collective outcomes of these individual decision processes. Theory presumes that there is an underlying rationality to this decision process even though it need not take the explicit form of a conscious weighing of alternatives.[13]

Capital punishment apparently makes sense to the extent that it is reasonable to believe that individuals will avoid certain acts if committing those acts would cost their lives.[14] However, this is a rather simplistic view of human behavior at best. The deterrence argument requires that humans be essentially rational beings, weighing all the possible consequences of their acts and rating the desirability of each possible consequence. Whether or not this view of humans is generally true is debatable, but in the instance of murderers it is most certainly untrue.

Murder is seldom a cold-blooded crime but it nearly always committed in the heat of violent passion, when the murderer is obviously incapable of rationally considering the consequences of his or her act. Experts (Bouza, 1976) assert that 80 percent or more of all homicides are emotional acts committed against a person known to or related to the killer.[15] Even for that small percentage of truly premeditated murders, one may find that the murderers are so convinced of their ability to escape detection that they rule out all thoughts of the consequences. In neither instance will the murderer be deterred from the

---

[13] Theory of General Deterrence. Criminal Justice Research Solicitation pamphlet, National Institute of Law Enforcement and Criminal Justice, 1977.

[14] Jaywardene, C. H. S., op. cit. The author makes a useful distinction between the problem of preventing the first homicide and preventing repetition by a murderer. In fact, few murderers who have been imprisoned ever repeat the act either in or out of prison.

[15] Confirmation of the accuracy of such estimates is hard to come by. One respected career police officer estimates that 72 percent of all homicides occur among people who know each other, 51.5 percent of homicide victims had either both alcohol and drugs in their bloodstream. Bouza, A. V., Deterrence-rehabilitation punishment: Do they work? *The Police Chief*, July 1976, 70–73.

crime by what may follow, because he or she either cannot or does not consider what those consequences are likely to be. Finally, even if one is aware of potential sanctions, the infrequent application of the death penalty makes it a rather empty threat.[16]

The ramifications of deterrence theory are many, as the supporter of the deterrence argument must believe that in order to keep individuals from murdering, society must constantly confront them with threats. The goal of any deterrence system then is to make the results of wrong doing so unpleasant to the offender that others will obey the law out of fear and not out of any intrinsic respect for the law. However, whenever the fear of punishment becomes the basic instructor of morality the danger exists that this fear will remain as the sole motivation of ethical behavior. But do we really refrain from killing out of fear?

Even those psychologists who believe strongly in the deterrent value of punishment in bringing about changes in behavior point out that the best arrangement for controlling behavior is to arrange training that will permit immediate punishment or the *immediate* avoidance of punishment. That is, to carry the argument to an extreme, if a person was certain that he or she would be killed on the spot after killing someone else, we might predict a certain hesitance in most people.[17] But this sort of fantasy lies at the root of primitive beliefs—presenting an unassailable commonsense analogy to counter a more complex reality.

The fantasy of perfect control or even perfect awareness by citizens sounds suspiciously like a police state and ignores what we know about the sudden emotional circumstances that seem to trigger most murders. Former New York City Deputy Police Commander Anthony Bouza, who generally supports capital punishment expressed the matter succinctly:

> it is manifestly ridiculous to conclude that any act we can take, in terms of punishment or rehabilitation, is going to impact a figure (the murder rate) that is largely determined by a spontaneous outburst that contains

[16] Jaywardene, C. H. S., op. cit., makes this point in light of the small percentage of people executed for a capital crime even in the years when execution was more common. "If a threat is an empty one that cannot or will not ever be actualized, it will not influence the conscious or unconscious deliberations of the individual. The capacity of a threat to act as a deterrent, hence, is dependent on the certainty of its actualization" (p. 21).

[17] Sommer, R. *The End of Imprisonment*, New York: Oxford University Press, 1976. The author uses the term *paleologic* to refer to patterns of thinking that are primitive, emotionally laden, and beyond the constraints of rational discourse. Sommer effectively analyzes many debates in the criminal justice system that founder on paleologic; referring to an analysis first used by Arieti, S., *Interpretation of Schizophrenia*, New York: Robert Brunner, 1955, p. 186.

no element of calculation—only passion. The bulk of murders cannot be prevented.[18]

Even if we assume that the death penalty plays a role in deterring murders, there are many other important motivational factors, such as love, desire for approval and acceptance, socialization processes, the environment, and culture, which serve to control and give direction to our social as well as our antisocial impulses.

The ramifications of the utilitarian position can be found in the implications that applying more and more severe sanctions will serve to eliminate forbidden behaviors, even to the extent of punishing the innocent in order to deter others. The key issue as pointed out by philosopher Hugo Bedau[19] is whether the death penalty is a superior deterrent to life imprisonment because those who oppose the death penalty grant the inevitability of *some* form of punishment. Utilitarians are compelled to follow the logic that increased punishments will serve as greater deterrents even to the extent that the death penalty would be applied to *all* crimes, for such severe sanctions would raise the risk so high as to eliminate those crimes. Furthermore, the utilitarian is committed to the logic that whenever society deems it necessary to set an example, even by punishing an innocent person, it must do so, for the sacrifice of one life is insignificant when compared to the benefits of deterring others from actually committing the crime.

Utilitarian thinking persists because it is so much a part of common sense, whether or not it works. Even though traditionalists retort that punishment should only be applied to those who have done something wrong and that it should then be no more than just and necessary to resolve some of the problems of utilitarianism, they make it all the more difficult to justify the extreme sanction of capital punishment. The problem of the death penalty being just is still an open question, but empirical data show that it is unnecessary to go to the extreme of death to produce the deterrence desired.

In some respects the deterrence argument is an anachronism with few serious adherents.[20] But court decisions are built on the precedence of extended arguments in the past—a past during which deterrence was the cornerstone of criminology. The first such evidence we shall

[18] Bouza, A. V., op. cit., p. 71.
[19] Bedau, H. A. *The Courts, the Constitution, and Capital Punishment*, Lexington, Mass.: Heath, 1977. This book is a chronological compilation of essays published by Bedau as one of the foremost abolitionists.
[20] By this we mean few adherents who seriously put forward an empirical justification for the deterrent effect of capital punishment. Bedau, ibid, notes that Ernest van den Haag (On deterrence and the death penalty, *Ethics*, 78. July 1968, 280–288) and other "retentionists" argue from ignorance, citing *possible* evidence rather than evidence in hand.

examine is of well-documented anecdotes, but such data are not the mainstay of the abolitionist viewpoint as it is of the retentionist argument. Little evidence beyond the personal beliefs and experiences of the advocates of capital punishment exists to support their view.

Numerous police officers and other law enforcement officials have reported quite a number of cases where a felon claims that he or she did not use a gun for fear of the death penalty. A formal survey conducted by the Los Angeles Police Department in 1971 supports this view, finding that of the 99 individuals interviewed who either carried no weapon or carried one they did not use in the perpetration of their crimes, half said that they had been deterred from using a gun by capital punishment.[21]

For every individual account tending to show the benefits of deterrence, there are many that indicate the contrary. Clinton Duffy, the former warden of San Quentin Prison, challenged the Los Angeles Police Department's findings when he reported that after interviewing thousands of prisoners convicted of homicide or armed robbery,[22] not one had thought of the death penalty before they acted. Those who had used unloaded guns or toy pistols told him that they did so merely because they did not want to hurt anyone and only wanted money. When asked why they told police officers that the fear of capital punishment motivated them, they typically responded that it seemed like a good thing to say at the time[23]—a familiar reaction to social psychologists who try to control the tendency of their research subjects who "tell the man what he wants to hear."

Anecdotes illustrating the death penalty's lack of deterrent value abound in the abolitionist literature. Charles Justice, an inmate in the Ohio State Penitentiary, suggested and designed improvements in the prison electric chair only to return a few months after his parole convicted of murder and sentenced to die in the chair he helped build. Similarly, a Delaware policeman who forcefully argued for the restoration of capital punishment in his state, based on its deterrent value, killed his wife just ten days after the penalty was restored in 1961.[24] Such examples are quite numerous, but they serve little purpose beyond

[21] Wilson, J. Q. The death penalty, *The New York Times Magazine*, October 28, 1973, 27–48.
[22] Hart Hearings, To Abolish the Death Penalty. Subcommittees on Criminal Law and Procedures, Committee on the Judiciary, U.S. Senate, 90th Congress, 2d Session, March–June, 1968. See also Hart, H. L. A., *Punishment and Responsibility*, New York: Oxford University Press, 1968.
[23] Ibid, Hart Hearings . . . p. 11.
[24] Cobin, T. Abolition and restoration of the death penalty in America. In H. A. Bedau (Ed.), *The Death Penalty in America*, New York: Doubleday (Anchor), 1964, p. 315.

Table 12.1 THE MYTHS OF CAPITAL PUNISHMENT ALL FOUND
TO BE FALSE

1. That states retaining the death penalty will have lower homicide rates than those abolishing it.
2. That the abolition of capital punishment would produce a rise in homicides and that its reintroduction would produce a decline.
3. That there will be fewer homicides in the period of time following an execution than before.
4. That the death penalty discourages the killing of policemen.
5. That murderers serving life sentences are an unacceptable risk to correctional employees and to other inmates.
6. That murderers released on parole present an unacceptable danger to society.

sensationalizing the debate for both sides of the controversy. Personal experiences and beliefs are often quite selective and biased, and interviewing apprehended criminals is rather dubious because these are individuals who evidently were *not* deterred. If deterrence meant anything to them, they would not have committed their crimes. Therefore we believe that the deterrence aspect of the capital punishment debate can only be settled through the careful study and research that the social scientist can offer. Common sense is not enough.

THE EVIDENCE ON DETERRENCE

An impressive body of data already exists which, although not conclusive, strongly opposes the deterrence theory in regard to capital punishment. Professor Thorsten Sellin[25] has been responsible for the most influential of these studies, but many others have also contributed toward exposing what we call the myths of deterrence[26] (see Table 12.1). Perhaps the most damaging evidence to the deterrence theory has been the comparison of murder rates between retentionist and abolitionist locales. The deterrence position implies that there exist a number of potential murderers among us who are motivated to commit murder but who are effectively deterred by the fear of death, so that it follows that murders should increase wherever capital punishment has been dispensed with.

Studies by Thorsten Sellin

The facts, however, do not bear this out, as the crime statistics of 1969 indicate that the three states with the lowest homicide rates and five of the lowest (homicide rates) seven states were abolition states,

[25] Sellin, T. (Ed.) *Capital Punishment*, New York: Harper & Row, 1967.
[26] Kakoullis, J. Myths of deterrence, *Social Action & the Law*, 1974, *1* (5), 5–6.

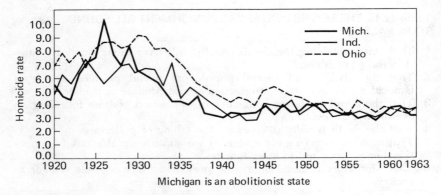

Michigan is an abolitionist state

Figure 12.1 Comparison of homicide rates in abolitionist state and two adjacent capital punishment states. (Source: After figure "Michigan is an abolitionist state" by Thorsten Sellin from *Capital Punishment,* edited by Thorsten Sellin, p. 136. © 1967 by Thorsten Sellin. Reprinted by permission of Harper & Row, Publishers, Inc.)

whereas the six states with the highest murder rates and twelve of the top thirteen had retained the death penalty.[27] It may be argued that figures of this sort reflect differing social and cultural variables, so that more sophisticated studies, such as those by Thorsten Sellin, have compared homicide rates in contiguous states where geography, history, and social and economic conditions are comparable. Thus by comparing such states, which differed only in the presence or absence of the death penalty between the years 1920 and 1963, Professor Sellin found that on the basis of homicide rates alone it would be impossible to identify which was the abolitionist state and which was the retentionist state (see Figure 12.1).

The homicide rates within each group of states appeared to be about the same and fluctuated in similar ways, regardless of whether or not the death penalty was available as punishment.[28] Following this same reasoning, one would expect that not only would the abolition of capital punishment produce a rise in homicides but its reintroduction should then produce a decline. Thorsten Sellin has studied the effect of the abolition and restoration of the death penalty in 11 states and found no evidence of the proposed effect. Some states, such as Delaware—which was one of the most recent states to abolish and then restore capital punishment—actually had a lower homicide rate during the period of abolition than before or after.[29]

[27] *Uniform Crime Reports,* Federal Bureau of Investigation, 1969, pp. 58–63.
[28] Sellin, T. Homicides in retentionist and abolitionist states. In T. Sellin (Ed.), *Capital Punishment,* op. cit., p. 138.
[29] Ibid, p. 124.

A further study by the United Nations—which included several American states and a number of European nations—examined the continuity of homicide rates during periods of abolition and restitution leading to the conclusion that the presence or absence of capital punishment had no effect on the already established trends in homicide rates, whether they were increasing or decreasing.[30]

In the light of such data, retentionists often retreat to the argument that whether or not the death penalty deters murder in general, it does discourage the killing of policemen, a claim vehemently supported by police officers themselves. No one doubts that police service involves a risk to life, but an analysis of the police homicide data fails to show any added protection for police officers in death penalty states. A study by Sellin for the years 1919–1954 showed that the police homicide rate was not significantly different for 182 cities in retentionist states (1.3 per 100,000 population) than in 82 comparable cities in abolitionist states (1.2 per 100,000 population).[31] His follow-up study for the years 1961–1963 revealed that of the 140 police officers killed by criminals or suspects, all but nine were in states that retained the death penalty. Furthermore, the percentages of police officers killed were quite comparable, as 1.31 officers per 10,000 officers were killed in abolition states and 1.32 officers per 10,000 were killed in the bordering retention states.[32]

Even though empirical research fails to show any support for the beliefs that the presence or absence of the death penalty will affect homicide rates in general, or even of police officers in particular, many supporters of the deterrence theory remain unconvinced. They put forth the argument that executions will have at least a short-term deterrent effect on homicides. However, the evidence once again fails to bear this assumption out, as a number of studies have shown that even highly publicized executions have no effect on homicide rates. A study done by Sellin (1969) investigated the supposition that an execution will have its greatest deterrent effect in a community where the person executed lived and where his crime, trial, and execution were well covered by the local press. Five such cases were located for the period between 1927 and 1932 so that an investigation revealed no differences in the homicide rates for the preexecution and the postexecution periods.[33]

---

[30] United Nations, *Capital Punishment*, New York: United Nations Publications, 1968.

[31] Sellin, T. *The Death Penalty*, Philadelphia, Pa.: American Law Institute, 1959, p. 34.

[32] Sellin, T. The death penalty and police safety. In T. Sellin (Ed.) *Capital Punishment*, op. cit., pp. 152–153.

[33] Ibid, Sellin, T. The inevitable end of capital punishment, pp. 246–247.

Another study performed in Philadelphia during the twenties and thirties found the exact opposite result from what deterrence theory would predict, that is, that there were significantly *more* homicides in the period after each of several well-publicized executions than in a comparable period before. However, the explanation of this phenomenon can be found in yet another study done in Chicago during 1962. In this study the homicide rates before and after each of three publicized capital cases were compared to the typical seasonal homicide patterns and it was found that the homicide rate fluctuated according to those patterns, independently of the executions.

Doubts on Deterrence

Thus deterrence fails to demonstrate any short-term effects as it also fails to show any longer term effects. However, the staunchest supporters of the deterrence theory have yet to be converted, for one final argument remains for them. These retentionists argue that murderers are dangerous individuals and that allowing them to live presents an unacceptable risk to correctional employees and to other inmates while they are in prison and that once paroled they present a danger to society on the whole.[34] The evidence, however, is overwhelmingly against them, as murderers generally make the best prisoners while incarcerated and are the least likely of all classes of offenders to return to crime once (if ever) released. A survey by Thorsten Sellin of prison homicides during 1965 firmly contradicted the view that life prisoners will kill because they have nothing to lose.[35] Prison life was found to be indeed hazardous, but most homicides in prison are committed by those serving sentences for crimes *other* than murder. Furthermore, prison life remained hazardous regardless of the presence or absence of the death penalty, thus it played no role in reducing those hazards.

Surveys of prison administrators, as done by Ehrmann, overwhelmingly present the view of life prisoners as the most reliable and best-behaved inmates of the institution.[36] A number of wardens were able to report that although their states had retained the death penalty for murder by life term prisoners, the law never needed to be invoked. Not a single abolition state official reported any special problems with life prisoners. Not only are life prisoners dependable in prison situations, but once released they become decent, law-abiding citizens.

[34] Dann, T. *The Deterrent Effect of Capital Punishment*, Committee of Philanthropic Labor of Philadelphia Yearly Meeting of Friends, Bulletin No. 29, 1935.
[35] Sellin, T. Prison homicides. In T. Sellin, (Ed.), *Capital Punishment*, p. 159.
[36] Ehrmann, M. The human side of capital punishment. In H. A. Bedau (Ed.), *The Death Penalty in America*, New York: Doubleday (Anchor), 1967, pp. 497–500.

Numerous studies have reached the same finding, that murderers have by far the lowest rate of parole violation of all classes of offenders. Paroled murderers almost never commit another murder and few of them ever commit another serious crime. A survey performed by Stanton of 63 murderers in New York who had had their sentences commuted between 1930 and 1961, revealed that by the end of 1962 only one had committed another crime—burglary.[37] This represents a 1.5 percent rate of criminal arrests for paroled murders as opposed to an 18.2 percent rate for all parolees during the same period. A California study confirmed this finding as it showed that only 2.6 percent of 342 murderers paroled between 1945 and 1954 committed new felonies.[38] This was by far the lowest rate of felony recidivism for any class of parolees as comparable rates for some other crimes were: auto theft, 31.2 percent; burglary, 25.6 percent; robbery, 20.8 percent. Many similar studies in other states, both retentionist and abolitionist, have produced the same results, thus rather firmly laying to rest the last of the retentionist claims to deterrence.

A vast body of scientific data now exists that tends to show that the death penalty fails as a deterrent to capital crimes. Although abolitionists admit that the evidence is far from conclusive, it is rather impressive because no body of data exists to oppose it. Arguments from personal experience and common sense are at best inconclusive and statistically meaningless, thus adding little support for the deterrence theory.

Perhaps the only way to settle the debate conclusively would be by an experiment whereby we would execute all the murderers in a random group of states and imprison the murderers in another random group of states, so that we could then observe the resultant homicide rates over a period of time.[39] Fortunately, we have yet to reach the ethical state that would permit the conduct of such an experiment, because the ultimate value endorsed by our society is the sanctity of human life. Such a controlled experiment would involve an unacceptable cost in human lives, both of innocent victims and of convicted murderers. However, because human life is held in such high regard and because the state can exercise a degree of control over the deaths of murderers that it cannot exercise in the case of their victims, retentionists must positively demonstrate a unique deterrent effect in capital punishment (as opposed to life imprisonment) before the state should be allowed to resume the execution of criminals.[40]

[37] Stanton, R. Murderers on parole, *Crime and Delinquency*, 1969, *15*, 149.
[38] California State Assembly, Problems of the death penalty and its administration, 1967.
[39] Wilson, J. Q., op. cit.
[40] Hart Hearings, op. cit. p. 65.

THE RETRIBUTION ARGUMENT

Beyond the deterrence theory, the only other major justification that remains for the death penalty is the retributive position. It is an argument that, although often difficult to define clearly, states that an offender deserves a particular penalty because he or she has committed an action for which he or she was responsible and that the penalty imposed will give satisfactions equal to the grievances caused by the offense. Retribution is perhaps the only argument in which one truly believes when attempting to justify capital punishment, as expressed so eloquently by Lord Justice Denning while speaking before the British Commission on Capital Punishment.

> The punishment inflicted for grave crimes should adequately reflect the revulsion felt by the great majority of citizens for them. It is a mistake to consider the objects of punishment as being deterrent or reformative or preventive. . . . The ultimate justification of any punishment is not that it is a deterrent, but that it is an emphatic denunciation of the community of crime; and from this point of view, there are some murderers which, in the present state of public opinion, demand the most emphatic denunciation of all, namely the death penalty.[41]

The retributivist position is often difficult to argue against as its case is generally presented with a deceptive simplicity, once again under the name of common sense. Supporters of retribution firmly believe that capital punishment possesses a certain moral fitness, particularly in brutal murders. They claim that the death penalty can be the only just penalty for murder as a murderer automatically forfeits his or her right to life. Furthermore, whenever a murderer is allowed to escape this standard and continue living, society's respect for life can only be lessened. However, this reasoning runs up against the fact that justice is a *relative* concept that changes with place and time.

If we look back through history, we shall find that capital punishment was once believed to be the only just penalty for thieves, adulteresses, heretics, and forgers, but today we consider the death penalty for such crimes to be excessive punishment. In our contemporary world a number of countries have abolished their death penalty statutes, but they can in no way be considered defective in their conception of justice because they choose to deal with their murderers in ways different from the retaliatory concept of "a life for a life" (an oversimplification of the Bible). One must consider that these nations believe that the killing of criminals may actually *decrease* our appreciation of the value of human life and that this value may better be supported by society's refusal to ever take a life, even in the case of

[41] Ibid.

the most brutal murders. Accordingly, whenever a society practices capital punishment, the executions may well serve as a morbid stimulus to further crimes. However, the point remains that justice can never be considered as a static, absolute standard but must be regarded as an ever-changing concept (and practice) applied differently according to the society enforcing it.

Therefore the fate of capital punishment must rest on the contemporary evaluation of its claims to justice. We must decide whether or not it is just to condemn one for injuring another while claiming that society is correct then to injure the offender. Despite all the arguments of the retributivists, it seems that both the offender's action and the act of punishing him or her are contraventions of the same principle, the protection of human life. It is not sufficient justification that the victim of societal punishment has himself or herself injured another nor is there a significant difference in the fact that in one case the injury is the work of a private individual whereas in the other it is the lawful work of officers of the condemning society. Thus one must concede that if the initial killing is to be considered wrong, then the succeeding execution must also be considered as an offense. However, even with such a concession, proponents of retribution argue that capital punishment is a necessary evil as it serves to preserve the balance of justice.[42]

THE PUBLIC WILL: MEASURING ATTITUDES TOWARD CAPITAL PUNISHMENT

Paralleling the rise in the national crime index for serious violent crimes, the rise in favorability toward the death penalty is a measure of a major change in public attitudes. In the 1960s when the Supreme Court was ruling against the death penalty laws in many states only a minority of the public favored capital punishment. In 1977 the pendulum had shifted to 67 percent of the population favoring the death penalty. The attitudes are complex enough in structure that when people are asked to qualify their answers the majority do not favor a mandatory death penalty (see Box 12.1).

As pointed out in the Harris survey, the general public believes that the death penalty deters murder in spite of the overwhelming evidence to the contrary.[43] In a recent study conducted in New York, a knowledge test was constructed to see how pro- and antideath penalty respondents would score on their concrete knowledge of the laws and

[42] Lehtiner, M. W. The value of life: An argument for the death penalty. *Crime and Delinquency*, 1977, 23 (3), 237–252. A well-written attack on social science data by an advocate of execution.
[43] See footnote 6.

BOX 12.1

DEATH PENALTY SURVEY

Recently, the Harris Survey asked the cross section:
  "Do you believe in capital punishment (death penalty) or are you opposed?"

CAPITAL PUNISHMENT

	Favor %	Oppose %	Not Sure %
1977	67	25	8
1973	59	31	10
1970	47	42	11
1969	48	38	14
1965	38	47	15

  "Do you feel that executing people who commit murder deters others from committing murder, or do you think such executions don't have much effect?"

DO EXECUTIONS DETER MURDER?

	Total Public %
Deters others	59
No such effect	34
Not sure	7

  "Suppose it could be proven to your satisfaction that the death penalty was NOT more effective than long prison sentences in keeping other people from committing crimes such as murder, would you be in favor of the death penalty or opposed to it?"

IF COULD BE PROVEN DEATH PENALTY DID NOT DETER MURDER

	Favor %	Oppose %	Not Sure %
Total public 1973	35	46	17
Total public 1977	46	40	14
By age			
18–29	42	47	11
30–49	45	40	15
50 and over	51	34	15
By race			
Black	25	51	24
White	49	39	12
By political philosophy			
Conservative	55	32	13
Middle of the road	45	41	14
Liberal	38	50	12

"Do you feel that all persons convicted of these crimes should get the death penalty, that no one convicted of these crimes should get the death penalty, or do you feel that whether or not someone convicted of the same crime gets the death penalty should depend on the circumstances of the case and the character of the person?"

MANDATORY USE OF THE DEATH SENTENCE

	All %	No One %	De-pends %	Not Sure %
Killing a policeman or prison guard				
1977	49	14	33	4
1973	41	17	38	4
First-degree murder				
1977	40	13	44	3
1973	28	16	53	3
Skyjacking				
1977	22	29	44	5
1973	27	27	41	5
Rape				
1977	20	27	48	5
1973	19	27	50	4
Mugging				
1977	8	44	43	5
1973	9	41	43	7

SOURCE: The Harris Survey, 1977.

the data on capital punishment.[44] Neither group had a very high average score but the antideath penalty group was more knowledgeable. There was a strong negative correlation between degree of knowledge and intensity of favorability toward the death penalty ($r = -0.62$, $p < 0.001$). These findings are consistent with the discussion in the prison chapter on "paleologic" which describes an attitude set that does not require consistency for strength. Politicians, sensing a gut issue were, in the 1970s, drawing election lines around each candidate's stand on the capital punishment (and the abortion issue).

The legal issue that has been raised in numerous death penalty cases by attorneys and social sciences is whether an individual committed to the pro- or antideath penalty position can be a fair and impartial juror. In most states the law requires that jurors be "death qualified"—if the juror is to sit in a trial that may require a verdict

[44] Buckhout, R. Unpublished study, 1978.

Table 12.2 COMPARISON OF ATTITUDES OF PRO- AND ANTIDEATH
PENALTY JURORS IN SUPREME COURT OF KINGS COUNTY, N.Y., 1976

SURVEY STATEMENT	GROUP	PERCENT AGREE	PERCENT DISAGREE
If the authorities go to the trouble of bringing someone to trial, he or she is probably guilty.	Pro	36.7*	63.3
	Anti	19.8	55.0
Defendants in a criminal case should be required to take the witness stand.	Pro	69.9*	30.1
	Anti	50.8	49.2
The defendant should prove his or her innocence or we should at least hear both sides try to prove their case.	Pro	70.9*	29.1
	Anti	57.5	42.5
A witness who takes the Fifth Amendment (refuses to testify) is probably hiding his or her guilt of a crime.	Pro	56.9	43.1
	Anti	45.0	55.0

* Significantly higher agreement than antideath penalty group ($p < 0.001$).

that leads to the death penalty, then that juror should be capable of voting for a verdict. Often, the test is whether the juror has scruples against the death penalty. If the juror does, he or she may be dismissed for cause. This issue is gone into in great detail in Resources File No. 11. The thrust of the legal memoranda presented there is that the death-qualified juror is more likely to convict than other jurors; a fact that mitigates against a fair trial.

We have found in our research that when people favoring the death penalty are questioned, those who remain committed to the death penalty without exception or qualification represent a *minority* of the jury-eligible public.[45] Hence the legal argument, extending a principle first enunciated in *Witherspoon* v. *Illinois* (1968), is that a death-qualified jury is made up of a nonrepresentative segment of the population that is conviction prone in violation of the Sixth Amendment and to a defendant's right to equal protection.

In Table 12.2 we present some data collected on jurors serving in a New York City court, which reflected the attitudes of jurors identified as either pro- or anticapital punishment.[46] Reflecting the national averages, the jury group was 59 percent pro- and 41 percent

[45] Buckhout, R. Model Deposition. See Resources File No. 11.
[46] Buckhout, R., et al. Jury attitudes and the death penalty, *Social Action & the Law*, 1977, 3 (6), 80–81.

Figure 12.2 Number of prisoners executed under civil authority in the United States, 1930-1976. (Source: National Criminal Justice Reference Service.) As of 1980, Utah and Florida had resumed executions.

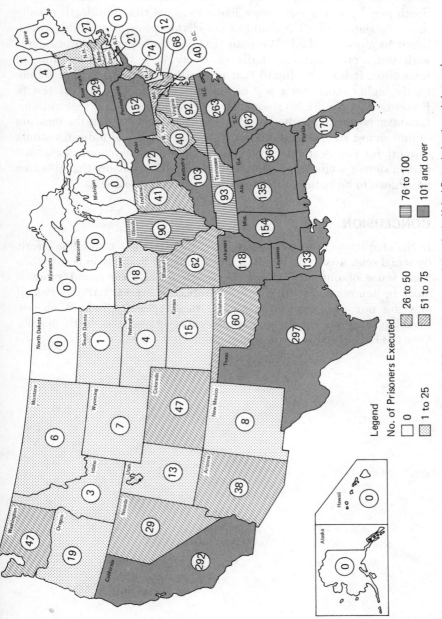

Legend

No. of Prisoners Executed

☐ 0	☐ 76 to 100
☐ 1 to 25	☐ 101 and over
☐ 26 to 50	
☐ 51 to 75	

Note: Excludes 33 Federal executions carried out in the United States during the period covered.

anticapital punishment. On each of the questions it is clear that pro-death penalty jurors were more likely to agree than antideath penalty jurors to statements that manifest conviction proneness; highly preju-dicial to any defendant. We note that prodeath penalty jurors agree with statements that essentially do away with the presumption of innocence. It was also found that prodeath penalty jurors had signifi-cantly higher scores on a test of authoritarianism (see text of test in Resource File No. 6). So frequently do psychologists find that authori-tarianism is equated with a stand on the death penalty that the measure of one almost stands for the other. When an individual indicates strong support for the death penalty under virtually all circumstances, that person signals a cluster of related attitudes and behaviors that research has shown to be better understood as conviction proneness.

CONCLUSION

In the chapter on expert witnessing, we describe some of the fine efforts by social scientists to do research and report the findings in court when their sense of outrage against the death penalty on moral grounds must be tempered by their role as unbiased experts. At the risk of masking our own opposition to the death penalty behind an un-shakable faith, we conclude that advocates against the death penalty have the bulk of social science findings on their side.

13

SOCIAL SCIENCE RESEARCH METHODS APPLIED TO THE LAW: A GUIDE FOR THE PRODUCER AND THE CONSUMER

This will not be easy. Social scientists and legal people indeed speak different languages. No where is this more important than in the case where both are trying to express their views about issues in numerical or statistical terms. The social scientist is trained to think with and use *inferential* statistics; the legal professional is usually more at home with anecdotal thinking of the specific case or "war story." Both forms of thinking have a very important place as we shall develop. In recent years statistical thinking has been making inroads into the criminal justice system and a torrent of numbers awaits those requesting them. The Law Enforcement Assistance Administration annually publishes a *Sourcebook of Criminal Justice Statistics*[1] which in 1976 had over 850

[1] Gottfredson, M. R., Hindelang, M. J., & Parisi, N. (Eds.), *Sourcebook of criminal justice statistics*, 1977. Washington, D.C.: U.S. Department of Justice, (LEAA), February 1978. An annual compendium of tables and valuable reference sections in the appendices describing just how the statistics were compiled. The source of the compilation effort is the Criminal Justice Research Center, Albany, New York, affiliated with the State University of New York, Albany. This massive work is provided free of charge to any subscriber to the National Criminal Justice

pages, mostly tables of data. The impact of the statistics avalanche on the thinking of the working legal professional is not so readily apparent.

NUMBERS

The untrained consumer of numbers (as well as some of the producers) not infrequently will be ignorant of the definitions of words used commonly by the (to them) "new" statisticians. Runyon (1977) gives a common example of how observers at a beauty contest talk about a woman's "vital statistics."[2] Such numbers as 36-23-34 are not statistics at all but are *data*. Only, for example, if one averaged all of the bust sizes of all contestants in the contest and came up with an arithmetic average or mean (e.g., 36.2″) would you really have a vital *statistic*. Another common misinterpretation is to take the single statistic and conclude from this that there is a *trend*. Knowing that this year's Miss America contestants had an average bust size of 36.2″, the untrained consumer might mistakenly conclude that busts are getting larger nowadays. Lacking the statistics of previous year's contestants, places this conclusion in the category of wishful thinking rather than a trend.

Population researchers, who are best described as overtrained in statistics, can get into furious arguments when it comes to trying to reach agreement on the fundamental data, statistics, and trends of their discipline.[3] For example, it would be of immense interest to politicians and the "man" on the street, if the "experts" could agree on whether the population will increase or decrease over the next 20 years. Instead, the technical literature has tended to reflect disagreements among the population experts in interpreting the fundamental data and statistics available. The rate of birth in the United States has showed a steady declining trend since 1960. It took about nine years for a majority of population experts to even agree that downward trend was occurring because many thought that a slight decline might be just due to chance

---

Reference Service (NCJRS), National Institute of Law Enforcement and Criminal Justice, Washington, D.C. 20531. We recommend that any practitioner sign up as a subscriber to the NCJRS service (or its replacement when the name changes) which sends out monthly a complete set of abstracts, publication notices, meeting notices, and the availability of free and paid documents in the field.

[2] Runyon, R. P. *Winning with Statistics*. Reading, Mass.: Addison-Wesley, 1977. A tongue in cheek presentation of the basic concepts of statistics that is invaluable to the consumer and a useful brushup on concepts for the producer of statistical data.

[3] Easterlin, R. A., Wachter, M. L., & Wachter, S. M. Demographic influences on economic stability: The U.S. experience. *Population and Development Review*, 1978, *4* (1), 1–22.

fluctuations in the collection of data. In 1977, with the birthrate still declining, some experts were predicting that the rate would soon show a rise as past trends in birthrate had indicated. The trends in birthrate, like the trends in the crime rate, depend heavily on the quality and general level of acceptance of theory among those who produce and interpret the data and statistics. Population experts look for cyclical trends; many of the criminal justice professionals usually expect straight line trends in the crime rate heading up. All producers of statistics have their most heated arguments over the issue of *prediction*.

Social scientists are taught that statistics can serve the dual functions of *description* and *inference*. Averages and percentages are examples of descriptive statistics; the consuming public is familiar enough with the radio and television news and sports broadcasts that spout statistics to all audiences—a baseball player's batting average, percentage of student loans defaulted, percent interest, rates of growth of stock value, and so on. People who might not be able to compute averages (or compound interest) are still able to use and understand descriptive statistics. Inferential statistics are the special province of a person trained to use statistics for scientific prediction. An *inference* can be thought of as an educated guess with a measurable degree of probability. Only in the daily weather forecasts do we routinely hear the results of applying inferential statistics as the weatherperson states that there is a 10 percent chance of rain on a given day. By comparing sample reports of rain on that day, the season and a set of immediate prior weather conditions, the weatherpeople predict the likelihood that it might rain. Although the prudent weatherperson is careful to qualify every statement with maybe, probability, or possibly, we of course mainly remember when the prediction is wrong. Nobody can predict the future you say? Maybe they can, says the scientist. Besides, we do it all the time.

The consumer of statistics in the criminal justice field is likely to be overwhelmed with both descriptive and inferential statistics and many fundamental policy decisions are based on how statistics are interpreted. An example might be the decision as to whether to appropriate money for a new prison. The data on the current prisoner count are compared with predictions of how fast the prison population is likely to grow, based in turn on the crime rate, arrest rate, average sentence time, percentage of paroles granted, conviction rate in all areas of crime, death rate of prisoners, and so on. Small wonder then that the expert on statistics is turned to at times to help to interpret these data. The expert's counterpart, fortified with the anecdotal evidence that "everything goes up including crime," may simply assert that we need new prisons. The two analysts coexist in any system.

DATA

Where do all the data come from? The principal source for data is the archives of bureaucratic agencies, where figures in raw form are collected for management purposes other than description or for making inferences. Unfortunately, most criminal justice agencies have turned to thoughts of doing research only after their archives have reached a state of utter chaos. Prodding from the federal government has forced these agencies to supply summary statistics to qualify for funding and thus paved the way for researchers who are accelerating the revolution in the use of statistics. The systematic collection of data with research and evaluation in mind is an old dream of many social scientists who think of the social agency as engaging in a social experiment whose impact demands good research in order to justify it. But the existence of usable research data in the files of criminal justice agencies remains the exception rather than the rule. The absence of good descriptive statistical data can lead to a situation where the agency really does not know what it is doing poorly or effectively—a situation we dwell on in other chapters.

A case in point occurred in the New York area when a Victim–Witness Assistance Center, heavily funded by the Law Enforcement Assistance Administration, was set up near a Criminal Court with the largest case load in the United States.[4] The purpose of the center was to keep track of criminal cases handled by the prosecutor's office in order to inform and schedule witnesses and victims of crime so that their time and inconvenience could be minimized. The center was mandated by law to do evaluation research on such matters as case load, time saved, costs, delays, and so on. The center personnel found that they first had to help create and streamline an accounting system for an overburdened prosecutor's office mired in the precomputer era of chaotic paper records. To show any improvement, the Victim–Witness Center first had to establish just what was going on; a question that the agency itself simply could not answer.

YIELDING TO THE COMPUTER

The criminal justice system may have been slow to adopt computers for everyday operation, but once the movement began billions of dollars were spent (especially in law enforcement) to install the devices throughout the country. Most of the computer programming efforts have been put into management—the handling of schedules, prisoner counts, court dockets, lists of people wanted on various charges (part

[4] Stern, S., & Sullivan, R. The victim witness assistance project. *Social Action and the Law*, 1976, 3 (2), 18.

of a national system), payrolls, and other administrative details. Only a small part of any agency's large computer budget is allocated to research, although, under federal law in the 1970s, the condition for the award of federal funds to local criminal justice agencies and courts was that some percentage of the budget be earmarked for evaluation research. Clark (1977) credits the Law Enforcement Assistance Administration (LEAA) with revolutionizing police agencies with money and computers over a period of ten years, beginning in 1968.[5] Clark and other observers see the computer as the harbinger of change in otherwise resistant agencies. Although agencies have adapted to the use of computers to generate descriptive statistics (for budget purposes), the next big step is to use the data as a basis for generating inferential statistics about processes.

SURVEY RESEARCH: SOME PROBLEMS AND ADVANTAGES

The criminal justice field overflows with the results of surveys, in spite of the claims by professionals that there are never enough data. Criminal justice topics have been included on national public opinion surveys for decades. It is possible, as we do in Chapter 12 to trace the ups and downs of favorability by the public toward the death penalty from 1960 to the present. Such surveys, competently done by the Gallup and Harris polling organizations, are preserved for use by scholars on public access computer tapes available in most university centers. In criminal justice, as in the field of politics, an enormous amount of faith has been placed on the results of such surveys, to the extent that the data obtained are often more trusted indicators than the data provided by such agencies as police departments.

One example is the annual compilation of the *Uniform Crime Reports* by the Federal Bureau of Investigation (FBI).[6] The so-called UCR is relied on by law enforcement agencies as a reliable source of national criminal statistics (with local breakdowns) for management purposes and by the public as an indicator of the level of criminality in society. It is a voluntary program of standardized data submitted to the FBI covering crimes in the following categories: murder and negligent manslaughter, aggravated assault, forcible rape, robbery,

---

[5] Clark, R. S. *Fundamentals of Criminal Justice Research.* Lexington, Mass.: Lexington Books, 1977. A very elementary how-to handle data book used to train people in data management. Statisticians will find it too lightweight.

[6] *Uniform Crime Reports for the United States,* 1976, issued by the Director, Federal Bureau of Investigation, U.S. Department of Justice, Washington, D.C., September 1977. Available from the Government Printing Office, this perennial is the bible of crime reporting.

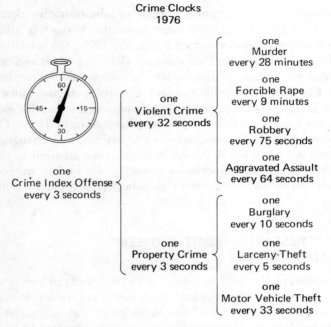

Figure 13.1 An Example of a "statistical" presentation from the *Uniform Crime Reports*. Published annually by the FBI.

burglary, larceny-theft and motor vehicle theft. A composite crime index is compiled and has come to be known as *the* crime rate or index. The FBI provides training to law enforcement personnel involved in compiling and reporting data in an effort to maintain quality control.[7]

One of the major problems with the UCR indices is that each year the number of agencies reporting increases and the quality of some of the reports improves. This creates some difficulty in interpreting year-to-year trends because an apparent rise in the crime rate may be attributed in part to improvements in reporting. It is in no way a sampling survey but, rather, an incomplete actuarial count of crimes by cooperating agencies. Another problem is the difference in recording practices in different police departments and the obvious fluctuations over time that probably reflect administrative or political pressures.[8]

[7] Ibid.

[8] Fox, J. A. *Forecasting Crime Data: An Econometric Analysis.* Lexington, Mass.: Lexington Books, 1978, p. 7: See also Beattie, R. H. Criminal statistics in the U.S., 1960. *Journal of Criminal Law, Criminology, and Police Science*, 1960, *51*, 49–65; Robinson, S. M. A critical view of the Uniform Crime Reports, *Michigan Law Review*, 1966, *64*, 1031–1054; Wolfgang, M. E., & Cohen, B., Uniform Crime Reports: A critical appraisal, *University of Pennsylvania Law Review*, 1963, *111*, 708–738.

Depending on election promises, it may behoove a reporting agency to show either an increase or decrease in *its* crime rate. Some critics feel that the reports are useless because they come only from law enforcement agencies which have a stake in appearing to be needed, suggesting an inflation of the true crime rate.[9] Other critics point to surveys of crime victims which suggest, if anything that the number of crimes has always been grossly underreported.

But criticisms or not, the UCR figures remain as one of the enduring "sacred cows" of criminal justice policy planning in the United States. Further, unlike the usual technical report on a statistical survey, the UCR comes replete with readily understood graphics and easily digested statements about the meaning of data (see Figure 13.1). Because these presentations are translated into easily read newspaper and television reports, the general public has become conditioned to expect the "FBI Crime Reports" at periodic intervals. In addition, scholars who have done research on such problems as deterrence have looked on the UCR crime rates (per 100,000 population) as the dependent variable to be predicted or influenced by independent variables ranging from the weather to the existence of the death penalty (see Chapter 12). It is somewhat disturbing to acknowledge in the UCR time series aggregate data that the old computer warning of GIGO (Garbage In-Garbage Out) may apply.

THE NATIONAL CRIME SURVEYS (NCS)

In 1972 when the Law Enforcement Administration (LEAA) was pouring out money into a wide variety of projects, the very ambitious National Crime Survey (NCS) was created to meet the need for valid crime data and to overcome some of the criticisms of the older methods such as those evident in the UCR.[10] Instead of sampling law enforcement agency data, the objective was to reach 60,000 households and 39,000 business establishments every six months and to conduct personal interviews with victims and potential victims. It is known that many crimes are not reported to the police and that the much used crime rate compiled in the UCR greatly underestimates certain crimes such as burglary and rape. Murder is still well reported with little difference between the UCR rates and the NCS victimization rates. But

---

[9] Fox, J. A., Ibid, p. 8.

[10] Penick, B. K., & Owens, M. E. B. (Eds.), *Surveying crime*. Washington, D.C.: National Research Council of the National Academy of Sciences, 1976; see also White, S. O., & Krislov, S. (Eds.), *Understanding crime*. Washington, D.C.: National Research Council of the National Academy of Sciences, 1977. Both reports deal critically with the programs to generate crime statistics and do not suffer from the bias that can afflict agency reports written by "the agency" itself.

when it came to rape, the NCS surveys indicated that only one in three rapes were reported to the police. Even fewer burglaries are reported because both individuals and business have reason to believe that reporting these crimes will gain little and cost a great deal in time, increased insurance premiums and inconvenience. A special review of the NCS program conducted by the National Research Council of the National Academy of Sciences generally applauded the NCS program as a step forward in accurately collecting social indicators of crime. The perspective of speaking of crime from the victim's point of view is a welcome one. Our only observation is that the expensive survey program appears to be oversampling the population and that the memory of victims may not be accurate enough to ensure reliability of the data collected.

NATIONAL PUBLIC OPINION SURVEYS

A substantial portion of the data shown in Resource File No. 12, is the results of surveys conducted by the Gallup poll, the Harris survey, and the Survey Research Center at the University of Michigan. To the researcher, the public access computer tapes containing the basic survey data from these and other files (in particular the National Opinion Research Corporation (NORC) files) are valuable aids that may save the cost of launching an expensive opinion survey for a supposedly new research challenge. In the "Law and Social Science Resources File" (particularly File No. 13), we have reprinted the sampling procedures used by Gallup and the Harris survey as model examples of how to conduct opinion surveys.[11] We would additionally recommend *Measures of Social Psychological Attitudes* as a basic reference work for developing the wording of questionnaires.[12] Some examples of questionnaires developed for use in research cited in other chapters are reprinted in other parts of the Resource Files.

SIMULATING THE LEGAL WORLD

At several points in the text we apologize to the legal world for the limitations in the data we discuss because so much of it has been generated from laboratory studies that purport to simulate the essence of the problem under discussion. Among the many examples are a respectably large set of studies of "mock juries" whose members are

---

[11] Gottfredson et al., op. cit.
[12] Robinson, J. P., & Shaver, P. R. *Measures of Social Psychological Attitudes.* Ann Arbor, Mich.: Survey Research Center, Institute for Social Research, The University of Michigan, 1973.

subjected to a condensed version of a court trial and then asked to render a verdict, "as if . . ." Subjects who serve in such experiments are generally aware of the fact that their role playing will have no real consequences for the life of a real person, hence a goodly amount of criticism has been directed at such studies. Yet the psychologist is operating under some practical and ethical restraints that preclude the conduct of research with either "high fidelity" realism or research directly conducted in the legal world.[13, 14]

In some of our research on the degree of reliability of the eye-witness to a crime, for example, one of the hypotheses we have tested concerns the extent to which a witness remains accurate as the level of stress during observation increases.[15] It is possible through careful simulation to provide a witness with a somewhat upsetting observation to make (e.g., an individual who is apparently bleeding) in one condition and compare the accuracy of eyewitness reports to a situation that is objectively less stressful. But the legal question posed by the court is whether a witness whose life is threatened by an assailant with a gun is less likely or more likely to recognize the "perpetrator's" face at a later date. We cannot ethically (or even legally) run around surprising witnesses, threatening them, and then test their perception. Thus the proper answer for a psychologist who is asked about the accuracy of a witness under such conditions is "I don't know." What the psychologist does know, based on the limited laboratory research approach already described, is that as the level of stress reported by witnesses increases, the accuracy of the eyewitness reports decrease. The simulations are probably all that can be safely done to test the hypothesis empirically. Of course, the findings of less accuracy remain controversial in legal circles because of the often quoted statement by highly stressed victims of crime to the effect that "I will never forget that face; it is burned into my mind." Common sense, however mistaken it might be, can only be countered with some research findings that come from studies that contain a limited amount of the mundane realism of the "real" world.

[13] Davis, J. H., Bray, R. M., & Holt, R. W. The empirical study of decision processes in juries: A critical review. In J. L. Tapp and F. J. Levine (Eds.), *Law Justice and the Individual in Society*. Holt, Rinehart and Winston, 1977, pp. 326–362.
[14] Streufert, S., & Suedfeld, P. Editorial: Simulation as research method: A problem in communication. *Journal of Applied Social Psychology*, 1977, 7 (4), 281–285; see also Dawson, R. E., Simulation in the social sciences. In H. Guetzkow (Ed.), *Simulation in Social Science: Readings*. Englewood Cliffs, N.J.: Prentice-Hall, 1972.
[15] Buckhout, R., and Greenwald, M. Witness Psychology, Imwinkelreid, J. (Ed.) *Handbook of Forensic Evidence*, New York: Practising Law Institute, 1980. In Press.

Applying social psychological research techniques to legal problems has resulted in great reliance on simulation either in the laboratory or in controlled field settings. Because social scientists can be naive about the needed level of realism, the consumer of research findings based on simulation research needs to be an informed consumer. A case in point is the simulation of the role of the juror in a trial. Far too many studies as noted by Gerbasi et al. (1977) have relied on the presentation of case summaries to *individuals* who then render an individual "verdict."[16] It is obvious that such a simulation of the real function of jurors is minimal, because the essence of the role is that the juror is a member of a group that will deliberate and vote on a (usually unanimous) verdict. The researcher who may be concerned about cost and efficiency as much as experimental validity is always in the position of making trade-off decisions. But a number of critics (Streufert and Suedfeld, 1977) make the point that some of the shortcuts to simulation raise serious doubts about the relevance of the research to the problem of jury behavior. For every one verdict a good mundanely realistic simulation would require 6 or 12 subjects, more time and more cost.

In the following section we present an edited text of a published mock jury study with interpolated comments intended to be a consumer's guide (and producer's warning guide) to the planning, interpretation, and use of findings from a simulated jury study.[17]

AN ANNOTATED SOCIAL SCIENCE PRODUCT, PLUS COMMENTS

Jury verdicts: Comparison of 6- vs. 12-person juries and unanimous vs. majority decision rule in a murder trial

ROBERT BUCKHOUT, STEVE WEG, VINCENT REILLY, and ROBINSUE FROHBOESE
*Center for Responsive Psychology, Brooklyn College, City University of New York,
Brooklyn, New York 11210*

A total of 180 jurors from the Kings County, New York, Jury Assembly room served as mock jurors in a murder trial presented on videotape. Subjects were randomly assigned to cells of a 2 by 2 design which varied jury size (6 vs. 12) and verdict decision rule (majority vs. unanimous). An ANOVA showed that jury verdicts became more severe as a result of deliberating in the smaller jury and under majority rule. The majority decision rule clearly resulted in more convictions. Empirical support for the smaller size jury effect was limited.

16 Gerbasi, K. C., Zuckerman, M., & Reis, H. T. Justice needs a new blindfold: A review of mock jury research. *Psychological Bulletin*, 1977, *84* (2), 323–345.
17 Buckhout, R., Weg, S., Reilly, V., & Frohboese, R. Jury verdicts: Comparison of 6 vs. 12-person juries and unanimous vs. majority decision rule in a murder trial. *Bulletin of the Psychonomic Society*, 1977, *10* (3), 175–178.

COMMENT 1   A note for the psychological researcher—to spell out carefully the range and limits of the study in the abstract. Every research study on law-related topics will be coded and filed into elaborate computer-based information systems solely on the basis of the information contained in the abstract and the title.[18] Further, the coding process and the extracting of key words to fit existing taxonomies will be done by people who are likely *never* to read the entire article. Thus the degree to which this research becomes available to the legal community (as well as the scientific community) depends heavily on how carefully the title and abstract are crafted.

Consumer Note   The journal in which this article is published is obscure —many of the social science journals are. The *Bulletin of the Psychonomic Society*, however, is abstracted in the standard reference work *Psychological Abstracts.* In addition, the table of contents of the *Bulletin* is reproduced along with almost every other psychological journal's table of contents in the behavioral sciences edition of *Current Contents,* a reference work that also lists the contents of all law journals (try to find the *Notre Dame Lawyer* in a New York law school library).

> The U.S. Supreme Court is hesitantly looking to social scientists to provide empirical data on which major decisions affecting jury trials can be based. Regretably, the court is not finding much data, either because the research has not been done or because some of the available research data are not adequate (Buckhout, Note 1). In the dubious search for efficiency, many state court systems have moved to the use of 6-person as opposed to 12-person juries and are experimenting with a relaxation of the unanimous decision rule in favor of a majority (usually 5/6) decision rule. Several challenges to these rule changes have arrived in the Supreme Court, and neither psychology nor the law has looked all that good in the written opinions of the court.
>
> The Supreme Court has displayed a profound ignorance of the meaning and value of empirical research in its recent decisions affecting juries. In Apodaca et al. vs. Oregon (1972) and Johnson vs. Louisiana (1971), the court studied the question of the obligation of the states to provide for a unanimous verdict in criminal trials, as opposed to some majority decision rule. The court held that, in other than federal cases, the unanimous decision rule is not guaranteed under the Constitution and, hence, may be left to the discretion of the states to establish. Justice Douglas, in a fierce dissenting opinion,

[18] Katzer, J., Cook, K. H., & Crouch, W. W. *Evaluating information: A guide for users of social science research.* Reading, Mass.: Addison-Wesley, 1978.

argued that the Court ignored the fact that nonunanimous juries convict about twice as often as unanimous juries do.

An equally fundamental question was raised in Williams vs. Florida (1970) and Colgrove vs. Battin (1973) concerning the right to trial by a 12-member jury. Here the Court similarly held that the size of a jury, in other than federal cases, is not guaranteed. In both instances the Court's conclusions were based on the presumption that changes in neither decision rule nor jury size would, in and of themselves, affect conviction rates. Both conclusions were drawn in the absence of firm empirical evidence, relying heavily on the data and opinions found in that wide-ranging, now classic book, *The American Jury*, by Kalven and Zeisel (1966) plus some law review articles (Berman & Coppock, 1973; Kessler, 1973; Mills, 1973).

COMMENT 2   Establishing both the legal relevance and the scientific relevance is no easy task. Scientific journal editors expect a certain amount of base-touching with the masters of the discipline or (perhaps uncharitably) with current trends among the "in" researchers. Scientific journal editors are only slowly learning the values and problems inherent in writing about cross-disciplinary research. In short, they need to be educated if the work is to find any acceptance. Further, we note that this is an unabashedly applied piece of research. A psychologist familiar with group dynamics and probability theory might well say, "My God! This is so obvious! Why do a research project at all? Why not generalize from all the simpler classic research on group size?" The answer must be that reviews of the technical literature (as reported in Chapter 7) reveal no such easy basis for generalization. In fact, most psychological research on groups that considered group size, dealt with smaller sizes than 12 and usually involved *consensus* decision rules around issues that were rather minor. An applied researcher hoping to make a scientific contribution to the dialogue before the court must be able to report findings that are based on situations (jury) that have a considerable degree of mundane realism.

Kalven and Zeisel pinpoint the nature and hazards of the type of study relied upon by the Court quite succinctly. In its optimal form, they explain, "It can be viewed as simply a retrospective controlled experiment. The cases are grouped *after the fact* by the critical variable to see if the variable has produced a difference . . . . The logic is precisely the same as for the experiment, except for one important and in the end ineradicable difficulty; one can never be sure that the groups of cases to be compared are comparable in all respects other than the critical variable" (pp. 89-90).

Zeisel (1974) bitterly criticized the Supreme Court for its statistical ignorance of the fact that "the smaller the size of the sample, the larger the margin of error." Further, he notes that smaller juries mean less representativeness of the community in seated juries. Saks (1974) noted that some of the studies cited in *Colgrove* actually reported data opposite to the interpretations made by the Court. His criticism, directed at both psychologists and lawyers, was ably summed up as follows: "The fact that reliable empirical evidence on these questions is lacking is largely the fault of social scientists who are insufficiently knowledgeable about the law to know what data the law needs. And the agents of the law are such strangers to empirical methods of understanding behavior they cannot tell that they have not been provided with the necessary empirical data."

More recently, Davis, Kerr, Atkin, Holt, and Meek (1975) reported no significant differences among student mock jury verdicts as a function of either size or decision rule. Valenti and Downing (1975) reported that, in prosecution-oriented cases, 6-person juries were more likely to convict than 12-person juries. Grofman (Note 2) reanalyzed the Valenti and Downing data, noting that the predeliberation verdicts of the 6-person juries were closer to a conviction than the 12-person juries. Grofman relegates the Valenti and Downing findings to inadequately controlled sampling, a problem exacerbated by the limited overall sample size.

Despite the absence of clear-cut empirical support, social scientists (e.g., Gelfand, 1977) maintain that the mathematics of the group sizes in a jury would force more decisions with a smaller jury and hence more convictions, since approximately 83% of all criminal juries convict (Kalven & Zeisel, 1966). Lempert (1975) points out that to detect a difference due to size would require a prohibitively large number of juries and he speculates on the possibility that the Supreme Court has contented itself with data which might mask a Type II error.

COMMENT 3 Here the review of literature points out the inadequacy of more recent relevant research efforts and the special problem posed by the tendency of legal professionals to equate the null hypothesis with the "proof" of any other hypothesis. The Supreme Court had been content with the acceptance by earlier researchers of a finding of no difference between 6 and 12 person juries, in spite of the possibility that a Type II error could be made. Social scientists are so overtrained to be careful about making the Type I error that they are not always clear in their explanation of results in which the null hypothesis is accepted. The world of applied research is one of the few areas in which negative scientific findings or *null hypothesis* results can even be published. Null hypothesis results simply are reports of no difference in scores between experimental and control groups.

Consumer Note   The *Type II error* is defined as a decision to accept the null hypothesis (a statement that there is no difference between experimental conditions) when in fact it is false. A finding of no difference in this study could mask the fact that in reality jury size does make a difference but that the demonstration of it is beyond the budget or even the skill of the researcher. The *Type I error* is made when a researcher decides to reject the null hypothesis, accept the hypothesis under test (here that jury size affects conviction rates) when, in reality, the null hypothesis is true. Because any experiment is an exercise in probabalistic decision making, the possibility of either error exists. Faith in results which avoid these errors stems from the repeatability of the findings and the adequacy of the methods employed.

> Our experiment suffers from some of the same problems noted above, since the sample size is limited. We ambitiously set out to compare the effects of jury size and decision rule in the real world—in a jury assembly room. Unfortunately, the Court withdrew permission for the research after we had tested a total of 20 juries in a 2 by 2 design. Comparing 6- vs. 12-person juries under a unanimous vs. majority decision rule, we tested whether a shift in procedure would affect jury verdicts. We offer these findings as an aid to other researchers who might gain from our experience under more favorable test conditions.

COMMENT 4   The candor here is necessary and speaks for itself. This research study obviously will not be the scientific breakthrough to settle the jury size and jury decision rule matter forever.

Reprints and background information, including a full transcript of the trial, may be obtained from the senior author at the Center for Responsive Psychology, Brooklyn College, CUNY, Brooklyn, New York 11210. An early report of this research was presented to the Eastern Psychological Association, New York, April 15, 1975. This research was supported (in part) by a grant from the Faculty Research Award Program of the City University of New York. Robinsue Frohboese is now at the Law-Psychology Program, University of Nebraska-Lincoln; 209 Burnett Hall, Lincoln, Nebraska 68508.

COMMENT 5 If an applied research study is taken seriously by people in the legal profession, the availability of the full details of the experiment becomes crucial. Because lawyers may well question how realistic the trial was, a full transcript of the words used as the independent variable or setting may be requested. If a psychologist had occasion to write a brief or to testify on the meaning of the research, details going beyond the limits of scientific publication might well be expected and should be easily secured from the authors.

METHOD

Subjects

A total of 180 jurors from the Jury Assembly in the Kings County, New York, Supreme Court were randomly assigned by the jury clerk to serve as mock jurors in the trial (as done for actual trials). The characteristics of the sample group matched the demographic profile of New York City jurors very closely. They were near the end of their 2-week term and were given the option of remaining in or leaving the experiment.

COMMENT 6 Discussion of social science findings before U.S. courts has been going on long enough for there to be a degree of sophistication about the sampling of subjects. Many judges share the concern of many scientists about the common practice of using college students as subjects in experiments. Because the average age of jurors is from 38–40, it is rather essential that any deviation from using subjects in the older range be justified. As it turns out, one of the authors (Weg) used a group of college students in the identical experiment and came up with completely different results. The students so rarely could agree on a verdict that most of the juries ended up with a "hung" verdict. This only served to confirm the warning that proper sampling in certain applied experiments is essential if we are to generalize the findings.

Procedure

The mock jurors completed demographic questionnaires. Each then read a brief summary of the case he would have to judge to compensate for the relative brevity of the videotaped presentation which was to follow. It was deemed important that the "facts" of the case be understood and that a preliminary briefing as to the testimony the jurors would hear would facilitate comprehension. Juror numbers were randomly assigned to each person, resulting in their assignment to an experimental condition.

Following the reading of the case summary, jurors viewed a videotaped presentation of a "mock" murder trial. In this case the defendant is accused of committing murder during the attempted commission of a robbery. The case, adapted from Vidmar (1972), is constructed in such a way that questions as to guilt arise from gross differences in the testimony of witnesses. Modifications allowing for locale (the original case was heard in Canada) were made. Furthermore, as no transcript was available, a script was extrapolated for use in the videotaping. In doing so, certain liberties were taken in adpating the case for dramatic presentation, in order to optimize the ambiguous nature of the testimony. Included in the script were the standard judge's instructions (New York State) concerning evidence and reasonable doubt, summations by prosecutor and defense attorney, and a final charge by the judge.

The presentation itself was taped on ½-in. black-white videotape and ran 32 min in length. Actual technical production was handled by the Brooklyn College Television Center. Taping was done with three ceiling-mounted television cameras in a small studio. Three separate microphones were placed around the studio to pick up the audio of all participants. The studio was equipped with an isolated control room. Actors were nonprofessional and consisted of a group of Brooklyn College students and psychology faculty members.

After viewing the videotaped presentation, subjects completed predeliberation verdict questionnaires. This was done to provide data on decision changes during the deliberation process. The option of verdicts available to the jurors were as follows: (1) guilty of first-degree murder, (2) guilty of second-degree murder, (3) guilty of reckless manslaughter, (4) guilty of negligent manslaughter, (5) not guilty. (Options 2-4 were lesser included verdicts.) The nature and definition of each of these charges were included in the questionnaire. They were also explained by the judge in her charge to the jury (the final segment of the videotaped presentation).

Allowing the jurors to decide the actual charge of the "guilty" verdict is not standard legal procedure in most jurisdictions, although in specified areas today, as well as historically, such practice has been made. More typically, the jury would only decide guilt or innocence of a single charge, specified by the court. In choosing the atypical procedure, two considerations were kept in mind. The first of these was that the greater sensitivity of this measure of verdict severity seemed desirable. Jurors differ in terms of how strongly they feel about their verdicts, and a simple "guilty/not guilty" measure would not expose these differences. Second, as the script of the mock trial has not been used previously in this context, there was no way of knowing which verdicts to expect. While ambiguity was emphasized, any quirks in the transcript might have swayed the verdicts too much in one direction to reasonably allow for choice on the parts of the jurors.

Following completion of the predeliberation verdict questionnaires, the juries were left unobserved to deliberate and arrive at group verdicts, according to the instructions from the experimenter concerning decision rules.

Subjects were assigned to one of four conditions. Assignment was made to either 12 or 6 juries, under decision rules of either unanimity or 5/6 quorum. There were 20 mock juries, with 5 juries in each of the following conditions: (1) 12-member juries, under a unanimous decision rule; (2) 12-member juries, under a 5/6 quorum decision rule; (3) 6-member juries, under a unanimous decision rule; (4) 6-member juries, under a 5/6 quorum decision rule. Instructions as to what would constitute a final verdict for a particular jury (i.e., the decision rule) were given by the experimenter, rather than by the judge (as would normally occur in a real trial).

Following deliberations, each juror completed a final questionnaire, asking for his jury's verdict, as well as for his individual verdict. Once again the nature and definition of each charge was included on the form.

COMMENT 7 This long methods section is familiar up to the point where there was one deviation made in the role given to jurors that might affect the generalizability of the results. The typical researcher's trade-off led the authors to give the jurors a continuous measure of verdict rather than the more familiar guilty/not guilty choice. A continuous measure permits more variability and allows for more sophisticated statistical analysis than dichotomous measures. In fact, verdict options are permitted in some states and jurors usually realize that the amount of sentence given on conviction is correlated with the seriousness of the charge. Exact simulation can be replaced by functional simulation of the juror role as long as the essence of the role is retained.

RESULTS

Decision Rule and Verdicts

By assigning scores of 1 through 5 (guilty through not guilty), we determined the mean verdict for each jury averaged over the five juries in each cell of the design. There were no significant differences in predeliberation verdict (F = .71, 3.06, .59; df = 1/16). The main dependent variable results, final jury verdicts of all 20 juries under the unanimous and nonunanimous verdict rules, are shown in Table 1. Under the unanimous verdict decision rule, there were only three convictions and seven hung juries, an outcome which may be regarded as the normally expected or control outcome by typical jurors in reaction to the weight of evidence in this particular trial. Changing the decision rule to a 5/6 or 10/12 majority rule resulted in nine (or three times as many) convictions, a finding which was highly significant (Z = 4.29, p < .001). Two of the six-person juries voted to convict the defendant of second-degree murder under the nonunanimous verdict rule. Only one nonunanimous rule jury reported that it was deadlocked.

COMMENT 8 The small number of juries results from the restrictions placed on the researchers by the court and the necessity of getting only one verdict per 6- or 12-person jury. The statistical test used is the Z test of a difference in proportion that is suitable for comparing small data set percentages and is a very useful statistic.[19]

[19] Siegel, S. *Nonparametric statistics for the behavioral sciences.* New York: McGraw-Hill, 1956.

Consumer Note These are the most difficult sections of any report to digest for anyone who lacks statistical training. In a legal hearing it is incumbent on the social scientist to translate the statistical tests used into coherent English. It can be done.

Jury Size and Verdicts

In Table 2, in a comparison of all 6-person and 12-person juries, the number of convictions was the same, but the severity of the final verdicts was somewhat higher in 6-person juries. The small number of juries tested contributed to a lack of statistical significance in the testing of the size variable. The combination of a nonunanimous verdict rule in a 6-person jury produced 100% convictions.

COMMENT 9 What the authors really mean is that they accepted the null hypothesis but are suspicious of the possibility that they too might be making a Type II error if they rested with this finding.

Table 1
Final Jury Verdicts as a Function of Decision Rule

	Decision Rule	
Convictions	Unanimous	Non-unanimous*
Second-Degree Murder		2
Reckless Manslaughter	3	6
Negligent Manslaughter		1
Hung Juries	7	1

5/6 or 10/12

Table 2
Final Jury Verdicts as a Function of Jury Size

	Jury Size	
Convictions	6-Person	12-Person
Second-Degree Murder	2	
Reckless Manslaughter	3	6
Negligent Manslaughter	1	
Hung Juries	4	4

Effects of Deliberation

Using the recorded verdict prior to the start of deliberation, the mean predeliberation verdict was computed for each jury in each cell of the experimental design. The average overall pre-verdict was 3.05, which

Table 3
Analysis of Variance of Changes from Pre- to Post-Verdicts Due
to Deliberation by Juries in a Metropolitan Supreme Court

Source	df	MS	F
Jury Size (s)	1	.8799	6.479*
Verdict Rule (V)	1	.9598	7.067*
S by V	1	.4148	3.055
Error	16	.1358	
Total	19		

*$p < .05$ Note—Mean shift: 6-person juries, $-.191$; 12-person juries, $+.228$; unanimous juries, $+.238$; nonunanimous juries, $-.200$.

averages out to conviction for reckless manslaughter with only a few votes for acquittal. The focus of the deliberations was destined to be on which of the levels of "guilty" would be voted for. To evaluate the effects of deliberating under variations in jury size and verdict rule, a 2 by 2 analysis of variance on the differences between mean predeliberation and mean postdeliberation individual verdicts for each jury was computed (see Table 3). The main effects of both verdict rule and jury size were significant ($p < .05$). In the case of jury size, the change in mean jury verdict was toward a more severe verdict in the 6-person condition and toward a less severe verdict in the 12-person condition. The nonunanimous decision rule produced a mean shift toward the more severe verdict, while the unanimous decision rule effected a shift toward a less severe verdict ($p < .05$). The interaction mean square fell short of significance. The importance of these deliberation effects can be better understood in light of the fact that, as expected, the final individual verdicts were significantly correlated with the pre-verdicts ($r = .54$, $p < .001$), though the relationship accounts for only 29% of the variance.

COMMENT 10   The authors' use of the analysis of variance is part of a reliance by social scientists on powerful statistical techniques. It adds very little to this report because it is much of an abstraction to take the mean verdict of a jury that, of course, has no legal standing whatsoever. The ANOVA may be useful to future researchers interested in the relative contributions of the two independent variables—jury size and decision rule. The meaning of the prepost verdict correlation is not clear and should have been explained in more detail. Correlations tend to be computed on the strength of two scores from every individual that, of course, removes them from the constraints of the jury within which they are deliberating. As such, correlations of this sort are rather misleading because they suggest that once a juror's mind is set, little can change it.

Within a given jury, the changing of two to four minds may completely change the verdict as a result of deliberation, and it matters little that the correlation of pre- to post-verdicts was high.

DISCUSSION

It is important to review at this point the fact that we attempted to conduct this study in the real world of a State Court jury assembly room in order to approximate the realism of jury trials as closely as practicable. Our mock trial was something that ordinary jurors were randomly assigned to, just as they would be assigned to any other trial. While we did not have the voir dire screening and selection by lawyers common to a real trial, the resulting demographic profile of our jurors showed them to be markedly similar to the typical juror who serves in the court in which we worked. Of course, they lacked the sense of urgency and involvement that a juror feels when he has a real defendant's life in his hands, but we were pleased to find that the jurors took the deliberations seriously and argued strongly for their points of view. Unfortunately, as happens in the real world, our research was cut short by the decision of an administrative judge who feared that our research might cause the jurors to think about their roles and in some way affect their later performance as jurors in real trials.

COMMENT 11 At least the authorities waited until a balance had been achieved in the assignments of jurors to treatment conditions. But the problem of conducting experimental research in the real world often leads to clashes as political or bureaucratic sensibilities are brushed against. A new administrative judge found out that his predecessor had granted permission to the authors to conduct their research, hence he felt that a show of authority was in order. The judge touched a point that we have heard before about jurors; that is, it is better to curse their ignorance than to light a candle, less they become too aware. We later learned that some lawyers had threatened to challenge any juror who had been in the study for cause if they showed up on a jury panel.

The results of this experiment clearly confirm the hypothesis that a change in decision rule from unanimous to a majority verdict is conducive to a greater number of convictions by criminal trial juries in the face of the same trial and the same evidence. The results provided only partial support for the predicted effects of reducing jury size from 12 to 6 persons. The number of convictions was the same, but the 6-person juries brought in more severe (second-degree murder) verdicts in two instances. These are the most important findings from the standpoint of the relevant Supreme Court decisions, supplying some of the "missing" empirical data noted in the dissent opinion of Justice Douglas (U.S., Johnson vs. Louisiana, 1971).

In the present study, the 12-person or the unanimous verdict conditions are the "control" conditions against which to judge the results. In the case of a unanimous verdict, the most likely outcome of this trial would have been a hung jury. But the majority (5/6 or 10/12) verdict rule clearly was more advantageous to the prosecution in that more convictions resulted.

Since the intent of the Supreme Court is that neither the state nor the defendant should gain advantage from a mere change in procedure, it is clear that the Court has incorrectly concluded that variations in size or decision rule have no effect on judicial finding. The anecdotal discussions of the Justices may now be supplemented by at least some hard data which support the proposition that both the 12-person jury and the unanimous verdict rule should be retained in criminal trials.

COMMENT 12   Having exercised caution and shown candor throughout the formal parts of the paper, it is reasonable for the authors to speculate and even to assert strongly the worthwhileness of their findings. Like the comments of a lawyer in court, comments in the discussion are *not* evidence. The social scientist would be well advised, however, to consult an attorney or judge in writing this part of the report so that his or her meaning is not completely misinterpreted by the legal professional trying to fit the findings into a legal brief.

REFERENCE NOTES

1. Buckhout, R. *The U.S. Supreme Court vs. social Science: The jury* (Report No. CR-28). Brooklyn, N.Y: Brooklyn College, Center for Responsive Psychology, April 1977.
2. Grofman, B. Personal communication, February 16, 1977.
3. Buckhout, R., Weg, S., Frohboese, R., & Reilly, V. *Jury verdicts: Six vs. 12 person juries, unanimous vs. majority decision rule in a murder trial* (Report No. CR-12). Brooklyn, N.Y: Brooklyn College, Center for Responsive Psychology, April 1977.

REFERENCES

Apodaca et al. vs. Oregon, 406 U.S. 404, 1971.

Berman, G., & Coppock, R. Outcomes of six and twelve member jury trials: An analysis of 128 civil cases in the State of Washington. *Washington Law Review*, 1973, **48**, 593-596.

Buckhout, R., et al. Jury without peers. In M. Reidel & P. A. Vales (Eds.), *Treating the offender: Problems and issues*. New York: Praeger, 1977.

Colgrove vs. Battin, 413 U.S. 149, 1973.

Davis, J. H., Kerr, H. L., Atkin, R. W., Holt, R., & Meek, D. The decision processes of 6- and 12-person mock juries assigned unanimous and 2/3 majority rules. *Journal of Personality and Social Psychology*, 1975, **32**, 1-14.

Gelfand, A. E. A statistical case for the twelve-member jury. *Trial*, 1977, **13**, 41-42.

Johnson vs. Louisiana, 406 U.S. 813, 1971.

Kalven, H., Jr., & Zeisel, H. *The American jury*. Boston: Little, Brown, 1966.

Kessler, J. An empirical study of six- and twelve-member jury decision-making process. *University of Michigan Journal of Law Reform*, 1973, **6**, 712-734.

LEMPERT, R. O. Uncovering "nondiscernible" differences: Empirical research and the jury size cases. *Michigan Law Review*, 1975, **73**, 643-708.

MILLS, L. R. Six member and 'twelve member juries: An empirical study of trial results. *University of Michigan Journal of Law Reform*, 1973, **6**, 671-711.

SAKS, M. J. Ignorance of science is no excuse. *Trial*, 1974, **10**, 18-20.

VALENTI, A., & DOWNING, L. Differential effects of jury size on verdicts following deliberation as a function of apparent guilt of the defendant. *Journal of Personality and Social Psychology*, 1975, **32**, 655-663.

VIDMAR, N. Effects of decision alternatives on the verdicts and social perceptions of simulated jurors. *Journal of Personality and Social Psychology*, 1972, **22**, 211-218.

Williams vs. Florida, 399 U.S. 78, 1970.

ZEISEL, H. Twelve is just. *Trial*, 1974, **10**, 13-15.

(Received for publication May 3, 1977.)

COMMENT 13   The reliance of the law on precedence serves as a warning to the researcher to err in the direction of quantity in citing references. The dual area of psychology and the law demands citations from both—especially relevant court decisions. If the courts are to rely on social scientific findings, they will expect to be able to establish that the findings are "generally accepted" in the particular discipline.

FIELD RESEARCH IN A COURTROOM

The main advantage of stimulating a trial, recording it on videotape, and then playing it back for mock juries to deliberate over is the assurance that all the mock jurors will have experienced the same evidence, the same trial, and the same set of facts and actors (judge, lawyers, etc.). The alternative of conducting a *field* experiment poses many problems, although there is no denying the increased degree of realism. But even if ethical constraints were relaxed and jurors were fooled into thinking that they were deciding a real case (although really being the subject of an experiment), we would have the problem of having each jury see a different live event. The lack of control over the independent variables would make comparisons difficult, to say the least.

One case in point is the fine study of the exercise of peremptory challenges by lawyers which was conducted by Professors Zeisel and Diamond (1978) in a federal district court.[20] Right from the beginning, compromises in sampling had to be made in the interest of time, costs, and permission from court officers. The purpose of the study was to

[20] Zeisel, H., & Diamond, S. S. The effect of peremptory challenges on jury and verdict: An experiment in a federal district court. *Stanford Law Review*, 1978, *30* (3), 491–531.

compare the ordinary *voir dire* exercise of challenges to an experimental situation in which a "shadow jury," made up of those jurors who had been excused, would sit as a parallel jury and hear the case as if they had been selected. A third jury was formed by random selection of the remaining jurors in the room—called the "English" jury. Each of 12 cases was thus heard by one "real" jury and two parallel juries whose verdict would not count. By treating all of the juries the same way, the investigators produced a great deal of ininvolvement and a rich source of comparative data on verdicts and the effectiveness of the challenges exercised by the lawyers in removing jurors from the real panel.

The resulting long paper, published in the *Stanford Law Review*, would probably not overly please the hard-nosed editor of a psychological or sociological journal, because formal experimental designs had to be abandoned in favor of a great deal of inventive but post hoc statistical analysis. Zeisel and Diamond are cautious enough to warn the reader that the 12 trials observed do not represent a probability sample—statisticians would call it an *opportunistic* sample. But the richness of the report comes from its superb mixture of theory, specific case example, and the creation of new ways of collecting data in the future which might help set a predictive equation or inferential approach. New measures are suggested and a certain amount of daring is displayed in testing them out with the data at hand.

Unfortunately, think pieces such as this one are not too welcome in technical journals in the social sciences, forcing the authors to turn to book chapters or law reviews. Social scientists do not hold law review publication in very high regard and do not read the reviews with any regularity. Yet the lengthy report of long but creative struggles to perform experiments in real-world settings deserve to be heard on their merits. For social scientists and legal professionals alike, it is possible that readable reports of relevant interdisciplinary research are more likely to be found in law reviews, books, or lengthy government technical reports than in quality professional journals. We are encouraged to note that some new journals are being founded to fill the gap, notably *Law and Human Behavior*.

An example of good complex data analysis is the presentation of four possible distributions of prejudice among jurors in a *venire* (jury panel) as compared to an ideal assumption of a normal symmetrical distribution of prejudice. The ideal model assumes a *normal* distribution of prejudice—the basis for the employment of most statistical tests. But the various comparison distributions illustrate what can happen when firmly rooted community prejudices exist in a community against certain class distinctions into which a defendant might fall. In our discussion on jury selection (Chapter 8) we discussed the case of pro-prosecution feelings generated by the fact that a given defendant was a Native American living in South Dakota, a black in a small southern town, or a deformed, Jewish man living in the heart of a very anti-Semitic community. It is possible (although rare) that a strong prodefendant prejudice could exist for a popular local citizen accused of harming a victim who was less popular. Zeisel and Diamond use this analysis and their direct observations to point out that "the *voir dire* as conducted in these trials did not provide sufficient information for attorneys to identify prejudiced jurors."[21] Their recommendations are for more questioning and flexibility in granting more challenges to the side that faces extreme prejudice in the community.

SUMMARY

We tried in the chapter to help create better informed consumers of social science (psychological) information among the members of the law and criminal justice communities. We dissected one of our own publications to aid in the translation process and referred our legal-minded readers to the fact that some landmark research papers are available in the legal literature where some social scientists have found a home for their longer works.

[21] Ibid.

LAW AND SOCIAL SCIENCES RESOURCE FILE

The purpose of this chapter is to present specific documents, questionnaires, legal briefs, outlines, and some data that have been found to be useful to the practitioner who works between the social sciences and the law. In a new interdisciplinary area many of the key contributions lie unpublished in the files of the practitioners or forgotten in the overwhelming pile of government reports that come out annually but are not adequately cataloged. We have also included some examples of service documents that are in use in criminal justice agencies.

This chapter is intended to supplement the main chapters with more advanced reading assignments and practical aids. In some ways, the selections in the Resource File represent materials which are obtainable through extensive digging in libraries or through reports available from the National Criminal Justice Reference Service. With respect to the specific checklists and questionnaires (in Files No. 2, 3, 6 and 8), these are not copyrighted and we encourage the reader to copy and use them without the need to get our permission.

RESOURCE FILE NO. 1

Official State Police Guide for Eyewitnesses to facilitate recall (N.J. State Police). (Figure 14.1) The focus of these aids is really to generate information useful in an investigation. They are at once too suggestive —encouraging overgeneration of details—and suggest stereotypes. The forms are also largely unavailable to the general public. See Chapter 6.

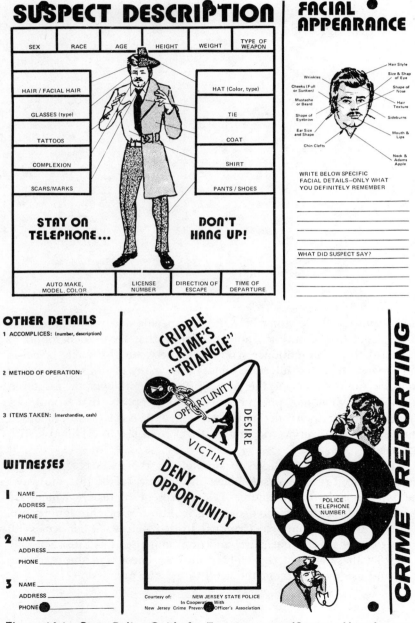

Figure 14.1   State Police Guide for Eyewitnesses. (Source: New Jersey State Police.)

RESOURCE FILE NO. 2

Reliability Checklist for Corporeal Lineups. To use the form, simply check the appropriate box after each question and total up the number of "yes" responses to determine a total unreliability score. Following the checklist is a set of detailed technical notes briefly indicating the scientific rationale for why the particular item is considered to be a source of unreliability in the lineup testing of eyewitnesses to crime. Reprinted from *Social Action and the Law*, 1975, 2 (2). See Chapter 7.

HOW FAIR IS YOUR LINEUP?

	YES	NO	UNKNOWN
1. Was the witness shown any photographs of the suspect prior to the lineup?	☐	☐	☐
2. Have the witnesses been shown prior lineups related to this case?	☐	☐	☐
3. Are there less than six people in the lineup?	☐	☐	☐
4. Are any of the participants in the lineup from a different race and/or ethnic background?	☐	☐	☐
5. Do the participants have different skin tones?	☐	☐	☐
6. Do the participants have different amounts and styles of facial hair?	☐	☐	☐
7. Are the participants widely varied in age?	☐	☐	☐
8. Do the participants differ in height?	☐	☐	☐
9. Do the participants have different body frames or stature (weight included)?	☐	☐	☐
10. Are the participants different in modes of dress?	☐	☐	☐
11. Do the participants have different styles of hair (example: braided, afro, D.A., partial balding)?	☐	☐	☐
12. Do any of the participants in the lineup differ from original description given by the witness?	☐	☐	☐
13. Did the officer in charge make the witness aware that a suspect is present in the lineup?	☐	☐	☐
14. If a suspect is present in a lineup, does the officer in charge know his position within the lineup?	☐	☐	☐
15. Is there more than one witness present at the lineup?	☐	☐	☐

	YES	NO	UNKNOWN
16. If there is more than one witness, did they have an opportunity to discuss the events of the case?	☐	☐	☐
17. If a positive identification is made, does the witness give a verbal response instead of writing down the choice on a form?	☐	☐	☐
18. Does the form lack a zero choice (a number representing a non-identification)?	☐	☐	☐
19. Is there anyone else in the lineup other than the one suspect who could be a suspect in this or related crimes?	☐	☐	☐
20. Was the witness told in any way that he or she was "correct" or "incorrect" in making an identification?	☐	☐	☐
21. Did the officer conducting the lineup suggest or emphasize any one individual through word, gesture, tone or number?	☐	☐	☐

Total Sources of Unreliability = the number of yes responses to all questions ☐

TECHNICAL NOTES FOR LINEUP CHECKLIST

1, 2. Photographs of the suspect or someone resembling the suspect may give cues to an identification "Regardless of how the initial misidentification comes about, the witness thereafter is apt to retain in his memory the image of the photograph rather than the person actually seen, reducing the trustworthiness of subsequent lineup or courtroom identification." In our view, the prior showing of a photograph or lineup is merely a practice session for the witness. (See Sobel, N. R., *Eye-Witness Identification*, Boardman, 1973.)

3. Having at least six participants in a lineup is a practical minimum which reduces the probability of error to 16.67% (Guessing level is 1/6). More participants would be better, for example, a lineup of twenty reduces the probability of error down to 5%. (See Wall, P., *Eyewitness Identification in Criminal Cases*, C. C. Thomas, 1965.)

4, 5. Distinctiveness of the slightest nature has been found to be a factor in encouraging unreliable eyewitness identification when the distinctive person was in fact innocent. Research indicates more mistakes when witness is of different race than suspect. (See Luce, T. "They All Look-A-Like to Me," *Psychology Today*, November 1974.)

6. In the case of *U.S. vs. Coulombe,* the defendant's photo array is a model case of the violation of every standard of witness testing. Various factors lead the witness to observe only two participants in the lineup who objectively match the original description. Since

Coulombe had a moustache, he was singled out. (See CR-5—Buck-hout and Freire, "Casebook," from the Center for Responsive Psychology, 1975.)

7. In the case of *U.S. vs. David Washington*, the defendant, 38 years old, was placed in a lineup with men in their early twenties. The defendant stood out in this lineup as a distinctive individual nearly ten years older than anyone else. (See CR-5.)

8, 9. In *N.Y. vs. Crippen*, the defendant, 5'4" in height was placed in a lineup with four cops (who must have a minimum height of 5'8"), and a friend. All of the participants in the lineup remained seated. The defendant, even seated, was distinctively the shortest person since the men surrounding the defendant have greater arm and leg extension, as well as broader shoulders, allowing the defendant to be unique in the lineup. (See Freire, V., "A Case History in Suggestivity on a Lineup," *Social Action and the Law*, 1975, Vol. 2, No. 2.)

10. Modes of dress can definitely influence a witness while viewing a lineup. In *R. vs. Shatford* the accused was not wearing glasses, yet 5 of the distractors wore glasses. The accused did not wear a tie, whereas the majority did. (See Doob, A., "Bias in Police Lineups . . . ," *Journal Police Science and Administration*, 1973, Vol. 1, No. 3).

11. In the case of *Fl. vs. Richard Campbell*, (armed robbery), only two people in the lineup had braids (platted hair) which the witness testified influenced her identification. The other person was logically rejected because of his height, leaving the defendant unique in appearing closest to the original description. (See CR-5.)

12. In many cases (*N.Y. vs. Crippen, U.S. vs. Coulombe*, etc.), the defendant is clearly identified because he is the only person who objectively matches the witnesses original description. (See CR-5.)

13. If a witness is lead to believe a suspect is present in a lineup, there is a scientifically greater likelihood that the witness will make a choice. (See CR-5.)

14. An officer's knowledge of the position of the suspect within the lineup may, accidentally or directly, by word or gesture, bias the identification. Rosenthal did research showing that test administrators who knew the "desired" answer, unconsciously biased subjects to pick that answer. (See Buckhout, "Eyewitness Testimony," *Scientific American*, December 1974.)

15, 16. Research shows that the individual reports become slightly more complete, and are marked by consensus on false details following group discussions. Other viewer of lineup may cause witness to conform to mistaken I.D. Group discussion leads to more mistaken I.D.'s. (See Rupp, A., et al., "Making the Blind See," Center Report No. CR-19, 1975.)

17. Writing down one's choice on a form has several advantages over a verbal response. This form permits an accurate record, reduces verbal interaction and help seeking which might lead to biasing by the test giver. (See "Eyewitness Testimony.")

18. A zero choice is crucial to an unbiased lineup. If not available, witness is more likely to pick a participant from the lineup, even if uncertain since he is forced to choose.

19. More than one suspect in a lineup is likely to confuse a witness and

most authorities agree that suspects in related crimes should be viewed in separate lineups. Further, the test is too easy in that 2 or more answers would be "right."

20. Any response given to a witness will influence his future role in the case. If a witness is told his identification is "correct," the witness is more likely to maintain his opinion regardless if it is correct or not.

21. A "biased" officer will obviously conduct a biased lineup. Beliefs on this matter dictate that the less interaction between officer and witness, the better. In this way the officer will not emphasize any individual within the lineup. (See Levine and Tapp, "The Psychology of Eyewitness Identification, 121, *Univ. of Pennsylvania Law Rev.,* 1973 at 1079.)

NOTE: All of the CR-Reports cited above can be ordered from the Center for Responsive Psychology, Brooklyn College, Brooklyn, New York 11210 for about $1.00 each.

RESOURCE FILE NO. 3

Reliability Checklist for Photospreads. In the United States, most of the testing of eyewitnesses to crimes is done with the use of books filled with "mug-shot" photos and a form of lineup testing, using six or more photos, is permitted. In general, research shows that photos are a less reliable test for recognition that live or corporeal lineups. To use the form, simply check the appropriate box after each question and total up the number of "yes" responses to get a total unreliability score. Following the checklist is a set of technical notes indicating the scientific rationale as to why the particular item is considered to be a source of unreliability in the testing of eyewitnesses to a crime. Reprinted from Buckhout, R. & Friere, V. Suggestivity in Lineups and Photo Spreads; A Casebook for Lawyers, *Center Monograph No. CR-5*, Center for Responsive Psychology, Brooklyn College, C.U.N.Y., June 1975. See Chapter 7.

A RELIABILITY CHECKLIST FOR PHOTOSPREADS

	YES	NO	UNKNOWN
1. Was the witness shown any photograph of the suspect prior to the photospread?	☐	☐	☐
2. Have the witnesses been shown prior photospreads related to this case?	☐	☐	☐
3. Are there less than six people in the photospread?	☐	☐	☐
4. Are any of the participants in the photospread from a different race or ethnic background?	☐	☐	☐
5. Do the participants have different skin tones?	☐	☐	☐
6. Are the participants widely varied in age?	☐	☐	☐
7. Do the participants have differing amounts and styles of facial hair?	☐	☐	☐
8. Do the participants differ in height?	☐	☐	☐
9. Do the participants have different body frames or stature (weight included)?	☐	☐	☐
10. Are the participants different in modes of dress?	☐	☐	☐
11. Do the participants have different styles of hair (example: braided, Afro, D.A., partial balding)?	☐	☐	☐

	YES	NO	UNKNOWN
12. Do any or all of the participants in the photospread differ from the original description given by the witness?	☐	☐	☐
13. Did the officer in charge make the witness aware that a suspect is present in the photospread?	☐	☐	☐
14. If a suspect is present in a photospread, does the officer in charge know his position within the photospread?	☐	☐	☐
15. Is there more than one witness present at the photospread viewing?	☐	☐	☐
16. If there is more than one witness, did they have an opportunity to discuss the events of the case?	☐	☐	☐
17. If a positive identification is made, does the witness give a verbal response instead of writing down the choice on a form?	☐	☐	☐
18. Does the form lack a zero choice (a number representing a nonidentification)?	☐	☐	☐
19. Are any photos in the spread mug shots?	☐	☐	☐
20. Is any information present on the photo (example: a date or name)?	☐	☐	☐
21. Are any photos in the spread unequal in size?	☐	☐	☐
22. Are any of the photographs distinctive in regard to their color or texture?	☐	☐	☐
23. Do the photographs vary widely in contrast (ratio of darkness to lightness)?	☐	☐	☐
24. Are both profile and frontal shots mixed within the photospread?	☐	☐	☐
25. Are any of the photographs placed in such a manner as to make it distinctive (example: is any photo slanted)?	☐	☐	☐
26. Are any of the photographs mutilated?	☐	☐	☐
27. Do the persons in the photographs differ in relative size of their image (distance from camera, filling the frame, etc.)?	☐	☐	☐
28. Is there anyone else in the photospread other than the one suspect who could be a suspect in this or related crimes?	☐	☐	☐
29. Was the witness told in any way that he or she was "correct" or "incorrect" in making an identification?	☐	☐	☐

	YES	NO	UNKNOWN

30. Did the officer conducting the photospread suggest or emphasize any one individual through word, gesture, tone or number? □   □   □

Total Sources of Unreliability = the number of yes responses to all questions □

TECHNICAL NOTES FOR PHOTOSPREAD CHECKLIST

1, 2. Photographs of the suspect or someone resembling the suspect may give cues to an identification "regardless of how the initial mis-identification comes about, the witness thereafter is apt to retain in his memory the image of the photograph rather than the person actually seen, reducing the trustworthiness of subsequent lineup or courtroom identifications." On our view, the prior showing of a photograph or lineup is merely a practice session for the witness. (See Sobel, N. R., *Eyewitness Identification*, Boardman, 1973. Note all notes are keyed to item numbers in the checklist.)

3. Having at least six participants in a photospread is a practical minimum which reduces the probability of error to 16.6% (guessing level is 1/6). More photos would be better, for example, a spread of twenty reduces the probability of error down to 5%. (See Wall, P., *Eyewitness Identification in Criminal Cases*, C. C. Thomas, 1965.)

4, 5. Distinctiveness of the slightest nature has been found to be a factor in encouraging unreliable eyewitness identification when the distinctive person was in fact innocent. Research indicates more mistakes when witness is of different race than suspect. (See Luce, T. "They All Look-A-Like to Me," *Psychology Today*, November 1974.)

6. In the case of *U.S. vs. David Washington*, the defendant, 38 years old, was placed in a lineup with men in their early twenties. The defendant stood out in this lineup as a distinctive individual nearly ten years older than anyone else. (See CR-5.)

7. In the case of *U.S. vs. Coulombe*, the defendant's photo array is a model case of the violation of every standard of witness testing. Various factors lead the witness to observe only two participants in the lineup who objectively match the original description. Since Coulombe had a moustache, he was singled out. (See CR-5—Buckhout and Freire, "Casebook," from the Center for Responsive Psychology, 1975.)

8, 9. In *N.Y. vs. Crippen*, the defendant, 5'4" in height was placed in a lineup with four cops (who must have a minimum height of 5'8"), and a friend. All of the participants in the lineup remained seated. The defendant, even seated, was distinctively the shortest person since the men surrounding the defendant have greater arm and leg extension, as well as broader shoulders, allowing the defendant to be unique in the lineup. (See Freire, V., "A Case History in Suggestivity on a Lineup," *Social Action & the Law*, 1975, Vol. 2, No. 2.)

10. Modes of dress can definitely influence a witness while viewing a lineup. In *R. vs. Shatford* the accused was not wearing glasses, yet five of the distractors wore glasses. The accused did not wear a tie,

whereas the majority did. (See Doob, A., "Bias in Police Line-ups . . . ," *Journal of Police Science and Administration*, 1973, Vol. 1, No. 3.)

11. In the case of *Fl. vs. Richard Campbell* (armed robbery), only two people in the lineup had braids (plaited hair) which the witness testified influenced her identification. The other person was logically rejected because of his height, leaving the defendant unique in appearing closest to the original description. (See CR-5.)

12. In many cases (*N.Y. vs. Crippen, U.S. vs. Coulombe,* etc.) the defendant is clearly identified because he is the only person who objectively matches the witnesses original description. (See CR-5.)

13. If a witness is lead to believe a suspect is present in a photospread, there is a scientifically greater likelihood that the witness will make a choice. (See CR-5.)

14. An officer's knowledge of the position of the suspect within the photospread may, accidentally or directly, by work or gesture, bias the identification. Rosenthal did research showing that test administrators who knew the "desired" answer, unconsciously biased subjects to pick that answer. (See Buckhout, "Eyewitness Testimony," *Scientific American,* December 1974.)

15, 16. Research shows that the individual reports become slightly more complete, and are marked by consensus on false details following group discussions. Other viewer of photospread may cause witness to conform to mistaken I.D. Group discussion leads to more mistaken I.D.'s. (See Rupp, A., et al., "Making the Blind See," Center Report No. CR-19, 1975.)

17. Writing down one's choice on a form has several advantages over a verbal response. This form permits an accurate record, reduces verbal interaction, and helps seeking, which might lead to biasing by the test giver. (See "Eyewitness Testimony.")

18. A zero choice is crucial to an unbiased photospread. If not available, witness is more likely to pick a participant from the array, even if uncertain since he is forced to choose.

19. Mug shots convey the message that the person in the photo is a criminal and increase the tendency of the witness to make a choice.

20. Recent dates suggest a recent arrest; old dates aid in rejecting some photos as unlikely.

21. Distinctiveness of any nature serves to single out a participant in a photospread. If any picture is unequal in size, the uniqueness will increase the probability of that picture's selection.

22, 23. An unbiased photospread must meet certain standards. Photographs should be similar in color, pose, contrast, texture and lighting. We recommend taking all pictures with the same camera and film stock.

24, 25. In one study, two layouts of photographs were presented to witnesses of a staged assault. In an unbiased spread the portraits were *aligned* and show similar *full-face* views. In the biased spread, the "culprit's" head is tilted and the portrait itself is placed at an angle. Whereas 40% of all witnesses picked the culprit, 61% of those who saw the biased spread did so. (See "Eyewitness Testimony.")

26. Mutilation of a picture may be an influencing factor in a photospread identification. In the case of *U.S. vs. Coulombe,* the photo of the defendant plus one other is a photo of a photo stapled to a wall, making them distinctive from all others which appear to be mug

shots (# 19). The facts around the Coulombe photospread, demon-strated a high level of suggestiveness which would cause the typical witness to be led to the pictures with the staples.

28. More than one suspect in a photospread is likely to confuse a wit-ness and most authorities agree that suspects in related crimes should be viewed in separate arrays. Further, the test is too easy in that 2 or more answers would be "right."

29. Any response given to a witness will influence his future role in the case. If a witness is told his identification is "correct," the witness is more likely to maintain his opinion regardless if it is correct or not.

30. A "biased" officer will obviously conduct a biased photospread test. Beliefs on this matter dictate that the less interaction between officer and witness, the better. In this way the officer will not emphasize any individual within the array. (See Levine and Tapp, "The Psy-chology of Eyewitness Identification," *121, University of Pennsyl-vania Law Rev.*, 1973, at 1079.)

RESOURCE FILE NO. 4

A Forensic Psychological Consultant's Report: "Factors affecting reliability of eyewitness identification testing in *U.S.* v. *Coulombe*." This is an example of a pretrial investigation report written for a defense attorney and used as a basis for conducting the defense. Part of the report was submitted as an affidavit at trial. Originally published as "Alfred Hitchcock Revisited: The Wrong Man in the Wrong Photospread," from Buckhout, R. and Friere, V. Suggestivity in Lineups and Photospreads, *Center Monograph No. CR-5*, Center for Responsive Psychology, Brooklyn College, C.U.N.Y., June 1975. See Chapters 6, 7.

FORENSIC PSYCHOLOGICAL CONSULTANT REPORT: FACTORS AFFECTING UNRELIABILITY IN U.S. V. COULOMBE

Robert Buckhout, Ph.D.

Brooklyn College, C.U.N.Y.

Facts of the Case. Charles R. Coulombe was indicted in Honolulu, Hawaii, for a robbery of a federally insured bank. The robbery occurred on June 9, 1972 at approximately 2:00 P.M. No weapons were displayed. The entire transaction apparently occurred quickly, involving a demand note by a man wearing a disguise and the over-the-counter exchange of approximately $1,279.00. Statements from 17 witnesses yielded a variety of widely varying descriptions.

Nearly one month after the day of the robbery, two of the bank tellers observed Mr. Coulombe, a regular customer of the bank, as he drove in to make a deposit. The tellers made this observation through a closed-circuit, black and white television screen. One teller called the other one over to the screen, suggesting that there was a customer who strongly resembled the robber. The second teller agreed to the strong resemblance. Neither teller was willing to positively identify Mr. Coulombe as the robber at this point.

On October 12, 1972 four months after the date of the alleged offense, a photospread consisting of fourteen pictures was shown to four tellers. Two positively identified the picture of Mr. Coulombe.

Initial Description. The following description was given by four women tellers of the robber: caucasian, male, stocky build, height— 5'10" to 6', 40–45 years old, wearing a mustache and a wig under a hat and an aloha (Hawaiian) shirt.

Length of Time. Descriptions were recorded from 7–14 days after the crime occurred. Scientific research on memory suggests that accuracy of report falls off dramatically in the first 24–48 hours after an event, decreasing still further as time goes on.[1] The key witness then viewed the defendant as a bank customer some 30 days after the crime. The passage of time in this case between the original perception and sighting of the defendant was long enough for substantial forgetting to interfere with the matching of the defendant's image to the witness's memory of the original event. This applies even more so to the viewing of the photospread some four months after the offense.

---

[1] Stevens, S. S. *Handbook of Experimental Psychology.* New York: Wiley, 1951.

Conformity. Consistent in the defense attorney's description of the facts is the active participation by the tellers in discussing the events, giving descriptions and in viewing (together) the defendant on a TV monitor screen. Psychological research on conformity among observers warns that groups can be influenced by the positive assertions of the majority or a highly credible minority to conclude on perceptions that are false, inaccurate, or unreliable. Research done by the Center for Responsive Psychology with eyewitnesses to simulated crimes demonstrated that individual reports become slightly more complete but were marked by a consensus on false details following group discussions.[2] The facts in this case parallel research on conformity to the extent that the viewing of the defendant on the TV monitor by one witness was signaled to the other witness. The opportunity for the witness to reinforce one another's suspicions at that point further erodes the reliability of subsequent independent in-court identification.

Suggestivity in the Lineup. The photospread used to test witnesses in *U.S. v. Coulombe* is a model case of the violation of every scientific and professional standard of witness testing. While a set of 14 photos would appear on its face to be difficult, only 3 of the photos bear even a passing resemblance to the original description by the tellers, with the majority of photos showing mug shots of young men in their 20's. Half of the photos were full color and half were black and white. The photo of the defendant plus one other is a photo of a photo stapled to a wall, making them distinctive from all others which appear to be mug shots. The facts around the Coulombe photospread demonstrated a high level of suggestiveness, which would very likely cause the typical witness to be led to the two photos with the staples. Since the witness had all mentioned a mustache, the "test"—now merely one out of the two photos—is further biased by the fact that only the defendant is pictured with a mustache. Thus the defendant is virtually the only participant in the photospread who objectively matches the original description given by the witnesses. As the investigation developed, we learned that the FBI administered the photospread more than one time, since they did not initially get positive identifications. To shore up the wavering witnesses, they made a composite drawing which included the disguise. This was shown to the witnesses who then made a positive identification. Examination of the drawing revealed that it showed a man with a double chin—a detail never mentioned in the original descriptions. The double chin could only have been suggested by the actual appearance of the defendant. Showing this doctored drawing to the witnesses was a highly suggestive (and wholly unprofessional) procedure.

[2] Buckhout, R. Eyewitness testimony. *Scientific American*, 1974, *231* (6), 23–31.

Test of Suggestivity. On February 6, 1975 we ran an experiment on the 14 photos. A group of nonwitnesses were informed only of the descriptions given by the original witnesses—the four tellers. The purpose of the experiment was to scientifically determine the degree of suggestivity in the photospread. The scientific justification for this procedure is that a nonwitness, lacking the original source of perception of the actual crime, would be merely guessing when confronted with the array of photos. A fair test with 14 photos should result in a nonwitness picking any single photo (e.g., the defendant) 1/14 or 6.8 percent of the time, a precedent established in Doob, 1973.[3]

Sixty-six college students, as in our previous reports, were tested under two conditions: (1) witnesses were told that the suspect might or might not be in the array, and (2) witnesses were biased—told that the suspect was definitely in the array (just as the tellers in the bank knew that the photo of the defendant was in the array). Each person was tested, given the original facts of the case and the witnesses' description, and asked if they recognized anyone in the lineup shown to them.

Overall 38 percent of the nonwitnesses picked out the defendant from the photo array as opposed to approximately 7 percent expected on the basis of chance. Thus there was a 5:1 greater likelihood that the defendant would be identified from this photospread.[4] Of the other identifications, it was noted that most people concentrated on the photos of older men (see table 14.1). As expected, when our witnesses were told that the suspect was definitely in the array, identifications of the defendant increased to 48 percent. The absence of a zero choice— ("He's not there.") creates more identifications and increases the possibility of mistaken identifications. The effects of this suggestivity are so strong that they create a substantial likelihood, to a scientific certainty, that the suggestiveness could have led to the identification of the defendant by the witness. This photospread says in effect, "Mr. Coulombe is the man." We concluded that the photospread was an unfair test of the eyewitness's ability to make an identification, and would tend to taint subsequent identifications in court.

Wade Suppression Hearing. Defense attorney Brook Hart presented a deposition of the above analysis by Dr. Buckhout to the judge who rejected the motion to suppress the identification, permitting introduction of the photospread and in-court identification.

Results of the Trial. On March 27, 1975 a federal court jury

---

[3] Doob, A. N. & Kirschenbaum, H. M. Bias in police lineups: Partial remembering, *Journal of Police Science and Administration*, 1973, *1*, 287–293.

[4] $x^2 = 107.21$, $p < 0.001$; a highly significant difference for the (1) condition; $x^2 = 246.04$, $p < 0.001$ for (2) condition.

Table 14.1 SUMMARY OF TEST OF PHOTOSPREAD IN *U.S.* V. *COULOMBE* ON NONWITNESSES WITH KNOWLEDGE OF THE WITNESS'S DESCRIPTION OF THE ROBBER

TEST CONDITION	EXPECTED % OF ID'S OF DEFENDANT (CHANCE LEVEL)	% OF WITNESS PICKING DEFENDANT	% OF WITNESS PICKING OTHER OLDER MEN	% OF WITNESS PICKING OTHERS	% OF WITNESS SAYING HE'S NOT THERE
Witness told the suspect may or may not be in photospread	6.6	33.2*	22.2	17.6	27
Witness told that suspect's photo is definitely in photospread	7	48.5**	42.4	9.1	0

* $p < 0.001$
** $p < 0.0001$

acquitted Charles Coulombe of the holdup of the Kahala branch of the Bank of Hawaii in 1972.

Comment. The defendant in this case was not actor Henry Fonda but a real person. Looking at a photospread to make an identification is a task of sorting alternatives, rejecting distractors and making a decision. Once again, we find that the witnesses were overly involved in suggesting a suspect on whom they would ultimately be tested. The photospread was outrageously biased and the authorities added their suggestions to the procedure. In this case the jury was convinced of the defendant's innocence from other evidence. Thus an innocent man spent excessive time, money, and anguish in fighting a charge which should never have been made.[5]

---

[5] See also Drury, K. Mandatory exclusion of identifications resulting from suggestive confrontations. *Boston University Law Review*, 1973, 53 (2), 433–452.

RESOURCE FILE NO. 5

U.S. Supreme Court Decisions involving Jury Selection. The text or summaries of these decisions are available in general as well as legal libraries. We have chosen those that have direct bearing on the material in the jury selection chapter. See Chapter 8.

U.S. SUPREME COURT DECISIONS INVOLVING JURY SELECTION

Strauder v. *West Virginia*, 100 U.S. 303 (1880).
Virginia v. *Rives*, 100 U.S. 313 (1880).
Ex Parta Virginia, 100 U.S. 339 (1880).
Neal v. *Delaware*, 103 U.S. 370 (1881).
Bush v. *Kentucky*, 107 U.S. 110 (1883).
Woods v. *Brush*, 140 U.S. 278 (1891).
Gibson v. *Mississippi*, 162 U.S. 565 (1896).
Smith v. *Mississippi*, 162 U.S. 592 (1896).
Carter v. *Texas*, 177 U.S. 442 (1900).
Tarrance v. *Florida*, 188 U.S. 519 (1903).
Brownfield v. *South Carolina*, 189 U.S. 426 (1903).
Rogers v. *Alabama*, 192 U.S. 226 (1904).
Martin v. *Texas*, 200 U.S. 316 (1906).
Rawlins v. *Georgia*, 201 U.S. 638 (1906) (exemptions for professionals).
Thomas v. *Texas*, 212 U.S. 278 (1909).
Norris v. *Alabama*, 294 U.S. 587 (1935).
Hollins v. *Oklahoma*, 295 U.S. 394 (1935).
Hale v. *Kentucky*, 303 U.S. 613 (1938).
Pierre v. *Louisiana*, 306 U.S. 354 (1939).
Smith v. *Texas*, 311 U.S. 128 (1940).
Glasser v. *United States*, 315 U.S. 60 (1942).
Hill v. *Texas*, 316 U.S. 400 (1942).
Akins v. *Texas*, 325 U.S. 398 (1945).
Thiel v. *Southern Pacific Co.*, 328 U.S. 217 (1946) (daily wage-earners).
Ballard v. *United States*, 329 U.S. 173 (1946) (women).
Fay v. *New York*, 332 U.S. 261 (1947) (blue-ribbon juries).
Patton v. *Mississippi*, 332 U.S. 463 (1947).
Moore v. *New York*, 333 U.S. 565 (1948) (blue-ribbon juries).
Cassell v. *Texas*, 339 U.S. 282 (1950).
Ross v. *Texas*, 341 U.S. 918 (1951).
Brown v. *Allen*, 344 U.S. 443 (1953).
Avery v. *Georgia*, 345 U.S. 559 (1953).
Hernandez v. *Texas*, 347 U.S. 475 (1954) (Hispanic).
Williams v. *Georgia*, 349 U.S. 375 (1955).
Reece v. *Georgia*, 350 U.S. 85 (1955).
Eubanks v. *Louisiana*, 356 U.S. 584 (1958).
Hoyt v. *Florida*, 368 U.S. 57 (1961) (women).
Arnold v. *North Carolina*, 376 U.S. 773 (1964).
Coleman v. *Alabama*, 377 U.S. 129 (1964).
Swain v. *Alabama*, 380 U.S. 202 (1965).
Whitus v. *Georgia*, 385 U.S. 545 (1967).
Coleman v. *Alabama*, 389 U.S. 22 (1967).

Jones v. *Georgia,* 389 U.S. 24 (1967).

Sims v. *Georgia,* 389 U.S. 404 (1967).

Duncan v. *Louisiana,* 391 U.S. 145 (1968) (6th Amendment extended to states).

Carter v. *Jury Comm. of Greene County,* 396 U.S. 320 (1970).

Turner v. *Fouche,* 396 U.S. 346 (1970).

Baldwin v. *New York,* 399 U.S. 66 (1970) (6th Amendment extended to states).

Williams v. *Florida,* 399 U.S. 78 (1970) (6-person juries allowed).

McKiever v. *Pennsylvania,* 403 U.S. 528 (1971) (no right to jury trial for juveniles).

Alexander v. *Louisiana,* 405 U.S. 625 (1972).

Johnson v. *Louisiana,* 406 U.S. 356 (1972) (less-than-unanimous verdicts allowed).

Apodaca v. *Oregon,* 406 U.S. 404 (1972) (less-than-unanimous verdicts allowed).

Peters v. *Kiff,* 407 U.S. 493 (1972) (standing).

Taylor v. *Louisiana,* 419 U.S. 522 (1975) (women).

RESOURCE FILE NO. 6

Jury Survey Questionnaire for Jury Selection. Used in New York Southern Federal Court District to determine potential juror attitudes in preparation for jury selection in the case of *U.S.* v. *Patricia Swinton*. See related materials in Resource File Nos. 7 and 8 and see Chapter 8. This survey was conducted with telephone interviews using a randomized system for generating numbers.

QUESTIONNAIRE FROM NEW YORK VOTER SURVEY FOR JURY SELECTION USED IN U.S. V. SWINTON, SOUTHERN DISTRICT, U.S. FEDERAL COURT

PHONE NUMBER° ☐☐☐☐☐☐☐

BUSY	NO ANSWER	REFUSED	TERMINATED
☐	☐	☐	☐

　　　　1. Male Answers ☐　　　　Female Answers ☐
MY NAME IS _____. I AM WORKING FOR SCHULMAN ASSOCIATES RESEARCH CORPORATION, AND I WOULD LIKE TO ASK YOU A FEW QUESTIONS.

2. ARE YOU A REGISTERED VOTER?
(If respondent answers YES, skip question #3 and　　YES ☐　　NO ☐
start with the questions.)

3. If the respondent answers NO ask:
ARE THERE ANY REGISTERED VOTERS
PRESENT?
(If the respondent answers YES, ask to speak with　　YES ☐　　NO ☐
them. If there are no registered voters present terminate the call.)

MEASURES OF ATTITUDES

If you get to speak to a registered voter say:

NOW I WILL READ YOU SOME OPINION STATEMENTS. PLEASE TELL ME WHETHER YOU AGREE VERY MUCH, AGREE SOMEWHAT, DISAGREE SOMEWHAT, OR DISAGREE VERY MUCH. THERE ARE NO RIGHT OR WRONG ANSWERS. READY?

(SCORE AS):	1	2	3	4	5
	AGREE VERY MUCH	AGREE SOME-WHAT	DISAGREE SOME-WHAT	DISAGREE VERY MUCH	DON'T KNOW
4 SUPREME COURT DE-CISIONS HAVE TIED THE HANDS OF LAW ENFORCEMENT AGENTS.	____	____	____	____	____

° Generated from random number list.

	1 AGREE VERY MUCH	2 AGREE SOME-WHAT	3 DISAGREE SOME-WHAT	4 DISAGREE VERY MUCH	5 DON'T KNOW
5. IF THE STATE GOES TO THE TROUBLE OF BRINGING SOMEONE TO TRIAL HE IS PROBABLY GUILTY.	____	____	____	____	____
6. POLICE SHOULD NOT HESITATE TO USE FORCE TO MAINTAIN ORDER.	____	____	____	____	____
7. MARIJUANA SHOULD BE LEGALIZED.	____	____	____	____	____
8. OBEDIENCE TO AUTHORITY IS THE MOST IMPORTANT VIRTUE CHILDREN SHOULD LEARN.	____	____	____	____	____
9. EVERY PERSON SHOULD HAVE COMPLETE FAITH IN GOD.	____	____	____	____	____
10. MOST PEOPLE ON WELFARE PREFER NOT TO HAVE JOBS.	____	____	____	____	____
11. ANYONE WHO GIVES TESTIMONY AGAINST A FRIEND TO THE GOVERNMENT IN EXCHANGE FOR LENIENCY SHOULD NOT BE BELIEVED.	____	____	____	____	____
12. NOW THAT THE VIETNAM WAR IS OVER, RESISTERS AND MILITARY DESERTERS SHOULD BE GIVEN SOME FORM OF AMNESTY.	____	____	____	____	____
13. PEOPLE SHOULD SUPPORT GOVERNMENT AUTHORITIES EVEN WHEN THEY FEEL THEY ARE WRONG.	____	____	____	____	____

	1 AGREE VERY MUCH	2 AGREE SOME- WHAT	3 DISAGREE SOME- WHAT	4 DISAGREE VERY MUCH	5 DON'T KNOW
14. MOST GOVERNMENT OFFICIALS CAN BE TRUSTED TO DO WHAT IS RIGHT.	____	____	____	____	____
15. SINGLE WOMEN WHO HAVE HAD INTIMATE RELATIONSHIPS WITH MORE THAN ONE MAN TEND TO BE UN- TRUSTWORTHY.	____	____	____	____	____
16. PRESIDENT FORD'S HANDLING OF THE MAYAGUEZ INCI- DENT—THE SHIP ATTACKED NEAR CAMBODIA—WAS PROPER UNDER THE CIRCUMSTANCES.	____	____	____	____	____
17. PEOPLE WHO FLEE FROM PROSECUTION ARE PROBABLY GUILTY OF THE CRIME CHARGED.	____	____	____	____	____
18. WOMEN ARE OFTEN LED ASTRAY BY THEIR MALE COMPANIONS.	____	____	____	____	____
19. WIRETAPPING BY ANY- ONE AND FOR ANY REASON SHOULD BE COMPLETELY ILLEGAL.	____	____	____	____	____
20. DEFENDANTS IN A CRIMINAL CASE SHOULD BE REQUIRED TO TAKE THE WITNESS STAND.	____	____	____	____	____
21. GOOD HEARTED PEOPLE OFTEN HELP PEOPLE WITHOUT CONSIDERING THEIR OWN INTEREST.	____	____	____	____	____

	1 AGREE VERY MUCH	2 AGREE SOME-WHAT	3 DISAGREE SOME-WHAT	4 DISAGREE VERY MUCH	5 DON'T KNOW
22. POLICE SHOULD BE ALLOWED TO ARREST AND QUESTION SUSPICIOUS LOOKING PERSONS TO DETER-MINE WHETHER THEY HAVE BEEN UP TO SOMETHING ILLEGAL.	____	____	____	____	____
23. CITIZENS NEED TO BE PROTECTED AGAINST EXCESSIVE POLICE POWER AS WELL AS AGAINST CRIMINALS.	____	____	____	____	____
24. A PERSON WHO FAILS TO REPORT TO THE POLICE ON THE CRIMI-NAL ACTIVITY OF SOMEONE ELSE IS PROBABLY EQUALLY GUILTY.	____	____	____	____	____
25. POLICE OR FBI IN-FORMERS ARE MORE LIKELY TO TELL THE TRUTH UNDER OATH THAN THE AVERAGE CITIZEN.	____	____	____	____	____
26. THE DEATH PENALTY IS MORE EFFECTIVE THAN A LIFE SEN-TENCE WITHOUT PAROLE IN KEEPING PEOPLE FROM COM-MITTING MURDER.	____	____	____	____	____

27. ARE YOU FAMILIAR WITH THE CASE OF THE ATTICA INMATES WHO ARE CHARGED WITH THE MURDERS THAT OCCURRED DURING THE ATTICA UPRISING OF 1971?   YES ☐   NO ☐

28. *BASED ON WHAT YOU KNOW ABOUT THE CASE, WHAT ARE THE ODDS, 1 OUT OF 10, THAT THE INMATES ARE GUILTY OF MURDER? ____ OUT OF 10.

* An attempt at a dependent measure to ascertain willingness to prejudge guilt.

POLITICAL EXPEDIENCY SCALE

ASSUME THAT YOU WERE STRONGLY OPPOSED TO GOVERN-
MENT POLICY—FOR EXAMPLE, BEING AGAINST THE VIETNAM
WAR. IN ORDER TO PROTEST AGAINST THIS POLICY, WOULD
YOU GIVE ME YOUR OPINION ON THE FOLLOWING TYPES OF
ACTION: WOULD YOU AGREE VERY MUCH OR DISAGREE VERY
MUCH WITH, FOR EXAMPLE:

	1 AGREE VERY MUCH	2 AGREE SOME-WHAT	3 DISAGREE SOME-WHAT	4 DISAGREE VERY MUCH	5 DON'T KNOW
29. WRITING TO YOUR CONGRESSMAN	____	____	____	____	____
30. PEACEFULLY PICKET YOUR CONGRESSMAN'S OFFICE.	____	____	____	____	____
31. GO TO WASHINGTON TO DEMONSTRATE.	____	____	____	____	____
32. LYING DOWN IN FRONT OF TROOP TRAINS.	____	____	____	____	____
33. THROWING BLOOD ON DRAFT RECORDS.	____	____	____	____	____
34. DESTROYING DRAFT OFFICES OR OTHER GOVERNMENT PROPERTY BY BOMBING.	____	____	____	____	____

HIGHEST RATING ____

36. CAN YOU PLEASE TELL ME WHAT NEWSPAPER YOU READ
REGULARLY? (Do not read) (Check one item only—if respondent
reads more than one, which one does he or she prefer.)
1 ____ NEW YORK POST
2 ____ NEW YORK NEWS
3 ____ NEW YORK TIMES
4 ____ SOME BRONX PAPER
5 ____ SOME WESTCHESTER PAPER
6 ____ DON'T READ ANY PAPER REGULARLY
7 ____ VILLAGE VOICE
8 ____ UNDERGROUND PAPER

37. IF YOU READ A PAPER REGULARLY, WHICH PART OF THE
PAPER DO YOU PAY MOST ATTENTION TO? (Do not read unless
you have to)
1 ____ EDITORIAL & NEWS

2 _____ SPORTS
3 _____ EVERYTHING ELSE
4 _____ NO PREFERENCE

DEMOGRAPHIC SECTION

38. NOW I'M SUPPOSED TO GET SOME BACKGROUND INFOR-
    MATION FOR STATISTICAL PURPOSES ONLY. REMEMBER,
    YOUR ANSWERS WILL BE CONFIDENTIAL, OF COURSE. (Read
    to respondent—check only one)
    DO YOU:
    _____ OWN A HOUSE
    _____ RENT
    _____ OWN A COOPERATIVE OR CONDOMINIUM
    _____ LIVE WITH PARENTS
    _____ LIVE WITH CHILDREN
    _____ LIVE ALONE
    _____ DON'T KNOW, NO ANSWER

39. WHERE DO YOU LIVE?
    _____ BRONX
    _____ MANHATTAN COUNTY
    _____ WESTCHESTER COUNTY
    _____ PUTNAM COUNTY
    _____ OTHER
    _____ NO ANSWER

40. HOW OLD ARE YOU? _____
    (If refuse to answer, try to probe for approximate age—over 50, under
    50, an age range, decade, etc.)

42. WHAT IS YOUR MARITAL STATUS? (Read list)
    _____ MARRIED
    _____ DIVORCED
    _____ WIDOWED
    _____ SINGLE
    _____ SEPARATED
    _____ DON'T KNOW, NO ANSWER

43. HOW MANY PERSONS LIVE IN YOUR HOUSEHOLD? _____

44. HOW MUCH SCHOOLING HAVE YOU COMPLETED? (Do not
    read list)
    _____ NONE, OR HIGH SCHOOL INCOMPLETE
    _____ HIGH SCHOOL COMPLETE
    _____ COLLEGE INCOMPLETE OR TWO YEAR DEGREE
    _____ FOUR YEAR COLLEGE COMPLETE
    _____ GRADUATE OR PROFESSIONAL SCHOOL COMPLETE
    OR INCOMPLETE

45. (If married) HOW MUCH SCHOOLING HAS YOUR HUSBAND/
    WIFE COMPLETED?
    _____ NONE, OR HIGH SCHOOL INCOMPLETE
    _____ HIGH SCHOOL COMPLETE

_____ COLLEGE INCOMPLETE OR TWO YEAR DEGREE
_____ FOUR YEAR COLLEGE COMPLETE
_____ GRADUATE OR PROFESSIONAL SCHOOL COMPLETE
OR INCOMPLETE

46. WHAT IS RESPONDENT'S SEX?   MALE _____   FEMALE _____

47. (If respondent is male use this   (If respondent is female use this
column—Read list)   column—Read list)

ARE YOU PRESENTLY   ARE YOU PRESENTLY
(Males only)   (Females only)

_____ EMPLOYED   _____ EMPLOYED
_____ UNEMPLOYED   _____ UNEMPLOYED
_____ RETIRED   _____ HOUSEWIFE
_____ STUDENT   _____ STUDENT

48. (If respondent is employed, unemployed or retired, ask the following.)

MALE RESPONDENT   FEMALE RESPONDENT

WHAT IS/WAS YOUR   WHAT IS/WAS YOUR
OCCUPATION   OCCUPATION
(Probe for specific job—   (Probe for specific job—record
record verbatim)   verbatim)

_____   _____
_____   _____
_____   _____
_____   _____

(If respondent is divorced, widowed, or separated, skip questions 49
and 50.)

49. NOW COULD YOU TELL ME IF YOUR SPOUSE IS:

RESPONDENT'S HUSBAND   RESPONDENT'S WIFE

_____ EMPLOYED   _____ EMPLOYED
_____ UNEMPLOYED   _____ UNEMPLOYED
_____ RETIRED   _____ RETIRED

50. (If respondent's spouse is employed, unemployed, or retired ask the
following.)

IF RESPONDENT IS MALE   IF RESPONDENT IS FEMALE

WHAT IS/WAS HER   WHAT IS/WAS HIS
OCCUPATION   OCCUPATION
(Probe for specific job—   (Probe for specific job—
record verbatim)   record verbatim)

_____   _____
_____   _____
_____   _____
_____   _____

51. WHAT IS YOUR RELIGION? (Probe for specific denomination and specific church if Protestant—record verbatim)

_____

52. HOW OFTEN DO YOU ATTEND RELIGIOUS SERVICES? (Do not read unless you have to)
    _____ MORE THAN ONCE A WEEK
    _____ WEEKLY
    _____ SEVERAL TIMES A MONTH
    _____ ONCE A MONTH OR LESS
    _____ NEVER
    _____ DON'T KNOW, NO ANSWER

53. EVERYBODY IS AN AMERICAN, BUT WHAT COUNTRY DOES YOUR FAMILY ORIGINALLY COME FROM? (If Canada, ask what European country—record first answer)

_____

54. HAS ANYONE LIVING IN YOUR HOUSEHOLD SERVED IN VIETNAM?
    YES _____ NO _____

55. DO YOU BELONG TO ANY SOCIAL OR CIVIC ORGANIZATION?
    _____ YES
    _____ NO
    _____ DON'T KNOW, NO ANSWER

56. COULD YOU PLEASE TELL ME YOUR APPROXIMATE TOTAL ANNUAL FAMILY INCOME. WHAT GROUP DOES IT FALL INTO? (Read groups)
    _____ UNDER $5,000
    _____ $5,000 to $9,000
    _____ $9,000 to $15,000
    _____ $15,000 to $25,000
    _____ $25,000 OR OVER
    _____ REFUSED
    _____ DON'T KNOW, NO ANSWER

57. COULD YOU PLEASE TELL ME WHAT POLITICAL PARTY YOU USUALLY SUPPORTED IN THE PAST. (Do not read—Don't worry if they refuse, go on to next question.)

    _____ REPUBLICAN   _____ INDEPENDENT
    _____ DEMOCRAT   _____ OTHER
    _____ LIBERAL   _____ REFUSED
    _____ CONSERVATIVE   _____ DON'T KNOW, NO
                                   ANSWER

58. HAVE YOU EVER BEEN CALLED TO SERVE AS A JUROR?
    YES _____ NO _____

59. HAVE YOU EVER SERVED AS A JUROR?
YES _____   NO _____

60. IF SERVED AS A JUROR, WAS IT A FEDERAL OR STATE CASE?
_____ FEDERAL
_____ STATE
_____ BOTH
_____ DON'T REMEMBER

61. WAS IT A CRIMINAL OR CIVIL CASE?
_____ CRIMINAL
_____ CIVIL
_____ BOTH

62. ARE YOU WHITE, BLACK, ASIAN AMERICAN, SPANISH AMERI-
CAN, OR NATIVE AMERICAN?
_____ WHITE
_____ BLACK
_____ ASIAN AMERICAN
_____ SPANISH AMERICAN
_____ NATIVE AMERICAN

THANK YOU VERY MUCH FOR YOUR COOPERATION

RESOURCE FILE NO. 7

Factor Analysis Results from a Jury Questionnaire. Results of a factor analysis of opinion statements collected in a survey of potential jurors in the Southern District of the U.S. Federal Court (Manhattan, Bronx, Westchester, and Putnam Counties), 1975. Provided by the National Jury Project and Center for Responsive Psychology, Brooklyn College, Brooklyn, N.Y. The text of the entire questionnaire is shown in Resource File No. 6. See Chapter 8.

U.S. V. SWINTON*

Factor Analysis of Opinion Statements in N.Y. Questionnaire

FACTOR ONE: EIGEN = 3.59		POLITICAL EXPEDIENCY
LOADING		ITEM
0.62	q. 30:	Endorsement of picketing congressmen (hi score = disagree)
0.57	q. 31:	Endorsement of demonstrations in Washington (hi score = disagree)
0.57	q. 32:	Endorsement of blocking troop trains (hi score = disagree)
0.54	q. 33:	Endorsement of throwing blood on draft records (hi score = disagree)
0.44	q. 7:	Marijuana should be legalized (hi score = disagree)
0.44	q. 12:	Draft resisters and deserters should be given some sort of amnesty (hi score = disagree)
0.42	q. 34:	Endorsement of bombing of draft offices, etc. (hi score = disagree)

Factor analysis of opinion statements in N.Y. Questionnaire.
* Respondents who score *high* on this factor are UNfavorable jurors while those scoring low are desirable. High disagreement implies unwillingness to consider radical alternatives.

FACTOR TWO: EIGEN VALUE = 1.95		AUTHORITARIANISM**
LOADING		ITEM
0.49	q. 8:	Obedience to authority is the most important virtue children learn (hi score = disagree)
0.44	q. 15:	Single women who have intimate relationships with more than one man tend to be untrustworthy (hi score = disagree)
0.44	q. 20:	Defendants in a criminal case should be required to take the witness stand (hi score = disagree)
0.43	q. 9:	Every person should have complete faith in God (hi score = disagree)

FACTOR TWO: EIGEN VALUE = 1.95		AUTHORITARIANISM**
LOADING		ITEM
0.43	q. 24:	People who fail to report criminal activity to the police are probably equally guilty (hi score = disagree)
0.43	q. 22:	Police should be allowed to arrest and question suspicious looking persons to determine whether they have been up to something illegal (hi score = disagree)
0.41	q. 6:	Police should not hesitate to use force to maintain order (hi score = disagree)
0.40	q. 26:	Death penalty is more effective than a life sentence in keeping people from commiting murder (hi score = disagree)
0.39	q. 25:	Police or FBI informers are more likely to tell the truth than the average citizen (hi score = disagree)

** High scores on the second factor are ANTI-authoritarians.

RESOURCE FILE NO. 8

In-Court Rating Instruments To Rate Jurors in *U.S.* v. *Patricia Swinton.* These forms were based on the demographic profiles related to the factor analyses presented in Resource File No. 7. An Automatic Interaction Detection (AID) analysis was run for both factors, labeled "political expediency" and "authoritarianism," assigning each respondent two factor scores. The resulting profile of major demographic predictors of favorable and unfavorable jurors for each factor are laid out in checklist fashion so that an observer can quickly check off and assign a quick score to each juror as information comes in. Such profiles vary with region and with the type of criminal case. See Chapter 8.

IN COURT INSTRUMENT
Political Expedience—*U.S. v. Swinton*

JUROR NAME _____ JUROR NO. _____ OBSERVER _____

SEX   MALE ☐   FEMALE ☐

	WORST	UNFAVOR-ABLE	FAVORABLE	BEST
1. AGE		☐ Over 40	☐ Under 40	
2. RELIGION	☐ Catholic		☐ Jewish Protestant	☐ No Preference
3. LOCATION		☐ Bronx Westchester	☐ Manhattan	
4. POLITICS		☐ Republican Conservative	☐ Democrat Liberal	
5. NEWSPAPER	☐ News	☐ Post	☐ Times Voice	
6. WHICH PART OF PAPER READ		☐ Other Sports	☐ Editorial News	
7. MARITAL		☐ Married Widowed	☐ Divorced Separated Single	

	WORST	UNFAVOR-ABLE	FAVORABLE	BEST
8. OCCUPATION	☐ White Collar Sales, Prof. (Over 40)	☐ White & Blue Collar Exec. (Under 40)	☐ Exec. Blue Collar (Over 40)	☐ Sales Prof. (Under 40)
9. EMPLOY-MENT STATUS	☐ Housewife (Over 40)	☐ Unemployed Retired*	☐ Employed	
10. EDUCATION		☐ Less than HS Over 40	☐ HS or better Over 40	
		☐ HS only Under 40	☐ HS & Grad & Prof. Under 40	

* Very hard to figure—can be radical.

IN COURT INSTRUMENT
Authoritarianism—*U.S. v. Swinton*

JUROR NAME _____ JUROR NO. _____ OBSERVER _____

	WORST	UNFAVOR-ABLE	FAVORABLE	BEST
1. RELIGION		☐ Catholic Baptist Evangel.	☐ Jewish Protestant	
2. EDUCATION		☐ HS or less Coll Incom.	☐ College Grad Prof. School	
3. AGE	☐ 50–68	☐ 75+	☐ 18–49 68–75	
4. EMPLOY-MENT STATUS	☐ Housewife Retired		☐ Employed Unemployed Student	
5. LOCATION		☐ Bronx Westchester	☐ Manhattan	
6. OCCUPATION		☐ Any other	☐ Professional	

	WORST	UNFAVOR-ABLE	FAVORABLE	BEST
7. INCOME		☐ Under 5,000 9–15,000	☐ 5–9,000 15,000 or over	☐* Refused 5–9,000
8. NEWSPAPER		☐ News Westchester Paper	☐ Times Post Don't read	
9. MARITAL		☐ Separated Married	☐ Divorced Widowed Single	
10. NO. OF PEOPLE IN HOME		☐ 2 or large family	☐ 1, 3, 5 (odd couples)	
11. ETHNIC		☐ Southern Europe Africa	☐ West/East Europe British Isles	

* Weird—May be disgruntled unemployed or welfare.

RESOURCE FILE NO. 9

Ethical Issues Raised for Psychologists and the Criminal Justice System. Adapted from Monahan, J. (Ed.), Report of the Task Force on the role of psychology in the criminal justice system, February 1978; available from the American Psychological Association, Washington, D.C. See Chapter 11.

ETHICAL ISSUES THAT THE CRIMINAL JUSTICE SYSTEM CREATES FOR PSYCHOLOGISTS

QUESTIONS OF LOYALTY

Recommendation 1. Psychologists in criminal justice settings, as elsewhere, should inform all parties to a given service of the level of confidentiality that applies and should specify any circumstances that would constitute an exception to confidentiality. This should be done in advance of the service and preferably in writing.

Recommendation 2. The ideal level of confidentiality of therapeutic services in criminal justice settings should be the same as the level of confidentiality that exists in voluntary noninstitutional settings.

Recommendation 3. Other than for legitimate research purposes, psychoassessments of offenders should be performed only when the psychologist has a reasonable expectation that such assessments will serve a useful therapeutic or dispositional function.

QUESTIONS OF COMPETENCE

Recommendation 4. Psychologists who work in the criminal justice system, as elsewhere, have an ethical obligation to educate themselves in the concepts and operations of the system in which they work.

Recommendation 5. Since it is not within the professional competence of psychologists to offer conclusions on matters of law, psychologists should resist pressure to offer such conclusions.

Recommendation 6. Psychologists should be clear about what they are trying to accomplish in the criminal justice system and the state of the empirical evidence in support of their ability to accomplish it.

Recommendation 7. There is an ethical obligation on psychologists who perform services in the criminal justice system, as elsewhere, to encourage and cooperate in the evaluation of those services.

Recommendation 8. Psychological research in prisons should conform to the ethical standards proposed by the National Commission for the Protection of Human Subjects.

ETHICAL ISSUES THAT PSYCHOLOGISTS
CREATE FOR THE CRIMINAL JUSTICE SYSTEM

Recommendation 9. Psychologists should be exceedingly cautious in offering predictions of criminal behavior for use in imprisoning or releasing individual offenders. If a psychologist decides that it is appropriate in a given case to provide a prediction of criminal behavior, he or she should clearly specify: (1) the acts being predicted, (2) the estimated probability that these acts will occur during a given time period, and (3) the factors on which the predictive judgment is based.

Recommendation 10. Psychologists should be strongly encouraged to offer treatment services to all offenders who request them.

IMPLEMENTING TASK FORCE RECOMMENDATIONS

Recommendation 11. The American Psychological Association should strongly encourage graduate and continuing education in the applied ethics of psychological intervention and research.

Recommendation 12. The American Psychological Association should strengthen its capacity to receive, investigate, and act on complaints of violations of its ethical standards. Formal advisory opinions should continue to be offered to psychologists requesting an interpretation of the standards in specific fact situations.

RESOURCE FILE NO. 10

A new Way For Jailers—An Inmate's View, by Edgar Smith, convicted murderer who successfully reversed a murder verdict, later confessed that he did it and was still later convicted of attempted murder. Reprinted from the *Bergen Record*, July 23, 1978. See Chapter 11. This article summarizes the start of the Determinate Sentencing Program in the California Prison system.

A NEW WAY FOR JAILERS— AN INMATE'S VIEW

Edgar Smith*

Crime is killing the American taxpayer. The most conservative estimate is that the total cost will exceed $20 billion this year.

For every tax dollar going to the public school system, nearly two will go to maintain the criminal justice system. For each dollar Americans give to their churches, the tax collector will take ten to finance a crime and punishment system mired in disproved theories, unworkable concepts, and counterproductive practices.

Rich and poor, young and old, black and white, taxpayer and welfare recipient—all are potential victims of crime, all bear the burden of the criminal justice system's failure.

Well-intentioned efforts to change the system, to make it work for the benefit of both society and the criminal, run into brick walls of public misunderstanding and seem only to exacerbate the problem.

Lawmakers and courts, goaded by angry, frustrated citizens or opportunistic politicians, have swung between the extremes of more prisons, harsher sentences and fewer paroles on one side, and less vindictiveness, greater use of probation and parole instead of prison sentences, and a more intensive effort in rehabilitation on the other.

None of this has helped. The crime rate continues to rise, and the majority of our prison inmates are repeat offenders.

All across the United States multimillion-dollar prison construction projects—an estimated $5 billion total—are under-way or planned by state and federal governments, spurred on by fears of rising crime, reduced efficiency on the part of courts and the police, all in the face of incontrovertible evidence that the system is inherently unfair.

Americans are for the most part a fair people with a deep-rooted sense of justice. One would suppose that a people who could put a man on the moon could solve any earthbound problem. Yet the solution to the crime menace seems as elusive today as it was 200 years ago.

Perhaps the fundamental assumptions about prisons are all wrong. Perhaps there is too little public understanding of what prisons can and should do.

Reprinted from *The Bergen Record,* July 23, 1978. This material first appeared in THE RECORD, Hackensack, N.J.

* Edgar Smith, 44, was sentenced to life in prison for kidnapping and attempted murder. He is in San Quentin Prison awaiting parole in 1982.

Nothing better illustrates the schizophrenic quality of our thinking about crime and punishment than to weigh California's recent decision to forgo new prison construction against New Jersey's current plans to spend about $60 million to rebuild the old Trenton State Prison at the astronomical cost of $50,000 per cell.

No real consideration was given by New Jersey to the fact that its prison system, one of the nation's oldest, has accomplished little more in 200 years than provide the state with low-cost license plates.

Nor have other states with budget-breaking prison construction projects given any real thought to whether their new institutions would be any more effective than the old.

The 1975 report of the National Advisory Commission on Criminal Justice, Standards, and Goals, says: "The prison, the reformatory, and the jail have achieved only a shocking record of failure. There is overwhelming evidence that these institutions create crime rather than reduce it."

Prison administrators and bureaucrats are little concerned with such details. Their watchword is MORE—more prisons, bigger prisons; more guards, higher salaries; more power, bigger staffs.

One bright spot seems to have emerged in the overall picture. California last year decided that enough was enough, that the old justice system did not work, would not work, and probably could not work.

Faced with demands for $79 million to build two new prison facilities, the California legislature hesitated, then refused, choosing instead to strike out on a new course. Doing so, however, was no easy task. It required abandoning the philosophical cornerstone upon which the American penitentiary system, the backbone of the justice system, has rested—the 200-year old precept that penitentiaries exist primarily to rehabilitate criminals and prepare them to return to society.

To appreciate fully the scope of the California decision to abandon the concept of rehabilitation, to weigh its possible implications for other states, including New Jersey, it is necessary first to understand the history of the American penitentiary system.

Prior to the latter third of the Eighteenth Century, criminals were not thought of as being fundamentally different from other men. Man was considered a basically imperfect creature prone to evil and the best society could ever hope to do was to deter him from his evil ways through the threat of severe punishment and public shame.

Punishment for crime tended to be along the lines of public whipping or mutilation, branding, the stocks and the pillory, or in extreme cases where the wrongdoer was thought beyond redemption, exile or death. Prisons of the time served two purposes: places where those in power isolated their personal and political enemies, or temporary places of confinement for those accused of crime, pending trial and punishment.

It was not until the Constitutional Convention of 1787 that the Philadelphia Society for Alleviating the Miseries of the Prisons (Quakers) finally prevailed and won general acceptance of their "reformist" views.

Man, the Quakers argued, was basically good because of his divine creation, and criminality resulted from evil influences outside Man's basic nature—bad environment, including corrupting family and friends; lack of work habits and skills leading to unemployment and indolence ("The Devil finds work for idle hands"); and a failure to know and understand the moral precepts imparted by Holy Scripture.

Remove the religious veneer and the 1787 Quaker philosophy is not unlike the modern sociological view that criminals are basically "good boys" who were led astray or never had a chance—the socio-environmental theory.

The Quaker solution to criminality was to isolate the offender totally from society and its evil influences, to force him to learn good work habits, and to confine him in absolute silence, with the Bible his only reading matter. In this way, it was thought, the basic good nature of man would manifest itself; the offender would reflect upon his wrongdoing and become penitent.

Thus arose the "House of Penitence," the penitentiaries, within whose walls the ostracized criminal would become a better man. Rehabilitation had been invented.

By the early 1800's medieval fortresslike penitentiaries had sprung up in Maryland, New Jersey, Pennsylvania, New York, and Connecticut, enormous monuments to the rapidity with which the Quaker theories took hold.

The new institutions were no low-budget afterthoughts built with crumbs salvaged from state treasuries. Eastern State Penitentiary in Pennsylvania, still standing today, was the largest structure then built in the New World, and the most expensive, a symbol of the young American republic's unique experiment.

Soon the system was in trouble. Within the first 50 years, the penitentiary concept began breaking down under the pressures of overcrowding and reform. Overcrowding made it impossible to isolate convicts in individual cells, silence could not be maintained under such conditions, and not enough work could be found to occupy every convict.

By the outbreak of the Civil War, the penitentiary system had for all practical purposes collapsed, and the prisons had become little more than warehouses for society's unwanted, much as they remain today.

California entered the prison business in 1853 with a penitentiary system based upon the concept of rehabilitation through confinement and retraining. Convicts were sentenced to fixed terms— ten years, for example—as they were in other states, including New Jersey, and served every day before release.

At about the turn of the century, it became the practice in California, as in most states, to sentence convicts to upper and lower terms—5-7 years, for example—the sentence supposedly representing the judge's best guess as to how long it would take the offender to become rehabilitated and fit for release back to society. The actual release date, somewhere within the limits of the sentence, was determined by parole boards—parole being a relatively new concept in prison reform.

In theory, the parole boards were supposed to monitor the convict's progress in prison and predict, with some degree of accuracy, his moral and psychological fitness for release.

While the theory of parole seemed fair and in the best interests of both the convict and society, the system had, in its discretionary nature, an inherent weakness. Persons with similar criminal backgrounds and convicted of similar crimes often received widely disparate sentences, sentences which too often depended almost entirely upon the personal prejudices of a given judge.

The unfairness of the system was so apparent that in 1948 California tried a new tack with the Indeterminate Sentencing Law (ISL).

While retaining rehabilitation as the ultimate goal of the penitentiary system, and leaving some sentencing discretion in the hands of judges, California's ISL provided that with few exceptions all persons convicted of felonies would receive a maximum sentence of life. Under the ISL, for example, an armed robber might receive a sentence of 5 years-to-life, with the parole board responsible for determining the actual release date.

The intent was good. Within a few years, however, it was discovered that the ISL had simply shifted the source of the unfairness. Convicts were less subject to the prejudicial sentencing whims of judges. Now they were subject to the unpredictability of the parole board, with release being more often than not based upon factors reflecting the personal and political prejudices of individual board members, having little to do with rehabilitation or the prognosis for the convict's readjustment to society.

Once again California found its prisons hotbeds of resentment and frustration. And no wonder, when convicts had little idea of how long their terms would be, or what they were expected to do to gain their release. In denying parole, the boards rarely gave any reason more illuminating than "not ready yet."

The final break with tradition came last year. The California prison system had grown to be the largest in America, and the most costly—14 institutions housing 21,000 convicts at an annual average cost of $9,100 per inmate.

The parole authority, responding to public concern over the rising crime rate, was granting fewer paroles. More prisoners serving longer sentences taxed the system's resources—as it has done in New Jersey—and corrections officials, always anxious to expand their domain, demanded $79 million to build two new prisons.

California had reached the penological crossroads.

The decision was made to reject the pleas for more prisons. Instead, the California legislature enacted a complex new formula of punishment for crime known as the Determinate Sentencing Law (DSL), which took effect July 1, 1977.

Unlike its predecessor law, the DSL holds, as a matter of state policy, that prison terms should serve the dual purpose of punishing the criminal and protecting the public, and that rehabilitation, while it may be a laudable goal, was not the state's primary responsibility. Self-rehabilitation was to be encouraged, but it would not be required as a precondition for release.

The DSL is a "same crime, same punishment" law. Virtually all sentencing discretion is taken from the judges, and only a minimal amount of release discretion is left to the parole authority, renamed the Community Release Board.

All crimes in California are now punishable under the DSL formula, and all persons convicted of similar crimes under similar circumstances, no matter where they are sentenced, or by whom, receive equal sentences and serve equal terms in the penitentiary.

The ultimate goal of the DSL is to release nonviolent offenders in the shortest possible time, while providing longer terms for repeat violent offenders.

Under the DSL formula, all crimes now have a "base term," which is the minimum term to be imposed for the criminal act before the circumstances of the act are considered. The base term for robbery, for instance, is set at three, four, or five years.

If the sentencing judge finds that mitigating circumstances existed in the commission of the crime, he may sentence the robber to the lower base term, three years, but he must state on the record of sentencing the specific mitigating factors which led to that sentence.

If the judge finds there were aggravating circumstances, he may sentence to the upper base term, five years, but again he must document his reasons.

Barring the finding of mitigating or aggravating circumstances, the judge *must* sentence to the middle base term, or four years.

Having once established the base term, the judge is then required to take into consideration all the factors of the offense and the background of the offender.

If the offender has a prior felony conviction, the judge must add one year to the base term. If a deadly weapon was used in the commission of the crime, the judge must add two years. And if the victim suffered bodily harm, the judge must add an additional three years. These added terms are known as "enhancements."

It is possible under the DSL formula for an offender to receive a longer sentence through the enhancement procedure than for the crime itself. A robber who has a prior felony record, who uses a gun and wounds his victim, would receive the middle base term of four years for robbery, but would receive an additional five years in enhancements, for a total of nine years.

To further the fairness of the new system, every man sentenced to the penitentiary must serve his entire sentence less time off for work and good behavior.

In theory, every convict should know the day he enters prison when he will be released, and two men convicted of the same crime under similar circumstances, and arriving at the penitentiary the same day, should be released the same day, barring in-prison disciplinary problems resulting in loss of work or of good-time credits.

As an added public protection, the Community Release Board is empowered to hold what are called Serious Offender Hearings for persons convicted of repeated crimes of violence. Upon a finding that a person is a serious offender, he may be required to serve an additional term under another DSL formula.

To maintain the fairness of the DSL system, and to insure that the Community Release Board does not abuse its discretion, convicts taken before these extrajudicial Serious Offender Hearings must be provided with free legal counsel, and the final decision is subject to multiple administrative and judicial reviews.

California's break with tradition went beyond sentencing revisions and included a major change in the state's parole system, previously the sacred cow of the criminal justice structure.

No longer are California convicts required to remain on parole until the expiration of the original maximum sentence, as is the case in most states. Now, no parolee serves more than one year on parole, with the single exception of life-term prisoners, who serve a maximum parole of three years. Moreover, no parolee can be reimprisoned for more than six months for a parole violation.

The new parole system does no more than reflect the fact that, under DSL, convicts will be serving their entire sentences before release. It recognizes the clear evidence that the majority of repeat offenders commit their new offenses within the first year after release. Those parolees who get past that first crucial year without a relapse into crime are unlikely ever to see the inside of a prison again, and it would prove counterproductive to keep them under the numerous disabilities parole imposes.

Data for the last full statistical year show that approximately 8,000 California convicts were serving sentences for nonviolent offenses—burglary, auto theft, bad checks, forgery, drugs, and related offenses. That number represented a shade over 40 percent of all prisoners.

Prisoners falling into the three major violent crime categories, as classified by the California Department of Corrections (homicide, various assaults, and rape); made up only 40.9 percent of the total prison population.

Robbery is the "swing" crime. If robbery is classified as a nonviolent crime, as it is classified by the California authorities, then the percentage of nonviolent offenders in the system rises to 58 percent. If, on the other hand, robbery is considered a violent crime, then the percentage of violent prisoners rises to the same level, give or take a fraction of one percent.

It is worth noting, perhaps, that more than 14 percent of all persons confined in California, both male and female, are serving sentences for marijuana and other controlled substance offenses.

Since the DSL took effect: The felon population has dropped 509 inmates; The number incarcerated for homicide dropped by 1; The number incarcerated for assault dropped by 18; The number incarcerated for rape dropped by 72; The major reductions were in theft, auto theft, forgery, the non-violent offenses, for a total of 492.

Whether the result of the DSL or not, the six-month period following implementation of the DSL did show a drop in the overall prison population, with the majority of the difference being in the non-violent offenses, while the proportion of violent offenders remained static.

The next survey, due in March, '79, should tell the story.

No one expects any significant increase in the number of violent offenders incarcerated under the DSL, barring some surprising and dramatic increase in the incidence of violent crime, but on a percentage basis, violent offenders are expected to make up a larger portion of the overall prison population. Indeed, corrections officials are so confident that the DSL will bring about smaller prison populations that planning has already begun to reduce the population of San Quentin by half.

Efforts to compare the characteristics of California's prison population with that of the New Jersey system have proved unavailing. The National Council on Crime and Delinquency, which encourages DSL sentencing formulas, says no similar statistical studies are presently available for the New Jersey system.

Most penologists agree, however, that the characteristics of prison populations vary only slightly from state to state, as the state socioeconomic structures vary. Thus, while New Jersey might have, for example, a greater percentage of inmates confined for homicide or rape, the overall ratio of violent to nonviolent offenders incarcerated probably varies only to a small degree from that of the California system.

Not everyone is happy with the DSL. Los Angeles Police Chief Ed Davis, and California Attorney General Evelle Younger, both gubernatorial candidates running law and order campaigns, have referred to the DSL as "The Great California Jail Break."

Convicts, on the other hand, tend to believe the new law is too harsh, particularly in the enhancements feature for serious offenders, but they applaud its general fairness and the "same crime, same punishment" provisions.

The truth probably lies somewhere in the middle. What seems certain, however, is that the DSL has been carefully designed to result in smaller, less-expensive-to-maintain prisons housing only the most violent, hardcore offenders, those who pose a real and immediate threat to society.

It is too early to tell if the California experiment will prove to be the national model for the future, though modified versions have been adopted in Arizona, Illinois, and Indiana. But certainly, for the taxpayers of those states proposing enormous new prison construction projects, like New Jersey, the possibility that the adoption of a DSL might render all or part of the new prison proposals unnecessary is a possibility worth considering.

One fact cannot be questioned: In having the courage to cast aside the 200-year-old myth of rehabilitation through confinement, the California legislature has shown the rest of the nation that there may well be an alternative to mortgaging the taxpayers' futures to maintain a prison system that every objective observer confirms does not work.

RESOURCE FILE NO. 11

Deposition By a Social Psychologist in Support of a Motion to Disallow the Death Qualification of Jurors. The first part is a model deposition, adapted from the trial of *North Carolina* v. *Joan Little* (1975) prepared by social scientists to present the scientific rationale of why it will reduce the impartiality of the jury if jurors are death qualified. The second part is the text of the actual legal motion, separate and distinct from the less legalistic deposition. A couple of sample exhibits of data are included. See Chapter 11.

		DEPOSITION OF PROF. ROBERT
		BUCKHOUT[1] IN REFERENCE TO
STATE OF NORTH CAROLINA		MOTION TO DISALLOW THE DEATH
v.		QUALIFICATION OF PROSPECTIVE
JOAN LITTLE		JURORS
		Filed in July 1975

PROFESSOR ROBERT BUCKHOUT, Ph.D., being duly sworn, deposes and says:

1. I am an Associate Professor of Psychology with the Department of Psychology of Brooklyn College located in Brooklyn, New York. . . .[2]

I have conducted jury studies and done research into the operation and functioning of juries, and I am fully familiar with research and studies conducted with respect to both civil and criminal trial juries by others. I am also fully familiar with other surveys and studies conducted in connection with the ascertaining of attitudes, feelings and opinions with respect to particular defendants in criminal cases.

My Ph.D. in psychology was obtained at Ohio State University in 1963.

As a forensic psychologist, I have done research, analysis and given testimony via deposition and direct appearances before juries in over 30 cases.

2. My purpose in writing this deposition is to answer questions raised by defendant's counsel about what empirical social science research findings since 1968 have to say about the attitudes of potential jurors toward the death penalty, and the effect of those attitudes on juror behavior in rendering a verdict. The 1968 date marks the *Witherspoon* v. *Illinois* 391 U.S. 510 (1968) decision in which the data were regarded by the court as ". . . too tentative and too fragmentary to establish that jurors not opposed to the death penalty tend to favor the prosecution in the determination of guilt," (391 at 516).

I agree with the court's description of the state of jury research of that time, but I wish to point out that the period of time from 1968 to the present has been marked by a very large increase in the amount of well controlled research on the attitudes and behavior of actual jurors and samples of voters who can be called as jurors. The amount and quality of this research is sufficient to allow a professional social scientist to offer reasoned opinions on the questions which interested

---

[1] This model deposition is modified from the original.

[2] Text continues with a biographical and professional resume of the expert. Complete documents are available from the CENTER.

the Supreme Court in *Witherspoon* and more specifically to offer an opinion on the questions raised by the defendant's attorney in *State* v. *Joan Little*.[3]

3. It is my opinion that the defendant cannot receive a fair trial in the State of North Carolina where the prosecution is permitted to challenge any juror for cause when the basis for such challenge is that juror's disbelief in or reservations concerning the penalty of death. It is my opinion that the exercise of such a challenge by one adversary to a court proceeding will shrink the size of the jury pool in a discriminatory manner, exclude a broad (majority) cross section of the attitudes of the community, and leave a (minority) jury pool with a unique cluster of attitudes which can best be described as "conviction proneness," and is hence inherently prejudicial to the defendant.

These opinions are predicated on the research of myself and my colleagues and on national and regional surveys of attitudes toward capital punishment as documented below and in the exhibits. I will use a question answer format to focus on the main issues before the court.

4. Social Science Research on the Questions Before the Court
   A. *Are Death Qualified Jurors More Likely to Convict?*
      YES. In a series of studies (see exhibits) social scientists have demonstrated conclusively that jurors who are qualified (in favor of the death penalty) are more likely to convict a defendant than nonqualified jurors in the face of the same evidence in criminal trials. Professor George L. Jurow found that jurors who were strongly in favor of capital punishment consistently voted to convict. (See Exhibit 2.) He noted that the bias existed very strongly in pro-death jurors in response to a case whose evidence aimed toward acquittal. In my own research I found that pro capital punishment jurors tended to disagree more with the presumption of innocence than jurors who did not favor the death penalty.[4]

Additional Studies:

In a study in the state of Georgia, Professor Faye Goldberg found that death-qualified jurors were more likely to convict than other jurors over a wide range of hypothetical cases.[5] Professor Edward J. Bronson,

---

[3] Or in a number of other cases including *House* v. *Stynchcombe*, State of Georgia, 1976.

[4] Buckhout, R. and Baker, E. Juror attitudes and the death penalty. *Social Action and the Law*, 1977, 3 (6), 70.

[5] Goldberg, F. Toward expansion of *Witherspoon*: Capital punishment scruples, jury bias and the use of psychological data to raise presumptions in the law. *Harvard Civil Rights Law Review*, 1969, 53.

who studied a large group of jurors in Colorado, found that the people who would be excluded by death qualification were those who were most favorably inclined toward the presumption of innocence.[6] Professor Hans Zeisel found that death qualified jurors in Kings County, N.Y. were significantly more likely to vote guilty on the first ballot in real cases.[7]

Opinion—The scientific evidence clearly supports a conclusion that death qualified jurors are more likely to convict and are prejudiced in favor of the prosecution in criminal cases.

B. *Do Death Qualified Jurors As a Group Represent a Majority of Society?*

NO. The results of scientific opinion surveys show conclusively that despite the majority of Americans favoring the abstract idea of the death penalty, when they are asked to put themselves in the role of jurors the majority of Americans (potential jurors) would *not* impose the death penalty. This point was clearly established in the 1973 Harris Poll which showed that only 39 percent pro-death penalty respondents would agree to vote guilty if such a vote meant an automatic death penalty as required by law in the case of the murder of a police officer.[8] In the most recent repeat testing by the Harris Organization, (February 1977) the percentage favoring the death penalty for all people convicted of murdering a police officer is still less than the majority.

Further Research Clarification:

The essence of the Harris Survey was to point out that most American potential jurors prefer discretion in the handing down of the death penalty and that the exercise of discretion depends upon the circumstances of the crime. This survey was superbly analyzed in an article by Professors Neil Vidmar and Phoebe Ellsworth writing in the *Stanford Law Review*.[9] In my own research on seated jurors in Kings County, N.Y. only 34 percent of the jurors were unequivocally in favor of the death penalty.[10]

Opinion—The real majority of the society is (a) a group of people who totally oppose capital punishment and (b) those who feel it should

---

[6] Bronson, E. On the conviction proneness and representativeness of the death qualified jury: An empirical study of Colorado veniremen. *University of Colorado Law Review*, 1970, *1*.

[7] Zeisel, H. Some data on juror attitudes toward capital punishment. Published by the Center for Studies in Criminal Justice, University of Chicago Law School.

[8] The complete 1977 Harris Poll of death penalty attitudes is shown in Table 1 on page 24 of this paper (Appendix A).

[9] Vidmar, N. and Ellsworth, P. Public opinion and the death penalty. *Stanford Law Review*, 1974, *26* (6), 1245–1270.

[10] Buckhout, R. and Baker, 1977, op. cit.

only be employed with discretion. According to the latest Harris Poll this represents at least 51 percent of society. Therefore it is possible that a substantial proportion of this majority of the population could be *disqualified* as jurors under the applicable law in the *State* v. *Joan Little*.

    C. *Do Death Qualified Jurors Have Attitudes Which Might Be Prejudicial to the Defendant?*

    YES. A body of social psychological research building since 1950 devoted to "the authoritarian personality" describes a person who is rigid, punitive moralistic, intolerant of deviant behavior, hostile toward low status persons, and likely to identify with those who would punish the deviant. Jurow[11] and others have found that those favoring capital punishment fit the authoritarian personality description. The defendant, as a poor, black, woman defendant accused of murder is likely to be the target of prejudice from authoritarian individuals who can choose from a number of labels on which their hostility might focus. In my research on jurors, pro-death penalty jurors had significantly higher authoritarianism scores than other jurors. Hence death qualification of jurors will in my opinion favor the selection of authoritarians and could very likely be prejudiced to the defendant.

    Further Research Clarification:

    The research on authoritarians, especially Professor Boehm[12] demonstrates that authoritarian (and death-qualified) jurors were conviction prone, overly "tough" (voting for unnecessarily high degrees of murder verdicts); and they relied heavily on subjective impressions of the defendant's character (which are of course legally irrelevant). Professor Boehm developed the Legal Attitudes Questionnaire (LAQ) which measures authoritarianism. I have personally used this test to select jurors of all types in a realistic mock murder trial.[13] I found that authoritarian jurors were more conviction prone than others and that they showed a rigidity in not changing their initial verdict even in the face of reasoned deliberations. Professors Mitchell and Byrne reported that authoritarian jurors showed a bias against a defendant they felt to be different from themselves.[14]

---

[11] Jurow, G. New data on the effect of a "death-qualified" jury on the guilt determination process. *Harvard Law Review*, 1971, 567.

[12] Boehm, V. Mr. Prejudice, Miss Sympathy, and the authoritarian personality: An application of psychological measuring techniques to the problem of jury bias. *Wisconsin Law Review*, 1968, 734.

[13] Alexander, M., and Licker, J. Jury selection: Finding rigid and flexible jurors and deciding if they're needed. Center for Responsive Psychology Report Number CR-18, July 1975.

[14] Mitchell, H. and Byrne, D. The defendant's dilemma: Effects of juror's attitudes and authoritarianism on judicial decisions. *Journal of Personality and Sociological Research.* 1973, 123.

Opinion—The more a juror favors the death penalty, the more punitive and prejudicial will be his/her attitude toward the accused.

    D. *Will Death Qualification of Jurors Tend to Systematically Exclude Cognizable Classes of People From Jury Service?*

    YES. "As opposition to the death penalty increases, the percentage of whites decreases . . ." (Bronson, p. 18).[15] This is but one of many findings which clearly show that the death penalty is not an "equal-opportunity attitude." Non-white people, women, people under 25, and poor people will be excluded disproportionately by death qualification due to greater opposition to the death penalty in those groups.

    Further Scientific Clarification:

Professor Bronson's data showed, despite the small percentage of people in his sample who were death qualified, that while the majority of white jurors were death qualified only 20 percent of blacks were. Goldberg notes that only 10 percent of those in her sample who could be death qualified were black. In the 1974 Gallup survey of national attitudes toward the death penalty it may be seen that 50 percent of non-whites and only 34 percent of whites oppose the death penalty and could be disqualified (see Exhibit 3). Women were more opposed than men (41 percent v. 31 percent); the poor were more opposed as were people 18–24. The more sophisticated Harris Poll (1973, 1977) showed a similar result: women—42 percent v. men—30 percent against; blacks 55 percent against v. whites 33 percent against. (See Exhibit 2.)

    Opinion—In summary the research studies and the polls indicate that death qualification mitigates against a jury of the peers of the defendant because of the systematic exclusion of relevant groups which have substantial sentiments against the death penalty.[16]

    E. *If Death Qualification Were Eliminated, Would the Court Face a Group of Acquittal-prone Jurors?*

    NO. There is no scientific evidence to support this usual justification of death qualification. In Professor Bronson's study of Colorado veniremen and in my own research the jurors who opposed capital punishment were split 50 percent-50 percent on conviction proneness and innocent proneness. This group contrasted sharply with those favoring capital punishment who, in the majority were conviction prone (Bronson, p. 19). This 50-50 division is what most psychologists regard as a normal outcome when asking any group of people how they might decide any controversial issue. The percentage of people who are absolutely opposed to the death penalty, whose role as a juror would be compromised is very small. In the Harris Poll (Table 1) only 23

15 Bronson, op. cit.
16 Buckhout, R., et al. A jury without peers. In M. Reidel, and P. A. Vales (Eds.), *Treating the Offender: Problems and Issues*. New York: Praeger Publishers, 1977.

percent said they would never return a death verdict. Goldberg found about 6 percent of such people. Some people who hold such views (or the other attitude of mandatory execution) mask their views and could only be detected with extensive questioning.

Opinion—The percentage of persons whose scruples against the death penalty prevent them from voting to convict in a capital case is too small to justify the risks in a fair trial which accompany the death-qualification procedure.

It is my professional opinion based on all of the foregoing that the interests of justice require that the Court refuse to allow the challenge of any juror for cause on the grounds of that juror's belief against or in favor of the death penalty. It is my opinion furthermore that elimination of death qualification of jurors will assure the defendant and the state of a jury which is more representative of a majority of the population and more representative of the attitudes of society. It is also my opinion that in eliminating the inherently prejudicial procedure of death qualification of jurors, the Court will be taking a step in the right direction of ensuring a fair trial for the defendant.[17]

Table 1

Recently, the Harris survey asked the cross section:
"Do you believe in capital punishment (death penalty) or are you opposed?"

CAPITAL PUNISHMENT	FAVOR %	OPPOSE %	NOT SURE %
1977	67	25	8
1973	59	31	10
1970	47	42	11
1969	48	38	14
1965	38	47	15

"Do you feel that executing people who commit murder deters others from committing murder, or do you think such executions don't have much effect?"

DO EXECUTIONS DETER MURDER?	TOTAL PUBLIC %
Deters others	59
No such effect	34
Not sure	7

[17] See additional readings on capital punishment and jurors elsewhere in this issue. Additional exhibits on each reference cited above in the form of Exhibit 1 are available from the CENTER. Also available is the Points of Law Brief from *North Carolina* v. *Joan Little*. The motion to eliminate death qualification was denied.

"Suppose it could be proven to your satisfaction that the death penalty was NOT more effective than long prison sentences in keeping other people from committing crimes such as murder, would you be in favor of the death penalty or opposed to it?"

IF COULD BE PROVEN DEATH PENALTY DID NOT DETER MURDER

	FAVOR %	OPPOSE %	NOT SURE %
Total public 1973	35	48	17
Total public 1977	46	40	14
By age			
18–29	42	47	11
30–49	45	40	15
50 and over	51	34	15
By race			
Black	25	51	24
White	49	39	12
By political philosophy			
Conservative	55	32	13
Middle of the road	45	41	14
Liberal	38	50	12

"Do you feel that all persons convicted of these crimes should get the death penalty, that no one convicted of these crimes should get the death penalty, or do you feel that whether or not someone convicted of the same crime gets the death penalty should depend on the circumstances of the case and the character of the person?"

MANDATORY USE OF THE DEATH SENTENCE

	ALL %	NO ONE %	DEPENDS %	NOT SURE %
KILLING A POLICEMAN OR PRISON GUARD				
1977	49	14	33	4
1973	41	17	38	4
FIRST-DEGREE MURDER				
1977	40	13	44	3
1973	28	16	53	3
SKYJACKING				
1977	22	29	44	5
1973	27	27	41	5
RAPE				
1977	20	27	48	5
1973	19	27	50	4
MUGGING				
1977	8	44	43	5
1973	9	41	43	7

EXHIBIT 1

EXPERT TESTIMONY ON JUROR QUALIFICATION

NAME

GEORGE L. JUROW

CREDENTIALS

Professor, City University of New York;
B.S. University of Pennsylvania;
LL.B. Yale University;
Ph.D. Clinical Psychology, Adelphi University

PUBLICATION

New Data on the Effect of a "Death Qualified" Jury on the Guilt Determination Process
84 Harvard Law Review 567 (1971)

STUDY

1. Under a grant from the Law Enforcement Assistance Administration 211 employees of Sperry Rand Corporation were used to compose the testing group.
2. Attitudes toward capital punishment were measured by two separate series of questions, one to measure general, and one to measure specific attitudes.
3. Jury performance was measured by reactions to two simulated trials where the evidence was approximately equal.

RESULTS

1. 10% of the group stated that in no circumstances could they return a death verdict; 16 out of 211 stated they would favor the return of a death penalty; and the remaining 132 stated they would consider the penalty.
2. Of the 10% who registered disapproval of the death penalty, only 33% voted to convict where the evidence was equal; however of the 16 who favored the death penalty, 80% voted to convict in *both* simulated cases.
3. 44% of all test subjects voted conviction in one case—while 58% of all subjects voted conviction in the second.

CONCLUSIONS

1. Death qualification of jurors allows the elimination of those persons who tend to be more skeptical toward conviction; however

it allows those persons to remain who have a very strong tendency to convict, even in the face of conflicting evidence.
2. The more in favor of capital punishment one is, the more likely that person is to be conservative, authoritarian, and punitive, (and, of course, the more conservative, authoritarian, and punitive, the more likely the juror is to be in favor of capital punishment.)

EXHIBIT 2

GALLUP POLL ON DEATH PENALTY

(From Gallup Magazine, Dec. 1974)
Date of Poll—October 18–21, 1974

I Favor the Death Penalty for Persons Convicted of Murder

I Oppose the Death Penalty for Persons Convicted of Murder

	Percent Favor	Percent Oppose		Percent Favor	Percent Oppose
NATIONAL	64	36	POLITICS		
SEX			Republican	72	28
Male	69	31	Democrat	61	39
Female	59	41	So. Democrat	65	35
RACE			Other Democrat	59	41
White	66	34	Independent	61	39
Non-White	50	50	RELIGION		
EDUCATION			Protestant	65	35
College	59	41	Catholic	67	33
High School	65	35	OCCUPATION		
Grade School	67	33	Prof. & Bus.	62	38
REGION			Clerical & Sales	64	36
East	63	37	Manual Workers	64	36
Midwest	63	37	Nonlabor Force	68	32
South	66	34	CITY SIZE		
West	63	37	1,000,000 & over	66	34
AGE			500,000–999,999	58	42
Total Under 30	52	48	50,000–499,999	62	38
18–24 years	49	51	2,500–49,999	65	35
25–29 years	56	44	Under 2,500, Rural	65	35
30–49 years	66	34			
50 & older	71	29			
INCOME					
$20,000 & over	65	35			
$15,000–$19,999	68	32			
$10,000–$14,999	67	33			
$ 7,000–$ 9,999	66	34			
$ 5,000–$ 6,999	64	36			
$ 3,000–$ 4,999	53	47			
Under $3,000	55	45			

By Jerry Paul, Attorney

STATE OF NORTH CAROLINA	IN THE GENERAL COURT OF JUSTICE
WAKE COUNTY	SUPERIOR COURT DIVISION

STATE OF NORTH CAROLINA	MOTION TO DISALLOW THE DEATH
V.	QUALIFICATION OF
JOAN LITTLE	PROSPECTIVE JURORS

Now comes the defendant by her attorneys and respectfully requests that the Court refuse to allow the prosecution to challenge any juror for cause when the basis for such challenge is that juror's disbelief in the penalty of death. As reasons for such request the defendant shows to this honorable court the following.

1. That in the case of *Witherspoon* v. *Illinois*, 391 U.S. 510 (1968), the Supreme Court took issue with the then current practice by prosecutors of challenging for cause those jurors who stated on *voir dire* that they were opposed to the death penalty. In determining that such disqualification was improper the Court, *at that time*, stated that the only constitutionally permissable challenges were if veniremen made it "unmistakably clear (1) that they would *automatically* vote against the imposition of capital punishment without regard to any evidence that might be developed at the trial of the case before them or (2) that their attitude toward the death penalty would prevent them from making an impartial decision as to the defendant's guilt." 391 U.S. at 522-23, n. 21.

2. That the *Witherspoon* opinion explicitly left open the question of whether or not a "death qualified" jury was impermissibly prone toward conviction (the data adduced by the petitioner, however, are too tentative and fragmentary to establish that jurors not opposed to the death penalty tend to favor the prosecution in the determination of guilt, 391 at 516) and that numerous studies since the decision in *Witherspoon* conclusively show that jurors which are "death qualified" are not representative of the community and are not unbiased, but are significantly prejudiced in favor of the prosecution and conviction.

3. That since the decision of *Furman* v. *Georgia*, 408 U.S. 238 (1972), as construed by the North Carolina Supreme Court in *State* v. *Waddell*, 282 N.C. 431 (1973), jurors no longer have the responsibility of considering a verdict in a capital case, the juror's only function being the determination of guilt or innocence, thus making the opinion or belief of prospective jurors in regard to the death penalty irrelevant.

4. That the Court in *Witherspoon* stated specifically that a jury in a capital case must as a constitutional requirement reflect the consensus of the community, which consensus is improperly represented by a jury from which the sizable portion of the community—that portion which does not believe in the death penalty—has been systematically excluded.

5. That the Court in *Witherspoon* required that a jury reflect a representative cross section of a community, and that the exclusion of persons who express a disbelief in the death penalty arbitrarily excludes significantly higher percentages of identifiable groups, specifically blacks and women.

6. That the exclusion of persons who do not believe in the death penalty results in a violation of the defendant's Sixth Amendment right to be free from unusual punishment, since those persons who remain on a "death-qualified" jury represent the beliefs of less than 50 percent of society.

7. That the allowance of any challenge for cause by the prosecution for a venireman's disbelief in the death penalty affords the prosecution an advantage in jury selection which is not afforded the defendant and is thus unconstitutional.

8. That to allow the prosecution to inquire into a juror's feelings as to punishment in death penalty situations—and to thereafter excuse for cause if the juror's attitudes are too favorable toward the defendant's position—while prohibiting the solicitor from making such inquiry as to punishment in any other criminal case, violates the capital defendant's right to Equal Protection.

9. That to allow a prospective juror's religion and moral beliefs to be questioned and to be grounds for excusal in a capital case, when religion and moral beliefs are not grounds for excusal in any other criminal proceeding is a denial of Equal Protection as to those who are on trial for their lives.

10. That a defendant in a capital case in North Carolina is further denied Equal Protection in that a substantial portion of the community —those who do not believe in the imposition of the death penalty— may be arbitrarily excluded from the jury which tries him, while all other criminal defendants have the benefit of a representative sample of the community drawn from a complete cross section.

WHEREFORE the defendant respectfully requests that this motion be granted and the State be prohibited from excusing for cause any prospective juror because of such juror's disbelief in the imposition of death as a penalty.

PAUL, KEENAN, ROWAN AND GALLOWAY
Post Office Box 1003
Durham, North Carolina

RESOURCE FILE NO. 12

Sample Statistical Presentation from the *Uniform Crime Reports* (1976). Produced by the Federal Bureau of Investigation. The crimes discussed are murder and negligent manslaughter. See Chapter 13.

MURDER AND NONNEGLIGENT MANSLAUGHTER

Definition

Murder is defined in the Uniform Crime Reporting Program as the willful killing of another. The classification of this offense, as in all of the other Crime Index offenses, is based solely on police investigation as opposed to the determination of a court, medical examiner, coroner, jury, or other judicial body.

Deaths caused by negligence, suicide, accident, or justifiable homicide are not included in the count for this offense classification. Attempts to murder or assaults to murder are scored as aggravated assaults and not as murder.

Trend

YEAR	NUMBER OF OFFENSES	RATE PER 100,000 INHABITANTS
1975	20,510	9.6
1976	18,780	8.8
Percent change	−8.4	−8.3

Features

Most frequent month	July
Most frequent weapon	Firearm
Most frequent victim:	
Age group	20–24
Sex	Male
Most frequent offender:	
Age group	18–22
Sex	Male

Volume

In 1976, there were an estimated 18,780 murders committed in the United States. This number of murders is approximately 2 percent of the total violent crimes.

An analysis of murder by month in 1976 shows that July had the greatest frequency of murder as compared to any other month of the year.

A geographic breakdown of murder by region showed 42 percent of the murders occurred in the Southern States, 23 percent in the North Central States, 18 percent in the Northeastern States, and 17 percent in the Western States.

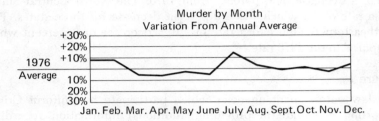

Murder by Month
Variation From Annual Average

Trend

The number of murders decreased 8 percent from 1975 to 1976.

Regionally, the number of murder offenses in 1976 decreased 10 percent in the Southern States, 9 percent in the North Central States, 8 percent in the Northeastern States, and 5 percent in the Western States.

Large core cities of 250,000 or more inhabitants had a 10 percent decrease in the number of murders in 1976 while the suburban and rural areas experienced decreases of 11 percent each.

The following chart reveals an increase of 1 percent from 1972 to 1976 in the murder counts.

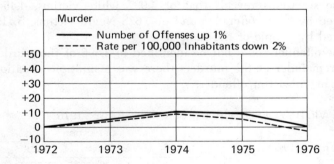

Murder
Number of Offenses up 1%
Rate per 100,000 Inhabitants down 2%

Rate

In 1976, there were 8.8 victims of murder for every 100,000 inhabitants in the Nation. This was a decrease of 8 percent from the murder rate of 9.6 per 100,000 inhabitants recorded in 1975.

The metropolitan areas reported a murder rate of 10 victims per 100,000 inhabitants, the rural areas a rate of 8 per 100,000 inhabitants, and cities outside metropolitan areas reported a murder rate of 5 per 100,000 inhabitants.

The number of murder victims in proportion to population was highest in the Southern States with 11.3 murders per 100,000 inhabitants. This is a decrease of 11 percent from the murder rate of that Region in 1975. In 1976, the Western States showed a murder rate of 8.5, a decrease of 6 percent from 1975. The North Central States had a rate of 7.4 which was a 9 percent decrease for those states. The Northeastern Region had a rate of 7.0, a decrease of 8 percent when compared to the 1975 rate.

Nature

The law enforcement agencies which participate in Uniform Crime Reporting cooperate in providing additional information regarding homicide so that a more in-depth analysis of this offense can be made. Through a supplemental reporting system information is provided regarding the age, sex, and race of the victim and offender; the weapon used in the murder; the circumstances surrounding the offense; and the relationship between the victim and offender.

The victims of murder in 1976 were male in approximately three out of four instances. This ratio of male to female victims is similar to the experience in the last several years. Approximately 51 out of 100 murder victims were white, 47 were Negro, and 2 percent were other races. Three of every ten murder victims were 20 through 29 years of age.

The victim and offender were identified in 10,847 cases during 1976, where there were a single victim and a single offender. A study of these situations reveals that of 4,997 white victims, 4,454 were murdered by white offenders and of 5,628 Negro victims, 5,412 were murdered by people of the same race.

The offender could not be identified in 3,596 of the murders and in the remainder of the murders there was a multiple situation with more than one victim/offender.

SINGLE VICTIM/OFFENDER BY SEX AND RACE, 1976

VICTIM	TOTAL	OFFENDER				
		SEX		RACE		
		MALE	FEMALE	WHITE	NEGRO	OTHER
Sex						
Male	8,190	6,432	1,758	3,442	4,583	165
Female	2,657	2,385	272	1,262	1,329	66
Race						
White	4,997	4,311	686	4,454	473	70
Negro	5,628	4,312	1,316	199	5,412	17
Other	222	194	28	51	27	144
Total	10,847	8,817	2,030	4,704	5,912	231

In 1976, firearms again predominated as the weapon most often used in homicide in the Nation. The accompanying chart illustrates a breakdown by type of weapon used in the commission of murder in the Nation. Firearms were used more frequently in the Southern States than in any other region with firearms used in more than seven of every ten murders. Nationwide, 64 percent of the homicides were committed through the use of firearms and 49 percent were committed with handguns. In 1975, 51 percent of the murders were through the use of handguns.

Murder, By Type of Weapon Used
1976

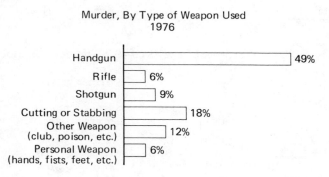

Cutting or stabbing weapons were used in 18 percent of the murders in the Nation. The Northeastern States reported the greatest use of knives or cutting instruments with one out of four murders being committed with this type of weapon. The North Central and Southern States had the least incidence of use of this type of weapon with less than two out of every ten murders. Other weapons such as blunt objects, poisons, explosives, arson, drowning, etc. were used in 12 percent of the murders. In the remaining 6 percent of the murders, personal weapons such as hands, fists, and feet were used.

A comparative study for the past five years shows a decrease from 66 percent of all homicides through use of firearms in 1972 to 64 percent of all homicides in 1976. A comparative analysis of weapons used to commit murder for 1972 through 1976 is shown in tabular form.

The activities resulting in murder vary from arguments to felonies. Murder is largely a societal problem beyond the control of law enforcement. The relationship of the murder victim to the offender emphasizes this point.

In 1976, 27 percent of the murder victims were related to the offenders and 54 percent were otherwise acquainted. During 1976, 6 percent of the murders resulted from drunken arguments and 4 percent resulted from arguments over money or property while 62 percent of the murders resulted from other arguments.

MURDER, TYPE OF WEAPON USED, 1976 [percent distribution]

REGION	TOTAL ALL WEAPONS USED	FIRE-ARMS	KNIFE OR OTHER CUTTING INSTRU-MENT	OTHER WEAPON; CLUB, POISON, ETC.	PERSONAL WEAPONS
Northeastern States	100.0	49.2	25.0	10.0	15.8
North Central States	100.0	66.4	15.1	13.3	5.2
Southern States	100.0	71.2	15.2	9.3	4.3
Western States	100.0	55.4	21.3	14.8	8.5
Total	100.0	63.8	17.8	12.2	6.2

MURDER, TYPE OF WEAPON USED, 1972–1976 [percent distribution]

YEAR	TOTAL NUMBER	TOTAL PERCENT	FIRE-ARMS	KNIFE OR OTHER CUTTING INSTRU-MENT	OTHER WEAPON; CLUB, POISON, ETC.	PERSONAL WEAPONS
1972	18,670	100.0	66.2	19.0	6.6	8.2
1973	19,640	100.0	67.0	17.8	6.6	8.6
1974	20,710	100.0	67.9	17.6	6.8	7.7
1975	20,510	100.0	65.8	17.7	7.5	9.0
1976	18,780	100.0	63.8	17.8	12.2	6.2

Felonious activities resulted in 20 percent of the murders and 8 percent were caused by suspected felonious activities. An analysis of the known felony-type murders reveal that 42 percent resulted from robbery offenses. Prostitution, commercialized vice, forcible rape, and other sex offenses accounted for 8 percent of the total.

RELATIONSHIP BY CIRCUMSTANCE, 1976 [percent distribution]

	RELATIVES	FRIENDS, NEIGHBORS, ACQUAINT-ANCES	STRANGERS	TOTAL
Total	27.2	54.4	18.4	100.0
Felony type	6.2	39.4	54.4	100.0
Suspected felony type	31.6	51.6	16.8	100.0
Romantic triangle	11.4	76.4	12.3	100.0
Argument over money or property	13.2	79.1	7.6	100.0
Other arguments	35.9	57.5	6.5	100.0
Unable to determine	21.6	51.1	27.4	100.0

Due to rounding percentages may not add to total.

Clearances

Nationally, police continue to be successful in clearing or solving by arrest a greater percentage of homicides than any other Crime Index offense. In 1976, 79 percent of the homicides were solved; and in 1975, 78 percent of all murder offenses were solved. Persons under 18 years of age were involved in 5 percent of the willful killings solved by police.

Since 1972, the clearance rate, nationwide, in homicide has decreased from 82 per 100 offenses to 79 per 100 offenses in 1976.

Persons Arrested

Based on reports submitted by law enforcement agencies, 9 percent of all persons arrested for murder were under 18 years of age and 43 percent were under 25. During the period 1972–1976, there was a 27 percent decrease in the number of persons under 18 years of age arrested for murder. The adult arrests increased 13 percent for murder offenses during this period. Numerically, the 18 to 22 year age group had the heaviest involvement during 1976 with 24 percent of the total arrests coming from within this age group. Negroes made up 53 percent of the arrests for murder in 1976.

Persons Charged

Law enforcement agencies' reports disclose that 71 percent of all adults arrested for murder in 1976 were prosecuted during the year. Forty-eight percent of the adults prosecuted were found guilty as charged, and 14 percent were convicted on some lesser charge. The remaining won release by acquittal or dismissal of the charges against them. Of all individuals processed for murder, 7 percent were juveniles who had their cases referred to juvenile court jurisdiction.

RESOURCE FILE NO. 13

Public Opinion Survey Sampling Procedures for National Samples. Technical information and explanations of the sampling strategies of the two major public opinion sampling organizations—Gallup and Harris. Adapted from *The Handbook of Criminal Justice Statistics* 1977, published by the U.S. Department of Justice. See Chapter 13.

The sampling procedures of two public opinion survey organizations are explained in this appendix: Gallup Polls and Harris Surveys.

GALLUP POLLS

All Gallup polls since 1950, excluding certain special surveys, have been based on a national probability sample of interviewing areas. Refinements in the sample design have been introduced at various points in time since then. However, over this period the design in its essentials has conformed to the current procedure, as follows:

1. The United States is divided into seven size-of-community strata: cities of population 1,000,000 and over; 250,000 to 999,999; and 50,000 to 249,999; with the urbanized areas of all these cities forming a single stratum; cities of 2,500 to 49,999; rural villages; and farm or open country rural areas.
2. Within each of these strata, the population is further divided into seven regions: New England, Middle Atlantic, East Central, West Central, South, Mountain, and Pacific Coast.
3. Within each size-of-community and regional stratum the population is arrayed in geographic order and zoned into equal-sized groups of sampling units.
4. In each zone, pairs of localities are selected with probability of selection proportional to the size of each locality's population—producing two replicated samples of localities.
5. Within selected cities for which population data are reported by census tracts or enumeration districts, these sample sub-divisions are drawn with probability of selection proportional to the size of the population.
6. For other cities, minor civil divisions, and rural areas in the sample for which population data are not reported by census tracts or enumeration districts, small, definable geographic areas are drawn, with the probability of selection proportional to size where available data permit; otherwise with equal probability.

7. Within each subdivision selected for which block statistics are available, a block or block cluster is drawn with probability of selection proportional to the number of dwelling units.

8. In cities and towns for which block statistics are not available, blocks are drawn at random, that is, with equal probability.

9. In subdivisions that are rural or open country in character, segments approximately equal in size of population are delineated and drawn with equal probability.

10. In each cluster of blocks and each segment so selected, a randomly selected starting point is designated on the interviewer's map of the area. Starting at this point, interviewers are required to follow a given direction in the selection of households, taking households in sequence, until their assigned number of interviews has been completed.

11. Within each occupied dwelling unit or household reached, the interviewer asks to speak to the youngest man 18 or older at home, or if no man is at home, the oldest woman 18 or older. This method of selection within the household has been developed empirically to produce an age distribution by men and women separately which compares closely with the age distribution of the population. It increases the probability of selecting younger men, who are at home relatively infrequently, and the probability of reaching older women in the household who tend to be underrepresented unless given a disproportionate chance of being drawn from among those at home. The method of selection among those at home within the household is not strictly random, but it is systematic and objective and eliminates interviewer judgment in the selection process.

12. Interviewing is conducted at times when adults are most likely to be at home, which means on weekends or if on week-days, after 4 P.M. for women and after 6 P.M. for men.

13. Allowance for persons not at home is made by a "times-at-home" weighting procedure rather than by "call-backs." This procedure is a standard method for reducing the sample bias that would otherwise result from underrepresentation of persons who are difficult to find at home.

14. The pre-stratification by regions is routinely supplemented by fitting each obtained sample to the latest available Census Bureau estimates of the regional distribution of the population. Also minor adjustments of the sample are made by educational attainment (by men and women separately), based on the annual estimates of the Census Bureau derived from their Current Population Survey.

SOURCE: The following information has been excerpted from George H. Gallup, *The Gallup Poll, Public Opinion 1935–1971*, Vol. 1, 1935–1948 (New York: Random House, 1972), pp. vi–viii; and Louis Harris and Associates, Inc., *The Harris Yearbook of Public Opinion 1970: A Compendium of Current American Attitudes* (New York: Louis Harris and Associates, 1971), pp. 511–514. Nonsubstantive editorial adaptations have been made.

The sampling procedure described is designed to produce an approximation of the adult civilian population living in the United States, except for those persons in institutions such as prisons or hospitals.

Prior to 1950, the samples for all Gallup surveys, excluding special surveys, were a combination of what is known as a purposive design for the selection of cities, towns, and rural areas, and the quota method for the selection of individuals within such selected areas.

The first step in obtaining the sample was to draw a national sample of places (cities, towns, and rural areas). These were distributed by six regions and five or six city size, urban-rural groups or strata in proportion to the distribution of the population of voting age by these regional-city size strata. The distribution of cases between the non-South and South, however, was on the basis of the vote in presidential elections.

Within each region the sample of such places was drawn separately for each of the larger States and for groups of smaller States. The places were selected to provide broad geographic distribution within States and at the same time in combination to be politically representative of the State or group of States in terms of three previous elections. Specifically they were selected so that in combination they matched the State vote for three previous elections within small tolerances. Great emphasis was placed on election data as a control in the era from 1935 to 1950.

Within the civil divisions in the sample, respondents were selected on the basis of age, sex and socioeconomic quotas. Otherwise, interviewers were given considerable latitude within the sample areas, being permitted to draw their cases from households and from persons on the street anywhere in the community.

HARRIS SURVEYS

Harris surveys are based on a national sample of the civilian population of the United States. Alaska and Hawaii, however, are not represented in the sample, nor are those in prisons, hospitals, or religious and educational institutions. The sample is based on census information on the population of each State in the country, and on the population living in standard metropolitan areas and in the rest of the country.

These population figures are updated by intercensal estimates produced annually by the Bureau of the Census, and sample locations are selected biennially to reflect changes in the country's demographic profile.

National samples are stratified in two dimensions—geographic region and metropolitan (and non-metropolitan) residence. Stratification insures that the samples will reflect, within 1 percent, the actual proportions of those living in the country in different regions and metropolitan (and non-metropolitan) areas. Within each stratum the selection of the ultimate sampling unit (a cluster of adjacent households) is achieved through a series of steps, a process which is technically called multistage cluster sampling. First States, then counties, and then minor civil divisions (cities, towns, townships) are selected with probability proportional to census estimates of their respective household populations.

Maps of the selected civil divisions are obtained and are partitioned by segments containing approximately the same number of households. This is generally done in the New York office, but for the smaller civil divisions segmenting may be performed in the field. At least one of the segments in each civil division is included in each survey.

The Harris Survey has six of these national samples, and they are used in rotation from study to study. The specific sample locations in one study generally are adjacent to those used in the next study. *For large surveys covering the entire country, more than one national sample may be employed. This avoids having too many respondents in one cluster.*

Interviews are conducted with randomly designated respondents in a minimum of 100 different locations throughout the country. Interviewers contact a designated number, generally 16, of households within each segment. Harris surveys of a *nationwide* sample, therefore, usually include a minimum of 1,600 respondents.

All interviews are conducted in person, in the homes of respondents. At each household the respondent is chosen by means of a random selection pattern, geared to the number of adults of each sex who live in the household. Interviews last approximately one hour in length. When the completed interviews are received in New York, a subsample of the respondents are recontacted to verify that the data have been accurately recorded. Questionnaires are edited and coded in the New York office. The coded questionnaires are keypunched and the data tabulated by standard computer equipment. In essence, the Harris sampling procedure is designed to produce a national cross-section which accurately reflects the actual population of the country

18 years of age and over living in private households. This means that the results of a survey among a national sample can be projected as representative of the country's civilian population 18 years old and above.

Special Surveys

The majority of the tables in this yearbook are based on nationwide surveys of the national adult population. In addition, tables are included that are based on surveys of five special population groups: businessmen, doctors, blacks, undergraduate college students, and youth. The survey of nationwide businessmen is based on interviews with 537 top executives drawn from the Fortune Directory of the largest U.S. corporations. That of nationwide doctors is based on interviews with 489 general practitioners, representing a national cross-section of their profession.

The opinions of nationwide blacks were obtained through interviews with 1,255 black men and women, representing a national cross-section of that minority. Some 820 full-time undergraduate students at 50 different 4-year colleges and universities were interviewed for the survey of nationwide undergraduate college students. And 1,220 interviews were conducted with a national cross-section of young people between the ages of 15 and 21 for the survey of nationwide youth.

The following table shows key dimensions involved in sample stratifications and respondent selection as well as the makeup of a national cross-section:

SELECTED DEMOGRAPHIC CHARACTERISTICS, NATIONWIDE—1970

	TOTAL PERCENT
Region[a]	
East	27
Midwest	28
South	28
West	17
Size of community[b]	
Cities	31
Suburbs	27
Towns	15
Rural	27
Sex	
Men	49
Women	51
Race	
White	89
Black	11

	TOTAL PERCENT
Age	
16 to 20	13
21 to 29	18
30 to 49	34
50 and over	35
Income	
Under $5,000	22
$5,000 to $9,999	38
$10,000 and over	40
Education	
8th (last grade completed: 1 to 8)	29
High school (last grade completed: 9 to 12)	51
College (last grade completed: Freshman-Postgraduate)	20
Religion	
White Protestant	63
White Catholic	23
Jewish	3
Party identification[c]	
Republican	28
Democrat	45
Independent	17

[a] East: Maine, New Hampshire, Vermont, New York, Massachusetts, Rhode Island, Connecticut, Pennsylvania, Maryland, New Jersey, Delaware, West Virginia. Midwest: North Dakota, South Dakota, Nebraska, Kansas, Minnesota, Iowa, Missouri, Wisconsin, Illinois, Michigan, Indiana, Ohio. South: Kentucky, Virginia, Tennessee, North Carolina, South Carolina, Georgia, Alabama, Mississippi, Florida, Louisiana, Arkansas, Oklahoma, Texas. West: Washington, Oregon, California, Idaho, Nevada, Utah, Arizona, Montana, Wyoming, Colorado, New Mexico.
[b] Cities: Central cities with populations of 50,000 or more. Suburbs: Urbanized areas surrounding central cities. Towns: Cities or towns with populations of less than 50,000 but larger than 2,500, that are not in the urbanized area of a central city. Rural: (Areas with populations of less than 2,500).
[c] Party identification: What people consider themselves, regardless of registration.

Sampling Error

Although many people find it hard to believe that a sample of 1,600 can represent the population of the United States, this is nonetheless statistically true. However, in reading the data, it should be kept in mind that the results are subject to sampling error, i.e., the difference between the results obtained from the sample and those which would be obtained by surveying the entire population. The size of a possible sampling error varies to some extent with the size of the sample and with the percentage giving a particular answer. The following table sets forth the range of error in samples of different sizes and at different percentages of response:

RECOMMENDED ALLOWANCE FOR SAMPLING ERROR (PLUS OR MINUS) AT 95 PERCENT CONFIDENCE LEVEL [percent]

RESPONSE	SAMPLE SIZE					
	1,600	1,200	900	500	250	100
10 (90)	2	2	2	3	5	7
20 (80)	2	3	3	4	6	10
30 (70)	3	3	4	5	7	11
40 (60)	3	3	4	5	7	12
50	3	3	4	5	8	12

For example, if the response for a sample size of 1,200 is 30 percent in 95 cases out of 100 the response in the population will be between 27 percent and 33 percent. This error accounts only for sampling error. Survey research is also susceptible to other errors, such as data handling and interviewer recording. However, the procedures followed by the Harris firm keep errors of this kind to a minimum.

Significance of Difference

When is a difference between two results significant? As in the case of sampling error, the answer depends on the size of the samples involved and percentage giving a particular answer. The following table has two charts, one showing the significance of difference between different size samples when the percent giving an answer is near 50 percent and the other showing the significance of difference when the percent giving an answer is near 20 to 80 percent:

RECOMMENDED ALLOWANCE FOR SIGNIFICANCE OF DIFFERENCE BETWEEN 2 PERCENTAGES AT 95 PERCENT CONFIDENCE LEVEL

1ST SAMPLE SIZE/ 2ND SAMPLE SIZE	[PERCENT NEAR 50]					
	1,600	1,200	900	500	250	100
1,600	4	4	5	6	8	12
1,200	—	5	5	6	8	12
900	—	—	6	7	8	12
500	—	—	—	7	9	13
250	—	—	—	—	11	14
100	—	—	—	—	—	17

1ST SAMPLE SIZE/ 2ND SAMPLE SIZE	[PERCENT NEAR 20 OR 80]					
	1,600	1,200	900	500	250	100
1,600	3	4	4	5	6	10
1,200	—	4	4	5	7	10
900	—	—	4	5	7	10
500	—	—	—	6	7	10
250	—	—	—	—	8	11
100	—	—	—	—	—	13

For example, if one group of size 900 had a response of 56 percent "yes" for a question and an independent group of size 250 had a response of 43 percent "yes" for the same question, in 95 cases out of 100, the difference in the "yes" response rate for these two groups would be 13 (56 minus 43), plus or minus 8, or between 5 and 21 percent.

RESOURCE FILE NO. 14

A Short Annotated Bibliography for Social Scientists Who Want to Understand Police. See Chapter 4.

1. Bittner, Egon. *The Functions of the Police in Modern Society.* Washington, D.C.: U.S. Government Printing Office, Public Health Service Publication #2059, 1970.
   One of the classic works on the role of police, this book examines factors such as the cultural background of policing, current practices, and suggestions for future directions. Of special interest is the chapter on "The relations of police work to scientific scholarship."

2. Kirkham, George. *Signal Zero.* Philadelphia: Lippincott, 1976.
   The autobiography of a criminology professor who becomes a police officer. Kirkham details the changes in attitude that come with socialization into the police role. It is particularly useful in demonstrating the slips between the cup of theory and the lip of practice. His work is very popular with police officers; some social scientists, however, point to it as an example of "co-optation:" the loss of "scientific objectivity."

3. Niederhoffer, Arthur. *Behind the Shield.* Garden City, N.Y.: Doubleday, 1967.
   A study of police cynicism and the conditions that encourage it.

4. Niederhoffer, Arthur, and Blumberg, Abraham (eds.). *The Ambivalent Force.* Hinsdale, Ill.: Dryden Press, 1967.
   A collection of articles covering many aspects of policing.

5. Rubinstein, Jonathan. *City Police.* New York: Farrar, Straus & Giroux, 1973.
   A journalist who trained as an officer and spent over a year riding in patrol cars in Philadelphia, Rubinstein gives a vivid account of the tasks police perform and their attitudes toward those tasks. One of the best books available.

6. Skolnick, Jerome H. *Justice Without Trial: Law Enforcement in Democratic Society.* New York: Wiley, 1966.
   Another classic. Skolnick analyzes the roles of police in America.

7. Task Force on the Police, The President's Commission on Law Enforcement and Administration of Justice. *Report: The Police.* Washington, D.C.: U.S. Government Printing Office, 1967.

8. Wambaugh, Joseph. *The Onion Field.* New York: Dell, 1973.
   The true story of an officer who was blamed for his partner's death. A prime example of the results of institutional dehumanization, we feel this is Wambaugh's best book.

9. Wambaugh, Joseph. *The Choirboys.* New York: Dell, 1975.
   A fictional account of the activities of a group of officers by a former lieutenant in the Los Angeles City Police Department. It is somewhat gruesome in spots, but with important insights. The chapters, "Tommy Rivers," and "Sergeant Dominic Scuzzi" are particularly good.

10. Wilson, James Q. *Varieties of Police Behavior: The Management of Law and Order in Eight Communities.* New York: Atheneum, 1971.

Presents a typology of styles of policing: watchman, legalistic, service. Wilson also comments on police discretion and the impact of politics on policing.

11. *The Police Chief.* Official publication of the International Association of Chiefs of Police, Inc.

    This journal presents articles on a variety of topics by officers, social scientists, and others concerned with police topics. An occasional perusal keeps one abreast of current trends and fads in policing.

12. "The Police Tapes."

    A cinema verite videotape, made in New York City's South Bronx in the mid-1970s. It gives a vivid picture of policing in one of the worst ghetto sections of the country. Available from Video-Verite, 927 Madison Avenue, New York, N.Y.

RESOURCE FILE NO. 15

Through Darkest Stacks: A brief guide to finding material in psychological and legal literature.

THE LEGAL CITATION

References to legal cases appear most commonly in the form: *Gideon* v. *Wainwright* [372 U.S. 335 (1963)]. This may be translated as

Plaintiff Versus Defendant Volume Legal text Page # Year of case

Gideon   v.   Wainwright   [372   U.S.   335   (1963)]

Thus a reader looking for specifics of the case that decided a defendant's rights to have an attorney present at all stages of the criminal justice process would go to volume 372, page 335 of the *United States Reports*.

Sometimes a longer form of citation is used: *Gideon* v. *Wainwright* [372 U.S. 335, 83 S. Ct. 792, 9 L. Ed. 2d 799 (1963)]. This means that in addition to the *United States Report*, the Gideon decision also may be found in volume 83, p. 792 of the *Supreme Court Reporter*, or volume 9, p. 799 of the *Lawyer's Edition* (2nd ed.).

THE PSYCHOLOGICAL ABSTRACTS
SOCIOLOGICAL ABSTRACTS, ETC.

Readers searching for material on a specific topic in the psychological or sociological literature are urged to consult the professional analogs to the *Reader's Guide to Periodic Literature*.

Psychological Abstracts is a monthly publication of the American Psychological Association. It is divided into three sections: Author Index, Subject Index, and Abstracts.

Subject Index. Entries in the Subject Index are in the form:
Child abuse

> Therapy for abused children 5214
> Causes and treatment 5216
> Child's role in abuse and development 5003

These numbers are references to entries in the Abstracts section. Turning to the entry numbered 5214, one finds the reference, Marris, A. Therapy for abused children. *Clin. Psych.* 1976, 29 (2), 23–25. This article may be found in volume 29, number 2 of *Clinical Psychologist*. In addition to the reference, there will be a short abstract:

This article reports on a program of treatment for physically abused children who have been taken from their homes and put into group homes. Special problems of runaways, assaultiveness among peers are discussed. Recommendations are made as to children most suitable for this type of placement.

In addition to the monthly issues, *Psychological Abstracts* also publishes a *Semi-Annual Index*, containing the same three sections. In the front of the *Semi-Annual Index* is a listing:

MONTH	ISSUE NUMBER	ABSTRACT NUMBER
Jan.	1	1–1709
Feb.	2	1710–3409
Mar.	3	3410–5859 etc.

Had one looked here first, and found the entry listed above: "therapy for abused children 5214", one would know to look in the March issue for the Abstract entry. (Entry numbers are sequential throughout a volume, which may be annual or semi-annual.)

Still confused? Librarians are marvellously helpful people.

RESOURCE FILE NO. 16

Syllabi from Key U.S. Supreme Court Decisions Involving Social Science Considerations.

These texts summarize the main issues in the following cases:

Brown et al. v. *Board of Education of Topeka et al.*, 349 U.S. 294 (1954): The first decision to involve social science input on the "separate but equal" issue.

Williams v. *Florida*, 399 U.S. 78 (1970): Decision on jury size discussed in Chapter 7.

Apodaca et al. v. *Oregon*, 406 U.S. 404 (1971). Decision approving a less than unanimous verdict (Chapter 7).

Johnson v. *Louisiana*, 406 U.S. 356 (1971): Decision parallel to *Apodaca*.

Colgrove v. *Battin*, 413 U.S. 149 (1973): Jury size decision discussed in Chapter 7.

O'Connor v. *Donaldson*, 422 U.S. 563 (1975): Landmark decision on the right to treatment of mental patients.

Our intention is to provide the instructor and the student with the actual texts of major decisions for concentrated reading by advanced students. The *U.S. Supreme Court Reporter* may be available in a local law or academic library, but these decisions will provide a start.

OCTOBER TERM, 1954.

Syllabus.   349 U.S.

BROWN ET AL. *v.* BOARD OF EDUCATION
OF TOPEKA ET AL.

NO. 1. APPEAL FROM THE UNITED STATES DISTRICT COURT
FOR THE DISTRICT OF KANSAS.*

Reargued on the question of relief April 11–14, 1955.—Opinion and
judgments announced May 31, 1955.

1. Racial discrimination in public education is unconstitutional, 347 U. S.
483, 497, and all provisions of federal, state or local law requiring or
permitting such discrimination must yield to this principle. P. 298.
2. The judgments below (except that in the Delaware case) are reversed
and the cases are remanded to the District Courts to take such proceedings and enter such orders and decrees consistent with this opinion as are
necessary and proper to admit the parties to these cases to public schools
on a racially nondiscriminatory basis with all deliberate speed. P. 301.

(a) School authorities have the primary responsibility for elucidating,
assessing and solving the varied local school problems which may require
solution in fully implementing the governing constitutional principles.
P. 299.

(b) Courts will have to consider whether the action of school authorities constitutes good faith implementation of the governing constitutional
principles. P. 299.

(c) Because of their proximity to local conditions and the possible
need for further hearings, the courts which originally heard these cases
can best perform this judicial appraisal. P. 299.

(d) In fashioning and effectuating the decrees, the courts will be
guided by equitable principles—characterized by a practical flexibility in
shaping remedies and a facility for adjusting and reconciling public and
private needs. P. 300.

* Together with No. 2, *Briggs et al.* v. *Elliott et al.*, on appeal from the United
States District Court for the Eastern District of South Carolina; No. 3, *Davis et al.*
v. *County School Board of Prince Edward County, Virginia, et al.*, on appeal from
the United States District Court for the Eastern District of Virginia; No. 4,
Bolling et al. v. *Sharpe et al.*, on certiorari to the United States Court of Appeals
for the District of Columbia Circuit; and No. 5, *Gebhart et al.* v. *Belton et al.*, on
certiorari to the Supreme Court of Delaware.

BROWN *v.* BOARD OF EDUCATION   295

(e) At stake is the personal interest of the plaintiffs in admission to public schools as soon as practicable on a nondiscriminatory basis. P. 300.

(f) Courts of equity may properly take into account the public interest in the elimination in a systematic and effective manner of a variety of obstacles in making the transition to school systems operated in accordance with the constitutional principles enunciated in 347 U. S. 483, 497; but the vitality of these constitutional principles cannot be allowed to yield simply because of disagreement with them.   P. 300.

(g) While giving weight to these public and private considerations, the courts will require that the defendants make a prompt and reasonable start toward full compliance with the ruling of this Court.   P. 300.

(h) Once such a start has been made, the courts may find that additional time is necessary to carry out the ruling in an effective manner. P. 300.

(i) The burden rests on the defendants to establish that additional time is necessary in the public interest and is consistent with good faith compliance at the earliest practicable date.   P. 300.

(j) The courts may consider problems related to administration, arising from the physical condition of the school plant, the school transportation system, personnel, revision of school districts and attendance areas into compact units to achieve a system of determining admission to the public schools on a nonracial basis, and revision of local laws and regulations which may be necessary in solving the foregoing problems.   Pp. 300–301.

(k) The courts will also consider the adequacy of any plans the defendants may propose to meet these problems and to effectuate a transition to a racially nondiscriminatory school system.   P. 301.

(l) During the period of transition, the courts will retain jurisdiction of these cases.   P. 301.

3. The judgment in the Delaware case, ordering the immediate admission of the plaintiffs to schools previously attended only by white children, is affirmed on the basis of the principles stated by this Court in its opinion, 347 U. S. 483; but the case is remanded to the Supreme Court of Delaware for such further proceedings as that Court may deem necessary in the light of this opinion.   P. 301.

98 F. Supp. 797, 103 F. Supp. 920, 103 F. Supp. 337 and judgment in No. 4, reversed and remanded.

91 A. 2d 137, affirmed and remanded.

78 OCTOBER TERM, 1969

WILLIAMS v. FLORIDA

CERTIORARI TO THE DISTRICT COURT OF APPEAL OF FLORIDA,
THIRD DISTRICT

No. 927. Argued March 4, 1970—Decided June 22, 1970

Florida has a rule of criminal procedure requiring a defendant who intends to rely on an alibi to disclose to the prosecution the names of his alibi witnesses; the prosecution must in turn disclose to the defense the names of witnesses to rebut the alibi. Failure to comply can result in exclusion of alibi evidence at trial (except for the defendant's own testimony) or, in the case of the State, exclusion of the rebuttal evidence. Petitioner, who was charged with robbery, complied with the rule after failing to be relieved of its requirements. His pretrial motion to impanel a 12-man jury, instead of the six-man jury Florida law provides for noncapital cases, was denied. At trial the State used a deposition of petitioner's alibi witness to impeach the witness. Petitioner was convicted and the appellate court affirmed. Petitioner claims that his Fifth Amendment rights were violated, on the ground that the notice-of-alibi rule required him to furnish the State with information useful in convicting him, and that his Sixth Amendment right was violated on the ground that the six-man jury deprived him of the right to "trial by jury" under the Sixth Amendment. *Held:*

1. Florida's notice-of-alibi rule does not violate the Fifth Amendment as made applicable to the States by the Fourteenth Amendment. Pp. 80–86.

(a) This discovery rule is designed to enhance the search for truth in criminal trials by giving both the accused and the State opportunity to investigate certain facts crucial to the issue of guilt or innocence and comports with requirements for due process and a fair trial. Pp. 81–82.

(b) The rule at most accelerated the timing of petitioner's disclosure of an alibi defense and thus did not violate the privilege against compelled self-incrimination. Pp. 82–86.

2. The constitutional guarantee of a trial by jury does not require that jury membership be fixed at 12, a historically accidental figure. Although accepted at common law, the Framers did not explicitly intend to forever codify as a constitutional requirement a feature not essential to the Sixth

Amendment's purpose of interposing between the defendant and the prosecution the commonsense judgment of his peers. Pp. 86–103.

224 So. 2d 406, affirmed.

Richard Kanner argued the cause and filed briefs for petitioner.

Jesse J. McCrary, Jr., Assistant Attorney General of Florida, argued the cause for respondent. With him on the brief were *Earl Faircloth,* Attorney General, and *Ronald W. Sabo,* Assistant Attorney General.

Jack Greenberg and *Michael Meltsner* filed a brief for Virgil Jenkins as *amicus curiae* urging reversal.

Mr. Justice White delivered the opinion of the Court.

JOHNSON *v.* LOUISIANA

APPEAL FROM THE SUPREME COURT OF LOUISIANA

No. 69–5035. Argued March 1, 1971—Reargued January 10, 1972— Decided May 22, 1972

A warrantless arrest for robbery was made of appellant at his home on the basis of identification from photographs, and he was committed by a magistrate. Thereafter he appeared in a lineup, at which he was represented by counsel, and was identified by the victim of another robbery. He was tried for the latter offense before a 12-man jury and convicted by a nine-to-three verdict, as authorized by Louisiana law in cases where the crime is necessarily punishable at hard labor. Other state law provisions require unanimity for five-man jury trials of offenses in which the punishment may be at hard labor and for 12-man jury trials of capital cases. The Louisiana Supreme Court affirmed the conviction, rejecting appellant's challenge to the jury-trial provisions as violative of due process and equal protection and his claim that the lineup identification was a forbidden fruit of an invasion of appellant's Fourth Amendment rights. Appellant conceded that under *Duncan* v. *Louisiana,* 391 U. S. 145, which was decided after his trial began and which has no retroactive effect, the Sixth Amendment does not apply to his case. *Held:*

   1. The provisions of Louisiana law requiring less-than-unanimous jury verdicts in criminal cases do not violate the Due Process Clause for failure to satisfy the reasonable-doubt standard. Pp. 359–363.

(a) The mere fact that three jurors vote to acquit does not mean that the nine who vote to convict have ignored their instructions concerning proof beyond a reasonable doubt or that they do not honestly believe that guilt has been thus proved. Pp. 360–362.

(b) Want of jury unanimity does not alone establish reasonable doubt. Pp. 362–363.

2. The Louisiana legal scheme providing for unanimous verdicts in capital and five-man jury cases but for less-than-unanimous verdicts otherwise, and which varies the difficulty of proving guilt with the gravity of the offense, was designed to serve the rational purposes of "facilitat[ing], expedit[ing], and reduc[ing] expense in the administration of justice," and does not constitute an invidious classification violative of equal protection. Pp. 363–365.

JOHNSON *v.* LOUISIANA   357

356   *Opinion of the Court*

3. Since no evidence constituting the fruit of an illegal arrest was used at appellant's trial, the validity of his arrest is not at issue and the lineup was conducted, not by the "exploitation" of the arrest, but under the authority of appellant's commitment by the magistrate, which purged the lineup procedure of any "primary taint." P. 365.

255 La. 314, 230 So. 2d 825, affirmed.

WHITE, J., delivered the opinion of the Court, in which BURGER, C. J., and BLACKMUN, POWELL, and REHNQUIST, JJ., joined. BLACKMUN, J., *post,* p. 365, and POWELL, J., *post,* p. 366, filed concurring opinions. DOUGLAS, J., filed a dissenting opinion, in which BRENNAN and MARSHALL, JJ., joined, *post,* p. 380. BRENNAN, J., filed a dissenting opinion, in which MARSHALL, J., joined, *post,* p. 395. STEWART, J., filed a dissenting opinion, in which BRENNAN and MARSHALL, JJ., joined, *post,* p. 397. MARSHALL, J., filed a dissenting opinion, in which BRENNAN, J., joined, *post,* p. 399.

Richard A. Buckley reargued the cause and filed a brief for appellant.

Louise Korns reargued the cause for appellee. With her on the brief were *Jack P. F. Gremillion,* Attorney General of Louisiana, and *Jim Garrison.*

MR. JUSTICE WHITE delivered the opinion of the Court.

Under both the Louisiana Constitution and Code of Criminal Procedure, criminal cases in which the punishment is necessarily at hard labor are tried to a jury of 12, and the vote of nine jurors is sufficient to return either a guilty or not guilty verdict.[1] The principal question

---

[1] La Const., Art. VII, § 41, provides:

"Section 41. The Legislature shall provide for the election and drawing of competent and intelligent jurors for the trial of civil and criminal cases; provided,

358   OCTOBER TERM, 1971

                        Opinion of the Court   406 U.S.

In this case is whether these provisions allowing less-than-unanimous verdicts in certain cases are valid under the Due Process and Equal Protection Clauses of the Fourteenth Amendment.

404   OCTOBER TERM, 1971

                              Syllabus   406 U.S.

APODACA ET AL. v. OREGON

CERTIORARI TO THE COURT OF APPEALS OF OREGON

No. 69–5046. Argued March 1, 1971—Reargued January 10, 1972—
Decided May 22, 1972

Petitioners, who were found guilty of committing felonies, by less-than-unanimous jury verdicts, which are permitted under Oregon law in non-capital cases, claim that their convictions, upheld on appeal, contravene their right to trial by jury under the Sixth and Fourteenth Amendments. *Held:* The judgment is affirmed. Pp. 410–414, 369–380.

---

however, that no woman shall be drawn for jury service unless she shall have previously filed with the clerk of the District Court a written declaration of her desire to be subject to such service. All cases in which the punishment may not be at hard labor shall, until otherwise provided by law, be tried by the judge without a jury. Cases, in which the punishment may be at hard labor, shall be tried by a jury of five, all of whom must concur to render a verdict; cases, in which the punishment is necessarily at hard labor, by a jury of twelve, nine of whom must concur to render a verdict; cases in which the punishment may be capital, by a jury of twelve, all of whom must concur to render a verdict."

La Code Crim. Proc., Art. 782, provides:

"Cases in which the punishment may be capital shall be tried by a jury of twelve jurors, all of whom must concur to render a verdict. Cases in which the punishment is necessarily at hard labor shall be tried by a jury composed of twelve jurors, nine of whom must concur to render a verdict. Cases in which the punishment may be imprisoned at hard labor, shall be tried by a jury composed of five jurors, all of whom must concur to render a verdict. Except as provided in Article 780, trial by jury may not be waived."

1 Ore. App. 483, 462 P. 2d 691, affirmed.

MR. JUSTICE WHITE, joined by THE CHIEF JUSTICE, MR. JUSTICE BLACKMUN, and MR. JUSTICE REHNQUIST, concluded that:

1. The Sixth Amendment guarantee of a jury trial, made applicable to the States by the Fourteenth (*Duncan* v. *Louisiana,* 391 U. S. 145), does not require that the jury's vote be unanimous. Pp. 410–412.

(a) The Amendment's essential purpose of "interpos[ing] between the accused and his accuser . . . the commonsense judgment of a group of laymen" representative of a cross section of the community, *Williams* v. *Florida,* 399 U. S. 78, 100, is served despite the absence of a unanimity requirement. Pp. 410–411.

(b) Petitioners' argument that the Sixth Amendment requires jury unanimity in order to effectuate the reasonable-doubt standard otherwise mandated by due process requirements is without merit since that Amendment does not require proof beyond a reasonable doubt at all. Pp. 411–412.

2. Jury unanimity is not mandated by the Fourteenth Amendment requirements that racial minorities not be systematically excluded from the jury-selection process; even when racial minority members are on the jury, it does not follow that their views will not be just as rationally considered by the other jury members as would be the case under a unanimity rule. Pp. 412–414.

MR. JUSTICE POWELL concluded that:

1. Although on the basis of history and precedent the Sixth Amendment mandates unanimity in a *federal* jury trial, the Due Process Clause of the Fourteenth Amendment, while requiring States to provide jury trials for

APODACA *v.* OREGON   405

404   Opinion of WHITE, J.

serious crimes, does not incorporate all the elements of a jury trial within the meaning of the Sixth Amendment and does not require jury unanimity. Oregon's "ten of twelve" rule is not violative of due process. Pp. 369–377.

2. Nor is the Oregon provision inconsistent with the due process requirement that a jury be drawn from a representative cross section of the community as the jury majority remains under the duty to consider the minority viewpoint in the course of deliberation, and the usual safeguards exist to minimize the possibility of jury irresponsibility. Pp. 378–380.

WHITE, J., announced the Court's judgment and delivered an opinion, in which BURGER, C. J., and BLACKMUN and REHNQUIST, JJ., joined. BLACKMUN, J., filed a concurring opinion, *ante,* p. 365. POWELL, J., filed an opinion concurring in the judgment, *ante,* p. 366. DOUGLAS, J., filed a dissenting

392 LAW AND SOCIAL SCIENCES RESOURCE FILE

opinion, in which BRENNAN and MARSHALL, JJ., joined, *ante*, p. 380.
BRENNAN, J., filed a dissenting opinion, in which MARSHALL, J., joined, *ante*,
p. 395. STEWART, J., filed a dissenting opinion, in which BRENNAN and
MARSHALL, JJ., joined, *post*, p. 414. MARSHALL, J., filed a dissenting opinion,
in which BRENNAN, J., joined *ante*, p. 399.

   Richard B. Sobol reargued the cause and filed briefs for petitioners.

   Jacob B. Tanzer, Solicitor General of Oregon, reargued the cause
for respondent. With him on the brief were *Lee Johnson*, Attorney
General, and *Thomas H. Denney*, Assistant Attorney General.

   Briefs of *amici curiae* urging reversal were filed by *James J. Doherty*
and *Marshall J. Hartman* for the National Legal Aid and Defender
Association, and by *Norman Dorsen, Melvin L. Wulf*, and *Paul R.
Meyer* for the American Civil Liberties Union.

   MR. JUSTICE WHITE announced the judgment of the Court and an
opinion in which THE CHIEF JUSTICE, MR. JUSTICE BLACKMUN, and MR.
JUSTICE REHNQUIST joined.

   Robert Apodaca, Henry Morgan Cooper, Jr., and James Arnold
Madden were convicted respectively of assault with a deadly weapon,
burglary in a dwelling, and grand larceny before separate Oregon

406   OCTOBER TERM, 1971

Opinion of WHITE, J.   406 U.S.

juries, all of which returned less-than-unanimous verdicts. The vote in
the cases of Apodaca and Madden was 11–1, while the vote in the
case of Cooper was 10–2, the minimum requisite vote under Oregon
law for sustaining a conviction.[1] After their convictions had been
affirmed by the Oregon Court of Appeals, 1 Ore. App. 483, 462 P. 2d
691 (1969), and review had been denied by the Supreme Court of
Oregon, all three sought review in this Court upon a claim that conviction of crime by a less-than-unanimous jury violates the right to trial
by jury in criminal cases specified by the Sixth Amendment and made
applicable to the States by the Fourteenth. See *Duncan* v. *Louisiana*,
391 U. S. 145 (1968). We granted certiorari to consider this claim,
400 U. S. 901 (1970), which we now find to be without merit.

   In *Williams* v. *Florida*, 399 U. S. 78 (1970), we had occasion to
consider a related issue: whether the Sixth Amendment's right to trial
by jury requires that all juries consist of 12 men. After considering the
history of the 12-man requirement and the functions it performs in

contemporary society, we concluded that it was not of constitutional stature. We reach the same conclusion today with regard to the requirement of unanimity.

COLGROVE *v.* BATTIN   149

Opinion of the Court

COLGROVE *v.* BATTIN, U. S. DISTRICT JUDGE

CERTIORARI TO THE UNITED STATES COURT OF APPEALS FOR
THE NINTH CIRCUIT

No. 71–1442.   Argued January 17, 1973—Decided June 21, 1973

Local federal court rule providing that a jury for the trial of civil cases shall consist of six persons comports with the Seventh Amendment requirement and the coextensive statutory requirement of 28 U. S. C. §2072 that the right of trial by jury be preserved in suits at common law, and is not inconsistent with Fed. Rule Civ. Proc. 48 that deals only with parties' stipulations regarding jury size.   Pp. 151–164.

456 F. 2d 1379, affirmed.

BRENNAN, J., delivered the opinion of the Court, in which BURGER, C. J., and WHITE, BLACKMUN, and REHNQUIST, JJ., joined. DOUGLAS, J., filed a dissenting opinion, in which POWELL, J., joined, *post*, p. 165. MARSHALL, J., filed a dissenting opinion, in which STEWART, J., joined, *post*, p. 166. POWELL, J., filed a dissenting opinion, *post*, p. 188.

Lloyd J. Skedd argued the cause and filed a brief for petitioner.

Cale Crowley argued the cause and filed a brief for respondent*

MR. JUSTICE BRENNAN delivered the opinion of the Court.

Local Rule 13(d)(1) of the Revised Rules of Procedure of the United States District Court for the District of Montana provides that

---

[1] Ore. Const., Art. I, § 11, reads in relevant part:

"In all criminal prosecutions, the accused shall have the right to public trial by an impartial jury in the county in which the offense shall have been committed; . . . provided, however, that any accused person, in other than capital cases, and with the consent of the trial judge, may elect to waive trial by jury and consent to be tried by the judge of the court alone, such election to be in writing; provided, however, that in the circuit court ten members of the jury may render a verdict of guilty or not guilty, save and except a verdict of guilty of first degree murder, which shall be found only by a unanimous verdict, and not otherwise. . . ."

* Briefs of *amici curiae* were filed by *William A. Wick, Alston Jennings,* and *John C. Elam* for the International Association of Insurance Counsel; by *Joseph W.*

a jury for the trial of civil cases shall consist of six persons.[1] When respondent District Court Judge set this diversity case for trial before a jury of six in compliance with the Rule, petitioner sought mandamus from the Court of Appeals for the Ninth Circuit to direct respondent to impanel a 12-member jury. Petitioner contended that the local Rule (1) violated the Seventh Amendment;[2] (2) violated the statutory provision, 28 U. S. C. § 2072, that rules "shall preserve the right of trial by jury as at common law and as declared by the Seventh Amendment . . .";[3] and (3) was rendered invalid by Fed. Rule Civ. Proc. 83

Cotchett, David Daar, Leonard Sacks, Siegfried Hesse, Edward I. Pollock, Theodore A. Horn, and *Marvin E. Lewis* for the California Trial Lawyers Assn.; by *Leonard Boudin* and *Alan Scheflin* for the National Emergency Civil Liberties Committee; and by the Nooter Corp.

[1] Rule 13(d)(1) provides:

"A jury for the trial of civil cases shall consist of six persons plus such alternate jurors as may be impaneled."

Similar local rules have been adopted by 54 other federal district courts, at least as to some civil cases. See the appendix to Fisher, The Seventh Amendment and the Common Law: No Magic in Numbers, 56 F. R. D. 507, 535–542 (1973) (the District Court of Delaware has since adopted a rule effective January 1, 1973). In addition, two bills were introduced in the 92d Congress to reduce to six the number of jurors in all federal civil cases. H. R. 7800, 92d Cong., 1st Sess. (1971); H. R. 13496, 92d Cong., 2d Sess. (1972). H. R. 7800, insofar as it related to civil juries, has received the approval of the Committee on the Operation of the Jury System of the Judicial Conference of the United States. 1971 Annual Report of the Director of the Administrative Office of the United States Courts 41. That Conference itself at its March 1971 meeting endorsed "in principle" a reduction in the size of civil juries. *Ibid.*

[2] The Seventh Amendment provides:

"In Suits at common law, where the value in controversy shall exceed twenty dollars, the right of trial by jury shall be preserved, and no fact tried by a jury, shall be otherwise reexamined in any Court of the United States, than according to the rules of the common law."

State court decisions have usually turned on the interpretation of state constitutional provisions. See Ann., 47 A. L. R. 3d 895 (1973).

[3] Title 28 U. S. C. § 2072 provides:

"The Supreme Court shall have the power to prescribe by general rules, the forms of process, writs, pleadings, and motions, and the practice and procedure of the district courts and courts of appeals of the United States in civil actions. . . .

"Such rules shall not abridge, enlarge or modify any substantive right and shall preserve the right of trial by jury as at common law and as declared by the Seventh Amendment to the Constitution."

COLGROVE *v.* BATTIN   151

149   Opinion of the Court

because "inconsistent with" Fed. Rule Civ. Proc. 48 that provides for juries of less than 12 when stipulated by the parties.[4] The Court of Appeals found no merit in these contentions, sustained the validity of local Rule 13(d)(1), and denied the writ, 456 F. 2d 1379 (1972). We granted certiorari, 409 U. S. 841 (1972). We affirm.

O'CONNOR *v.* DONALDSON   563

Syllabus

O'CONNOR *v.* DONALDSON

CERTIORARI TO THE UNITED STATES COURT OF APPEALS FOR
THE FIFTH CIRCUIT

No. 74–8.   Argued January 15, 1975—Decided June 26, 1975

Respondent, who was confined almost 15 years "for care, maintenance, and treatment" as a mental patient in a Florida state hospital, brought this action for damages under 42 U. S. C. § 1983 against petitioner, the hospital's superintendent, and other staff members, alleging that they had intentionally and maliciously deprived him of his constitutional right to liberty. The evidence showed that respondent, whose frequent requests for release had been rejected by petitioner notwithstanding undertakings by responsible persons to care for him if necessary, was dangerous neither to himself nor others, and, if mentally ill, had not received treatment. Petitioner's principal defense was that he had acted in good faith, since state law, which he believed valid, had authorized indefinite custodial confinement of the "sick," even if they were not treated and their release would not be harmful, and that petitioner was therefore immune from any liability for monetary damages. The jury found for respondent and awarded compensatory and punitive damages against petitioner and a codefendant. The Court of Appeals, on broad Fourteenth Amendment grounds, affirmed the District Court's ensuing judgment entered on the verdict. *Held:*

[4] Fed. Rule Civ. Proc. 48 provides:
"The parties may stipulate that the jury shall consist of any number less than twelve or that a verdict or a finding of a stated majority of the jurors shall be taken as the verdict or finding of the jury."
Fed. Rule Civ. Proc. 83 provides:
"Each district court by action of a majority of the judges thereof may from time

1. A State cannot constitutionally confine, without more, a non-dangerous individual who is capable of surviving safely in freedom by himself or with the help of willing and responsible family members or friends, and since the jury found, upon ample evidence, that petitioner did so confine respondent, it properly concluded that petitioner had violated respondent's right to liberty. Pp. 573–576.

2. Since the Court of Appeals did not consider whether the trial judge erred in refusing to give an instruction requested by petitioner concerning his claimed reliance on state law as authorization for respondent's continued confinement, and since neither court below had the benefit of this Court's decision in *Wood* v. *Strickland*, 420 U. S. 308, on the scope of a state official's qualified immunity under 42 U. S. C. § 1983, the case is

564   OCTOBER TERM, 1975

                    Opinion of the Court   422 U.S.

vacated and remanded for consideration of petitioner's liability *vel non* for monetary damages for violating respondent's constitutional right. Pp. 576–577.

493 F. 2d 507, vacated and remanded.

STEWART, J., delivered the opinion for a unanimous Court. BURGER, C. J., filed a concurring opinion, *post*, p. 578.

Raymond W. Gearey, Assistant Attorney General of Florida, argued the cause for petitioner *pro hac vice*. With him on the briefs were *Robert L. Shevin*, Attorney General, and *Daniel S. Dearing*, Special Assistant Attorney General.

Bruce J. Ennis, Jr., argued the cause for respondent. With him on the brief was *Morton Birnbaum.**

---

to time make and amend rules governing its practice not inconsistent with these rules. . . . In all cases not provided for by rule, the district courts may regulate their practice in any manner not inconsistent with these rules."

* *William F. Hyland*, Attorney General, *Stephen Skillman*, Assistant Attorney General, and *Joseph T. Maloney*, Deputy Attorney General, filed a brief for the State of New Jersey as *amicus curiae* urging reversal.

Briefs of *Amici curiae* urging affirmance were filed by *E. Barrett Prettyman, Jr.*, for the American Psychiatric Assn.; by *Francis M. Shea, Ralph J. Moore, Jr., John Townsend Rich, James F. Fitzpatrick, Kurt W. Melchior, Harry J. Rubin, Sheridan L. Neimark*, and *A. L. Zwerdling* for the American Association on Mental Deficiency; and by *June Resnick German* and *Alfred Berman* for the Committee on Mental Hygiene of the New York State Bar Assn.

William J. Brown, Attorney General, and *Andrew J. Ruzicho* and *Barbara J. Rouse*, Assistant Attorneys General, filed a brief for the State of Ohio as *amicus curiae.*

MR. JUSTICE STEWART delivered the opinion of the Court.

The respondent, Kenneth Donaldson, was civilly committed to confinement as a mental patient in the Florida State Hospital at Chattahoochee in January 1957. He was kept in custody there against his will for nearly 15 years. The petitioner, Dr. J. B. O'Connor, was the hospital's superintendent during most of this period. Throughout

O'CONNOR *v.* DONALDSON   565

563   Opinion of the Court

his confinement Donaldson repeatedly, but unsuccessfully, demanded his release, claiming that he was dangerous to no one, that he was not mentally ill, and that, at any rate, the hospital was not providing treatment for his supposed illness. Finally, in February 1971, Donaldson brought this lawsuit under 42 U. S. C. § 1983, in the United States District Court for the Northern District of Florida, alleging that O'Connor, and other members of the hospital staff named as defendants, had intentionally and maliciously deprived him of his constitutional right to liberty.[1] After a four-day trial, the jury returned a verdict assessing both compensatory and punitive damages against O'Connor and a codefendant. The Court of Appeals for the Fifth Circuit affirmed the judgment, 493 F. 2d 507. We granted O'Connor's petition for certiorari, 419 U. S. 894, because of the important constitutional questions seemingly presented.

---

[1] Donaldson's original complaint was filed as a class action on behalf of himself and all of his fellow patients in an entire department of the Florida State Hospital at Chattahoochee. In addition to a damages claim, Donaldson's complaint also asked for habeas corpus relief ordering his release, as well as the release of all members of the class. Donaldson further sought declaratory and injunctive relief requiring the hospital to provide adequate psychiatric treatment.

After Donaldson's release and after the District Court dismissed the action as a class suit, Donaldson filed an amended complaint, repeating his claim for compensatory and punitive damages. Although the amended complaint retained the prayer for declaratory and injunctive relief, that request was eliminated from the case prior to trial. See 493 F. 2d 507, 512–513.

BIBLIOGRAPHY

Aaronson, D. E., Kittrie, N. N., Saari, D. J., & Cooper, C. S. *Alternatives to Conventional Criminal Adjudication: Guidebook for Planners and Practitioners.* Washington, D.C.: National Institute of Law Enforcement and Criminal Justice, LEAA, 1977.

Abrahamson, D. A. *The Psychology of Crime.* New York: Columbia University Press, 1960.

Adler, F. Socioeconomic factors influencing jury verdicts, *New York University Review of Law and Social Change,* Winter 1973, *3*, 1.

Adorno, T. W., Frenkel-Brunswik, E., Levinson, D. J., & Sanford, R. N. *The Authoritarian Personality.* New York: Harper & Row, 1950.

Alker, H. R., & Barnard, J. J. Procedural and social biases in the jury selection process. *The Justice System Journal,* 1978, *3* (3), 220–241.

Alker, H. R., Hosticka, C., & Mitchell, M. Jury selection as a biased process, *Law and Society Review,* 1976, *11* (1), 9–41.

Allport, G. W., & Postman, L. The basic psychology of rumor. *Transcriptions of the New York Academy of Sciences,* Series 11, 1945, *8,* 61–81.

Alper, A., Buckhout, R., Chern, S., Harwood, R., & Slomovits, M. Eyewitness identification: Accuracy of individuals vs. composite recollection of a crime. *Bulletin of the Psychonomic Society,* 1976, *8,* 147–149.

Amir, M. *Patterns in Forcible Rape.* Chicago: University of Chicago Press, 1971.

Anastasi, Ann. *Psychological Testing* (2nd ed.). New York: Macmillan, 1961.

Arieti, S. *Interpretation of Schizophrenia.* New York: Robert Brunner, 1955.

Asch, S. E., Opinions and social pressure. *Scientific American,* 1955, *193,* (5).

Ash, M. On witnesses: A radical critique of criminal court procedures. *Notre Dame Law Review,* December 1974, *48,* 386–425.

Bailey, W. C. An evaluation of one hundred reports. In L. Radzinowicz and M. E. Wolfgang (Eds.), *The Criminal in Confinement* (Vol. III). New York: Basic Books, 1971.

Baker, L. Concern over I.Q. testing. *San Francisco Chronicle,* March 5, 1970.

Balch, R. W., Griffiths, C. T., Hall, E. L., & Winfree, L. T. The socialization of jurors: The voir dire as a rite of passage. *Journal of Criminal Justice,* 1967, *4,* 271–283.

Bane, M. J., & Jencks, C. Five myths about your IQ. *Harpers,* February 1973, 28–40.

Banuazizi, A., & Movahedi, S. Interpersonal dynamics in a simulated prison: A methodological analysis. *American Psychologist,* 1975, *30,* (2), 152–160.

Bard, M. Extending psychology's impact through existing community institutions. *American Psychologist,* 1969, *24,* 610–612.

Bard, M. *Training Police as Specialists in Family Crisis Intervention.* Washington, D.C.: U.S. Government Printing Office, 1970.

Bard, M. Immediacy and authority in crisis management. Paper presented at NIMH Crisis Intervention Seminar, Washington, D.C., June 22–24, 1973.

Bard, M. Implications of collaboration between law enforcement and the social sciences. Paper presented at a symposium on Law Enforcement in a Changing Society, Palo Alto, Calif. February 20, 1974.

Bard, M., & Ellison, K. Crisis intervention & investigation of forcible rape. *The Police Chief,* May 1974.

Bard, M., & Zacker, J. Assaultiveness and alcohol use in family disputes: Police perceptions. *Criminology,* November 1974, *13* (3), 281–292.

Bard, M., Zacker, J., & Rutter, E. Police family crisis intervention and conflict management: An action research analysis. Monograph prepared for the U.S. Department of Justice, Law Enforcement Assistance Administration, April 1972.

Bartholomew, A. A., Badger, P., & Milte, K. L. The psychologist as expert witness in the criminal courts. *Australian Psychologist,* 1977, *12* (2), 133–150.

Bartlett, F. C. *Remembering.* Cambridge, Eng.: Cambridge University Press, 1932.

Bassili, J. Facial motion in the perception of faces and of emotional expression. *Journal of Experimental Psychology: Human Perception and Performance.* 1978, *4* (3), 373–379.

Bazelon, D. L. Psychiatrists and the adversary process. *Scientific American,* 1974, *230* (6), 18–23.

Beattie, R. H. Criminal statistics in the U.S., 1960. *Journal of Criminal Law, Criminology, and Police Science*, 1960, *51*, 49–65.

Bedau, H. A. *The Courts, the Constitution, and Capital Punishment.* Lexington, Mass.: Heath, 1977.

Bedau, H. A., & Pierce, C. M. (Eds.). *Capital Punishment in the United States.* New York: AMS Press, 1976.

Beeghey, L., & Butler, E. W. The consequences of intelligence testing in the public schools before and after segregation. *Social Problems*, 1974, *21*, (5), 740–754.

Bem, D. J. *Beliefs, Attitudes and Human Affairs.* Belmont, Calif.: Brooks/Cole, 1970.

Bennett-Sandler, G., & Ubell, E. Time bombs in blue. *New York Magazine*, March 21, 1977, 47–51.

Benson, H. *The Relaxation Response.* New York: Morrow, 1975.

Berg, K., & Vidmar, N. Authoritarianism and recall of evidence about criminal behavior. *Journal of Research in Personality*, 1975, 9, 147–157.

Berk, R. A. Social science and jury selection: A case study of a civil suit. In G. Bermant, C. Nemeth, and N. Vidmar (Eds.), *Psychology and the Law.* Lexington, Mass.: Heath, 1976.

Berk, R. A., Hennessy, M., & Swan, J. The vagaries and vulgarities of "scientific" jury selection: A methodological evaluation. *Evaluation Quarterly*, 1977, *1* (1), 143–158.

Berman, G., & Coppock, R. Outcomes of six and twelve member jury trials: An analysis of 128 civil cases in the State of Washington. *Washington Law Review*, 1973, *48*, 593–596.

Berman, J., & Sales, B. D. A critical evaluation of the systematic approach to jury selection. Paper presented to the American Psychological Association, Washington, D.C., 1976.

Berscheid, E., & Walster, E. Physical attractiveness. In L. Berkowitz (Ed.), *Advances in Experimental Social Psychology* (Vol. 7). New York: Academic Press, 1974.

Bittner, E. The Functions of the Police in Modern Society. Washington, D.C.: U.S. Government Printing Office: Public Health Service Publication # 2059, 1970.

Block, R. A. Remembered duration: Effects of event and sequence complexity. *Memory and Cognition*, 1978, *6* (3), 320–326.

Bloom, M. L. The witness: Forgotten man. *National Civic Review*, October 1974.

Boland, B., & Wilson, J. Q. Age, crime and punishment. *The Public Interest*, 1978, *51*, 22–34.

Bolz, F. Hostage taking. Paper presented at the annual meeting of the International Association of Women Police, Minneapolis, Minn., November 1975.

Boros, D. C. (Ed.). The Seventh Mental Measurements Yearbook, Vols. I and II. Princeton, New Jersey: Gryphon Press, 1972.

Bouza, A. V. Deterrence-rehabilitation-punishment: Do they work? *The Police Chief*, July 1976, 70–73.

Bower, G. H., & Karlin, M. B. Depth of processing pictures of faces and recognition memory. *Journal of Experimental Psychology*, 1974, *103*, 751–757.

Brams, S. J., & Davis, M. D. A game-theory approach to jury selection. *Trial*, December 1976, 47–49.

Brodsky, S. L. *Psychologists in the Criminal Justice System*, Urbana: University of Illinois Press, 1973.

Brodsky, S. L. Prison notes. *APA Monitor*, September/October 1976, 24.

Brodsky, S. L. Psychology at the interface of law and corrections. *Law and Psychology Review*, 1977, *3*, 1–14.

Brodsky, S. L. The mental health professional on the witness stand: A survival guide. In B. D. Sales (Ed.), *Psychology in the legal process*. New York: Spectrum, 1977.

Brodyaga, L., Gates, M., Singer, S., Tucker, M., & White, R. *Rape & its victims: A report for citizens, health facilities, and criminal justice agencies*. Washington, D.C.: U.S. Government Printing Office, 1975.

Brooks, W. N., & Doob, A. N. Justice and the jury. *Journal of Applied Social Psychology*, 1975, *31* (3), 171–182.

Brown, E., Deffenbacher, K., & Sturgill, W. Memory for faces and the circumstances of encounter. *Journal of Applied Psychology*, 1977, *62*, 311–318.

Brown, Lee P., & Martin, E. E. Neighborhood team policing: A viable concept in Multnomah County. *The Police Chief*, May 1976.

Brown, R., & Kulik, J. Flashbulb memories. *Cognition*, 1977, *5*, 73.

Brownmiller, S. *Against Our Wills: Men, Women, & Rape*. New York: Simon & Schuster, 1975.

Bruner, J., & Postman, L. On the perception of incongruity: A paradigm. *Journal of Personality*, 1949, *18*, 206–223.

Buckhout, R. Eyewitness testimony. *Scientific American*, 1974, *231* (6), 23–31. See also *Jurimetrics*, 1975, *15*, 171.

Buckhout, R. Nearly 2000 witnesses can be wrong. *Bulletin of the Psychonomic Society*, 1980, *16*, (4), 307–310.

Buckhout, R. Nobody likes a smartass. *Social Action and the Law*, 1976, *3* (4), 41–53.

Buckhout, R. Psychology and eyewitness identification. *Psychology and Law Review*, 1976, *2*, 75–93.

Buckhout, R. Jury without peers. *Center Monograph No. CR-2*, 1973, Center for Responsive Psychology, Brooklyn, N.Y. An expanded version of paper published in M. Reidel and P. Vales (Eds.), *Treating the Offender: Problems and Issues*. New York: Praeger, 1977.

Buckhout, R. *U.S. v. Swinton:* A case history of jury selection, *Social Action and the Law*, 1978, *4* (4) 27–29.

Buckhout, R. Unpublished Study, 1978.

Buckhout, R. et al. A jury without peers. In M. Reidel and P. Vales (Eds.), *Treating the Offender: Problems and Issues*. New York: Praeger, 1977.

Buckhout, R. et al. Jury attitudes and the death penalty. *Social Action and the Law*, 1977, *3* (6), 80–81.

Buckhout, R., Alper, A., Chern, S., Silverberg, G., & Slomovitz, M. Determinants of eyewitness performance on a lineup. *Bulletin of Psychonomic Society*, 1974, *4*, 191–192.

Buckhout, R., & Baker, E. Surveying the attitudes of seated jurors. *Social Action and the Law*, 1977, *4*, (6), 98–101.

Buckhout, R., & Friere, V. Suggestivity in lineups and photospreads, *Center for Responsive Psychology Monograph No. CR-5*, 1975. New York: Brooklyn College C.U.N.Y.

Buckhout, R., Weg, S., & Cohen, R. Case study of the presumption of guilt in jurors. *Center Monograph No. CR-8*, Center for Responsive Psychology, 1975. New York: Brooklyn College, C.U.N.Y.

Buckhout, R., Weg, S., Reilly, V., & Frohboese, R. Jury verdicts: Comparison of six vs. twelve person juries, unanimous vs. majority decision in a murder trial. *Center for Responsive Psychology Report No. CR-12*, 1976. *Bulletin of the Psychonomic Society*, 1977, *10* (3), 175–178.

Burger, W. Psychiatrists, lawyers and the courts. *Federal Probation*, 1967, *28* (3), 7.

Burgess, A., & Holstrom, L. Rape: *Victims of Crisis*. Bowie, Md.: Robert J. Brady, 1974.

Burns, W. C. Personnel testing and the courts. Presentation to the American Psychology-Law Society, San Francisco, Calif., June 1974.

Cady, H. M. On the psychology of testimony. *American Journal of Psychology*, 1924, *35*, 110–112.

California State Assembly, Problems of the Death Penalty and Its Administration, 1967.

Campbell, D. T. Legal reforms as experiments. *Journal of Legal Education*, 1971, *23*, 217–239.

Cannavale, F. J., & Falcon, W. D. (Eds.). *Witness Cooperation*. Lexington, Mass.: Lexington Books, 1976.

Cannavale, F. J., & Falcon, W. D. (Eds.). Improving witness cooperation: Summary report of the District of Columbia witness survey and a handbook for witness management. Washington, D.C.: U.S. Government Printing Office (NILE/CJ), August 1976.

Capital Punishment 1976, National Prisoner Statistics Bulletin SD-NPS-CP-5, November 1977, Law Enforcement Assistance Administration, National Criminal Justice Information and Statistics Service.

Caplan, G. *Principles of Preventive Psychiatry*. New York: Basic Books, 1964.

Carrol, J. S., & Payne, J. W. Judgments about crime and the criminal: A model and method for investigating parole decisions. In B. D. Sales (Ed.), *Perspectives in Law and Psychology, Vol. I: The Criminal Justice System*. New York: Plenum Press, 1977, pp. 191–239.

Cawley, Donald F. Anatomy of a siege. *The Police Chief*, January 1974, 23–26.

Christie, R. Probability v. precedence: The social psychology of jury selection. In G. Bermant, C. Nemeth, and N. Vidmar, *Psychology and the Law*. Lexington, Mass.: Heath, 1976.

Clark, L., & Lewis, D. Rape: The price of coercive sexuality. Toronto, Canada: Women's Press, 1977.

Clark, R. S. *Fundamentals of Criminal Justice Research*. Lexington, Mass.: Lexington Books, 1977.

Clifford, B. R., & Bull, R. *The Psychology of Person Identification*. London: Routledge & Kegan-Paul, 1979.

Cobin, P. Abolition and restoration of the death penalty in America. In H. A. Bedau (Ed.). *The Death Penalty in America*. New York: Doubleday (Anchor), 1964, 315.

Conklin, J. E. *The Impact of Crime*. New York: Macmillan, 1975.

Conrad, J. P. Citizens and criminals. *Law and Psychology Review*, 1977, 3, 14–23.

Craik, F. I. M., & Lockhart, R. S. Levels of processing a framework for memory research. *Journal of Verbal Learning and Verbal Behavior*, 1972, 11, 671–684.

Cronbach, L. J. Five decades of public controversy over mental testing. *American Psychologist*, 1975, 30 (1), 1–14.

Cronin, R. Six member juries tried in Massachusetts District Courts, *Journal of the American Judicial Society*, 1958, 42, 136.

Cross, J., Cross, J., & Daly, J. Sex, race, age and beauty as factors in recognition of faces. *Perception and Psychophysics*, 1971, 10, 393–396.

Crowne, D. P., & Marlowe, D. *The Approval Motive*. New York: Wiley, 1964.

Culley, J. A. Hostage negotiations. *FBI Law Enforcement Bulletin*, October 1974.

Cumming, E., Cumming, I., & Edel, L. Policeman as philosopher, guide and friend. *Social Problems*, 1965, 17, 276–286.

Curtis, L. Victim precipitation and violent crime. *Social Problems*, 1974, 21, 4.

Dann, C. *The Deterrent Effect of Capital Punishment*, Committee of Philanthropic Labor of Philadelphia Yearly Meeting of Friends, Bulletin No. 29, 1935.

Davis, J. H., Bray, R. M., & Holt, R. W. The empirical study of decision processes in juries: A critical review. In J. L. Tapp, and F. J. Levine (Eds.), *Law Justice and the Individual in Society*. New York: Holt, Rinehart and Winston, 1977, pp. 326–362.

Davis, J. H., Kerr, N. L., Atkin, R. W., Holt, R., & Meek, D. The decision processes of 6- and 12-person mock juries assigned unanimous and 2/3 majority rules. *Journal of Personality and Social Psychology*, 1975, 32 (1), 1–14.

Dawson, R. E. Simulation in the social sciences. In H. Guetzkow (Ed.), *Simulation in social science: Readings*. Englewood Cliffs, N.J.: Prentice-Hall, 1972.

DeCani, J. S. Statistical evidence in jury discrimination cases. *The Journal of Criminal Law and Criminology*, 1974, 65 (2), 234–238.

Deinstitutionalization. *Corrections Magazine*, 1975, 2 (2), 3–28.

Denno, D., & Cramer, J. A. The effects of victim characteristics on judicial decision making. In W. F. McDonald (Ed.), *Criminal Justice and the Victim*. Beverly Hills, Calif.: Sage, 1976.

Devlin Report. Report to the Secretary of State for the Home Department of the Departmental Committee on Evidence of Identification in Criminal Cases, House of Commons, April 26, 1976, Chairman: Rt. Hon. Lord Devlin, London: Her Majesty's Stationery Office.

Diamond, Shari, S. A jury experiment reanalyzed. *University of Michigan Journal of Law Reform.* 1974, 7 (2), 520–532. *Id.*

Dierking, A. What should the police do in spouse abuse cases? *Social Action and the Law*, July 1978, 4, 8.

Dohrenwend, B. S., & Dohrenwend, B. P. (Eds.). *Stressful Life Events: Their Nature and Effects.* New York: Wiley, 1974.

Doob, A. N., & Kirschenbaum, H. M. Bias in police lineups—partial remembering. *Journal of Police Science and Administration*, 1973, 1, 287–293.

Doob, A. N., & Kirschenbaum, H. M. Some empirical evidence of the effect of S. 12 on the Canada Evidence Act on an accused. *Criminal Law Quarterly*, 1972, 15, 88–96.

Driscoll, J. M., Meyer, R. G., & Schanie, C. F. Training in family crisis intervention. *Journal of Applied Behavioral Science*, 1973, 9, 62–82.

DuBow, F. L., & Becker, T. M. Patterns of victim advocacy. In W. F. McDonald (Ed.), *Criminal Justice and the Victim.* Beverly Hills, Calif.: Sage, 1976.

Dunnette, M. D., & Motowidlo, S. J. *Police Selection and Career Assessment.* Washington, D.C.: U.S. Department of Justice, LEAA, November 1976.

Easterlin, R. A., Wachter, M. L., & Wachter, S. M. Demographic influences on economic stability: The U.S. experience. *Population and Development Review*, 1978, 4 (1), 1–22.

Editorial: Wrong results from I.Q. tests. *San Francisco Chronicle*, January 27, 1970.

Ehrmann, The human side of capital punishment. In H. A. Bedau (Ed.), *The Death Penalty in America.* New York: Doubleday (Anchor), 1967, 497–500.

Ellison, K. W. Psychologist in court: Testimony on rape in the Joan Little trial. *Social Action and the Law*, 1975, 2 (6), 5.

Ellison, K. W. The "just world" in the "real world." Unpublished doctoral dissertation. City University of New York, 1976.

Ellison, K. W., & Genz, J. L. The police officer as burned out samaritan. *FBI Law Enforcement Bulletin*, March 1978, 47 (3), 1–7.

Ennis, B. J., & Litwack, T. R. Psychiatry and the presumption of expertise: Flipping coins in the courtroom. *California Law Review*, 1974, 62 (3), 693–752.

Ennis, P. H. Criminal victimization in the United States (Field Survey II. A Report of a National Survey. President's Commission on Law Enforcement and Administration of Justice). Washington, D.C.: U.S. Government Printing Office, 1967.

Erdelyi, M. H., & Kleinbard, J. Has Ebbinghaus decayed with time? The growth of recall (hypermnesia) over days. *Journal of Experimental Psychology: Human Learning and Memory*, 1978, 4, 275–289.

Erikson, E. H. *Childhood and Society.* New York: Norton, 1950.

Erikson, K. T. *Everything in Its Path: Destruction of Community in the Buffalo Creek Flood.* New York: Simon & Schuster, 1976.

Etzioni, A. Science: Threatening the jury trial. *Washington Post,* May 26, 1974.

Eugenio, P., Kostes, S., Buckhout, R., & Ellison, K. W. Hypermnesia and the eyewitness to crime. Paper presented to the American Psychological Association Convention, September 1979.

Fanselow, M. How to bias an eyewitness. *Social Action and the Law,* 1975, 2 (3), 3–4.

Farmer, M. W. Jury composition challenges. *Law and Psychology Review,* 1976, 2, 45–74.

Faust, R., & Carlson, J. The impact of age and other stratification variables on attitudes toward justice, *Center Monograph No. CR–32,* 1977, Center for Responsive Psychology. New York: Brooklyn College, C.U.N.Y.

Fields, M. Quoted in Dierking, A. What should the police do in spouse abuse incidents? *Social Action and the Law,* July 1978, 4, 6.

Fighting federal prisons. *Jericho.* Newsletter of the *National Moratorium on Prison Construction,* 1978, 1 (13), 6–7.

Fisher, H. R. The Seventh Amendment and the common law: No magic in numbers. *Federal Rules and Decisions,* January 1973, 56, 507–534.

Footlick, J. K. The bail debate. *Newsweek,* May 23, 1977.

Foss, R. D. A critique of jury simulation research. Paper presented at the American Psychological Association Meeting, Chicago, Ill., September 1975.

Fox, D., Lorge, I., Weltz, P., & Herrold, K. Comparison of decisions written by large and small groups. *American Psychologist,* 1953, 8, 351.

Fox, J. A. *Forecasting Crime Data: An Econometric Analysis.* Lexington, Mass.: Lexington Books, 1978, p. 7.

Friedman, H. Trial by jury: Criteria for convictions, jury size and Type I and Type II errors. *The American Statistician,* 1972, 26, 21–23.

Galper, R., & Hochberg, H. Recognition memory for photographs of faces. *American Journal of Psychology,* 1971, 84, 351–354.

Garcia, J. I.Q.: the conspiracy. *Psychology Today,* September 1972, 40–43, 94.

Gay, W. G., Woodward, J. P., Day, H. T., O'Neil, J. P., & Tacher, C. J. *Issues in Team Policing: A Review of the Literature.* Washington, D.C., National Sheriffs' Association, 1975.

Gaylin, W., & Blatte, H. Behavior modification in prisons. *The American Criminal Law Review,* 1975, 13 (11), 11–35.

Geis, Gilbert. Crime victims and victim compensation programs. In W. F. McDonald (Ed.), *Criminal Justice and the Victim.* Beverly Hills, Calif.: Sage, 1976.

Gelb, Barbara. A cool-headed cop who saves hostages. *New York Times,* April 17, 1977.

Gelfand, A. E. A statistical case for the twelve member jury. *Trial,* 1977, 13 (2), 41–42.

Gerbasi, K. C., Zuckerman, M., & Reis, H. T. Justice needs a new blindfold: A review of mock jury research. *Psychological Bulletin*, 1977, *84* (2), 323–345.

Gianutsos, R. Whither intelligence. *Social Action*, 1974, *7* (3), 1, 7–9.

Glass, David. Stress, competition and heart attacks. *Psychology Today*, December 1976, 86–92.

Goertzel, T. The myth of the normal curve. Unpublished paper. Available from the author, Department of Sociology, Rutgers University, Camden, N.J. 08102.

Goffman, E. *The presentation of self in everyday life*. Garden City, N.Y.: Doubleday, 1959.

Goffman, E. *Asylums*. New York: Doubleday (Anchor), 1961.

Goldman, P., & Holt, D. How justice works: *The People v. Donald Payne*. *Newsweek*, March 8, 1971.

Goleman, D. Proud to be a bleeding heart. *Psychology Today*, 1978, *12* (1), 80.

Goldstein, A. G. The fallibility of the eyewitness: Psychological evidence. In B. D. Sales (Ed.), *Psychology in the Legal Process*. New York: Spectrum, 1977, 223–247.

Goldstein, A. G., & Chance, J. Measuring psychological similarity of faces. *Bulletin of the Psychonomic Society*, 1976, 7, 407–408.

Goldstein, A. G., Johnson, K. S., & Chance, J. Face recognition and verbal description of faces from memory. Paper presented to the Psychonomic Society, Washington, D.C., November 1977.

Goldstein, A. G., & Lesk, A. B. Man machine interaction in human face identification. *The Bell System Technical Journal*, 1972, *51* (2), 399–427.

Goodrich, G. A. Should experts be allowed to testify concerning eyewitness testimony in criminal cases? *The Judges Journal*, 1975, *14* (4), 70–71.

Gordon, R. A study in forensic psychology: Petit jury verdicts as a function of the number of jury members. Doctoral dissertation, University of Oklahoma, Ann Arbor, Michigan: University Microfilms, 1968, No. 68–13250.

Gottfredson, M. R., Hindelang, M. J., & Parisi, N. (Eds.). *Source-book of Criminal Justice Statistics, 1977*. Washington, D.C.: U.S. Department of Justice (LEAA), February 1978.

Grano, J. D., Kirby, B., & Ash, L. Do any constitutional safeguards remain against the danger of convicting the innocent. *Michigan Law Review*, 1974, 72 (4).

Grofman, B. Communication: Differential effects of jury size revisited. *Social Action and the Law*, 1977, *4* (2), 5–9.

Greenwood, P. W., Chaiken, J. M., & Petersilia, J. *The Criminal Investigation Process*. Lexington, Mass.: Heath, 1978.

Hall, Calvin, S., & Lindzey, G. *Theories of Personality* (2nd Ed.). New York: Wiley, 1970.

Hallie, P. O. Justification & rebellion. In N. Sanford and C. Comstock (Eds.), *Sanction for Evil*. San Francisco: Jossey-Bass, 1971.

Hampden-Turner, C. *Sane Asylum*. San Francisco: San Francisco Book, 1976.

Hampton, D. R., Summer, C. E., & Webber, R. A. Organizational behavior and the practice of management. Glenview, Ill.: Scott, Foresman, 1978.

Haney, C., & Zimbardo, P. G. The socialization into criminality—on becoming a prisoner and a guard. In J. L. Tapp and F. J. Levine (Eds.), *Law Justice and the Individual in Society.* New York: Holt, Rinehart and Winston, 1977.

Hare, A. P. Interaction and consensus in different sized groups. *American Sociological Review*, 1952, *17*, 261–267.

Harmon, L. D. The recognition of faces. *Scientific American*, 1973, *229* (5), 70–82.

Harris, R. Answering questions containing marked and unmarked adjectives and adverbs, *Journal of Experimental Psychology*, 1973, 97, 399–401.

Hart, H. L. A. *Punishment and Responsibility.* New York: Oxford University Press, 1968.

Hart Hearings, To abolish the death penalty. Subcommittee on Criminal Law and Procedures, Committee on the Judiciary, U.S. Senate, 90th Congress, 2nd Session, March–June 1968.

Hassel, C. V. The hostage situation: exploring the motivation and cause. *The Police Chief*, September 1975, 320–323.

Hays, W. L. *Statistics for Psychologists.* New York: Holt, Rinehart and Winston, 1963.

Hendricks, C. Effects of pleading the fifth amendment on the perceptions of guilt and morality. *Bulletin of the Psychonomic Society*, 1975, *6* (5), 449–452.

Herrnstein, R. I.Q. *Atlantic*, 1971, *228* (3), 43–64.

Hicks, R. E., Miller, G. W., & Kinsbourne, M. Prospective and retrospective judgments of time as a function of amount of information processed. *American Journal of Psychology*, 1976, *89*, 719–730.

Hilgard, E. R., & Loftus, E. F. Effective interrogation of the eyewitness. *International Journal of Clinical and Experimental Hypnosis*, 1979, in press.

Hindelang, M., & Gottfredson, M. The victim's decision not to invoke the criminal justice process. In W. F. McDonald (Ed.), *Criminal Justice and the Victim.* Beverly Hills, Calif.: Sage, 1976.

Hintzman, D. L. Repetition and memory. In G. L. Bower (Ed.), *The Psychology of Learning and Motivation* (Vol. 10). New York: Academic Press, 1972.

Hochberg, J., & Galper, R. E. Recognition of faces: 1. An exploratory study. *Psychonomic Science*, 1967, *9*, 619–620.

Holden, C. Butner: Experimental U.S. prison holds promise, stirs trepidation. *Science*, 1974, *185*, 423–427.

Hudson, J., & Galaway, B. *Restitution in Criminal Justice.* Lexington, Mass.: Lexington Books, 1975.

Hursch, C. J. The trouble with Rape. Chicago: Nelson/Hall, 1977.

International Association of Chief of Police—Training Key #67, Witness Perception, 1967. Available from 1319 18th St. N.W. Washington, D.C. 20036.

I.Q. *Science for the People*, 1974, *6*, 2–entire issue.

Jackson, G. *Soledad Brother, The Prison Letters of George Jackson*. New York: Dell, 1971.

Jackson, T. P. Presenting expert testimony. *Trial*, Winter 1975, 41–44.

Jacobi, J. H. Reducing police stress: A psychiatrist's point of view. In W. H. Kroes, & Hurrell, J. J. (Eds.), *Job Stress and the Police Officer*. Monograph, U.S. Department of HEW, December 1975.

Jacobson, J. L., & Wirt, R. D. MMPI profiles associated with outcomes of group psychotherapy with prisoners. In J. N. Butcher (Ed.), *MMPI: Research Developments and Clinical Applications*. New York: McGraw-Hill, 1969.

Jayewardene, C. H. S. *The Penalty of Death: The Canadian Experiment*. Lexington, Mass.: Heath, 1977.

Jensen, A. R. How much can we boost I.Q. and scholastic achievement. *Harvard Educational Review*, 1969, 39 (1), 1–123.

Jensen, A. R. The differences are real. *Psychology Today*, December 1973, 80–84.

Jones, C., & Aronson, E. Attribution of fault to a rape victim as a function of respectability of the victim. *Journal of Personality and Social Psychology*, 1973, 26 (3), 415–419.

Jury Verdict Research, Inc., Personal Injury Valuation Handbooks, Vol. VIII, *Psychological Factors Affecting Verdicts-Jurors*, J.V.R., 1969.

Kadish, M. R., & Kadish, S. H. The institutionalization of conflict: Jury acquittals. *Journal of Social Issues*, 1971, 27 (2), 199–218.

Kagan, J. The magical aura of the I.Q. *Saturday Review*, December 4, 1971, 92–93.

Kairys, D., Schulman, J., & Harring, S. *The Jury System: New Methods for Reducing Prejudice*, National Jury Project and the National Lawyers Guild, 1975.

Kakoulis, J. The Myths of Capital Punishment. *Center Monograph No. CR-13*, June 1974, *Center for Responsive Psychology*. New York: Brooklyn College, C.U.N.Y.

Kakoulis, J. Myths of deterrence. *Social Action and the Law*, 1974, 1 (5), 5–6.

Kalven, H., Jr., & Zeisel, H. *The American Jury*. Boston: Little, Brown, 1966.

Kalven, H., & Zeisel, H. *The American Jury*. Chicago: The University of Chicago Press, 1971.

Kamin, Leon. *The Science and Politics of I.Q.* Potomac, Md.: Erlbaum, 1974.

Kaplan, J. *Criminal Justice* (2nd Ed.). Mineola, N.Y.: Foundation Press, 1978, 570–571.

Kassenbaum, G., Ward, D., & Wilner, D. *Prison Treatment and Parole Survival: An Empirical Assessment*. New York: Wiley, 1971.

Katzer, J., Cook, K. H., & Crouch, W. W. *Evaluating Information: A Guide for Users of Social Science Research*. Reading, Mass.: Addison-Wesley, 1978.

Kelley, C. *Crime in the United States, 1976. The Uniform Crime Report*. Washington, D.C.: U.S. Government Printing Office, 1977.

Kelley, H. H., & Thibaut, J. W. Group problem solving. In G. Lindzey and

E. Aronson (Eds.), *The Handbook of Social Psychology* (Vol. 4, 2nd Ed.). Reading, Mass.: Addison-Wesley, 1969, 1–101.

Kessler, J. An empirical study of six and twelve-member jury decision-making process. *University of Michigan Journal of Law Reform*, 1973, 6 (3), 671–711; Institute of Judicial Administration.

Kessler, J. The social psychology of jury deliberations. In R. J. Simon (Ed.), *The Jury System in America*. Beverly Hills, Calif.: Sage, 1975.

Kling, S. G. *Sexual Behavior & the Law*. New York: Bernard Geis, 1965.

Knudten, R. D., Meade, A., Knudten, M., & Doerner, W. The victim in the administration of criminal justice: Problems and perceptions. In W. F. McDonald (Ed.), *Criminal Justice and the Victim*. Beverly Hills, Calif.: Sage, 1976.

Kobetz, R. W. Hostage incidents: the new police priority. *The Police Chief*, May 1975.

Kroes, W. H. *Society's Victim—the Policeman*. Springfield, Ill.: Thomas, 1976.

Kroes, W. H., & Hurrell, J. J. *Job Stress and the Police Officer*. U.S. Department of Health, Education, and Welfare (NIOSH), 1975.

Kuehn, L. L. Looking down a gun barrel: Person perception and violent crime. *Perceptual and Motor Skills*, 1974, 39, 1159–1164.

Landy, D., & Aronson, E. The influence of the character of the criminal and his victim on the decisions of simulated jurors. *Journal of Experimental Social Psychology*, 1969, 5, 141–152.

Lefkowitz, J. Psychological attributes of policemen: A review of research and opinion. *Journal of Social Issues*, 1975, 31 (1), 3–26.

Lefkowitz, J. Industrial-Organizational Psychology and the Police. *American Psychologist*, May 1977, 32 (5), 346–364.

Lehtinen, M. W. The value of life: An argument for the death penalty. *Crime and Delinquency*, 1977, 23 (3), 237–252.

Leippe, M. R., Wells, G. L., & Ostrom, T. M. Crime seriousness as a determinant of accuracy in eyewitness identification. *Journal of Applied Psychology*, 1978, 63 (3), 345–351.

Lempert, R. O. Uncovering "nondiscernible" differences: Empirical research and the jury size cases. *Michigan Law Review*, 1975, 73 (4), 643–708.

Lerner, M. J. Evaluation of performance as a function of performer's reward & attractiveness. *Journal of Personality and Social Psychology*, 1965, 1, 355–360.

Lerner, M. J., & Simmons, C. H. Observers' reaction to the innocent victim: Compassion or rejection? *Journal of Personality and Social Psychology*, 1966, 4, 203–210.

Lerner, M. J. The desire for justice & reactions to victims. In J. Macaulay, and L. Berkowitz (Eds.), *Altruism and Helping Behavior*. New York: Academic Press, 1970.

Levinson, D. J. *The Seasons of a Man's Life*. New York: Knopf, 1978.

Levy, R. J. Predicting police failures. *Journal of Criminal Law, Criminology and Police Science*, 1967, 58, 265–275.

Levy, R. J. A method for the identification of the high-risk police applicant. In J. R. Snibbe, and R. M. Snibbe (Eds.), *The Urban Policeman in Transition*. Springfield, Ill.: Thomas, 1973.

Levine, A. G., & Schweber-Koren, C. Jury selection in Erie County: Changing a sexist system. *Law and Society Review*, 1976, *11* (1), 43–55.

Levine, F. J., & Tapp, J. L. The psychology of criminal identification: The gap from *Wade* to *Kirby*. *University of Pennsylvania Law Review*, May 1973, (5), 1079–1120.

Levine, R. I., Chein, I., & Murphy, G. The relation of the intensity of a need to the amount of perceptual distortion. *Journal of Psychology*, 1942, *13*, 283–293.

Lindemann, E. Symptomatology & management of acute grief. *American Journal of Psychiatry*, 1944, *101*, 141–148.

Lipton, J. P. On the psychology of eyewitness testimony. *Journal of Applied Psychology*, 1977, *62*, 90–95.

Loftus, E. F. *Eyewitness Testimony*. Cambridge, Mass.: Harvard University Press, 1980.

Loftus, E. F., & Palmer, J. C. Reconstruction of automobile destruction: An example of the interaction between language and memory. *Journal of Verbal Learning and Verbal Behavior*, 1974, *13*, 385–589.

Loftus, E. F., & Zanni, G. Eyewitness testimony: The influence of the wording of a question. *Bulletin of the Psychonomic Society*, 1975, *5*, 86–88.

Loftus, E. R. Reconstruction of memory: The incredible eyewitness. *Jurimetrics Journal*, 1975, *15* (3), 188–193.

Loftus, G. R. Eye fixations and recognition memory. *Cognitive Psychology*, 1972, *3*, 525–557.

McClelland, D. C. Testing for competence rather than for "intelligence." *American Psychologist*, 1973, *28* (1), 1–14.

McConahay, J. B., Mullin, C. J., & Fredrick, J. The Uses of social science on trials with political and racial overtones: The trial of Joan Little. *Law and Contemporary Problems*, 1977, *41* (1), 10–17.

McDonald, W. F. Criminal justice & the victim: An introduction. In W. F. McDonald (Ed.), *Criminal Justice and the Victim*. Beverly Hills, Calif.: Sage, 1976.

McGregor, D. *The Human Side of Enterprise*. New York: McGraw-Hill, 1960.

Maris, L., & Maris, M. The mechanics of stress release: the transcendental stress. *Police Work*, April 1978, 48–56.

Marshall, J. *Law and psychology in conflict*. New York: Doubleday (Anchor), 1969.

Marshall, M., & Oskamp, S. Effects of kind of question and atmosphere of interrogation on accuracy and completeness of testimony. *Harvard Law Review*, 1971, *84*, 1620.

Martinson, R. What works?— Questions and answers about prison reform. *The Public Interest*, 1974, *35*, 22–54.

Maslach, C. Burned out. *Human Behavior*, September 1976, 330–336.

Meehl, P. E. Psychology and the criminal law. *University of Richmond Law Review*, 1970, *5*, 1–30.

Meehl, P. E. Law and the fireside induction. In J. L. Tapp and F. J. Levine (Eds.), *Law, Justice and the Individual in Society*. New York: Holt, Rinehart and Winston, 1977, 10–28.

Megargee, E. I. A critical review of theories of violence. *U.S. National Com-*

mission on Causes & Prevention of Violence. New York: Braziller, 1969, *13*, 1037–1115.

Mehrabian, A. *Non-verbal communication.* New York: Prentice-Hall, 1970.

Meltsner, M. *Cruel and Unusual: The Supreme Court and Capital Punishment.* New York: Murrow Paperback, 1973.

Menninger, K. *The Crime of Punishment.* New York: Viking Press, 1966.

Mercer, J. R. I.Q. the legal label. *Psychology Today,* 1972, *6* (9), 44–47, 95–97.

Milgram, S. *The individual in a social world.* Reading, Mass.: Addison-Wesley, 1977.

Miller, G. A., & Buckhout, R. *Psychology: The Science of Mental Life.* New York: Harper & Row, 1973, 165–170.

Miller, J. G. The abandonment of rehabilitation in corrections: Some thoughts and dilemmas. *Law and Psychology Review,* 1977, *3* (25), 29.

Miller, W. B. Lower Class Culture as a Generating Milieu of Gang Delinquency. In S. Dinitz, R. R. Dynes, and A. C. Clark (Eds.), *Deviance: Studies in the Process of Stigmatization and Societal Reaction.* New York: Oxford University Press, 1969, 158–172.

Mischel, W. Toward a cognitive social learning reconceptualization of personality. *Psychological Review,* 1973, *80*, 252–283.

Mitford, J. Kind and usual punishment in California. *Atlantic Monthly,* 1971.

Mitford, J. *Kind and Usual Punishment.* New York: Knopf, 1973.

Model Rules: Eyewitness Identification, Police Foundation, Washington, D.C., 1974.

Monahan, J. (Ed.). Report of the task force on the role of psychology in the criminal justice system. *American Psychological Association,* February 1978.

Monahan, J. The prevention of violence. In J. Monahan (Ed.), *Community Mental Health and the Criminal Justice System.* New York: Pergamon Press, 1976.

Morris, N. Who should go to prison. In B. D. Sales (Ed.), *Perspectives in Law and Psychology, Vol. I: The Criminal Justice System.* New York: Plenum Press, 1977, 151–160.

Moskowitz, M. J. Hugo Munsterberg: A study in the history of applied psychology. *American Psychologist,* 1977, *32* (10), 824–842.

Mossman, K. Jury selection: An expert's view. *Psychology Today,* 1973, *6*, 78–79.

Mueller, J. H., Carlomusto, M., & Goldstein, A. G. Orienting task and study time in facial recognition. *Bulletin of the Psychonomic Society,* 1978, *11* (5), 313–316.

Muensterberg, H. *On the Witness Stand.* New York: Doubleday, 1908.

Mungham, G., & Bankowski, Z. The jury in the legal system. *Sociological Review Monograph,* No. 23, 1977, 202–225.

Munn, N. M. *Psychology.* New York: Harcourt Brace Jovanovich, 1952.

Murphy, G. *Historical introduction to psychology.* New York: Appleton-Century-Crofts, 1949, 244–245.

Murphy, J. J. Current practices in the use of psychological testing by police agencies. *Journal of Criminal Law, Criminology and Police Science,* 1972, *63,* 570–576.

Murphy, P., & Bloch, P. The beat commander. *The Police Chief,* May 1970.

Murton, T. One year of prison reform. *The Nation,* January 12, 1970, 12–17.

Muscio, B. The influence of the form of a question, *British Journal of Psychology,* 1915, *8,* 351–389.

Nagel, W. G. A statement on behalf of a moratorium on prison construction. *Law and Psychology Review,* 1977, *3,* 31–51.

Nagel, S., & Neef, C. Deductive modeling to determine an optimum jury size and fraction required to convict. *Washington University Law Quarterly,* 1975, 973–976.

Nass, D. R. *The Rape Victim.* Dubuque, Iowa: Kendall/Hunt, 1977.

New Jersey experiments with the six man jury. *Bulletin of the Section on Judicial Administration of the American Bar Association,* 1966, 9.

New Jersey Police Manual, 1962.

Newsweek, September 20, 1970. Tests that destroy.

Nickerson, R. S. Short-term memory for complex meaningful visual configurations. *Canadian Journal of Psychology,* 1965, *19,* 155–160.

Niederhoffer, Arthur. *Behind the Shield.* Garden City, N.Y.: Doubleday, 1967.

O'Hara, C. E. *Fundamentals of Criminal Investigation* (3rd Ed.). Springfield, Ill.: Thomas, 1973.

Opton, E. M. How to witness expertly. *Newsletter of the Society for the Psychological Study of Social Issues,* Fall 1973.

Opton, E. M. Institutional behavior modification as a fraud and a sham. *Arizona Law Review,* 1975, *17* (1), 20–28.

Opton, E. M. When psychiatry goes to prison, law is the loser. *Social Action and the Law,* 1975, *2* (5), 7–8.

Pabst, W. R. What do six-member juries really save? *Judicature: Journal of the American Judicature Society,* 1973, 57 (1), 6–11.

Pacht el al. The current status of the psychologist as an expert witness. *Professional Psychology,* 1973, *4,* 409.

Padawer-Singer, A., & Barton, A. H. The impact of pretrial publicity on jurors' verdicts. In R. J. Simon (Ed.), *The Jury System in America.* Beverly Hills, Calif.: Sage, 1975, 123–142.

Penick, B. K., & Owens, M. E. B. (Eds.). *Surveying Crime.* Washington, D.C.: National Research Council of the National Academy of Sciences, 1976.

Perlin, M. L. The legal status of the psychologist in the courtroom. Paper presented to the American Psychological Association Meetings, Washington, D.C., September 1976.

Peters, A. (1917) cited in H. Ellis, Recognizing faces. *British Journal of Psychology,* 1975, *66,* 409–426.

Petersilia, J. Developing programs for the habitual offender: New directions in research. In R. C. Huff (Ed.), *Contemporary Corrections.* Beverly Hills, Calif.: Sage, 1977.

Phillips, S. Justice for whom? *Psychology Today,* March 1977, 23–27.

Platt, A., & Pollock, R. Channeling lawyers: The careers of public defenders.

In G. Bermat, C. Nemeth, and N. Vidmar, *Psychology and the Law.* Lexington, Mass.: Heath, 1976.

Pope, C. E. *Crime-Specific Analysis: An Empirical Examination of Burglary Offense and Offender Characteristics.* Washington, D.C.: U.S. Department of Justice (LEAA), NILE/CJ, 1977.

President's Commission on Law Enforcement and Administration of Justice. The Challenge of Crime in a Free Society. Washington, D.C.: U.S. Government Printing Office, 1967.

Rappaport, J. *Community Psychology: Values, Research and Action.* New York: Holt, Rinehart and Winston, 1977.

Remer, L. Criminologist for the defense. *Human Behavior,* December 1977, 57–59.

Rhead, C., Abrams, A., Trasman, H., & Margolis, P. The psychological assessment of police candidates. *American Journal of Psychiatry,* 1968, *124,* 1575–1580.

Rice, B. The high cost of thinking the unthinkable. *Psychology Today,* December 1973, 89–93.

Richert, J. P. Jurors' attitudes toward jury service. *The Justice System Journal,* 1977, *273,* 233–245.

Robinson, J. P., & Shaver, P. R. *Measures of Social Psychological Attitudes.* Ann Arbor, Mich.: Survey Research Center, Institute for Social Research, the University of Michigan, 1973.

Robinson, S. M. A critical view of the Uniform Crime Reports. *Michigan Law Review,* 1966, *64,* 1031–1054.

Rogosin, H. R. *The Grings v. Duke Power Case.* Conference paper—available from The Community Relations Education Federation, 4034 Buckingham Road, Los Angeles, California 90008.

Rokeach, M., & Widmar, N. Testimony concerning possible jury bias in a Black Panther murder trial. *Journal of Applied Social Psychology,* 1973.

Rosenblatt, Julia C. Should the size of the jury in criminal cases be reduced to six? An examination of psychological evidence. *The Prosecutor: Journal of the National District Attorney's Association,* 1972, 8 (4), 309–314.

Rosenman, S. The paradox of guilt in disaster victim populations. *Psychiatric Quarterly Supplement,* 1956, *30,* 181–221.

Rosenthal, R. *Experimenter Effects in Behavioral Research.* New York: Appleton-Century-Crofts, 1966.

Roy, M. *Battered Wives.* New York: Van Nostrand Reinhold, 1977.

Rubin, Z., & Peplau, L. A. Who believes in a just world? *Social Issues,* 1975, *31* (3), 65–90.

Rubinstein, J. *City Police.* New York: Farrar, Straus & Giroux, 1973.

Runyon, R. P. *Winning with Statistics.* Reading, Mass.: Addison-Wesley, 1977.

Ryan, W. *Blaming the Victim.* New York: Random House, 1971.

Scarr-Salaptek, S. Race, social class and I.Q. *Science,* 1971, *174,* (4015), 1223–1228.

Saks, M. *Jury Verdicts.* Lexington, Mass.: Lexington Books, 1977.

Saks, M. Social scientists can't rig juries. *Psychology Today,* 1976, 9 (8), 48–57.

Saks, M. Social psychological contributions to a legislative sub-committee on organ and tissue transplants. *American Psychologist,* 1978, *33* (7), 680–690.

Saks, M. J. Ignorance of science is no excuse. *Trial,* 1974, *10* (6), 18–20.

Saks, M. J. The limits of scientific jury selection: ethical and empirical, *Jurimetrics Journal,* 1976, *17* (1), 3–22.

Schilling, C. G. Behavioral science services for police. *The Police Chief,* April 1978, 28–32.

Schneider, Anne L., Burcat, Janie M., and Wilson, L. A. "The Role of Attitudes in the Decision to Report Crimes to the Police." In McDonald, W. F. (Ed.), *Criminal Justice and the Victim.* Beverly Hills: Sage, 1976.

Schulman, J. Strategies and issues in systematic jury selection, Unpublished paper, 1976.

Schulman, J., Shaver, P., Colman, R., Emrich, B., Christie, R. Recipe for a jury, *Psychology Today,* 1973, *6*, 37–84, available at *Center Monograph No. CR-16, Center for Responsive Psychology.* Brooklyn College, Brooklyn, N.Y. 11210.

Schulman, J. A systematic approach to successful jury selection. *Guild Notes,* 1973, Vol. II (7), 13–20.

Schulman, J. Personal communication, 1976.

Schwartz, H., & Jackson, B. Prosecutor as public enemy. *Harper's,* February 1976.

Scull, A. T. *Decarceration.* Englewood Cliffs, New Jersey: Prentice-Hall, 1977. See also "Deinstitutionalization," *Corrections Magazine,* 1975, *2* (2), 3–28.

Sellin, T. (Ed.) *Capital Punishment,* New York: Harper & Row, 1967.

Sellin, T. "Homicides in Retentionist and Abolitionist States," in T. Sellin (Ed.), *Capital Punishment.* New York: Harper & Row, 1967.

Sellin, T. "Prison Homicides," in *Capital Punishment, Supra,* Note 25, 159.

Sellin, T. "The Death Penalty and Police Safety," from T. Sellin (Ed.), *Capital Punishment,* New York: Harper & Row, 1967, 52–153.

Sellin, T. *The Death Penalty.* Philadelphia, Pennsylvania: American Law Institute, 1959, 34.

Selnick, G. J., & Steinberg, S. *The Tenacity of Prejudice: Anti-semitism in Contemporary America.* New York: Harper & Row, 1969.

Selye, Hans. *The Stress of Life.* New York: McGraw-Hill, 1976.

Selye, H. The stress concept: Its philosophical and psychosocial implications. *Bioscience Communication,* 1975, *1*, 131–145.

Shah, S. The criminal justice system. In S. E. Golann, & C. Eisdorfer (Eds.), *Handbook of Community Mental Health.* New York: Appleton-Century-Crofts, 1972.

Shapley, D. Jury selection: Social scientists gamble in an already loaded game. *Science,* 1974, *185*, (September 20), 1033–1071.

Shaver, K. G. *Principles of Social Psychology.* Cambridge, Mass.: Winthrop Publishers, 1977, 136.

Sheehy, G. *Passages: Predictable Crises of Adult Life.* New York: E. P. Dutton, 1976.

Shepard, R. N. Recognition memory for words, sentences and pictures. *Journal of Verbal Learning and Verbal Behavior,* 1967, *6*, 156–163.

Siegel, S. *Nonparametric Statistics for the Behavioral Sciences.* New York: McGraw-Hill, 1956.

Silber, D. E. The place of behavior therapy in correction. *Crime and Delinquency,* April 1976, 211–217.

Silberman, C. E. *Criminal Violence and Criminal Justice.* New York: Random House, 1978.

Skinner, B. F. *The Cumulative Record.* New York: Appleton-Century-Crofts, 1960.

Skolnick, Jerome H. *Justice Without Trial: Law Enforcement in Democratic Society.* New York: Wiley, 1966.

"Smaller Juries Increase; Divided Verdicts Allowed," *New York Times,* July 21, 1975 by Lesley Oelsner.

Smith, E. A new way for jailers. *The Bergen Record,* July 23, 1978, B-5.

Smith, M. Percy Foreman: top trial lawyer. *Life,* 1966, *60,* 92–101.

Sobel, N. *Eyewitness Identification.* New York: Boardman, 1976, Supplement, 870.

Sommer, R. *The End of Imprisonment.* New York: Oxford University Press, 1976.

Sorce, J. F., & Campos, J. J. The role of expression in the recognition of a face. *American Journal of Psychology,* 1974, *87* (1–2), 71–82.

Spielberger, Charles D. (Ed.) *Police Selection & Evaluation: Issues & Techniques.* Washington: Hemisphere, 1979.

Stanton, M. Murderers on parole. *Crime and Delinquency,* 1969, *15,* 149.

Steinmetz, Suzanne K. "Wifebeating, Husbandbeating—A Comparison of the Use of Physical Violence Between Spouses to Resolve Marital Fights." In Roy, M., (Ed.), *Battered Women.* New York: Van Nostrand, Reinhold, 1977.

Stern, S., & Sullivan, R. The victim/witness assistance project. *Social Action & the Law,* 1976, *3* (2), 18.

Stevens, S. S. *Handbook of Experimental Psychology.* New York: Wiley, 1950.

Streufert, S., & Suedfeld, P. Editorial: simulation as research method: A problem in communication. *Journal of Applied Social Psychology,* 1977, *7* (4), 281–285.

Strnad, B. N., & Mueller, J. H. Levels of processing in facial recognition memory. *Bulletin of the Psychonomic Society,* 1977, *9* (1), 17–18.

Strodtbeck, F., James R., and Hawkins, C. Social status in jury deliberations. *American Sociological Review,* 1957, *22,* 713–719.

Sue, S. Effects of inadmissible evidence on the decision of simulated jurors— A moral dilemma. *Journal of Applied Social Psychology,* 1973, *3* (4), 345–353.

Sutherland, S., & Scherl, D. Patterns of response among rape victims. *American Journal of Orthopsychiatry,* 1970, *40,* 504.

Stotland, E., & Berberich, J. "The Psychology of the Police." In H. Toch (Ed.), *The Psychology of Crime and Criminal Justice.* New York: Holt, Rinehart and Winston, 1979.

Symonds, M. The accidental victim of violent crime. Paper presented at Symposium on Violence, Georgetown Hospital, Washington, D.C., October 1973.

Tate, E., Hawrish, E., & Clark, S. Communication Variables in Jury Selection. *Journal of Communication*, 1974, *24* (3), 130–139.

"Theory of General Deterrence" Criminal Justice Research Solicitation pamphlet, *National Institute of Law Enforcement and Criminal Justice*, 1977.

Thomas, E., & Fink, C. Effects of group size. *Psychological Bulletin*, 1963, *60*, 371–384.

Timothy, M. *Jury Woman*. Palo Alto, California: EMTY Press, 1974.

Toch, H. (Ed.). *Psychology of Crime and Criminal Justice*. New York: Holt, Rinehart & Winston, 1979.

Toch, H. *Living in Prison: The Ecology of Survival*. New York: The Free Press, 1977.

Topoff, H. "Genes, Intelligence and Race," in E. Tobach et al. (Eds.). *The Four Horsemen: Racism, Sexism, Militarism and Social Darwinism*, New York: Behavioral Publications, 1974.

Trotter, S. Patuxent: Therapeutic prison faces test. *APA Monitor*, May 1975, *6* (5), 1.

Tuddenham, R. D. The nature and measurement of intelligence. In L. Postman (Ed.), *Psychology in the Making*. New York: Alfred A. Knopf, 1963.

Uniform Crime Reports, Federal Bureau of Investigation, 1969, 58–63.

Uniform Crime Reports for the United States, 1976, issued by the Director, Federal Bureau of Investigation, U.S. Department of Justice, Washington, D.C., September, 1977.

United Nations, *Capital Punishment*. New York: United Nations Publications, 1968.

U.S. Department of Justice, LEAA, NCJISS. Patterns of Robbery Characteristics and Their Occurrence Among Social Areas. Washington, D.C.: U.S. Government Printing Office, 1976.

U.S. Department of Justice, LEAA, NCJISS. Criminal Victimization Surveys in Eight American Cities: A Comparison of 1971/72 and 1974/75 Findings. Washington, D.C.: U.S. Government Printing Office, November 1976.

U.S. Department of Justice, LEAA, NCJISS. Criminal Victimization in the United States, 1973. Washington, D.C.: U.S. Government Printing Office, December 1976.

U.S. Department of Justice, LEAA, NCJISS. Local Victim Surveys: A Review of the Issues. Washington, D.C.: U.S. Government Printing Office, 1977.

U.S. Department of Justice, LEAA, NCJISS. Criminal Victimization in the United States: A comparison of 1975 and 1976 findings. Washington, D.C.: U.S. Government Printing Office, November 1977.

U.S. Department of Justice. LEAA, National Criminal Justice Information & Statistics Service. Criminal victimization in the United States, 1975: A National Crime Survey Report. Washington, D.C.: U.S. Government Printing Office, December 1977.

U.S. Department of Justice, LEAA, NCJISS. Criminal Victimization in the United States, 1974. Washington, D.C.: U.S. Government Printing Office, December 1977.

U.S. Department of Justice, LEAA, NCJISS. Public opinion about crime: The attitudes of victims and nonvictims in selected cities. Washington, D.C.: U.S. Government Printing Office, December 1977.

U.S. Department of Justice, Law Enforcement Assistance Administration, National Criminal Justice Information and Statistics Service. *Sourcebook of Criminal Justice Statistics, 1978*. Washington, D.C.: U.S. Government Printing Office, June 1979.

U.S. News & World Report, May 10, 1976.

U.S. News & World Report, June 20, 1977. Interview with Norval Morris, Dean, University of Chicago Law School.

Valenti, A., & Dowling, L. Differential effects of jury size on verdicts following deliberation as a function of apparent guilt of the defendant. *Journal of Personality and Social Psychology*, 1975, *32*, 655–663.

Vanden Haag, E. On deterrence and the death penalty. *Ethics*, July 1968, *78*, 280–288.

Van Dyke, J. M. *Jury Selection Procedures: Our Uncertain Commitment to Representative Panels*, Cambridge, Mass.: Ballinger, 1977, 24–25.

Verdicts linked to speech style, *New York Times*, December 13, 1976.

Viano, E. C., Jacquin, D., Jones, H. C., Neuse, M., Spaid, O., & Steinberg, S. *Victim/Witness Services: Participant's Handbook*. Washington, D.C.: University Research, 1977.

Virzera, V. Plan of Action. *Spring 3100*, January/February 1974.

Von Hentig, H. *The Criminal and His Victim*. New Haven: Yale University Press, 1948.

Waldron, R. J., Uppal, J. C., Quarles, C. L., McCauley, R. P., Harper, H., Frazier, R. L., Benson, J. C., & Altemose, J. R. *The Criminal Justice System: An Introduction*. Boston: Houghton Mifflin, 1976.

Wall, P., *Eyewitness Identification in Criminal Cases*. Springfield, Ill.: Thomas, 1965.

Walster, E. Assignment of responsibility for an accident. *Journal of Personality and Social Psychology*, 1966, *3* (1), 73–79.

Watkins, M. J., Ho, E., & Tulving, E. Context effects in recognition memory for faces. *Journal of Verbal Learning and Verbal Behavior*, 1976, *15*, 505–517.

Webster, W. Crime in the United States, 1977: *FBI Uniform Crime Reports*. Washington, D.C.: U.S. Government Printing Office, 1978.

Wechsler, David. Intelligence defined and undefined: A relativistic appraisal. *American Psychologist*, 1975, *30* (2), 135–139.

Weis, K., & Borges, S. S. Victimology & rape: The case of the legitimate victim. *Issues in Criminology*, 1973, *8* (2), 71–115.

Wells, G. L. Applied eyewitness-testimony research: System variables and estimator variables. *Journal of Personality and Social Psychology*, 1978, *36* (12), 1546–1557.

Wexler, D. Behavior modification and the legal developments. *American Behavioral Scientist*, 1975, *18* (5), 679–684.

White, S. O., & Krislov, S. (Eds.). *Understanding Crime*. Washington, D.C.: National Research Council of the National Academy of Sciences, 1977.

Wickelgreen, W. A. *Learning and Memory*. Englewood Cliffs, N.J.: Prentice-Hall, 1977.

Wiehl, R. The six man jury, *Gonzaga Law Review*, 1968, *4*, 35.

Williams, K. M. The effects of victim characteristics on the disposition of violent crimes. In W. F. McDonald (Ed.), *Criminal Justice and the Victim*. Beverly Hills, Calif.: Sage, 1976.

Williams, R. L. Scientific racism and I.Q.: The silent mugging of the black community. *Psychology Today*, May 1974, 32.

Wilson, C. R. Psychological opinions on the accuracy of expert testimony. *The Judges Journal*, 1975, *14* (4), 72–74.

Wilson, J. Q. *Varieties of Police Behavior: The Management of Law and Order in Eight Communities*. Cambridge, Mass.: Harvard University Press, 1968.

Wilson, J. Q. The death penalty. *New York Times Magazine*, October 28, 1973, 27–48.

Wilson, J. Q. *Thinking About Crime*. New York: Basic Books, 1975.

Wolfgang, M. E. *Patterns in Criminal Homicide*. Philadelphia: University of Pennsylvania Press, 1958.

Wolfgang, M. E. The social scientist in court. *The Journal of Criminal Law and Criminology*, 1974, *65* (2), 239–247.

Wolfgang, M. E. Real and perceived changes of crime and punishment, *Daedalus*, 1978, *107* (1), 143–157.

Wolfgang, M. E., & Cohen, B. Uniform Crime Reports: A critical appraisal, *University of Pennsylvania Law Review*, 1963, *111*, 708–738.

Wolfgang, M. E., & Ferracuti, F. *The Subculture of Violence: Toward an Integrated Theory in Criminology*. London: Lanistock, 1967.

Woocher, F. D. Did your eyes deceive you? Expert psychological testimony on the unreliability of eyewitness identifications. *Stanford Law Review*, 1977, *29* (5), 969–1030.

Yarmey, A. D. The effects of attractiveness, feature saliency, and liking on memory for faces. In M. Cook and G. Wilson (Eds.), *Love and Attraction: An International Conference*, Toronto: Pergamon Press, 1978, 51–53.

Yarmey, A. D. *The Psychology of Eyewitness Testimony*. New York: Free Press, 1979.

Yin, R. K. Looking at upside-down faces. *Journal of Experimental Psychology*, 1969, *81*, 141–145.

Zanzola, L. The role of pretrial publicity in the trial process and jury deliberations. Unpublished master's thesis, Northern Illinois University, 1977.

Zeisel, H. And then there were none: The diminution of the federal jury. *University of Chicago Law Review*, 1971, *39*, 710–728.

Zeisel, H. Twelve is Just. *Trial*, 1974, *10* (6), 13–15.

Ziegenhagen, E. Toward a theory of victim-criminal justice system interactions. In W. F. McDonald (Ed.), *Criminal Justice and the Victim*. Beverly Hills, Calif.: Sage, 1976.

Zeisel, H., & Diamond, S. S. Convincing empirical evidence on the six member jury. *University of Chicago Law Review*, 1974, *41*, 281.

Zeisel, H., & Diamond, S. S. The jury selection in the Mitchell-Stans conspiracy trial. *American Bar Foundation Research Journal*, 1976, *1* (1), 151–174.

Zeisel, H., & Diamond, S. S. The effect of peremptory challenges on jury and verdict: An experiment in a federal district court. *Stanford Law Review*, 1978, *30* (3), 491–531.

Zimbardo, P. G., Haney, C., Banks, C., & Jaffee, D. The mind is a formidable jailer: A pirandellian prison. *New York Times Magazine*, April 8, 1973.

Ziskin, J. *Coping with psychiatric and psychological testimony* (2nd Ed.). Beverly Hills, Calif.: Law and Psychology Press, 1975.

CASE CITATIONS

Allegheny Airlines v. *U.S., et al.,* U.S. Federal District Court, Indianapolis, Indiana.

Apodaca, et al. v. *Oregon,* 406 U.S. 404 (1971), pp. 404–425.

Ballew v. *Georgia,* 435 U.S. 223 (1978), pp. 1–26.

Blunt v. *U.S.,* 389, F. 2d 545, 547 (D.C. Cir. 1967).

Boulden v. *Holman,* 394 U.S. 478, 89 Supreme Court 1138 (1969).

Bruton v. *United States,* 391 U.S. 123, 88 Supreme Court 1620 (1968).

Chance v. *Board of Examiners,* 458, F. 2d 1167, (2nd Cir., 1972).

Colgrove v. *Battin,* 413, U.S. 149, 1973.

Florida v. *Richard Campbell* (Armed robbery), 74–2777, Circuit Court of Palm Beach County, Florida (April 24, 1975). (*Wade* hearing and trial).

Frazier v. *Cupp,* 89 Supreme Court 1420, 394 U.S. 731 (1969).

Furman v. *Georgia,* 408 U.S. 238 (1972).

Grings v. *Duke Power,* 945 U.S. 849 (1971).

Iberia, Hampton, administratrix, etc. et al. v. *Edward Hanrahan et al.,* No. 70c 1384 consolidated, 1978.

Jenkins v. *United States,* 307, F. 2d 637, 651, 652 (D.C. Cir. 1961), Bastian, J. dissenting).

Michigan v. *Hall & McGill,* Circuit Court, County of Ingham, No. 75–25859–FY (October 8, 1975).

People v. *Attica Brothers: Ernest Bixby et al.*, Superior Court of New York, Erie County (July 2, 1974).

People v. *Richard Boldon* (Attempted murder), No. 3180–74, Queens County Supreme Court, New York (April 8, 1975).

People v. *Castle* (Armed robbery), Superior Court, Contra Costa County, California (April 1, 1974).

People v. *Chavez* (Rape-robbery), Superior Court, Alameda County, California (July 15, 1970).

People v. *Angela Y. Davis* (Murder), Superior Court, Santa Clara County, California (May 23, 1972).

People v. *Davis*, No. 52613, Santa Clara County Superior Court, California (May 27, 1972).

People v. *Eugene Duncan* (Murder), No. 71–112, County Court, Tomkins County, Ithaca, New York (June 19, 1975).

People v. *Guzman*, 47 CA 3d 380 (1975).

People v. *Kincy et al.* (Assault with deadly weapon), Superior Court, San Bernardino County, California (on April 3, 8, 1974).

People v. *Ernest Montgomery, R. Woods, and L. Whitehead* (Attempted murder), Bronx Supreme Court, New York (1976).

People v. *Moultrie* (Rape), Kings County Supreme, New York (July 1976).

People v. *Lyles*, 526 P. 2d 1332, 1334–1335, Colorado Supreme Court (1974).

People v. *Pratt* (Murder), Superior Court, Los Angeles (June 27, 1972).

People v. *Richardson and Williams* (Armed robbery), Superior Court, Alameda County, California (October 29, 1971).

People v. *Milton Rucker* (Armed robbery), New York County Supreme Court (September 19, 1975).

People of the State of New York v. *Gramaglia et al.*, (1978), Erie County Superior Court, Buffalo, N.Y.

People v. *Edward Stevens* (Rape), Orange County Court, Goshen, New York (March 15, 1976).

People v. *Kenneth Wilson* (Armed robbery), Queens County Supreme Court, New York (October 6, 1975).

People v. *Daniel Woodbery*, Queens County Supreme Court, New York, Q520577/75 (June 1976).

People v. *Valentine, Brown, Young and Petty*, 6 AD 1, F #17, 287, New York Appellate Division (1976).

Sheppard v. *Maxwell*, 384 U.S. 333 (1966).

Spencer v. *State of Texas*, 87 Supreme Court 648, 385 U.S. 567 (1967).

State v. *Chaisson* (Fraud, grand larceny), Douglas County Court, Omaha, Nebraska (June 5, 1975).

State v. *Leo McGill and John Hall* (Murder), Ingham County District Court, Lansing, Michigan (October 8, 1975).

U.S. v. *Amaral*, 488 F. 2d 1148 (CA 9, 1973).

U.S. v. *Brown*, 501 F. 2d 146 (CA 9, 1974).

U.S. v. *Busic*, U.S. Federal Court, Eastern District, Brooklyn, New York (June 1977).

U.S. v. *Green*, 373 F. Supp. 149, 158 (E. D. pa. 1974).

U.S. v. *Jackson,* District of Columbia Superior Court, Cr. No. 16158–74 (1975).

U.S. v. *Jarvik* (Robbery), U.S. District Court, Eastern District, Brooklyn, New York (July 19, 1976).

U.S. v. *Roszoryk* (Extortion), U.S. District Court, Western Michigan, Grand Rapids, Michigan (June 1, 1976).

U.S. v. *Richard Coleman Smith* (Armed robbery), Central District of California, Case No. 10171–HP–CD (August 30, 1972).

U.S. v. *Soliah* (Robbery), U.S. District Court, Eastern District of California, Sacramento, California (April 1976).

U.S. v. *Soliah,* U.S. District Court, Sacramento, California (1977).

U.S. v. *Telfaire,* 469 F. 2d 552 (1972).

Williams v. *Florida,* 399, U.S. 78C (1970), pp. 78–113.

GLOSSARY OF
CRIMINAL JUSTICE TERMS

acquittal. A judgment of a court, based either on the verdict of a jury or a judicial officer, that the defendant is not guilty of the offense(s) for which (s)he has been tried.

adjudicated. Having been the subject of completed criminal or juvenile proceedings and convicted or adjudicated a delinquent, status offender, or dependent.

appeal. A request by either the defense or the prosecution that a case be removed from a lower court to a higher court in order for a completed trial to be reviewed by the higher court.

arraignment. The appearance of a person before a court in order that the court may inform him/her of the accusation(s) against him/her and enter his/her plea. The meaning of arraignment varies widely among jurisdictions. An arraignment may extend over several appearances and in some cases may include reading formal charges, advising the defendant of his/her rights, appointing counsel, entering a plea and other actions. Commonly, arraignment is used to refer to the appearance of the defendant at a hearing in which he/she is informed of the charges against him/her but which does not include the entering of a plea.

arrest warrant. See *warrant, arrest*.

assault. Unlawful intentional inflicting or attempted or threatened inflicting of injury on another. Assaults are most commonly classified as *aggravated assault* and *simple assault* by their seriousness. *Aggravated assault* involves intentional inflicting of serious bodily injury or threatening serious bodily injury or death with a deadly weapon. *Simple assault* involves intentional threatening, attempt, or inflicting of less than serious bodily injury in the absence of a deadly weapon.

bench warrant. See *warrant, bench.*

booking. A police administrative action officially recording an arrest and identifying the person, the place, the time, the arresting authority, and the reason for the arrest.

burglary. Unlawful entry of a structure (building) with or without force, with intent to commit a felony or larceny.

complaint. A formal written accusation made by a person, often a prosecutor, and filed in a court, alleging that a specified person(s) has committed a specific offense(s).

charge. A formal allegation that a specific person(s) has committed a specific offense(s).

charging document. A formal written accusation, filed in a court, alleging that a specified person(s) has committed a specific offense(s). There are three types of charging document. A *complaint* is an accusation made by any person, but often by a *prosecutor*. An *information* is an accusation made by a prosecutor. An *indictment* is an accusation made by a *grand jury*. The filing of a charging document in a court initiates criminal proceedings against the accused. Complaints, informations, and indictments are sometimes collectively spoken of as "indictments."

convict (n.). An adult who has been found guilty of a felony and who is confined in a federal or state confinement facility. *Inmate* or *prisoner* are preferred terms.

conviction. A judgment of a court, based either on the verdict of a jury or a judicial officer or on the guilty plea of the defendant, that the defendant is guilty of the offense(s) for which he/she has been tried.

crime. An act committed or omitted in violation of a law forbidding or commanding it for which an adult can be punished, on conviction, by incarceration and other penalties or a corporation penalized, or for which a juvenile can be brought under the jurisdiction of a juvenile court and adjudicated a delinquent or transfer to adult court.

defendant. A person against whom a criminal proceeding is pending.

delinquency. Juvenile actions or conduct in violation of the criminal law, and, in some contexts, status offenses.

delinquent. A juvenile who has been adjudicated by a judicial officer of a juvenile court as having committed a delinquent act, which is an act for which an adult could be prosecuted in criminal court.

delinquent act. An act committed by a juvenile for which an adult could be prosecuted in a criminal court, but for which a juvenile can be adjudicated in a juvenile court or prosecuted in a criminal court if the juvenile court transfers jurisdiction.

dependent. A juvenile over whom a juvenile court has assumed jurisdiction because the court has found his/her care by parent, guardian, or custodian to fall short of a legal standard of proper care. Reasons for finding of dependency may include unintentional neglect, where the responsible adult is mentally disabled or lacks financial resources, or willful child neglect or abuse.

disposition. The action by a criminal or juvenile justice agency that signifies that a portion of the justice process is complete and jurisdiction is relinquished or transferred to another agency, or which signifies that a decision has been reached on one aspect of a case and a different aspect comes under consideration, requiring a different kind of decision.

diversion. The official halting or suspension at any legally proscribed processing point after a recorded justice system entry, or formal criminal or juvenile justice proceedings against an alleged offender, and a referral of that person to a treatment or care program administered by a nonjustice agency or a private agency. It also can mean that no referral is made, the case is just taken from the system.

excusable homicide. See *homicide, excusable.*

expunge. The sealing or purging of arrest, criminal, or juvenile record information.

extortion. Unlawfully obtaining or attempting to obtain the property of another by the threat of eventual injury or harm to that person, or his/her property, or another person. Extortion differs from *robbery* in that the harm is not imminent. If there is no threat of injury or force the offense is *larceny*. Thus if an offender says, "Give me $100 dollars by this afternoon or I'll break your arm," the offense is extortion, if (s)he says, "if you don't give me your money right now, I'll break your arm," the offense is robbery.

felony. A criminal offense punishable by death or by incarceration in a state or federal confinement facility for a period of which the lower limit is prescribed by a statute in a given jurisdiction, typically one year or more. It is one of the two major classes of crimes, the other being *misdemeanors*. The particular acts described as felonies vary among different jurisdictions, although most felonies are regarded as more harmful than most misdemeanors.

fraud. An element of certain offenses, consisting of deceit or intentional misrepresentation with the aim of depriving a person illegally of his/her property or legal rights. Crimes that contain the element of fraud include check fraud, counterfeiting, forgery, embezzlement, and credit card fraud.

homicide. Any killing of one person by another. *Criminal homicide* is the term used for causing the death of another person without justification or excuse, and includes *murder, voluntary* (nonnegligent) *manslaughter,* and *involuntary* (negligent) *manslaughter.* Some state statutes also include *justifiable homicide* and *excusable homicide* to describe noncriminal homicides.

homicide, excusable. The intentional but justifiable causing of the death of another or the unintentional causing of the death of another by accident or misadventure, without gross negligence. Not a crime.

homicide, justifiable. The intentional causing of the death of another in the legal performance of an official duty or in circumstances defined by law as constituting legal justification. Not a crime. Typically, this category includes execution of a death sentence or the killing of a fleeing felon by a law enforcement officer. It may also include killing to defend oneself or others against the threat of death or serious violence.

indictment. A formal written accusation made by a *grand jury* and filed in a court, alleging that a specified person(s) has committed a specific offense(s). The other two types of charging document are *complaint* and *information.*

information. A formal written accusation made by a prosecutor and filed in a court, alleging that a specified person(s) has committed a specific offense(s). An information, like an indictment, is usually used in *felony* cases. Not all jurisdictions use the information. In some, all felony accusations must be made by grand jury indictment.

infraction. An offense punishable by fine or other penalty, but not by incarceration. May also be called "violations." Traffic offenses are typical infractions.

jail. A confinement facility usually administered by a local law enforcement agency, such as the city or county, intended for adults but sometimes also containing juveniles, which holds persons detained pending adjudication and/or persons committed after adjudication for sentences of 1 year or less. May also be called "county farm," "honor farm," "work camp," "road camp." A "county jail" is usually administered by a sheriff's department, a "city jail" by a city police department.

judgment. The statement of the decision of a court that the defendant is convicted or acquitted of the offense(s) charged. It is often used to refer to any court decision.

judicial officer. Any person exercising judicial powers in a court of law. There are two types of judicial officer: *judge* and *subjudicial officer.* The latter type includes those probation officers who exercise judicial powers. Justices of the peace, magistrates, or hearing officers may also be subjudicial officers.

jurisdiction. The territory, subject matter, or person over which lawful authority may be exercised. Jurisdiction may be determined by constitutional provision or by statute.

justifiable homicide. See *homicide, justifiable.*

juvenile. A person subject to juvenile court proceedings because a statutorily defined event was alleged to have occurred while his/her age was below the statutorily specified limit of original jurisdiction of a juvenile court. Jurisdiction is determined by the age at the time of the event, not at the time of judicial proceedings, and continues until the case is terminated. Although the age limit varies in different states, it is most often the 18th birthday. Thus a 20-year-old on trial for a crime committed when he was 17, will still be tried in juvenile court.

juvenile court. A cover term for courts that have original jurisdiction over persons statutorily defined as juveniles and alleged to be delinquents, status offenders, or dependents.

jury, grand. A body of persons who have been selected and sworn to investigate criminal activity and the conduct of public officials and to hear the evidence against an accused person(s) to determine whether there is sufficient evidence to bring that person(s) to trial. A *trial jury* is distinguished from a grand jury in that a trial jury hears a case and renders a verdict of guilty or not guilty. A grand jury is asked only to decide whether there is sufficient evidence to cause a person to be brought to trial for a crime. The decision of a grand jury that there is sufficient evidence results in an *indictment* or "true bill."

jury, trial. A statutorily defined number of persons selected according to law and sworn to determine certain matters of fact in a criminal action and to render a verdict of guilty or not guilty. A jury delivers its verdict according to the evidence presented at the trial and the judge's instructions as to the law. A trial jury's powers and duties are to determine matters of fact, not to interpret the law of the cases. Also called a petit jury.

kidnapping. Unlawful transportation of a person without his/her consent, or without the consent of his/her guardian, if a minor. Sometimes used to include *unlawful confinement* as in hostage-taking situations.

larceny (larceny-theft). Unlawful taking or attempted taking of property, other than a motor vehicle, from the possession of another. Intent to deprive the owner of property *permanently* is a crucial element. Includes pocket picking, purse snatching, shoplifting, thefts from motor vehicles, and so on.

manslaughter, involuntary (negligent manslaughter). Causing the death of another by recklessness or gross neglect. There is no standard definition for amount and type of negligence or recklessness necessary. Typically includes unintentionally causing death while committing a misdemeanor, negligently handling dangerous instruments, and so on. See *homicide*.

manslaughter, voluntary (nonnegligent manslaughter). Intentionally causing the death of another with reasonable provocation. See *homicide*.

misdemeanor. An offense usually punishable by incarceration in a local confinement facility for a period of which the upper limit is prescribed by statute in a given jurisdiction, typically limited to a year or less. See also *felony*.

motion. An oral or written request made by a party to an action, before, during, or after a trial, that a court issue a rule or order.

murder. Intentionally causing the death of another without reasonable provocation or legal justification, or causing the death of another while committing or attempting to commit another crime. See *homicide*.

nolo contendere. A defendant's formal answer in court to the charges in a complaint, information, or indictment, in which (s)he states that (s)he does not contest the charges and which, while not an admission of guilt, subjects him/her to the same legal consequences as a plea of guilty.

offender, criminal. An adult who has been convicted of a criminal offense. An *alleged offender* is a person who has been charged with a specific criminal offense(s) by a law enforcement agency or court but has not been convicted.

parole. The status of an offender conditionally released from a confinement facility prior to the expiration of his sentence and placed under the supervision of a parole agency.

petit jury. See *jury, trial.*

petition. A document filed in juvenile court alleging that a juvenile is delinquent, a status offender, or a dependent and asking that the court assume jurisdiction over the juvenile, or asking that the juvenile be transferred to a criminal court for prosecution as an adult. A juvenile need not have been taken into custody for a petition to be filed.

plea. A defendant's formal answer to the charge brought against him/her in a complaint, information, or indictment. There are three kinds of pleas: guilty, not guilty, and *nolo contendere.*

prison. A confinement facility having custodial authority over adults sentenced to confinement for more than a year.

probable cause. A set of facts and circumstances that would induce a reasonably intelligent and prudent person to believe that an accused person had committed a specific crime. Probable cause requires "reasonable grounds to believe," whereas proof of guilt requires "belief beyond a reasonable doubt."

probable cause hearing. A proceeding before a judicial officer in which arguments, witnesses, or evidence is presented and in which it is determined whether there is sufficient cause to hold the accused for trial or if the case should be dismissed. May also be called "preliminary hearing," "preliminary examination," "felony preliminary," or "examining trial."

probation. The conditional freedom granted by a judicial officer to an alleged offender or adjudicated adult or juvenile as long as the person meets certain conditions of behavior. Probation is a *court* ordered freedom, whereas *parole* is a conditional freedom granted either by a parole authority or by statute after confinement.

pro se (in *propria persona*). Acting as one's own defense attorney in criminal proceedings; representing oneself.

prosecutor. An attorney employed by a government agency or subunit whose official duty is to initiate and maintain criminal proceedings on behalf of the government against persons accused of committing criminal offenses. The terms, "U.S. Attorney," "district attorney," and "state's attorney," may also be used.

public defender. An attorney employed by a government agency or subdivision, whose official duty is to represent defendants unable to hire private counsel. Other types of defense attorneys are *assigned counsel* and private counsel. Assigned counsel is one who may be paid by the government for defending a client in a particular case but is not regularly employed by the government. Private counsel is paid by the client.

rape. Unlawful sexual intercourse with a female by force or without legal or factual consent. Some states now include all violent or forced sexual contact, whether the victim is male or female in the category of rape. Statutory rape is sexual intercourse with someone who has consented but is not considered legally capable of consent, usually because of age.

recidivism. The repetition of criminal behavior; habitual criminality.

search warrant. See *warrant, search.*

status offender. A juvenile who has been adjudicated by a judicial officer of a juvenile court, as having committed a status offense, which is an act or conduct that is an offense only when committed or engaged in by a juvenile. A typical status offense is truancy.

status offense. An act or conduct that is declared by statute to be an offense, but only when committed or engaged in by a juvenile, and which can be adjudicated only by a juvenile court. Typical offenses are violation of curfew, running away from home, truancy, possession of an alcoholic beverage, incorrigibility, having delinquent tendencies, leading an immoral life, and being in need of supervision.

subpoena. A written order issued by a judicial officer requiring a specified person to appear in a designated court at a specified time in order to serve as a witness in a case under the jurisdiction of that court or to bring material to that court.

summons. A written order issued by a judicial officer requiring a person accused of a criminal offense to appear in a designated court at a specified time to answer the charge(s). In contrast, a document issued by a law enforcement officer requiring a court appearance is a *citation*, in some, but not all jurisdictions.

suspect. A person, adult, or juvenile considered by a criminal justice agency to be one who may have committed a specific criminal offense but who has not been arrested or charged.

theft. Larceny, or in some legal classifications, the group of offenses including larceny, and robbery, burglary, extortion, fraudulent offenses, hijacking, and other offenses sharing the element of larceny.

transfer to adult court. The decision by a juvenile court, resulting from a transfer hearing, that jurisdiction over an alleged delinquent will be waived and that (s)he should be prosecuted as an adult in a criminal court. Juvenile courts usually waive jurisdiction over alleged delinquents only when a serious felony has been alleged and when the juvenile is near the statutory age limit between juvenile and adult. At a transfer hearing probable cause to believe the juvenile committed the offense must be shown.

trial. The examination of issues of fact and law in a case or controversy, beginning when the jury has been selected in a jury trial or when the first witness is sworn or the first evidence is introduced in a court trial and concluding when a verdict is reached or the case is dismissed.

UCR. An abbreviation for the Federal Bureau of Investigation's uniform crime reporting program. The annual reports are entitled, "Crime in the United States."

venue. The geographical area from which the jury is drawn and in which trial is held in a criminal action. Venue is usually the county in which the crime is alleged to have been committed.

verdict. In criminal proceedings the decision made by a jury in a jury trial, or by a judicial officer in a court trial, that a defendant is either guilty or not guilty of the offense(s) for which (s)he has been tried. In entering a judgment, a judicial officer has the power to reject a jury verdict of *guilty,* but must accept a verdict of not guilty. Thus a verdict of not guilty results in a judgment of *acquittal,* but a verdict of guilty does not necessarily result in a judgment of *conviction.*

voir dire (to see, to say). A hearing conducted before a magistrate to inquire into the qualifications of prospective jurors or witnesses (usually expert witnesses). In Federal Court, questioning of jurors is conducted by the judge, while opposing attorneys conduct the questioning in other courts. In jury selection, questions may be asked to gain information as a basis for peremptory challenges and challenges for cause. Witnesses are *voir dired* (v.) to permit the judge to rule on the admissibility of their proffered testimony or their qualifications to testify.

warrant, bench. A document issued by a judicial officer directing that a person who has failed to obey an order or notice to appear be brought before the court.

warrant, search. A document issued by a judicial officer that directs a law enforcement officer to conduct a search of specified property or persons at a specific location, to seize the property or persons, if found, and to account for the results of the search to the issuing judicial officer.

GLOSSARY OF
PSYCHOLOGY TERMS

attribution (theory). The act of ascribing or imputing a characteristic to oneself or to another person. The development of the theory of attribution is a prominent topic in modern social psychology and personality psychology. At root, the concept is a study of the nature of perceived causality.

catharsis (cathartic). The belief that the verbal or fantasy expression of an impulse leads to its reduction. A key concept in psychodynamic (Freudian) theory.

confabulation. The act of filling in memory gaps with statements that make sense but are in fact untrue. A person who confabulates believes that his/her statements are true.

correlation. A statistic that indicates the degree of relationship between variables.

dependent variable. A response; any behavior, attitude, situation, or object that "depends on" or varies with a stimulus. See also *independent variable*.

Durham rule. An 1954 decision of the U.S. Court of Appeals (2nd District) stating that an individual should not be held responsible for a criminal act if the act was a result of "mental disease or deficiency."

Gestalt (psychology). A school of psychology; emphasizes the importance of looking at whole behavior patterns to understand the "parts."

hypermnesia. An apparent improvement in memory after an event over time as indicated by an increase in the amount of information recalled.

independent variable. A stimulus; any behavior, attitude, situation, or object that is under the control of the investigator. See also *dependent variable.*

long-term memory (LTM). Memory system in which information is organized (encoded) and stored indefinitely.

M'Naughten rule. A legal concept of responsibility for an act sometimes called the insanity rule. Since 1843 the M'Naughten rule has been used as a precedent; a person should be considered irresponsible if unaware of the nature and consequence of the act, or if incapable of realizing the wrongness of the act. See *Durham rule.*

paradigm. According to philosopher of science Thomas Kuhn, a theory or approach that is so successful in dealing with the subject matter of a field of science that it almost completely determines both which phenomena are studied and how they are studied. Also a particular method of research, called a research paradigm.

perception. A two-stage process of sensation (seeing, hearing, etc.) and mental organization (the cognitive process of giving meaning to various sensations).

psychodynamic. Psychoanalytic theory or Freudian approach to describing personality; idea that personality is the dynamic interaction of id, and superego.

recall (memory). The amount of information remembered—quantifiable and checkable in a research setting.

recognition (memory). In memory experiments, recognizing an item that has previously been presented.

reliability. Extent to which subjects will receive approximately the same scores each time a particular test is given.

stress. Generalized physiological or psychological response to environmental demands.

restriction of range. A statistical concept referring to limits on the extent to which numbers can vary.

self-fulfilling prophecy. A belief, prediction, or expectation that operates to bring about its own fulfillment.

set (perceptual). Tendency to make a habitual response; tendency of a preceding event to affect current perceptual responses.

short-term memory (STM). Memory system that holds all information that is in an activated state at a given moment. Has limited capacity and short duration.

social learning theory. A cognitive theory that emphasizes learning by watching others do things (modeling), seeing them rewarded or punished, and noting the probable consequences of one's own behavior.

tachistoscope. A device used in the study of memory that controls the exposure time of a visual stimulus by means of a shutter in front of a lens plus timing equipment. Brief flashes of visual stimuli down in the millisecond range can be presented to the visual field.

validity. Extent to which a test really measures what it is intended to measure.

NAME INDEX

Aaronson, D. E., 37, 38
Abrahamsen, D., 11, 48
Adler, F., 186
Adorno, T. W., 191
Albee, G., 228, 237
Alker, H. R., 186, 196
Allport, G. W., 100, 101
Alper, A., 108, 110
Alpert, J., 192
Amir, M., 48, 49
Anastasi, A., 74
Ardrey, R., 10
Aronson, E., 50, 51, 138, 139, 165
Asch, S. E., 111
Ash, H., 45, 212

Badger, P., 204
Bailey, F. L., 175
Bailey, W. C., 247
Baker, E., 145, 176, 191
Baker, P., 15
Baker, R., 3
Balch, R. W., 144
Bandura, A., 12–14
Bane, M. J., 230

Bankowski, Z., 130
Banks, C., 251
Banuazizi, A., 251
Bard, M., 21, 53–55, 61, 66–69, 121
Barnard, J. J., 196
Baron, R., 13
Bartholemew, A., 204
Bartlett, F. C., 108
Barton, A. H., 184
Bassili, J., 93
Bateson, G., 13
Bazelon, D., 204–205
Beattie, R. H., 288
Becher, T., 44, 63
Bedau, H. A., 264, 269
Beeghley, L., 235
Bem, D. J., 263–264
Bem, S., 50
Bennett-Sandler, G., 73–74
Benson, H., 76
Bentham, J., 266
Berberich, J., 65
Berg, K., 192
Berrigan, P., 174
Berk, R., 180

Petersilia, J., 44, 45, 259
Piaget, J., 50
Pierce, C. M., 264
Platt, A., 152
Pollack, S., 193
Pollock, R., 152
Postman, L., 99–101, 229

Race, S., 228
Radzinowicz, L., 247
Rappaport, J., 248
Reidel, M., 144, 154, 191
Reilly, V., 159, 292
Reis, H. T., 137, 186, 292
Remer, L., 206
Rice, B., 229
Richert, J. P., 189
Robinson, J. P., 290
Robinson, S. M., 288
Rogosin, H. R., 230
Rokeach, M., 191
Rosenblatt, J. C., 131, 156
Rosenman, S., 49
Rosenthal, R., 112, 117
Roy, M., 21, 69
Rubinstien, J., 21, 44
Runyon, R. P., 284
Rupp, A., 120
Rutter, E., 67–69
Ryan, W., 49

Saks, M. J., 31, 131, 156, 162, 178, 208
Sales, B. D., 90, 139, 190, 207, 259
Sanford, R. N., 191
Scarr-Salaptek, S., 228
Schanie, C., 69
Scherl, D., 54, 55
Schilling, C., 75
Schlosberg, H., 71
Schnee, C., 123
Schorr, D., 182, 186
Scott, B., 95, 97, 139
Scull, A. T., 260
Sellin, T., 263, 271–274
Selye, H., 94
Shah, S., 18, 20
Shapely, D., 180
Shaver, K. G., 49, 191
Shaver, P., 173, 290
Sheehy, G., 53
Shepard, R. N., 89
Shepart, J., 125
Shulman, J., 166, 172–173, 175–177, 180–181
Siegel, S., 299
Sigall, H., 138
Silber, D. E., 257
Silberman, C. E., 66
Silverberg, G., 108

Simon, R. J., 135, 155, 184
Sirica, J., 181
Skinner, B. F., 202
Skolnick, J., 65
Slomovitz, M., 108, 111
Smith, E., 250, 261
Sobel, N. R., 223
Soliah, S., 114–115
Sommer, R., 133, 144, 242–243, 268
Sorce, J. F., 119
Sparling, J., 179
Spencer, 167, 168, 169, 170
Spielberger, C., 72
Spivak, D., 123, 127
Stantan, R., 275
Steinmetz, S., 69
Stern, S., 62, 286
Stevens, S. S., 86
Stotland, E., 65
Streufert, S., 291
Strnad, B. N., 85, 93
Strodtbeck, F., 132–133, 136, 156
Sturgill, W., 103, 126
Sue, S., 170
Suedfeld, P., 291
Sullivan, R., 62, 284
Sutherland, S., 54–55
Swan, J., 180
Swinton, P., 192–193, 195
Symonds, M., 54–55, 61

Tapp, J., 82, 137, 201, 219, 252
Tarde, G., 13
Tate, E., 178
Terman, L., 231
Thibaut, J. W., 265
Thomas, E., 156
Thomas, M. H., 15
Timothy, M., 130, 150–151
Tinbergen, L., 10
Tobach, E., 229
Toch, H., 12, 250
Topoff, H., 229
Trotter, S., 255
Tuddenham, R., 229

Ubell, E., 73, 75

Valenti, A., 158, 159
Vales, P., 144, 154, 191
van den Haag, E., 269
Van Dyke, J. M., 186, 189
Viano, E., 46, 47, 61, 62
Vidman, N., 152, 177, 180, 191, 192
Virzera, V., 70–71
Von Hentig, H., 48

Wachter, M. L., 284
Wachter, S. M., 284

SUBJECT INDEX

81 82 83 9 8 7 6 5 4 3 2 1